Revised and Updated

on

daily inspiration
or the history
ouff, the trivia
over, and the
nnately curious

this
day

HOWARD BOOKS
A DIVISION OF SIMON & SCHUSTER
New York London Toronto Sydney

carl d. windsor

Our purpose at Howard Books is to:
• *Increase faith* in the hearts of growing Christians
• *Inspire holiness* in the lives of believers
• *Instill hope* in the hearts of struggling people everywhere
Because He's coming again!

Published by Howard Books, a division of Simon & Schuster, Inc.
1230 Avenue of the Americas, New York, NY 10020
www.howardpublishing.com

On This Day © 2006 by Carl D. Windsor

13 Digit ISBN: 978-1-58229-654-8; 10 Digit ISBN: 1-58229-654-5

10 9 8 7 6 5 4 3 2 1

Manufactured in the United States of America

For information regarding special discounts for bulk purchases, please contact Simon & Schuster Special Sales at 1-800-456-6798 or business@simonandschuster.com.

Edited by Between the Lines
Cover design by John Lucas
Interior design by Stephanie D. Walker

To Tyrun
On Tyour
36th Birthday!
up Tyour other!
Keep this other!
your luck in so hard
want and so keep you
everyday crazy
prospective! crazy
this world.
I love you and
am so proud of
you

Mother!
Mom

To God,
"who was, and is, and is to come"
(Revelation 4:8)

Contents

Acknowledgments

Credit is due to many people who have been an inspiration and encouragement to me and thus have contributed to this effort.

To Denny and Philis Boultinghouse and all the fine people at Howard Books and Dawn Brandon at Between the Lines, whose suggestions helped make this a better book.

To Leonard and Thelma Spinrad, whose book *The Instant Almanac* inspired the format for this book.

To veteran author Dr. Harold Willmington for making the Bible come alive and for his assistance in scripture selection, in writing, and in publication.

To expert researcher Jeff Dull, whose broad knowledge and thorough investigative skills made this book as comprehensive as it is.

To Jerry Edwards, whose encouragement launched *A Quiet Place* radio ministry that formed the basis for this book.

To my pastor, Marvin Suitt, whose vivid stories and examples make the message of the Bible come alive.

To my many students, colleagues, and friends, from whom I've learned so much over the years.

Most of all to my wonderful wife, Beverly; my children, Trent, Todd, Heather, and son-in-law Anthony; and my lovely granddaughter Layla Cuellar, all of whose support and encouragement enabled this book to be completed.

Foreword

Historic events recorded in this book are meant only to be representative of activities occurring on that date and are in no way exhaustive. Not every significant event occurring on each date could be included due to space limitations. Also, not every date had activities of sufficient interest to be included here. Inclusion of a given event in this book does not imply endorsement of that event.

Birthdays were chosen from available information for those persons believed to be of greatest interest to readers of this book. Inclusion within this book is for information purposes only and does not necessarily imply endorsement of the lifestyle or activities of the persons listed. (Likewise, exclusion does not imply disapproval of a given individual.)

Efforts have been made to provide a balanced listing between historic and contemporary figures of general interest from such fields as religion, education, entertainment, the arts, politics, athletics, and government.

Reasonable efforts have been made to authenticate all information contained herein. However, all listings are subject to errors at the data source over which the author has no control.

Because illustrations have been used, reused, and published in many different forms over the years, it is nearly impossible to determine the originator of such stories. Every effort has been made to credit the originator of illustrations where such information is readily available. It is the author's intention to provide credit where the original source can be determined. Sources who can verify the originality of their work contained herein will be given credit in future printings. For those not wishing their content to be published, their content will be deleted.

Readers desiring further information or having questions or suggestions for future editions are encouraged to submit them via this Web site: www.onthisdayonline.com.

Preface

Throughout history people have used stories from life to make abstract truths clearer. In *On This Day* I've used numerous illustrations (much like what the Bible calls parables) to illustrate spiritual principles. It is my prayer that in reading these, you will find enjoyment and might better understand eternal, biblical truths.

On This Day also lists various significant "firsts" and key historical events on the day they occurred in history. Space considerations have limited the number of events that could be included. (Inclusion of an event is for information purposes only and does not necessarily imply endorsement of the event, lifestyle, or activities of the persons or groups named. Likewise, exclusion does not necessarily imply disapproval of a given individual, activity, or event.)

Efforts have been made to provide a balanced listing of historic and contemporary figures of general interest from such fields as religion, education, entertainment, the arts, politics, athletics, and government.

I trust you will find *On This Day* to provide information, guidance, and inspiration for years to come.

Ways to Use *On This Day*

Family Devotions—Encourage each member of your family to participate by reading the Scripture passage and one or more segments from *On This Day*—great for developing a greater appreciation of our nation's heritage and God's historic plan.

Office or Group Devotions—Unite fellow workers around God's Word each day. Reading *On This Day* will help develop group cohesiveness and productivity as it focuses on the importance of an individual's accomplishments in shaping world events.

In the Classroom—Teach responsibility and proper use of time by beginning each class with a selection from *On This Day*. Help students become more effective as they see the roles others before them have played in shaping history.

As a Contest for Trivia Lovers—Select a quotation from a day's reading and have others "Guess who said . . ." (then read the quotation). Or guess in what year an event occurred or the year in which a public figure was born.

Finding Your Special Day—Discover events that happened on family birthdays, anniversaries, graduation dates, and so forth. Write these dates in the Our Family Heritage and Memorable Dates section on page 15, and then look them up in *On This Day*.

Individually, along with Scripture, as a personal, daily quiet time with God—Begin each day with the inspiring thoughts in *On This Day*, and watch your outlook improve.

. . . all in less than ten minutes a day!

Our Family Heritage

NAME: _____ DATE: _____

Grandparents: _____
_____
_____
_____

Father: _____
Mother: _____
Brothers/Sisters: _____
_____
_____
_____

Children: _____
_____
_____
_____

Grandchildren: _____
_____
_____
_____

Anniversaries: _____
_____
_____

OTHER MEMORABLE DATES

_____
_____
_____
_____

On This Day

I have only just a minute
Only sixty seconds in it
Forced upon me, can't refuse it
Didn't seek it, didn't choose it
But it's up to me to use it
I must suffer if I lose it
Give account if I abuse it
Just a tiny little minute
But eternity is in it.

—Author Unknown

TODAY IN HISTORY

1863—Slaves freed by Emancipation Proclamation
1892—Ellis Island opened to welcome immigrants
1921—First religious broadcast (on KDKA Pittsburgh)
1959—Cuban government toppled by Fidel Castro's revolt
1990—Debut of World Wide Web
2000—New Millennium Y2K scare proved groundless

BORN TODAY

Patriot Paul Revere . . . . 1735 Author J. D. Salinger 1919
U.S. flag maker Betsy Ross . . . . . . 1752 Actor Frank Langella 1940
FBI director J. Edgar Hoover . . . . 1895 Actor Verne Troyer 1969

TRUE FREEDOM

When president Abraham Lincoln prepared to sign the Emancipation Proclamation, he took his pen, held it in place for a moment, and then dropped it. Lincoln explained: "If my name goes into history, it will be for this act, and if my hand trembles when I sign it, there will be some who will say, 'he hesitated.'" Lincoln then turned to the table, took up the pen again, and slowly, boldly wrote his famous signature.

As you begin a new year, don't hesitate to embrace the new possibilities. Boldly turn the page to a new chapter in your life, leaving behind the bondage and mistakes of the past and seeking the One who offers true spiritual freedom. No matter what last year was like, regardless of your background, you can find true freedom in Jesus. Writing in *The Word God Sent,* author Paul Scherer noted, "We find freedom when we find God. We lose it when we lose him." The Bible assures us, "If the Son sets you free, you will be free indeed" (John 8:36).

Throughout this new year, why not celebrate your emancipation in Christ and proclaim freedom and God's love to others? Ask God to give you strength and wisdom to act upon all the challenges and opportunities to proclaim your spiritual freedom that may arise in this New Year.

TODAY'S POWER POINT

Life's greatest freedom is experienced as we find true liberty in Jesus.

TODAY IN HISTORY

1776—First U.S. flag flown

1778—Fourth state, Georgia, added to Union

1893—First commemorative postage stamp issued

1968—First successful heart transplant performed

1970—Clifton Wharton Jr. became first African American president of a major U.S. university (Michigan State University)

1974—President Richard Nixon signed 55-mph speed-limit law to save fuel

BORN TODAY

General James Wolfe 1727

Composer Michael Tippett. 1905

Author and scientist Isaac Asimov. . .1920

Singer Roger Miller 1936

House Speaker Dennis Hastert. . . 1942

Actor Cuba Gooding Jr. 1968

Hockey player Brian Boucher. . . . 1977

MY WAY OR THE HIGHER WAY

Have you ever heard the saying "When life hands you lemons, make lemonade"? As you go through life, you may well discover that what seemed at the time to be a great setback actually paved the way for a tremendous opportunity you otherwise might never have had. Such is the story of Wilson Johnson, founder of Holiday Inn hotels. At age forty Johnson was working at a sawmill when he was abruptly fired. Not knowing what to do, he became increasingly despondent. One day, after talking with his wife, Johnson decided to take charge of his life, mortgage their home, and start a business. He initially built several small structures but gained rapid success, becoming a multimillionaire within just five years.

Years later Johnson observed, "At the time it happened, I didn't understand why I was fired. Later I saw that it was God's unerring and wonderful plan to get me into the way of his choosing."

God is so much bigger than we are. His perspective is all-encompassing and all-wise. God knows what he's doing, and we'd be smart to trust his superior wisdom and knowledge. "'My thoughts are not your thoughts, neither are your ways my ways,' declares the LORD. 'As the heavens are higher than the earth, so are my ways higher than your ways and my thoughts than your thoughts'" (Isaiah 55:8–9). So when you come to a bend in life's road and are suddenly facing events not of your own choosing, look up for God's leading.

TODAY'S POWER POINT

Experience is not what happens to you; it is what you do with what happens to you.—Aldous Huxley

January 3

TODAY IN HISTORY

1870—Brooklyn Bridge construction started
1921—First weather-forecast broadcast
1924—King Tut's mummy discovered in Egypt
1952—Television premiere of *Dragnet*
1959—Forty-ninth state, Alaska, added to Union
2000—Last new *Peanuts* cartoon strip published
2004—Successful landing on Mars by U.S. spacecraft *Spirit*
2006—Key Washington DC lobbyist Jack Abramoff pleaded guilty to fraud and corruption charges

BORN TODAY

Orator Cicero. . . . . 106 BC
British politician Clement Attlee. . . 1883
Actor Ray Milland 1905
Comedian Victor Borge 1909
Hockey player Bobby Hull 1939
Musician Steven Stills. 1945
Actor and producer Mel Gibson. . . 1956

THE RIGHT KIND OF CONFIDENCE

Placing our confidence in the right person can mean the difference between success and failure. A man was driving along a winding mountain road behind a long line of cars. Ahead a fully loaded truck labored slowly up the narrow road. No one could see beyond the curve ahead, so no one dared pass, and it didn't take long for drivers to lose patience. Finally, as the convoy reached the crest of the hill, the truck driver, who could now see quite some distance, waved his hand to signal that all was clear ahead.

Consider this: a group of drivers who had never met the driver of the truck were willing to trust their lives to his judgment and good heart. How much more should we be willing to trust our future to the God who created the universe and gave his own Son to redeem us? When you put your confidence in God instead of other people or even your own abilities, you'll discover the power and strength to face life's challenges today and every day.

TODAY'S POWER POINT

Overconfidence in one's own ability is the root of much evil.—Alice Foote MacDougal

January 4

TODAY IN HISTORY

1790—First State of the Union Address
1885—First appendectomy performed
1896—Forty-fifth state, Utah, added to Union
1954—Eighteen-year-old Elvis Presley made first recording (for his mother)
2004—Afghanistan adopted new constitution giving women rights

BORN TODAY

Physicist Sir Isaac Newton 1643
Author Jacob Grimm 1785
Blind reading originator Louis Braille
. . . . 1809
Writer J. R. R. Tolkien 1892
Football coach Don Shula 1930
Boxer Floyd Patterson. 1935
Actor Dave Foley 1963

WHEN THE LAST WILL BE FIRST

Someone has said, "It is possible to be too big for God to use you, but never too small for God to use you." The Bible reminds us that the people whom the world considers the lowliest are often the greatest in God's eyes.

Pastor A. J. Gordon spoke of a man in his congregation who could quote the Bible from cover to cover. Yet when asked to tell what the Lord was doing in his life, he was speechless. Gordon later discovered that the man was involved in activities that were not of good character and that greatly damaged his testimony.

Another man in the same congregation labored in the coal mines and often had to hurry to arrive in time for the midweek service after work. Because of this he frequently was unkempt and dirty when he arrived. Yet when he spoke of the Lord, the congregation paid attention. He lived faithfully for God and served him every day. Often he talked with his coworkers about God. Despite this man's humble appearance, he was a shining example of God's love at work. It was clear to all he met that Christ was real in his life.

God doesn't grant status based on how religious we are. He's more concerned with how faithful we are. Jesus said, "Many who are first will be last, and the last first" (Mark 10:31). Ask God to help you be faithful so that in the end you'll come in first with him.

TODAY'S POWER POINT

When a man is wrapped up in himself, he makes a pretty small package.—John Ruskin

January 5

TODAY IN HISTORY

1914—Five-dollar-a-day minimum wage established by Henry Ford
1925—Nellie Tayloe Ross, first woman governor, took office (in Wyoming)
1933—Construction started on Golden Gate Bridge in San Francisco
1997—Major flooding caused widespread damage in western United States
1998—Singer and politician Sonny Bono killed in skiing accident

BORN TODAY

War of 1812 naval hero Stephen Decatur 1779
Disposable-razor inventor King Gillette 1855
Actor Robert Duvall 1931

TV host Charlie Rose 1942
Actress Diane Keaton 1946
Actor Ted Lange 1949
Actress Pamela Sue Martin 1954
Football player Warrick Dunn . . . 1975

THE WAY

As we try to find our way in an increasingly complex world, thousands of messages, promises, and sales pitches compete for our attention in this information age. A quick search of the Internet reveals millions of entries for articles, books, and programs touting "The Way to Happiness," "The Way to Peace," "The Way to Save for College," "The Way to Clean Air," and "The Way to Paradise"—and a plethora of others. But in the overload of information, some from dubious sources, it's easy to lose our way. That's why it's essential to be loyal followers of the God who knows the way. Our prayer should be that of the psalmist: "Tell me clearly what to do, and show me which way to turn" (Psalm 5:8 NLT).

Jesus not only knows the way, he *is* the Way! More than just an all-knowing guide, Jesus is the path to everything worthwhile—truth, life, joy, and peace. Author Dan Crawford wrote of a guide who led him along an unfamiliar trail. He asked his guide where the path led. "You want to know the way? *I* am the way!" smiled the guide, pointing to his head, where the knowledge of their path was stored. Crawford later had an opportunity to share with his guide the One who is the true and living Way.

Each day make it a point to communicate with God, who can see beyond tomorrow. Ask him to guide you, then follow where he leads you. He knows what he's doing and the best way to get you to your final destination.

TODAY'S POWER POINT

The people to fear are not those who disagree with you, but those who disagree with you and are too cowardly to let you know.—Napoleon

TODAY IN HISTORY

1759—George Washington married Martha Dandridge Custis

1838—First telegraph system demonstrated by inventor Samuel F. B. Morse

1912—Forty-seventh state, New Mexico, added to Union

1942—First around-the-world flight completed (Pan Am's *Pacific Clipper*)

1973—First electoral vote cast for a woman (Theodora Nathan for vice president)

1975—Television premiere of game show *Wheel of Fortune*

1994—Figure skater Nancy Kerrigan attacked and injured two days before national championships

BORN TODAY

Joan of Arc 1412

Poet Carl Sandburg 1878

Philosopher Khalil Gibran 1883

Entertainer Danny Thomas 1914

Pollster Lou Harris 1921

Football coach Lou Holtz 1937

Football player and sportscaster

    Howie Long 1960

FREE TO READ

Reading the Bible each day is a privilege many people around the world cannot experience. When the Americans first arrived in the Philippines in 1898, after the Spanish-American war, many political prisoners were freed. Among the "crimes" some had committed was reading the Bible. The threat of persecution had been so great previously, that one day a man came to a missionary and asked quietly if it was true that he could now read his Bible in peace. The missionary pointed to a nearby American flag and said, "As long as you see that flag flying overhead, you can read the Bible on your roof if you want, and no one can molest you."

Americans have the freedom to worship God and to read the Bible at any time and in any place, but too few avail themselves of this privilege. Deuteronomy 17:19–20 describes how daily Bible reading benefits a king—or any person: "That way he will learn to fear the LORD his God by obeying all the terms of this law. This regular reading will prevent him from becoming proud and acting as if he is above his fellow citizens. It will also prevent him from turning away from these commands in the smallest way" (NLT).

Have you considered that not utilizing your freedom to read the Bible might be just as bad as not having the freedom at all? Recognize the freedom you have to read God's Word wherever and whenever you wish. Thank God for your freedoms—and make the most of them—today.

TODAY'S POWER POINT

Do only what is required of you and remain a slave. Do more than is required and become free.

January 7

TODAY IN HISTORY

1782—First commercial bank opened in United States
1789—George Washington elected America's first president
1839—First practical camera, the daguerreotype, introduced
1904—Radio distress signal established
1927—Transatlantic phone service began
1996—Record-setting blizzard paralyzed eastern United States, killing one hundred
1999—Impeachment trial of President Bill Clinton opened

BORN TODAY

President Millard Fillmore	1800	Actor David Caruso	1956
Singer Paul Revere	1938	News anchor Katie Couric	1957
Singer Kenny Loggins	1948	Actor Nicolas Cage	1964

FOLLOWING GOOD LEADERS

Reading the Bible and going to church help us better learn how to follow Christ. Not only is Jesus, our ultimate example, revealed to us through God's Word and the teaching of his Word at church, but we also can benefit from seeing Christ's example lived out in the lives of other Christians. In 1 Corinthians 11:1 Paul told the believers, "Follow my example, as I follow the example of Christ." A mature follower of Christ can make it easy for us to see and understand what it means to follow Jesus in our daily lives.

But we must be careful whom we follow, or we will be led astray. The great motivator Dale Carnegie told a story that illustrates this truth: "As a boy in the Midwest, I used to amuse myself by holding a stick across a gateway that the sheep had to go through. After the first few sheep had jumped over the stick, I took it away; but all the other sheep leaped through the gateway over an imaginary barrier. The only reason for their jumping was that those in front had jumped."

Don't jump just because someone in front of you did. Instead, let Jesus set the bar. Then your habits of Bible-reading, prayer, and church attendance will help you easily clear every hurdle.

TODAY'S POWER POINT

Once a use, forever a custom.—English proverb

TODAY IN HISTORY

1889—Electric punch-card tabulating machine (early computer) patented
1918—President Woodrow Wilson unveiled post–World War I peace plans
1962—*Mona Lisa* made first appearance in the United States
1965—First woman state supreme-court chief justice named, in Arizona
1987—Dow Jones Industrial Average exceeded two thousand for the first time
1998—Ramzi Yousef sentenced to life for masterminding 1993 World Trade Center
     bombing
2002—Death of Wendy's founder Dave Thomas, age sixty-nine

BORN TODAY

Financier Nicholas Biddle. 1786   Physicist Stephen Hawking 1942
Publisher Frank Doubleday 1862   Musician David Bowie 1947
Singer Elvis Presley 1935   Baseball player Jason Giambi 1971

TRUSTING THE FATHER

Some time ago a family was watching home movies of a daughter's first steps. Over and over she cautiously tried to walk a step or two before collapsing once again in a heap. While such an experience would cause most adults to quit trying, the young girl trusted Mom or Dad to walk along beside her; and she kept trying and trusting them until she had finally mastered the art of walking on her own.

The girl outgrew her need for her parents to help her walk, but she will never outgrow her need to trust them. Likewise, even as adults and maturing Christians, we never outgrow our need to trust God. The Old Testament prophet Abraham is a case in point. Abraham's name means "Father of Nations," yet in his old age he and his wife Sarah were still childless. But God told Abraham, "'Look up at the heavens and count the stars—if indeed you can count them.' Then he said to him, 'So shall your offspring be'" (Genesis 15:5–6).

It took almost fifteen more years—Abraham was nearly one hundred—until Isaac, the son of God's promise, was born.

As we begin this new year, we can say, "I don't know what the future holds, but I know who holds my future—and he's worthy of my trust."

TODAY'S POWER POINT

Fear is simply unbelief parading in disguise.—Source Unknown

January 9

TODAY IN HISTORY

1788—Fifth state, Connecticut, added to Union

1894—*The Sneeze* became first movie to be copyrighted

1945—General Douglas MacArthur returned to free the Philippines from Japanese control

1951—United Nations opened new headquarters in New York City

2005—Mahmoud Abbas chosen to succeed Yasser Arafat as Palestinian leader

BORN TODAY

President Richard Nixon 1913

Guitarist Les Paul. 1915

Football player Bart Starr 1934

Actor Bob Denver 1935

Folk singer Joan Baez 1941

Singer Crystal Gayle. 1951

Musician Dave Matthews. 1967

SPEAKING CAREFULLY

Researchers have determined that the average articulate adult says some thirty thousand words per day. These words, if put into print, would fill a full-length book a day. Over a lifetime, these daily "books" would be enough to establish a good-sized library.

How much are your words worth? When President Ronald Reagan once gave two twenty-minute talks during a visit to Japan, he was paid two million dollars. That amounts to $50,000 per minute!

Scientists say the sound waves begun by our voices carry on into the vastness of space and that, having sufficiently sensitive instruments, we might be able someday to retrieve them again and reconstruct all the words we've ever said. How careful should we be, then, to choose our words wisely?

Every time you speak, remember that God hears everything you say and that you must someday account to him for every word you've spoken.

TODAY'S POWER POINT

Let nobody speak mischief of anybody.—Plato

TODAY IN HISTORY

1901—Oil first discovered in the United States (in Texas)
1911—First photographs taken from a plane
1920—League of Nations established
1951—First jet airplane passenger trip
1967—Edward Brooks (Massachusetts) became first African American U.S. senator
1971—Television premiere of *Masterpiece Theater*
1980—Death of labor leader George Meany, age eighty-five
1998—AOL announced plans to purchase TimeWarner

BORN TODAY

Patriot Ethan Allen. 1738
Scientist George Washington Carver
. . . . 1864
Composer Johnnie Ray 1927

Musician Rod Stewart 1940
Boxer George Foreman. 1949
Singer Pat Benatar 1953
Basketball player Glenn Robinson. . . 1973

THE BOOK OF BOOKS

When newsman Henry Stanley began his pilgrimage across Africa in search of missionary Dr. David Livingstone, he took with him seventy-three books that weighed nearly two hundred pounds. After three hundred miles of his wearying trek, he found it necessary to lighten the load and throw away some of his baggage. As the journey went on, his library grew smaller and smaller until only one book remained: the Bible. Stanley refused to part with this book, reading it through three times during his lengthy trip.

In the jungle's extreme conditions, Stanley recognized the unique and true value of the Bible and refused to be without it. The Bible is a guide, inspiration, teacher, example, challenger, comforter, companion, and letter from a Loved One. Of all the books ever written, none can compare to the Bible.

This year, why not resolve to make Bible study an important part of your days?

TODAY'S POWER POINT

The Bible will keep you from sin, or sin will keep you from the Bible.—Dwight L. Moody

January 11

TODAY IN HISTORY

1935—Amelia Earhart completed solo flight across Pacific Ocean
1964—U.S. surgeon general warned cigarette smoking causes health problems
1973—Baseball's designated-hitter rule approved
1980—Honda announced plans to build its first U.S. car plant, in Ohio
1993—Ross Perot formed political watchdog group United We Stand America

BORN TODAY

Founding Father Alexander Hamilton 1757
Educator Ezra Cornell 1807
Writer William James 1842
TV producer Grant Tinker 1926

Singer Naomi Judd 1946
Golfer Ben Crenshaw 1952
Singer Mary J. Blige 1971
Actress Amanda Peet 1972

LOVING OBEDIENCE

When Thomas Edison was looking for a way to record and reproduce the sound of a human voice, he sketched out his idea and asked that his assistant build a working model by following his specifications. The workman looked over the drawing and shook his head adamantly. "Impossible," he said. "That thing will never work. No one has ever made a machine that could talk."

But Edison would not be deterred. "Build what I have sketched," Edison insisted, "and let me be the loser if it doesn't work."

God has a similar offer for us. However, when we obey God, neither he nor we are the losers. We may even find that things work out better than we ever thought possible. Like Edison's assistant, we don't always have to understand the reason for what God asks of us. The only thing required of us is to love him. Obedience springs from genuine love. Jesus said, "If anyone loves me, he will obey my teaching. My Father will love him, and we will come to him and make our home with him. He who does not love me will not obey my teaching" (John 14:23–24).

Do you love God? If so, you'll strive to obey him in all you do and say. What has God commanded you to do today?

TODAY'S POWER POINT

Our greatest need is not more knowledge, but to put into practice what we already know.—Source Unknown

TODAY IN HISTORY

1773—First U.S. museum opened in Charleston, South Carolina
1932—Arkansans elected Hattie Caraway, first woman U.S. senator
1945—Battle of South China Sea launched
1971—Premiere of television show *All in the Family*
1976—Death of mystery writer Agatha Christie in London, age eighty-five
1990—Communist Party outlawed in Romania
1991—Congress authorized military action against Iraq

BORN TODAY

Massachusetts Bay Colony governor
  John Winthrop 1588
Author Jack London 1876
Civil-rights leader James Farmer . . 1920

Boxer Joe Frazier 1944
Talk-show host Rush Limbaugh . . 1951
Actress Kirstie Alley 1955
Amazon.com founder Jeff Bezos . . 1964

MAKING MISTAKES

Anyone who has ever made a mistake can identify with the poor bank janitor who accidentally put a box containing checks worth $840,000 next to the trash shredder. In a matter of minutes, the shredder operator had turned thousands of negotiable checks into confetti. Realizing the mistake, bank officials quickly mobilized dozens of employees to reconstruct all eight thousand checks. Imagine the task they faced, all because of an honest mistake.

Some mistakes are time-consuming and difficult to fix, but others can be deadly. One taxidermist was bitten by a "frozen" rattlesnake. The man was in the habit of buying live snakes, freezing them to death, and then stuffing and selling them. Normally he would tape the deadly snake's mouth shut before beginning his procedure, but just one time he failed to do so—a crucial oversight.

Read 2 Samuel 6:1–8 to find out how a man named Uzzah died because of a simple mistake. It's a tragic story, but when we look a little closer, we realize that Uzzah's death could have been prevented with a little care and obedience. In Exodus 25:10–16 and Numbers 4:4–20, God gave detailed instructions on how to move the ark of the covenant. The Israelites were also warned that failing to treat these holy items in the manner and with the care God demanded would result in death. Uzzah found that out the hard way.

Let's be honest, we all make mistakes. Even though "to err is human," let's be careful never to consciously violate God's commands.

TODAY'S POWER POINT

The only people who never make mistakes are those who never do anything.
—Lloyd Morris

January 13

TODAY IN HISTORY

1910—First radio broadcast (New York City)
1953—Nine physicians arrested for plot against Russian leader Joseph Stalin
1957—First Frisbees produced
1972—President Richard Nixon announced seventy thousand U.S. troops to be withdrawn from Vietnam
1984—Death of McDonald's founder Ray Kroc, age eighty-one
1990—Virginian Douglas Wilder became first African American U.S. governor
1997—Seven African American soldiers awarded Medal of Honor for World War II valor

BORN TODAY

Chief justice Salmon Chase 1808
Author Horatio Alger 1834
Actor Charles Nelson Reilly 1931
Sculptor Frank Gallo 1933
TV executive Brandon Tartikoff . . 1949
Actress Julia Louis-Dreyfus 1961
Actor Patrick Dempsey 1966

TRUTH

Author and teacher Vernon Grounds wrote that in 1636, "when Harvard University was founded, its motto was *Veritas Christo et Ecclesiae*—'Truth for Christ and the Church.' Its crest showed three books, one face down to symbolize the limitation of human knowledge. But in recent decades that book has been turned face up to represent the unlimited capacity of the human mind. And the Harvard motto has been changed to *Veritas*—'Truth.'"

How would you define truth? While preparing to take a comprehensive exam, a graduate student's colleagues cautioned that he could expect a challenging line of questioning regarding the "definition of truth." While the world might find this a challenging concept, every believer's answer should be, "Your [God's] word is truth" (John 17:17).

Look to the Bible to discover truth for your situation in life.

TODAY'S POWER POINT

The truth is no less true if it cannot be explained.—Source Unknown

TODAY IN HISTORY

1639—First colonial constitution adopted (in Connecticut)
1784—Treaty of Paris ratified by Continental Congress, ending the American Revolution
1919—Germany freed allied prisoners of war
1952—Premiere of television's *Today* show, with Dave Garroway as host
1980—Death of composer Andre Kostelanetz, age seventy-eight
1990—Premiere of television's *America's Funniest Home Videos*
2004—Libya signed nuclear-test-ban treaty

BORN TODAY

Colonial traitor Benedict Arnold. . . 1741
Nobel Peace Prize winner Albert Schweitzer. 1875
German anti-Nazi theologian Martin Niemöller 1892
Commentator Andy Rooney 1919
Actress Faye Dunaway 1941
Director Stephen Soderbergh 1963
Actor Jason Bateman 1969

OVERCOMING TEMPTATION

Sometimes when we are forbidden to do or have something, that alone makes the thing seem almost irresistible. The more off-limits the territory, the more enticing it becomes.

But however strong that attraction may be, we can be encouraged to know that many others have survived similar temptations without giving in. The *Christian Herald* once told of a man who had responsibility for large sums of money in a major organization. Knowing that it would be a long time before an audit was due, he was tempted to temporarily transfer some funds to his personal account. He didn't do it, but he felt he must talk with someone to share the anguish he went through before he could overcome that temptation. So he called the man who had held the position before him. To his relief the man did not reprimand him but rather shared how he had undergone similar temptations, without giving in, when he held the position.

Believers are not alone in being enticed. Being tempted is not wrong, but yielding to it is always sin. The Bible reminds us that Christ himself "has been tempted in every way, just as we are—yet was without sin" (Hebrews 4:15). With God's help you can conquer temptation, regardless of how irresistible it may seem.

TODAY'S POWER POINT

We gain the strength of the temptation we resist.—Ralph Waldo Emerson

January 15

TODAY IN HISTORY

1559—Queen Elizabeth I crowned
1870—First depiction published of the donkey as symbol of the Democratic Party
1967—NFL's first Super Bowl (Green Bay beat Kansas City)
1974—Premiere of television's *Happy Days*
1981—Premiere of television's *Hill Street Blues*
1991—UN deadline passed for Iraq to withdraw from Kuwait, setting stage for launching of Operation Desert Storm
1992—First Web browser introduced

BORN TODAY

Dramatist Molière 1622
Physicist Edward Teller. 1908
Actor Lloyd Bridges 1913
Broadcast journalist Rod MacLeish . . . 1926

Civil-rights leader Dr. Martin Luther King Jr. 1929
Actress Margaret O'Brien 1937
Football player Mike Minter. 1974

THE BURDENS OF LIFE

Attempting to explain the meaning of the text "My yoke is easy," a teacher asked her class, "Who can tell me what a yoke is?"

One child answered, "A yoke is something they put on the necks of animals."

"Good," said the teacher. "What do you think is the yoke God puts on us?"

With just a moment's thought, a little girl eagerly raised her hand and responded, "It's God putting his arms around our necks."

That's the story of God's love for us—when we are beaten down and discouraged by all the troubles and problems of life, God reaches down and puts his sustaining arms of strength around us.

God's Word assures us: "Give your burdens to the LORD, and he will take care of you. He will not permit the godly to slip and fall" (Psalm 55:22 NLT). If you are discouraged and struggling in what seems to be an uphill battle, consider whether you've given your situation to the Lord and asked your heavenly Father for help. This is the secret of overcoming life's difficulties. With God's help you can handle anything life throws at you today.

TODAY'S POWER POINT

The world is full of willing people: some willing to work, the rest willing to let them.—Robert Frost

TODAY IN HISTORY

1866—Clamp-on metal roller skate patented
1883—U.S. civil-service system organized
1920—Alcoholic beverages prohibited under Eighteenth Amendment
1959—Fidel Castro assumed power in Cuba
1976—Premiere of television's *Donny & Marie Show*
1991—Desert Storm launched with massive U.S. air strikes on Iraqi targets,
      following Iraqi invasion of Kuwait
1997—Israel gave up major area on West Bank

BORN TODAY

Industrialist Andre Michelin	1853	Author Susan Sontag	1933
Olympic runner Eric Liddell	1902	Racer A. J. Foyt	1935
Musical actress Ethel Merman	1909	Singer Aaliyah	1979
Zoologist Dian Fossey	1932	Actress Yvonne Zima	1989

MISDIRECTED COMMUNICATION

A department-store manager in England wrote a note of congratulations to his employee, Gwen James, who worked as a clerk at the store's china counter. He put the note in an envelope and addressed it to: "Mrs. James in china." Two months and ten thousand miles later, the message finally reached its intended destination. The note had traveled around the world to China, was postmarked in Peking, and stamped "Return to Sender."

Such confusion isn't limited to the mail. President John F. Kennedy told of being awakened early one morning by the ringing of the emergency phone near his bed. Kennedy answered and said, "This is the president." At the other end of the line, a hesitant voice responded timidly, "I'm sorry; I was trying to reach a French laundry," and hung up. White House technicians never were able to discover how the call had gotten misdirected to the presidential hot line.

It's amazing what mix-ups can occur in this age of rapid communication. But we can be thankful that God never mixes things up, fails to understand us, or gets things wrong. His prayer "hot line" is open twenty-four hours a day, from any location. His line is never busy, and you'll never get a wrong number or be disconnected.

Have you communicated with God through prayer today? He's waiting to hear from you.

TODAY'S POWER POINT

Great minds discuss ideas; average minds discuss events; small minds discuss people.—Eleanor Roosevelt

January 17

TODAY IN HISTORY

1871—Cable car patented
1917—Virgin Islands acquired from Denmark
1955—First nuclear-powered undersea voyage launched, USS *Nautilus*
1984—Home videotaping of TV programs ruled legal
1995—Kobe, Japan, rocked by earthquake, more than five thousand dead

BORN TODAY

Statesman and inventor Benjamin
   Franklin 1706
Novelist Anne Brontë 1820
Dramatist Anton Chekhov 1860

Actor James Earl Jones 1931
Talk-show host Maury Povich . . . 1939
Boxer Muhammad Ali 1942
Actor Jim Carrey 1962

WORDS OF HOPE

It's amazing how effective a bit of encouragement can be to those who are in need of hope. The mother of a severely crippled boy was helping him learn to walk. His spindly legs were nearly covered by heavy metal braces that caused him to hobble along, one halting step at a time. As he strained to move, his mother encouraged each improvement, no matter how small. At her every word the youngster would try still harder.

The boy's confidence increased, and one day he said to his mother, "Watch me. I'm going to run." He did well for a few steps, but then his brace caught and he would have tumbled to the ground had his mother not caught him at the last moment. She wrapped the dejected boy up in her arms, kissed him, and said, "You did fine! And I know you'll do even better next time!"

Our heavenly Father is like that—ready to lift us up when we've fallen, there with support and encouragement when we're ready to quit. The Bible tells us, "We are more than conquerors through him who loved us" (Romans 8:37). Let God encourage your heart today. With his help you can win the race of life.

TODAY'S POWER POINT

Winners never quit and quitters never win.—Vince Lombardi

TODAY IN HISTORY

1535—Lima, Peru, founded by Francisco Pizzaro
1911—First plane landing on a navy ship
1948—Premiere of *Ted Mack's Original Amateur Hour*
1966—Indira Ghandi elected Indian prime minister
1975—Premiere of television's *The Jeffersons*
1993—Martin Luther King Jr. holiday first observed in all fifty states
1998—Four Golden Globes awarded to motion picture *Titanic*

BORN TODAY

Orator Daniel Webster 1782
Linguist Peter Roget 1779
Author A. A. Milne 1882
Comedian Oliver Hardy 1892
Actor Cary Grant 1904

Actor Kevin Costner 1955
Hockey player Mark Messier 1961
Actress Alison Arngrim (Nellie Oleson)
. . . . 1962

TEACHERS

Great teachers are rarely popular. "I have long ago maintained that any college can raise its standards simply by firing annually whichever professor is voted Best Liked by the graduating class," author and critic Clifton Fadiman once wrote.

Whether teachers are well liked or not, they have an awesome responsibility. *The Mediator* reported on a study at Johns Hopkins University: a professor asked his graduate students to locate two hundred inner-city boys and predict their future. Their conclusion? They predicted that 90 percent of the boys would eventually serve time in jail.

Twenty-five years later a similar group of students tracked down the original subjects of the study, locating all but a few. Much to their amazement, they discovered that only four had ever been to jail. How had these high-risk kids managed to stay out of trouble? Further probing led to one woman who had taught most of them in class. When pressed for the secret of her success, the elderly woman replied only that she had truly loved her students. Those youths had experienced firsthand what makes the difference between a good teacher and a great teacher.

Exodus 18:20 gives advice pertinent for anyone who would be a great teacher: "Teach them the decrees and laws, and show them the way to live." Everyone has something to teach others. Whom are you teaching? What are they learning from you? Become a faithful example (teacher) to your family and others around you, accurately mirroring God's love at work in your life. Remember that love is the key that opens the hearts and minds of students.

TODAY'S POWER POINT

A teacher affects eternity; he can never tell where his influence stops.—Henry Brooks Adams

January 19

TODAY IN HISTORY

1825—Food-canning process patented
1937—Transcontinental flight record set by Howard Hughes
1955—First televised news conference held by President Dwight Eisenhower; premiere of television's *The Millionaire*
1988—Premiere of television's *48 Hours*
2000—Death of actress Hedy Lamarr, age eighty-six

BORN TODAY

Engineer James Watt 1736
General Robert E. Lee 1807
Author Edgar Allan Poe 1809
Painter Paul Cézanne 1839
Actress Jean Stapleton. 1923
Singer Phil Everly. 1942
Singer Janis Joplin 1943
Singer and actress Dolly Parton . . 1946
Musician and actor Desi Arnaz Jr.. . .1953
Actress Jodie Sweetin 1982

PEACE AT HOME

Helping people keep their home and work lives in balance is an increasing concern of both business and government. Douglas MacArthur II once served as the U.S. ambassador to Japan. A hard-working man, he also had once served in the State Department under the equally ambitious John Foster Dulles.

On one occasion Dulles called the MacArthur residence to speak to Douglas. Mrs. MacArthur, who answered the call, thought Dulles was an aide and shouted, "MacArthur is where MacArthur always is, weekdays, Saturdays, Sundays, and nights—in the office!"

Dulles immediately called MacArthur's office and urged him, "Go home at once, boy. Your home front is crumbling."

Peace at home is vital not just for nations but for individuals as well. Thank God for those in your home, and seek his help in keeping your family in the right place on your priority list.

TODAY'S POWER POINT

He is happiest . . . who finds peace in his home.—Goethe

TODAY IN HISTORY

1801—John Marshall appointed as U.S. chief justice

1887—U.S. acquired land for naval base at Pearl Harbor

1892—First basketball game

1961—John F. Kennedy became youngest elected U.S. president (at age forty-three)

1980—U.S. threatened to withdraw from Summer Olympics if not moved from Moscow

1981—Iran freed fifty-two U.S. hostages held for 444 days

1986—France and Britain announced joint effort to tunnel under English Channel

1996—Yasser Arafat elected Palestinian president

2000—Official start of Census 2000 in Alaska

2001—George W. Bush sworn in as forty-third U.S. president

2004—Estate of McDonald's heir Joan Kroc donated record $1.5 billion to Salvation Army

BORN TODAY

Comedian George Burns	1896	Socialite Ivana Trump	1949
Director Federico Fellini	1920	Comedian Bill Maher	1956
Actress Patricia Neal	1926	Actor Lorenzo Lamas	1958
Director David Lynch	1946	TV host Melissa Rivers	1969

PEACE IN THE MIDST OF TURMOIL

A man who helped create the atomic bomb was once asked if there were any defense against the weapon. "Certainly," he replied. "Peace!"

In a world where everyone desires peace, how much peace has actually been experienced throughout recorded history? The *Personnel Journal* reported that since Creation, the world has been entirely at peace only 8 percent of the time. In more than 3,100 years of recorded history, only 286 years have been without war; and eight thousand treaties have been broken during this time.

But what about inner peace? Theologian Paul Lee Tan noted that the "peace that passes our comprehension is not a quality of life which excludes us from the stresses and strains of human society. It is not a sheltered withdrawal from the wrongs that rack our world. Nor is it a cloistered existence in which we are cut off from the calamities and conflicts of our generation. The place of peace to which God our Father calls us is that intimate inner acquaintance with himself, whereby we come to know so assuredly, 'Father, You are here! And all is well!'"

That is true peace. Today pray for peace—not only world peace but also the God-given peace of mind which passes all understanding.

TODAY'S POWER POINT

I will lie down and sleep in peace, for you alone, O Lord, make me dwell in safety.—Psalm 4:8

January 21

TODAY IN HISTORY

1915—Kiwanis issued first club charter
1924—Death of first Soviet Union premier Vladimir Lenin, age fifty-four
1950—Alger Hiss, former state-department employee, convicted of perjury
1954—U.S. Navy launched first nuclear-powered submarine, USS *Nautilus*
1959—Death of producer Cecil B. DeMille, age seventy-eight
1976—Concorde aircraft began regular transatlantic passenger service
1977—President Jimmy Carter pardoned Vietnam-era war protesters
1995—O. J. Simpson trial opened in California
1998—First visit of a pope to Cuba (John Paul II)
2000—Grandmothers of Elian Gonzalez appeared in U.S. court to plead for six-
     year-old's return to Cuba

BORN TODAY

Inventor John Fitch 1743
Confederate general Thomas "Stonewall"
     Jackson 1824
Designer Christian Dior 1905
Actor Telly Savalas 1927
Radio personality Wolfman Jack . . 1939
Golf champion Jack Nicklaus 1940
Opera singer Placido Domingo . . 1941
Actress Geena Davis 1957
Basketball player Hakeem Olajuwon
     1963

AT PEACE

President Dwight Eisenhower once noted, "All the world wants peace." This is especially true today, but violence and wars make peace seem elusive. Still, the longing for peace is a basic human desire, and the striving for peace represents the best and noblest of our human nature. Such efforts have been among the finest moments in human history.

Christian Victory reported that the motto of the *Apollo 11* moon flight was, "We come in peace for all mankind." This was inscribed on the plaque that was placed on the moon after the lunar module landed in the Sea of Tranquility, where there had never been any humans to disturb the peace.

In a world populated by many troublemakers, it's safe to say that millions are searching for stability and peace. Christians hold the answer to the world's quest for peace. Isaiah 52:7 says, "How beautiful on the mountains are the feet of those who bring good news, who proclaim peace, who bring good tidings, who proclaim salvation." Share God's good news of peace with those you meet today.

TODAY'S POWER POINT

The wisdom that comes from heaven is first of all pure; then peace-loving, considerate, submissive, full of mercy and good fruit, impartial and sincere.
—James 3:17

TODAY IN HISTORY

1881—Cleopatra's Needle, a gift from Egypt, erected in New York City's Central Park

1901—Death of Britain's Queen Victoria, age eighty-two

1944—Allies stormed ashore at Anzio Beach, Italy

1972—European Common Market expanded to ten nations

1973—Supreme Court legalized abortion in *Roe v. Wade* decision; death of former president Lyndon Johnson, age sixty-four

1997—Man-made space junk first struck a human (in Tulsa, Oklahoma)

1998—Justice Department announced partial settlement with Microsoft in antitrust suit

BORN TODAY

English statesman and philosopher
    Francis Bacon 1561

Physicist Andre Ampere 1775

Poet George Byron 1788

Director D. W. Griffith 1875

Aviator Willa Brown Chappell . . . 1906

Actress Ann Sothern 1911

Singer Steve Perry 1949

Actress Olivia D'Abo 1967

Actor Christopher Masterson 1980

Actress Robyn Richards 1987

PLEASURE

One of Americans' favorite amusements is riding roller coasters. The first "switchback" roller coaster was built by former Sunday-school teacher Lemarcus Thompson; it opened at Coney Island, New York, in 1884. The coaster traveled at only six miles per hour, and its biggest drop was just thirty feet, but it attracted much attention and plenty of riders. It eventually led to the high-speed coaster that opened at Coney Island in 1927.

Americans spend ever-increasing amounts of money each year on amusements and pleasure. While there's nothing wrong with relaxation and recreation (indeed, both are essential to well-rounded living), something *is* wrong when the pursuit of pleasure becomes our major obsession in life. It's easy to get so caught up in temporary thrills that we forget that the truest pleasures are spiritual, not physical. King David knew the source of true pleasure. In Psalm 16:11 he wrote: "You have made known to me the path of life; you will fill me with joy in your presence, with eternal pleasures at your right hand."

So take a break, relax, and enjoy yourself from time to time. But don't forget to find the pleasure that can be yours only in the presence of God.

TODAY'S POWER POINT

It now costs more to amuse a child than it once did to educate his father.— Vaughan Monroe

January 23

TODAY IN HISTORY

1793—First aid organization established (Humane Society of Philadelphia)
1849—First U.S. woman physician awarded MD degree (Dr. Elizabeth Blackwell)
1950—Israel proclaimed Jerusalem its capital
1968—North Korea seized intelligence ship USS *Pueblo*
1973—President Richard Nixon announced end to Vietnam War
1974—Panel ruled erasure of key Nixon White House conversation from tape was not accidental
1997—As new secretary of state, Madeline Albright became highest-ranking female U.S. official
2005—Viktor Yuschenko sworn in to head Ukraine

BORN TODAY

Declaration of Independence signer
  John Hancock. 1737
Painter Edouard Manet 1832
Comedian Ernie Kovacs 1919

Actress Jeanne Moreau 1928
Actress Chita Rivera 1933
Radio host Laura Schlessinger . . . 1947
Actress Tiffany Amber Thiessen . . 1974

A BETTER IDEA

F. W. Woolworth, a young hardware clerk, got permission to set up a counter of miscellaneous items that he priced at just ten cents. The items sold quickly, and Woolworth urged his boss to open an entire store offering similar low-cost products. The boss said the plan would never work because there weren't enough items to sell for a dime. Undeterred, Woolworth launched the first "five-and-dime store"—the high-volume discount store of his day.

Years later former dime-store owner Sam Walton expanded on that concept to establish the world's largest retail chain, Wal-Mart—now a megacorporation with thousands of locations worldwide.

Similarly, Ray Kroc believed that by selling large volumes of carry-out food at a low profit margin, he could build a successful business. The popularity today of the McDonald's golden arches proves he was right.

The Bible addresses the subject of business in a number of passages. In Luke 2:49 (NKJV), a twelve-year-old Jesus asked his parents, "Did you not know that I must be about My Father's business?"

There is room for good business practices in this life, as well as being about our Father's business, the rewards of which will last forever. The key is to find and maintain the proper balance. Ask God to give you the wisdom to balance those things that last eternally with all the other activities of your daily life.

TODAY'S POWER POINT

Human progress has often depended on the courage of a man who dared to be different.—Herbert Prochnow

January 24

TODAY IN HISTORY

1848—Gold discovered in California
1907—New motorcycle land-speed record set (136 mph)
1908—Boy Scouts founded
1922—Eskimo Pie ice-cream bar patented
1946—U.S. Army sent first radar signal to moon and back
1958—American-British scientific team triggered first thermonuclear reaction
1965—Death of British leader Winston Churchill, age ninety-one
1981—Millions in Poland went on strike in support of Solidarity union
1984—Apple's first Macintosh personal computer went on sale (for $2,495, with
       128 KB memory)
1986—U.S. space probe *Voyager II* sent back pictures of Uranus
1996—FDA approved fat substitute Olestra

BORN TODAY

Prussian king Frederick the Great . 1712
Author Edith Wharton 1862
Producer Mark Goodson 1915
Actor Ernest Borgnine 1917
Evangelist Oral Roberts 1918
Singer Neil Diamond 1941
Comedian John Belushi 1949
Gymnast Mary Lou Retton 1968
Actress Mischa Barton 1986

PRESSING ON

Thomas A. Edison earned a total of 1,098 patents during his lifetime, but only after years of frustrating setbacks and thousands of largely unsuccessful experiments. When asked if he became discouraged by all his failures, Edison replied, "I have not failed. I've just found ten thousand ways that won't work."

Does it seem that you're having more than your share of failures, while everyone else seems to be doing well? If so, recognize that everyone makes mistakes; everyone has failed—probably many times—before finding success. Edison, who could be the poster child for perseverance in the face of failure, said, "Many of life's failures are men who did not realize how close they were to success when they gave up."

So don't give up in the face of what feels like failure. You may be closer to success and victory than you realize. Keep going. The apostle Paul wrote, "Forgetting what is behind and straining toward what is ahead, I press on toward the goal to win the prize" (Philippians 3:13–14). Press on! When you fall short of your expectations, remember that failure is simply deferred success, and with God's help, pick yourself up, dust yourself off, and move on to win the prize.

TODAY'S POWER POINT

Anyone can make a mistake; the key to success is not to make the same mistake again.—Source Unknown

January 25

TODAY IN HISTORY

1890—Reporter Nellie Bly traveled around the world (in record time of seventy-two days, six hours, eleven minutes)

1915—First transcontinental telephone call (Alexander Graham Bell called San Francisco from New York City)

1961—First live televised presidential news conference (John F. Kennedy)

1974—South African surgeon Dr. Christian Barnard completed first human heart transplant

1980—U.S. Navy hovercraft set warship speed record of 103 mph

1985—U.S. broke ties with Libya over continued terrorism

2002—The *Guiding Light* achieved a record-breaking daily run of sixty-five consecutive years on radio and TV

BORN TODAY

Poet Robert Burns 1759
Novelist Somerset Maugham 1874
Author Virginia Woolf 1882
Sportscaster Ernie Harwell 1918
Actor Dean Jones 1931
Philippine president Corazon Aquino 1933
Actress Leigh Taylor-Young 1945
Basketball player Vince Carter . . . 1977
Singer Alicia Keys. 1981

A GOOD REPUTATION

A young man, called upon to preach on short notice, chose as his text, "Thou shalt not steal" (Exodus 20:15 KJV). The next day he boarded a bus, handed the driver a dollar bill, took his change, and walked to the back of the bus. Before taking his seat, the young man paused to count his change and noticed he had been given an extra dime. His first thought was that the bus company would never miss it. But he soon decided he must return the coin, so he went to the front of the bus and handed the coin back to the driver. "You gave me too much change," he said.

"Yes," the driver replied, "I gave it to you purposely. I heard your sermon yesterday, and I watched in my mirror as you counted your change. Had you kept it, I never again would have had confidence in any preacher."

You can never tell who might be watching what you do each day. What a great opportunity you have to influence those around you—even when it seems no one is watching. So, as the apostle Peter said, "Be careful how you live among your unbelieving neighbors. Even if they accuse you of doing wrong, they will see your honorable behavior, and they will believe and give honor to God" (1 Peter 2:12 NLT).

TODAY'S POWER POINT

People may doubt what you say, but they will always believe what you do.
—Source Unknown

January 26

TODAY IN HISTORY

1778—First British settlement established in Australia

1837—Twenty-sixth state, Michigan, joined Union

1875—Electrically powered dental drill patented

1911—Naval aviator Glenn Curtiss made first successful water takeoff

1934—Historic Apollo theater opened in Harlem, New York

1940—Actor Ronald Reagan married actress Jane Wyman

1945—Lt. Audie Murphy, most-decorated World War II soldier (awarded thirty-seven medals and ribbons) wounded in France

1949—First high-speed audiotape duplicator introduced

1979—Death of former vice president Nelson Rockefeller, age seventy

1988—Australia celebrated its bicentennial

1996—Major arms-reduction treaty approved by U.S. Senate

BORN TODAY

General Douglas MacArthur 1880

Actor Paul Newman 1925

Cartoonist Jules Feiffer 1929

Sportscaster Bob Uecker 1935

Actor Scott Glenn 1942

Film critic Gene Siskel 1946

Musician Eddie Van Halen 1955

Singer Anita Baker 1958

Hockey player Wayne Gretzky . . . 1961

Gospel singer Kirk Franklin 1970

BEING CHRISTLIKE

Bible teacher Warren Wiersbe told the story of the pious church member who visited the sixth-grade Sunday-school class. He asked the students, "Why do you think people call me a Christian?" An embarrassing silence was finally broken by a small voice from the back of the class: "Because they don't know you?"

That honest answer hits most Christians right between the eyes at one time or another.

The term *Christian* (literally, "little Christs") was first applied to believers at Antioch, Greece. These people had such great moral fortitude and backbone that, in all, they seemed Christlike. What a challenge to us today! Do you live your life in such a way that God is glorified by your character, or is he ashamed of your behavior? What a tragedy to be considered of poor character by Christ. Ask him to make you worthy of his name today—in your thoughts, words, and deeds.

TODAY'S POWER POINT

Holiness is not the way to Christ; Christ is the way to holiness.—Source Unknown

January 27

TODAY IN HISTORY

1785—First state university chartered (University of Georgia)
1880—Incandescent electric bulb patented
1888—National Geographic Society established
1918—First *Tarzan* movie released
1943—U.S. Army Air Force launched first World War II air attack on Germany
1945—Soviet troops freed Auschwitz prisoners
1948—First tape recorder sold
1959—First candidates for manned U.S. space program selected, including John Glenn
1967—Three U.S. astronauts killed in a flash fire aboard *Apollo I* spacecraft
1973—Official end of Vietnam War (longest U.S. war)
1976—Premiere of TV series *Laverne and Shirley*
2003—UN weapons inspectors reported Iraq's "noncompliance"

BORN TODAY

Composer Wolfgang Amadeus Mozart 1756
Theologian David Strauss 1808
Author Lewis Carroll 1832
Composer Jerome Kern 1885

Actress Donna Reed 1921
Actor Troy Donahue 1936
Sportscaster Chris Collinsworth . . 1959
Actress Bridget Fonda 1964
Country singer Tracy Lawrence . . 1968

YOUNG ACHIEVERS

Many of history's greatest achievers showed signs of future greatness at an early age. Josiah became king of Judah when he was just eight. Jeremiah was likely a teenager when God called him to be a prophet. Joan of Arc did all her work and was burned at the stake by the age of nineteen. Charles Spurgeon built the great Metropolitan Tabernacle in London when he was twenty-seven.

Clearly God can use young people when their lives are surrendered to him. Youth or lack of experience is never an acceptable excuse for not answering God's call. When God told Jeremiah he had appointed him to be a prophet, Jeremiah protested, "I do not know how to speak; I am only a child." But God would hear none of it. "Do not say, 'I am only a child.' You must go to everyone I send you to and say whatever I command you. Do not be afraid of them, for I am with you" (Jeremiah 1:6–8).

Jeremiah became one of the greatest prophets of the Old Testament because he was willing to accept God's calling on his life. What is God calling you to do today? You're just the right age to do what he asks.

TODAY'S POWER POINT

Don't let anyone look down on you because you are young, but set an example for the believers in speech, in life, in love, in faith and in purity.—1 Timothy 4:12

January 28

TODAY IN HISTORY

1871—Germans conquered Paris
1878—Publication of first college newspaper, *Yale Daily News*; first telephone switchboard installed
1902—Carnegie Institution launched with $10 million gift
1915—U.S. Coast Guard founded
1916—Louis Brandeis became first Jew appointed to U.S. Supreme Court
1938—Rudolf Caracciola set world speed record of 268 mph on a public highway (the German autobahn)
1960—First photograph of the moon (transmitted from Hawaii to Washington DC)
1969—Offshore oil well sprang a leak, causing first disastrous oil spill (covering two hundred miles of California coastline)
1986—U.S. spacecraft *Challenger* exploded moments after liftoff, killing seven-member crew

BORN TODAY

Printer John Baskerville 1706
Evangelist R. A. Torrey 1856
Pianist Artur Rubinstein 1887
Impressionist Jackson Pollock 1912
Sculptor Claes Oldenburg 1929
Actor Alan Alda 1936
Singer Nick Carter 1980
Actor Elijah Wood 1981

PREJUDICE

Maxwell Droke tells of a trial in England that was just about to start when it was noticed that only eleven people were in the jurors' box. When questioned by the lord chancellor about the missing juror, the foreman said, "Don't worry. He was called away by an urgent message, but it'll be all right. He left his verdict with me."

Clearly the juror had already made up his mind before hearing all the evidence. We shake our heads in disapproval at such a story, but we reveal our own prejudices when we judge a person based on skin color, race, gender, age, religion, economic status, or appearance.

It's important to refrain from premature conclusions. We can't really know all the facts or what a person is truly like on the inside. First Corinthians 4:5 instructs us, "Judge nothing before the appointed time; wait till the Lord comes. He will bring to light what is hidden in darkness and will expose the motives of men's hearts." Ask God to help you shed those remnants of prejudice that keep you from loving others as God loves you.

TODAY'S POWER POINT

Prejudices are the chains forged by ignorance to keep men apart.—The Countess of Blessington

January 29

TODAY IN HISTORY

1845—Edgar Allan Poe's *The Raven* published
1861—Thirty-fourth state, Kansas, joined Union
1876—Electoral commission named to decide Hayes-Tilden presidential election
1924—First ice-cream cone rolling machine patented (in Cleveland, Ohio)
1936—First five players named to National Baseball Hall of Fame: Ty Cobb, Babe
        Ruth, Honus Wagner, Christy Mathewson, and Walter Johnson
1963—Death of poet Robert Frost, age eighty-eight
1979—United States signed peace accord with China
1980—Islamic conference condemned Soviet intervention in Afghanistan; six
        Americans escaped from Iran posing as Canadian diplomats; death of
        comedian Jimmy Durante, age ninety-seven
1993—President Bill Clinton modified ban on homosexuals in the military
        (adopting the "Don't Ask, Don't Tell" policy)
1998—Thick fog triggered three-hundred-car pileup in Western Europe, killing six

BORN TODAY

Political writer Thomas Paine 1737
Banker John D. Rockefeller Jr. . . . 1874
Comedian W. C. Fields 1880
Actor Victor Mature 1913
Actor John Forsythe 1918

Actor Tom Selleck 1945
Talk-show host Oprah Winfrey . . 1954
Swimmer Greg Louganis 1960
Actor Nick Turturro 1962
Actress Heather Graham. 1970

DOING GOOD

Don't put off doing acts of kindness as the opportunities arise, for you may never pass this way again. Over one hundred years ago the French-born nobleman Stephen Grellet expressed that idea well in this epic theme: "I shall pass through this life but once. Any good that I can do, or any kindness that I can show to any human being, let me do it now and not defer it. For I shall not pass this way again."

Determine to say that kind word and perform your acts of kindness before it's too late. Pray that God will let you see others through his eyes and love them as he does. Then look for someone who needs your help and encouragement today.

TODAY'S POWER POINT

As the purse is emptied, the heart is filled.—Victor Hugo

TODAY IN HISTORY

1835—First presidential assassination attempt (on Andrew Jackson)

1911—First airplane rescue at sea (biplane pilot John McCurdy rescued ten miles off Havana, Cuba)

1933—Adolf Hitler installed himself as chancellor of Nazi Germany; premier of *The Lone Ranger* on WXYZ radio, Detroit

1948—Assassination of Mahatma Gandhi

1973—Three former aides to President Richard Nixon convicted in Watergate trial

1975—Rubik's Cube patented

1979—Iranian Ayatollah Khomeini freed to return from exile in France

1993—Subway service began in Los Angeles

1996—AIDS named leading cause of death for young Americans

1998—FDA panel approved a new glue to replace stitches in surgery

2000—Kenya Airways crash killed 169

2006—Death of Coretta Scott King, widow of Martin Luther King Jr.

BORN TODAY

Composer Walter Damrosch	 1862	Actress Vanessa Redgrave;	
President Franklin D. Roosevelt	.. 1882	chess player Boris Spassky	 1937
Historian Barbara Tuchman	 1912	Vice President Dick Cheney	 1941
Comedian Dick Martin	 1922	Comedienne Brett Butler	 1958
Actor Gene Hackman	 1930	Basketball player Jalen Rose	 1973

REBELLION

Evangelist J. Wilbur Chapman told the story of a ship that left Boston harbor in a blinding storm in November 1898 and never returned. Just why it sailed no one has ever been able to say. Despite all the danger signals (the government agent at the signal office had advised vessels to remain in port, and even the vessel's owners had ordered the ship to remain docked), the vessel set out to sea. The ship was lost, and all aboard died because of someone's stubborn rebellion against authorities.

Rebellion is caused by pride—an arrogance in thinking that we know more than others, or even more than God. How dangerous it is to believe we have greater knowledge than the Creator of the universe. Is it any wonder, then, that God considers rebellion to be sin? It is serious stuff. First Samuel 15:23 tells us that rebellion is right up there with the big sins: "Rebellion is as bad as the sin of witchcraft, and stubbornness is as bad as worshiping idols" (NLT). Call upon God, asking him to keep your heart sensitive and open to his leading today so you'll never rebel against what he knows is best.

TODAY'S POWER POINT

Civilization is always in danger when those who have never learned to obey are given the right to command.—Fulton J. Sheen

January 31

TODAY IN HISTORY

1863—First black Civil War regiment mustered into U.S. army

1865—Thirteenth Amendment, abolishing slavery, passed by Congress

1915—Poison gas used in combat for first time (by Germany)

1940—First social security check issued

1943—German troops surrendered at Stalingrad, Russia (first major defeat of World War II)

1949—First daytime TV soap opera aired (*These Are My Children*, NBC)

1958—First U.S. satellite launched

1968—Vietcong troops held U.S. embassy staff hostage for six hours

1990—First McDonald's restaurant in Soviet Union opened in Moscow

2006—Senate confirmed Ben Bernanke to head Federal Reserve (replacing Alan Greenspan, who held the post for eighteen years)

BORN TODAY

Composer Franz Schubert 1797

Comedian Eddie Cantor 1892

TV host Garry Moore 1915

Baseball legend Jackie Robinson . . 1919

Author Norman Mailer 1923

Director Stuart Margolin 1940

Baseball player Nolan Ryan 1947

Actress Kelly Lynch 1959

Actress Minnie Driver 1971

Singer Justin Timberlake 1981

THE BEST DEFENSE

It's ironic that a World War II bomb used for ten years as a blacksmith's anvil exploded when it was moved. A similar fiery end lay in store for a gigantic weapon of war built in the sixteenth century. It was a huge cannon with a massive twenty-five-inch bore that could be fired only seven times a day because it took so long to reload. Piles of powder were required for each shot. Though the big gun could shoot up to a mile, it could be heard more than twelve miles away. In all, 650 men were required to move and operate the cannon. But anyone who trusted that weapon to keep him safe would have been disappointed. When it was put into service during the siege of Constantinople, it didn't last long or live up to its hype. It exploded in a fiery inferno, killing its creator, a man named Orban. To this day it is known as Orban's Folly.

While the Bible is clear in its support for us to defend our families and property, we're foolish if we rely on man-made weapons to keep us safe instead of on the God who made man. When we begin to lose sight of God's power and instead try to do things ourselves, we are bound to fail. Only God never fails. Won't you trust him today?

TODAY'S POWER POINT

The problem with the world is not with the bomb. The problem of the world is man.—Clement Attlee

TODAY IN HISTORY

1790—United States Supreme Court first convened

1861—Texas voted to secede from the Union

1865—Abraham Lincoln signed Thirteenth Amendment, abolishing slavery

1887—120-acre tract called "Hollywood" unveiled by developer

1893—First motion-picture studio opened

1898—First car-insurance policy issued

1919—First Miss America crowned in New York City

1949—RCA released first 45 rpm single record

1954—Premiere of first TV soap opera, *Secret Storm*

1959—Swiss men voted against women's right to vote

1965—Martin Luther King Jr. and demonstrators arrested in Selma, Alabama

1978—Harriet Tubman became first black woman honored on a U.S. postage stamp

2003—Breakup of space shuttle *Columbia* over Texas

BORN TODAY

Composer Victor Herbert. 1859

Director John Ford. 1895

Actor Clark Gable 1901

Author Langston Hughes 1902

Russian leader Boris Yeltsin 1931

Singer Don Everly 1937

Actor Sherman Hemsley. 1938

Actor and producer Bill Mumy. . . 1954

Actress Laura Dern. 1967

Singer Lisa Marie Presley 1968

IGNORANCE

One of the most unusual animals in the zoo is the tall, spindly legged bird that attempts to escape danger by sticking its head into the sand. "That's foolish!" you say? Yet many people seem to think that by not attending church or ignoring spiritual things, they can live happily, free of the natural consequences.

Often ignorance of the facts produces unexpected results. There was a story some years ago of a West German man whose wife gave birth to six children in seven years. The man, in his fifties, was angry that the contraceptive pills didn't seem to be working and complained bitterly that "modern medicine is just no good." Upon investigation, his doctor discovered that the man, not his wife, had been taking the pills.

God has given us instructions for life in the Bible. But if we choose to ignore them, we can expect to bear the consequences.

TODAY'S POWER POINT

We live on an island surrounded by a sea of ignorance. As our island of knowledge grows, so does the shore of our ignorance.—John A. Wheeler

TODAY IN HISTORY

1653—New York City incorporated as New Amsterdam
1848—Treaty of Guadalupe Hidalgo ended the Mexican-American War
1863—Samuel Clemens used pseudonym "Mark Twain" for the first time
1876—Baseball's National League established
1880—First electric streetlight installed
1887—First Groundhog Day in Punxsutawney, Pennsylvania
1897—Pennsylvania state capitol destroyed by fire
1912—World's first stuntman performed on film
1913—Grand Central train station officially opened in New York City
1923—Leaded gasoline first sold
1935—First test of polygraph machine (lie detector) in Portage, Wisconsin
1950—Premiere of TV quiz show *What's My Line?*
1982—Premiere of NBC's *Late Night with David Letterman*
1989—Final Russian armored columns left Afghanistan
1998—Budget surplus and first balanced budget in thirty years announced by
          President Bill Clinton
2004—Ricin scare: white powder found in an office of Senate Majority leader Bill Frist

BORN TODAY

Novelist James Joyce. 1882
Violinist Jascha Heifetz. 1901
Author Ayn Rand. 1905
Gossip columnist Liz Smith 1923
Comedian Tom Smothers. 1937
Musician Graham Nash 1942
Actress Farrah Fawcett 1947
Model Christie Brinkley. 1954
Actor Michael T. Weiss. 1962
Basketball player Sean Elliott 1968

DOING IT YOURSELF

Some readers may recall the TV commercial in which a mother, attempting to be helpful, was rebuked by her adult daughter, shouting, "Mother, I'd rather do it myself." Such was not the case with a young girl years ago who seemed to always have problems understanding her math homework. The frustrated girl met a helpful neighbor and often sought his assistance. Her mother, becoming increasingly alarmed at the girl's boldness, finally went to the neighbor, scientist Albert Einstein, to apologize. Einstein said, "You don't have to apologize. I have learned more from the conversations with the child than she has from me."

Although our heavenly Father knows what we need even before we ask, he nonetheless wants to hear from us and is ready to assist anytime, 24/7, if we will but call upon him. Don't let your pride and independence keep you from trusting God!

TODAY'S POWER POINT

The more meek that a man is and the more subject to God, the more wise shall he be in all things.—Thomas à Kempis

TODAY IN HISTORY

1690—Paper money first issued in the United States (Massachusetts)
1783—Spain recognized independence of the United States
1809—Territory of Illinois created
1870—Right to vote extended to all races through Fifteenth Amendment
1889—"Bandit Queen" Belle Starr murdered in Oklahoma
1894—First steel sailing ship launched
1913—Federal income tax authorized by Sixteenth Amendment
1919—First League of Nations meeting (in Paris)
1924—Death of President Woodrow Wilson, age sixty-seven
1938—Abbott and Costello made first radio broadcast
1959—Death of pop singers Buddy Holly, Ritchie Valens, and "The Big Bopper"
      Richardson in snowy Iowa plane crash
1966—Soviets' first soft moon landing
1969—Yasser Arafat appointed leader of Palestinian Liberation Organization
1994—Nineteen-year trade ban against Vietnam lifted
2000—Alan Greenspan confirmed to fourth term as Federal Reserve chairman

BORN TODAY

Composer Felix Mendelssohn. . . . 1809
Newspaperman Horace Greeley . . 1811
Artist Norman Rockwell. 1894
Author James Michener 1907
Football player Fran Tarkenton. . . 1940

Actress Blythe Danner 1943
Sportscaster Bob Griese 1945
Actress Morgan Fairchild 1950
Actor Nathan Lane. 1956

PEACE

Just how long, exactly, has the world been at peace? Although statistics differ, they all point to the same trend: since the end of World War I, there has been an average of just two minutes of peace worldwide for every three years of war. Clearly, peace is a much-sought-after, but elusive, goal in this life. How wonderful then to know the Prince of Peace, whom to know is life eternal.

During the Cold War years a popular chorus sung by Christian youth said, "What though wars may come with marching feet and beat of the drum, for I have Christ in my heart." This kind of peace is what the apostle Paul described as the peace "which surpasses all understanding" (Philippians 4:7 NKJV).

God's Word promises inner peace now for those who follow him and the assurance of everlasting peace in the world to come.

TODAY'S POWER POINT

With God in charge of our defenses, there will be peace within.—T. T. Faichney

TODAY IN HISTORY

1789—Electoral votes cast to officially make George Washington first U.S. president-elect

1826—*The Last of the Mohicans,* by James Fennimore Cooper, published

1861—Confederate States of America established

1932—Winter Olympics first held in the United States at Lake Placid, New York

1962—St. Jude Children's Research Hospital opened

1974—Publishing heiress Patty Hearst kidnapped from her California apartment

1997—O. J. Simpson found liable in civil trial for deaths of former wife, Nicole Brown, and her friend

2003—Yugoslavia formally disbanded by lawmakers

BORN TODAY

Aviator Charles Lindbergh 1902

Theologian Dietrich Bonhoeffer . . 1906

Civil-rights pioneer Rosa Parks . . . 1913

Feminist Betty Friedan 1921

Argentine president Isabel Perón . 1931

Comedian David Brenner 1945

Vice President Dan Quayle 1947

Musician Alice Cooper 1948

Boxer Oscar de la Hoya 1973

EXPERIENCE

What a difference a little experience makes! According to the story, famed pianist Paderewski was walking through a small Connecticut town one day when he noticed a sign reading, "Miss Jones, piano lessons—25 cents an hour." Listening, he heard someone inside trying to play one of Chopin's nocturnes but not doing very well. So the great pianist walked up to the door and offered to assist. Immediately the delighted teacher recognized the famed musician and invited him in to play. After spending about an hour correcting the woman's mistakes, he moved on. Some months later Paderewski was again in town and strolled by the same house, where he noticed a new sign: "Miss Jones (pupil of Paderewski), piano lessons—$1.00 an hour."

Some years ago *The Gospel Banner* looked into the accomplishments of 400 famous achievers. Their findings? "Of the group's greatest achievements, 35 percent came when the men were between 60 and 70; 23 percent when they were between 70 and 80; and 8 percent when they were more than 80. In other words, 66 percent of the world's greatest work has been done by men past 60."

The Bible recognizes varying levels of Christian maturity and even has suggestions for how to gain spiritual strength through spiritual growth and experience. How experienced are you?

TODAY'S POWER POINT

Experience is a wonderful thing. It helps you to recognize a mistake when you make it again.—Source Unknown

TODAY IN HISTORY

1846—First U.S. newspaper published on the West Coast (*Oregon Spectator*)

1881—Phoenix, Arizona, incorporated

1924—First U.S. president buried in Washington DC (Woodrow Wilson)

1983—Musical score authenticated as Mozart's first symphony (composed at age nine)

1988—Panama's military strongman Manuel Noriega indicted on drug-smuggling charges

1994—White supremacist Byron De La Beckwith convicted of 1963 murder of civil-rights leader Medgar Evers

1999—Boxing champ Mike Tyson sentenced to a year in prison for assaulting two motorists

2001—Kelly Ripa announced as new cohost of *Live with Regis and Kelly*

2004—Secretary of State Colin Powell revealed new intelligence before the United Nations as evidence against Iraq

BORN TODAY

Clergyman John Witherspoon . . . 1723

Evangelist D. L. Moody 1837

Politician Adlai Stevenson 1900

Author William Burroughs. 1914

Baseball player Hank Aaron 1934

Quarterback Roger Staubach 1942

Racer Darrell Waltrip 1947

Writer Christopher Guest. 1948

Singer Elton John. 1949

Actress Jennifer Jason Leigh 1962

Baseball player Roberto Alomar . . 1968

Musician and actor Bobby Brown. . 1969

Twin actors Jeremy and Jessica Sumpter
. . . . 1989

JUSTICE

Justice sometimes takes on unusual forms. A loud commotion erupted on a Japanese street one day as one man leaped upon another and beat him furiously. "Confess!" he yelled. "No," gasped his struggling victim, "I didn't do it!" An investigation revealed how the attacker had been wrongly imprisoned for twenty-three years for a crime he did not commit. Following his release, his search for his accuser led to the street battle in which he unleashed all the anger pent up for more than twenty years. Eventually the man was fully exonerated, yet there was no way he could recover the decades he'd lost in prison.

Human justice sometimes moves slowly, and occasionally it's simply not just. But God offers not only his justice but also his grace to those who believe in him.

TODAY'S POWER POINT

"Injustice will not end," Socrates once said, until "those who are not wronged feel as indignant as those who are."

February 6

TODAY IN HISTORY

1788—Sixth state, Massachusetts, ratified U.S. Constitution
1891—First train robbery by the Dalton gang
1911—First old-age home opened for pioneers in Arizona
1921—Movie *The Kid* released (starring Charlie Chaplin and Jackie Coogan)
1935—Board game Monopoly first sold
1948—First radio-controlled airplane flown
1952—Princess Elizabeth, age twenty-six, crowned as Queen Elizabeth II
1971—Alan Shepard hit first golf ball on the moon
1991—Death of comedian Danny Thomas, age seventy-seven
1998—National Airport in Washington DC renamed Reagan National Airport
2000—Former First Lady Hillary Clinton declared candidacy for U.S. Senate

BORN TODAY

Vice President Aaron Burr 1756
Baseball great Babe Ruth 1895
President Ronald Reagan 1911
Archeologist Mary Leakey 1913
Actress Zsa Zsa Gabor 1919
Actor Mike Farrell 1939
Broadcast journalist Tom Brokaw . 1940
Singer Fabian 1943
Reggae artist Bob Marley 1945
Singer Natalie Cole 1950
Actress Kathy Najimy 1957
Singer Axl Rose 1962

THE LITTLE THINGS

Late one night, years ago, a tired elderly couple approached the desk clerk at a small, humble hotel in Philadelphia and pleaded for a room. But a convention was in town, and every available room was booked. The old man inquired, "Are there any rooms left anywhere?" Upon thinking, the young clerk realized that, since he worked the overnight shift, his room would be available, so he offered it to the weary travelers.

At breakfast the next morning the couple summoned the kindly clerk. "You're too good a hotel man for this place," the man said. "How would you like for me to build a big, beautiful, luxurious hotel in New York City?" The clerk, stunned at first, finally blurted out, "Why, it sounds wonderful!" Later he would learn that the elderly man was none other than John Jacob Astor, who went on to build the famed Waldorf-Astoria Hotel. Because of his faithfulness in the little things, that lowly night clerk eventually became one of the greatest hoteliers in all the world.

God has prepared a wonderful place for you to live, if you're willing to choose faithfulness to him over the temporary, fleeting pleasures of this life.

TODAY'S POWER POINT

A true friend has been defined as "the one who walks in when the whole world has gone out."

TODAY IN HISTORY

1904—Fire leveled Baltimore, more than 1,500 businesses destroyed

1948—General Dwight D. Eisenhower resigned as army chief of staff, replaced by General Omar Bradley

1964—Arrival in New York of British rock group the Beatles

1984—First untethered space walk (astronauts Bruce McCandless Jr. and Robert L. Stewart)

1985—"Baby Doc" Duvalier fled Haiti

1990—Collapse of the Soviet Union; Central Committee agreed to give up its power monopoly

1992—European Union formed

1999—Jordan's Crown Prince Abdullah became king upon the death of his father, King Hussein

2000—Sixth straight PGA tour event won by golfer Tiger Woods

2002—President George W. Bush announced faith-based initiatives plan

BORN TODAY

Manufacturer John Deere 1804
Author Charles Dickens 1812
Author Laura Ingalls Wilder 1867
Novelist Sinclair Lewis 1885
Actor Buster Crabbe 1907

Baseball player Dan Quisenberry . 1953
Singer Garth Brooks 1962
Comedian Chris Rock 1965
Basketball player Juwan Howard . 1973
Actor Ashton Kutcher 1978

RAISING CHILDREN

Today, more than ever, children are being influenced by outside forces their predecessors could never even have imagined.

One highly successful parent from an earlier era was Susannah Wesley, mother of John and Charles Wesley—and fifteen others. John Wesley, writing in his journal, recalled several of his mother's rules for children: "When turned a year old, they were taught to fear the rod and to cry softly to forego further punishment. In order to form the child's mind, their will must first be conquered," he wrote, for "by neglecting timely correction, they will contract a stubbornness and obstinacy which is hardly ever after conquered. . . . Self-will is the root of all sin and misery, so whatever checks it promotes their future happiness."

What a tremendous responsibility is child-raising! As a parent it's important for you to do your best to make sure your kids are exposed to good influences—ones that will help them to know God and do what is right.

TODAY'S POWER POINT

A father of ten was asked why he had so many children. "Because," he said, "we never wanted the youngest one to be spoiled!"

February 8

TODAY IN HISTORY

1587—Execution of Mary, Queen of Scots
1861—Confederate States of America formed
1910—U.S. Boy Scouts organized
1915—Premiere of classic film *Birth of a Nation*
1924—First coast-to-coast radio broadcast
1926—Walt Disney Studios formed
1936—First NFL draft: Jay Berwanger selected first by Philadelphia Eagles
1963—Dallas Texans became the Kansas City Chiefs
1969—*Saturday Evening Post*'s last issue published
1983—Wayne Gretzky set NHL all-star record, four goals in one period
1998—First women's ice-hockey game in Olympics history: Finland beat Sweden 6-0

BORN TODAY

Author Jules Verne 1828
Author Kate Chopin 1851
Actor Jack Lemmon 1925
Actor James Dean. 1931
Broadcast journalist Ted Koppel . . 1940
Actor Nick Nolte 1941
Actress Mary Steenburgen 1953
Author John Grisham. 1955
Actor Gary Coleman 1968
Basketball player Alonzo Mourning
. . . . 1970
Actor Seth Green 1974

WEATHER

Sometimes it seems nothing is as changeable as the weather. Many dramatic shifts in weather patterns have been noted in recent years. One confirmation of how the weather can be affected is shown in a 1974 Soviet military plan that described "(1) creating holes in the ozone layer of the upper atmosphere, (which would let in deadly radiation) (2) setting off a nuclear explosion under the polar ice caps (likely triggering a meltdown that could put 'whole areas' underwater), and (3) creating acoustic fields on the sea surface to combat naval vessels." According to the Soviet official, these were not idle proposals but real scientific likelihoods.

The Bible predicts that weather patterns will become increasingly erratic as we approach the last days. How important it is, then, to trust in an unchanging God in these uncertain times. In the book of Matthew, Jesus assured us we can do just that: "Do not worry, saying, 'What shall we eat?' or 'What shall we drink?' or 'What shall we wear?' . . . But seek first his kingdom and his righteousness, and all these things will be given to you as well. Therefore do not worry about tomorrow" (Matthew 6:31–34). Put your hope in the God who made heaven and earth (including the weather).

TODAY'S POWER POINT

The world hates change, yet it is the only thing that has brought progress.
—Charles F. Kettering

TODAY IN HISTORY

1775—English parliament declared Massachusetts colony in rebellion

1825—Election (in the House of Representatives) of President John Quincy Adams, first son of a former president to be elected

1861—Jefferson Davis chosen president of Confederate States

1867—Nebraska became thirty-seventh state

1870—Launch of Federal Meteorological Service (National Weather Service)

1942—American clocks turned ahead one hour for "War Time"

1943—President Franklin D. Roosevelt ordered workweeks of at least forty-eight hours in critical war industry

1951—Pitcher Satchel Paige signed by St. Louis Browns at age forty-five

1964—First appearance of the Beatles on *Ed Sullivan Show*; GI Joe character created

1971—Pitcher Satchel Paige, first negro-league player, inducted into sports hall of fame

1999—*The Simpsons* eclipsed *The Flintstones* as the longest-running primetime animated series

BORN TODAY

Ninth president William Henry Harrison 1773
Poet Amy Lowell 1874
Singer Ernest Tubb 1914
Broadcast journalist Roger Mudd . 1928
Musician Smokey Robinson 1940

Singer and songwriter Carole King 1942
Actor Joe Pesci 1943
Actress Mia Farrow 1945
Actress Judith Light 1949
Country singer Travis Tritt 1963

GRACE ENOUGH

One day evangelist Charles Spurgeon was returning home after a hard day's work, feeling tired and depressed. Suddenly the words from Scripture, "My grace is sufficient for thee," entered his mind. Spurgeon then thought of the fish who might be afraid lest they drink the river dry but who hear the reassuring word, "Drink up, little fish, my stream is sufficient for thee." Or the mouse who, in Joseph's grain bins in Egypt, worried about depleting the supply of grain only to be reassured, "Cheer up, little mouse, my granaries are sufficient for thee." Or a mountain climber fearing lest he exhaust all the thin oxygen in the atmosphere being reassured, "Breathe away, young man, and fill thy lungs, for My atmosphere is sufficient for thee." Spurgeon said then, for the first time, "I experienced the joy that Abraham felt when he rejoiced in God's provision."

Whatever challenges you're facing, God's grace is more than enough to meet your need.

TODAY'S POWER POINT

Man is born to live and not to prepare to live.—Boris Pasternak

February 10

TODAY IN HISTORY

1763—Treaty of Paris ended French and Indian War; France ceded Canada to England
1847—Mormon exodus to Utah began
1870—Young Women's Christian Association (YWCA) founded in New York City
1897—*New York Times* first published slogan "All the news that's fit to print"
1906—Britain launched first modern battleship
1931—New Delhi became capital of India
1933—First singing telegram delivered
1962—United States exchanged captured U2 pilot Gary Powers for a Soviet spy
1967—Twenty-Fifth Amendment concerning presidential disability and succession ratified
1989—Ron Brown became first black chairman of major U.S. party (Democrats)
1996—IBM computer Deep Blue defeated chess champion Garry Kasparov
1997—O.J. Simpson civil jury reached decision for $25 million punitive damages

BORN TODAY

Comedian Jimmy Durante 1893
Actor Lon Chaney Jr. 1905
Actor Robert Wagner 1930
Singer Roberta Flack 1939
Swimmer Mark Spitz 1950
Golfer Greg Norman 1955
Political commentator George
   Stephanopoulos 1961
Actress Laura Dern 1967
Football player Ty Law 1974

INVESTING IN FRIENDS

Edgar A. Guest liked to tell the story of a rich man who was "almost friendless. His life had been one long round of bickering and lawsuits. Friendships apparently meant nothing to him as he was busy making his fortune."

Later, Guest recalled, "the rich man encountered someone with whom he had had a bitter quarrel many years before. 'I don't understand it,' the wealthy man said, 'you have hundreds of friends, while I have almost no one to whom I can turn.' The old acquaintance replied, 'Sir, I was busy making friends years ago, while you were busy making money.'"

In this age of "every man for himself," we need to go the extra mile in showing neighborliness by offering encouragement and a helping hand to others. Remember, as someone has said, "Prosperity begets friends, adversity proves them."

As in earlier times, may it be said of us today, "Each helps the other and says to his brother, 'Be strong'" (Isaiah 41:6). Ask God to give you a spirit of love and concern for people you meet each day, then look for ways to help these, your neighbors.

TODAY'S POWER POINT

It is easier to love humanity than to love one's neighbor.—Eric Hoffer

February 11

TODAY IN HISTORY

1752—First hospital in United States opened in Pennsylvania
1790—Society of Friends petitioned Congress for abolition of slavery
1852—First public female toilet opens in Britain
1922—Use of insulin to treat diabetes first announced
1929—Vatican City designated an independent state
1941—First gold record awarded (Glenn Miller—"Chattanooga Choo Choo")
1942—Debut of *Archie* comic book
1960—Jack Paar walked off his television show in feud over censorship
1975—First woman (Margaret Thatcher) elected to lead British Conservative Party
1990—Anti-apartheid leader Nelson Mandela freed after twenty-seven years in jail
1993—Janet Reno appointed U.S. attorney general
2006—Vice President Dick Cheney shot friend Harry Whittington in hunting
    accident (Whittington not seriously injured)

BORN TODAY

Abolitionist and author Lydia Maria Child . . . 1802
Inventor Thomas Edison . . . 1847
Boxer Max Baer . . . 1909
Author Joseph Mankiewicz . . . 1909
Novelist Sidney Sheldon . . . 1917
Actress Eva Gabor . . . 1921
Actor Burt Reynolds . . . 1936
Musician Sergio Mendes . . . 1941
Singer Sheryl Crow . . . 1962
Actress Jennifer Aniston . . . 1969
Singer and actress Brandy . . . 1979

MAJORITY RULE

While the will of the majority is what makes a democracy function, just because the majority is for something doesn't make it right; in fact, the opposite is sometimes true. Famed lawyer William Jennings Bryan once said, "Never be afraid to stand with the minority which is right, for the minority which is right will one day be the majority; always be afraid to stand with the majority which is wrong, for the majority which is wrong will one day be the minority."

Believers need to fearlessly stand up for God, regardless of the consequences. Like the sixteen-year-old Russian girl in the Young Communist League newspaper who, under the caption "The one who has gone astray," was quoted as saying, "I have [young communist] members pass me without greeting. Let them look on me with contempt. My brothers and sisters in God treat me very well. I believe them and I believe God."

The Bible clearly states that those who trust in God and do right will be in the minority. In whom do you believe—in the majority or in God?

TODAY'S POWER POINT

The two World Wars came in part . . . because men, whose nature is to tire of everything . . . tired of common sense and civilization.—F. L. Lucas

February 12

TODAY IN HISTORY

1870—Women gained right to vote in Utah Territory

1878—Baseball catcher's mask patented

1879—Opening of first artificial ice-skating rink (Madison Square Garden, New York City)

1909—NAACP founded

1915—Lincoln Memorial cornerstone laid

1924—Premiere of Gershwin's "Rhapsody in Blue"; first sponsored network radio program, *The Eveready Hour*

1973—First metric mileage signs posted on a state highway (Ohio)

1986—Jewish advocate Anatoly Sharansky released by Soviets

1999—U.S. Senate acquitted President Bill Clinton on charges of perjury and obstruction of justice

2004—Mattel announced breakup of Barbie and Ken

BORN TODAY

President Abraham Lincoln;
naturalist Charles Darwin 1809

Actor Lorne Greene 1915

Director Franco Zeffirelli 1923

Sportscaster Joe Garagiola 1926

Basketball player Bill Russell 1934

Author Judy Blume 1938

Comedian Arsenio Hall 1955

INTEGRITY

It's been said that integrity describes what we do when we think no one is looking. President Abraham Lincoln certainly can be said to have been a man of integrity. When he once received a request for 500,000 additional troops to fight in the Civil War, political advisors strongly recommended he turn down the request, as to grant it would likely block his reelection. But Lincoln's decision was firm. "It is not necessary for me to be reelected," he said, "but it is necessary for the soldiers at the front to be reinforced by 500,000 men, and I shall call for them. If I go down . . . I will go down with my colors flying."

Theologian Carl Henry once asked evangelist Billy Graham, "What do you consider the most important thing in life?" Immediately Graham responded, "Integrity." Pressing him further, Henry asked, "Suppose you could choose between a billion-dollar gift to be spent for Christian causes, conversion of Nikita Khrushchev to Jesus Christ, or an open door to evangelize the Communist world—which would you take?" "Still integrity," Graham insisted. "I believe the gospel allows no other answer."

When God looks down on earth and sees into your heart, will he be pleased or saddened by the integrity (or lack of it) he sees?

TODAY'S POWER POINT

Character is what you are in the dark.—Dwight L. Moody

February 13

TODAY IN HISTORY

1747—First magazine published in America
1789—University of North Carolina, first state university, opened
1837—New York riot over price of flour
1866—Jesse James's first bank robbery (Liberty, Missouri)
1867—Premiere of Johann Strauss's "Blue Danube Waltz" in Vienna
1914—American Society of Composers, Authors, and Publishers (ASCAP)
    established
1937—NFL's Boston Redskins moved to Washington DC
1959—Barbie doll went on sale
1965—Peggy Fleming won U.S. Women's Figure Skating Championship
1974—Dissident Alexander Solzhenitsyn expelled from USSR
1991—Authentication announced of long-missing partial manuscript of Mark
    Twain's *Huckleberry Finn*
2000—Final original Sunday *Peanuts* comic strip published (one day after the death
    of cartoonist Charles Schulz)

BORN TODAY

Painter Grant Wood 1892
Singer Tennessee Ernie Ford 1919
Singer Eileen Farrell 1920
Test pilot Chuck Yeager 1923
Actress Kim Novak 1933
Actor George Segal 1934
Actress Stockard Channing;
    talk-show host Jerry Springer . 1944
Singer Peter Gabriel 1950
Actress Kelly Hu 1967

ALL THINGS NEW

A young woman was being questioned about her salvation experience by the church board reviewing her application for membership. When she admitted that she still sinned even after becoming a Christian, they asked, "If you sinned before you were a Christian and you sin since you became a Christian, how has Christ made a difference in your life?" The woman thought for a moment and then replied, "It's like this: before I became a Christian, I ran after sin. Now I run from it, though sometimes I'm still overtaken."

George Müeller was known as a drinker and thief while in college, yet after he turned his life over to God, he was so radically changed that he was reported as giving over $135,000 to the Lord's work (in 1800s dollars!) during his lifetime. Yet when Müeller died, the value of all his possessions combined totaled less than $1,000. Clearly, God had revolutionized his life.

Has God's forgiveness changed your life?

TODAY'S POWER POINT

Forgiveness is the fragrance the violet sheds on the heel that has crushed it.
—Source Unknown

TODAY IN HISTORY

1849—First photograph taken of a president in office (James Polk)
1859—Thirty-third state, Oregon, admitted to Union
1884—Theodore Roosevelt's wife and mother died
1907—United Parcel Service (UPS) formed
1912—Forty-eighth state, Arizona, added to Union
1920—League of Women Voters formed in Chicago
1929—Valentine's Day Massacre: seven gangsters killed in Chicago
1946—Pioneering ENIAC computer introduced
1949—First Knesset session opened in Jerusalem
1962—First Lady Jacqueline Kennedy conducted TV tour of White House
1989—Iran's Ayatollah Khomeini called on Muslims to kill *The Satanic Verses*
        author, Salmon Rushdie
1990—Solar system photographed by *Voyager I* space probe

BORN TODAY

Abolitionist Frederick Douglass . . 1818
Inventor George Ferris (Ferris wheel)
. . . . 1859
Comedian Jack Benny 1894
Author Edmund Love 1912
Broadcaster Hugh Downs. 1921

New York City mayor Michael
        Bloomberg 1942
Journalist Carl Bernstein 1944
Pitcher Dave Dravecky. 1956
Quarterback Drew Bledsoe. 1972
Quarterback Steve McNair. 1973

TRUE LOVE

A grandmother once told the secret of her long and happy marriage: "I decided to make a list of ten of my husband's faults which, for the sake of our marriage, I would overlook." When asked what some of these faults were, the grandmother replied, "To tell you the truth, I never did get around to listing them. But whenever my husband did something that made me hopping mad, I would say to myself, 'Lucky for him that's one of the ten!'"

True love is faithful. W. F. Allan told of a young woman who promised her lover that she would keep a light burning in her window every night until he returned. He sailed forth the next day, but neither he nor his ship were ever heard from again. Still, his true love was faithful and kept the light burning in her window every night until her death some fifty years later.

Our heavenly Father is always loving. Best of all, he shows his love by doing something only he can do—forgiving us of our wrongs through his marvelous grace.

TODAY'S POWER POINT

Love isn't like a reservoir—you'll never drain it dry. It's much more like a natural spring. The longer and the farther that it flows, the stronger and deeper and clearer it becomes.—Eddie Cantor

TODAY IN HISTORY

399—Philosopher Socrates sentenced to death
1758—Mustard first advertised in the United States
1799—First printed ballot authorized (in Pennsylvania)
1842—Gummed postage stamps introduced
1879—Congress authorized women lawyers to practice before the Supreme Court
1898—Explosion of Battleship *Maine*
1903—Teddy bear first introduced in the United States
1919—American Legion organized in Paris
1950—Release of Walt Disney's *Cinderella*
1978—Leon Spinks beat Muhammad Ali in fifteen rounds for world heavyweight crown
1984—500,000 Iranian soldiers moved into Iraq
1990—Baseball owners locked out players
1992—Jeffrey Dahmer found sane and guilty of killing fifteen people
1998—Dale Earnhardt won Daytona 500

BORN TODAY

Astronomer Galileo 1564
Inventor Cyrus McCormick 1809
Feminist Susan B. Anthony 1820
Actor John Barrymore 1882
Composer Harold Arlen 1905
Actor Cesar Romero 1907
Actor Harvey Korman 1927
Singer Melissa Manchester;
    actress Jane Seymour 1951
Cartoonist Matt Groening 1954
Comedian Chris Farley 1964
Actress Renee O'Connor 1971

GOLD

Few things so convey an image of beauty and wealth more than pure gold. Robert Ripley tells of a structure built on two underpinnings of solid gold, each thirty-five feet square and twelve feet deep. This magnificent foundation, built in 1920, is said to still be standing in India. A total of fifty thousand gold bricks, weighing over 37,500 pounds (and worth well over $240 million today), were used to construct the foundation. That's not all—the largest pure gold nugget ever found was two feet long and one foot across and weighed more than 150 pounds. It was discovered by two explorers in Australia. Tests revealed the chunk was 98.66 percent pure gold!

The Bible speaks of our heavenly home, where gold will be so commonplace, it'll be used to pave the streets! We can scarcely begin to imagine a place of such overwhelming splendor and beauty as this. Yet it belongs to all who put their faith and trust in God.

TODAY'S POWER POINT

A word aptly spoken is like apples of gold in settings of silver.—Proverbs 25:11

February 16

TODAY IN HISTORY

374—Ninth recorded perihelion passage of Halley's Comet
600—Pope Gregory decreed the correct response to a sneeze is "God bless you"
1857—Gallaudet College, first school in the world for advanced education for deaf students, incorporated
1862—General Ulysses S. "Unconditional Surrender" Grant captured Fort Donelson
1878—Silver dollar became legal tender in the United States
1883—*Ladies Home Journal* began publication
1923—Howard Carter unsealed the burial chamber of King Tut
1937—Nylon, the world's first synthetic fiber, patented
1945—U.S. troops landed on Corregidor Island
1950—Premiere of long-running TV game show *What's My Line?*
1968—First 911 phone system started service in Haleyville, Alabama
1980—Speed skater Erick Heiden set Olympic record in 5K race
2000—German president asked Israelis to forgive his country for atrocities against Jews during World War II
2005—NHL announced cancellation of season due to labor dispute

BORN TODAY

Composer Johann Strauss. 1866
"Father" of the documentary,
   Robert Flaherty. 1884
Ventriloquist Edgar Bergen. 1903
Singer Patty Andrews 1920

Entertainer Sonny Bono. 1935
Rap singer Ice-T. 1958
Tennis player John McEnroe 1959
Football player Jerome Bettis 1972
First cloned calf, Mr. Jefferson . . . 1998

GIVING SUPPORT

Rich or poor, famous or unknown, who doesn't want to be admired? Perhaps you feel like the British prime minister Lord Melbourne, who criticized a London newspaper editor for not supporting him sufficiently. In reply, the editor said he always supported Melbourne's party when he thought it was in the right. Melbourne responded, "We don't want support when we are in the right—what we want is a little support when we are in the wrong!"

Whether we're in the right or are wrong, we're all fond of being liked. How often do you go out of your way to show kindness to the outcasts of society—those who most need encouragement?

Ask God to lead you to someone who needs encouragement, and give that person your time, attention, and support.

TODAY'S POWER POINT

The person who tries to live alone will not succeed as a human being. His heart withers if it does not answer another heart. His mind shrinks away if he hears only the echoes of his own thoughts and finds no other inspiration.—Pearl S. Buck

TODAY IN HISTORY

1801—Thomas Jefferson elected president (over Aaron Burr) by House of Representatives on thirty-sixth ballot

1817—Baltimore became first U.S. city lighted by gas streetlights

1820—Senate passed Missouri Compromise for slavery issue

1864—First submarine sinking of an enemy ship (Confederate sub sank Union warship *Housatonic*)

1865—Columbia, South Carolina, burned as Sherman's Union forces moved in

1911—Cadillac introduced self-starting car engine

1933—*Newsweek* first published

1947—*Voice of America* beamed first broadcast to Soviet Union

1996—Garry Kasparov, world chess champ, beat IBM supercomputer Deep Blue in Philadelphia

2005—John Negroponte named first Director of National Intelligence

BORN TODAY

Businessman Montgomery Ward . . .1843
Chocolatier William Cadbury . . . 1867
Sportscaster Walter "Red" Barber . . .1908
Actor Hal Holbrook 1925
Football player Jim Brown 1936
Actress Rene Russo. 1954
Actor Lou Diamond Phillips 1962
Basketball player Michael Jordan. . . 1963
Singer Bryan White 1974
Heiress and celebrity Paris Hilton . . 1981

LIFE'S SCARS

Life leaves us with many scars, only some of which are visible. It is said that when the knights of King Arthur's court returned from battle, they were expected to bear some scar of the battle. If not, the king would send them back out, telling them, "Go get your scar!"

Do you have any scars as a result of doing spiritual battle for your heavenly King? A story in *Westminster Quarterly* tells of a harried preacher who was so troubled by his church members that he went to his superiors to resign. His bishop thought things over for a moment and then asked thoughtfully, "Do your people ever spit in your face?" "No, of course not," the preacher replied. "Do they ever hit you? Have they mocked and belittled you?" "No," he said. "Have they stripped and scourged you, crowned you with thorns?" The minister soberly responded, "No sir, and God helping me, until they do, I'll carry on."

When we think of what others, including our Savior, have suffered and endured in God's name, we will indeed feel humbled, and all of our persecutions will suddenly seem insignificant in comparison.

TODAY'S POWER POINT

The highest reward for a man's toil is not what he gets for it, but what he becomes by it.—John Ruskin

TODAY IN HISTORY

1564—Death of artist Michelangelo in Rome
1678—John Bunyan's *The Pilgrim's Progress* published
1735—First opera performed in United States (*Flora*, in Charleston, South Carolina)
1804—Ohio University chartered as first U.S. land-grant institution
1861—Jefferson Davis inaugurated as president of Confederate States of America
1885—Mark Twain's *Adventures of Huckleberry Finn* first published in United States
1929—First Academy Awards presented
1930—Pluto discovered
1977—Maiden flight of U.S. space shuttle, piggybacked aboard 747 jet
2001—Driver Dale Earnhardt Sr. killed in crash during Daytona 500

BORN TODAY

Artist and designer Louis Tiffany. . . 1848
Football player George "The Gipper"
    Gipp. 1895
TV host Bill Cullen;
    actor Jack Palance 1920
Author Helen Gurley Brown 1922

Actor George Kennedy. 1925
Actress Cybill Shepherd 1950
Actor John Travolta 1954
TV personality Vanna White 1957
Actor Matt Dillon 1964
Actress Molly Ringwald 1968

MOTIVATED GIVING

Have you ever been asked to give to a worthy cause? Although God owns all the world's resources (including ours), it's important to remember that we should not give in order to receive the recognition of men, but rather because we love God.

James Duff described this motivation for giving in the life of English theologian Andrew Fuller. Writing in *Flashes of Truth*, Duff recalled the occasion when Fuller returned to his hometown to raise funds for missions. On contacting an old friend for a donation, the man said, "Well Andrew, seeing it's you, I'll give you five dollars." Fuller replied, "I can't take your money seeing it is for me," and handed the donation back.

Fuller was right. The Bible tells us, "When you give to the needy, do not let your left hand know what your right hand is doing, so that your giving may be in secret. Then your Father, who sees what is done in secret, will reward you" (Matthew 6:3–4).

Remember, in God's eyes, it's not how much we give but why we give that counts.

TODAY'S POWER POINT

Whatever you do, work at it with all your heart, as working for the Lord, not for men, since you know that you will receive an inheritance from the Lord as a reward. It is the Lord Christ you are serving.—Colossians 3:23–24

TODAY IN HISTORY

1738—Methodist church established
1830—Song "Mary Had a Little Lamb" written by Sarah Hale
1844—First telegraph message: "What hath God wrought"
1878—Phonograph patented by Thomas Edison
1883—Brooklyn Bridge opened
1913—Cracker Jack first included prize
1945—U.S. Marines landed on island of Iwo Jima
1961—Freedom Riders arrested in Jackson, Mississippi
1985—Cherry Coke first introduced in bottles and cans
1986—Soviet Union launched Mir space station
1989—Premiere of *Indiana Jones and the Last Crusade*
2001—Okalahoma City National Memorial Center dedicated in honor of bombing
     victims
2003—German court convicted first 9/11 terrorist

BORN TODAY

Astronomer Nicolaus Copernicus	. . 1473	Britain's Prince Andrew	 1960
Actor Lee Marvin	 1924	Actress Justine Bateman	 1966
Singer Smokey Robinson	 1940	Actor Benicio Del Toro	 1967
Singer Lou Christie	 1943	Actress Haylie Duff	 1985
Actor Jeff Daniels	 1955		

A LASTING MARRIAGE

Dr. James Dobson, perhaps one of Christianity's best-known spokesmen, is often asked questions concerning marriage. In his book *Straight Talk to Men and Their Wives*, Dr. Dobson related an excerpt from the letter his father wrote to his mother just before they were married: "I have been taught that the marriage vows are inviolable, and by entering them, I am binding myself absolutely and for life. . . . I am fully aware of the possibility, unlikely as it now appears, that mutual incompatibility or other unforeseen circumstances could result in extreme mental suffering. If such becomes the case, I am resolved for my part to accept it as a consequence of the commitment I am now making, and to bear it, if necessary, to the end of our lives together."

Dobson's father recognized the truth that when God is the center of the home and we "seek first his kingdom and his righteousness," then "all these things will be given to you as well" (Matthew 6:33). If you can trust God for the hereafter, you certainly can trust him in your marriage.

TODAY'S POWER POINT

A successful marriage requires falling in love many times—but always with the same person.—Dennis De Haan

February 20

TODAY IN HISTORY

1792—President George Washington signed Postal Service Act
1937—First car-airplane tested
1938—Anthony Eden resigned as British foreign minister to protest British appeasement of Nazis
1962—John Glenn became first American to orbit Earth
1974—Cher filed for separation from husband, Sonny Bono
1989—Total eclipse of the moon
1998—Tara Lipinski won Olympic figure-skating gold medal
2001—FBI agent Robert Hanssen arrested and charged with spying for Russia for fifteen years
2004—Hardliners won election to Iranian parliament
2005—Israeli leaders voted to withdraw troops and settlers from Gaza Strip

BORN TODAY

Automotive designer Enzo Ferrari . . 1898
Photographer Ansel Adams 1902
Fashion designer Gloria Vanderbilt 1924
Actor Sidney Poitier 1927
Singer Nancy Wilson 1937
Folksinger Buffy Sainte-Marie . . . 1941
Actress Sandy Duncan 1946
Actress Jennifer O'Neill 1948
Kidnapping victim Patty Hearst Shaw 1954
Basketball player Charles Barkley . . .1963
Supermodel Cindy Crawford 1966
Basketball player Stephon Marbury 1977

FREE ENTERPRISE

Despite its general unpopularity in the world today, hard work and free enterprise have historically built some of our most successful businesses. One such example is the young Cincinnati grocer who had $372 and an idea: sell many goods at a small mark-up each to obtain a large overall profit. Today Bernard Kroger's grocery chain boasts more than 2,500 stores in thirty-two states.

F. W. Woolworth was another man with a unique idea. His boss asked him to gather up some items and sell them to get what he could. Woolworth posted a sign offering any article on the counter for just five cents. The items quickly sold out, thus giving Woolworth the idea for the first five-and-ten-cent store (an idea Sam Walton would later adapt to propel Wal-Mart into becoming the world's largest retailer).

Every day presents new opportunities, and each of us must choose whether to seize them or let them slip away. With God as your guide, step out and follow your dreams. You never know what good things might be in store.

TODAY'S POWER POINT

He who gathers money little by little makes it grow.—Proverbs 13:11

February 21

TODAY IN HISTORY

1842—Sewing machine patented
1848—*Communist Manifesto* published by Karl Marx
1858—First electric burglar alarm installed (Boston)
1866—First woman graduate from dental school
1878—First telephone directory published
1885—Washington Monument dedicated
1916—Battle of Verdun in France began
1925—First issue of the *New Yorker* magazine published
1965—Malcolm X, age thirty-nine, gunned down at New York rally
1975—John Mitchell, H. R. Haldeman, and John Ehrlichman sentenced to prison
    for Watergate break-in
1992—Kristi Yamaguchi won Olympic women's figure-skating gold medal for US
2001—Britain stopped milk and meat exports to halt spread of hoof-and-mouth
    disease
2002—FBI confirmed death of reporter Daniel Pearl in Afghanistan

BORN TODAY

Guitarist Andres Segovia 1893
Humorist Erma Bombeck 1927
Actress Rue McClanahan 1934
Actor Gary Lockwood 1937
Record executive David Geffen. . . 1943
Actor Alan Rickman;
    actress Tyne Daly 1946
Actor Kelsey Grammer. 1955
Actor William Baldwin. 1963
Singer Charlotte Church 1986

ANGER

C. E. McCartney noted that anger weakens a person. It puts one at a disadvantage in every undertaking. When legendary sailor Sinbad and his crew landed on a tropical island, they spotted coconuts, which could quench their thirst and satisfy their hunger. The coconuts were high up in the treetops, far out of reach of the men but not of a group of chattering apes. So the men came up with an idea. Picking up nearby rocks, they threw them toward the apes, making them angry. In response, the apes grabbed the nearby coconuts and threw them at the men on the ground. In their anger the apes provided food for the entire party.

In much the same way, when we lose our temper, we play right into the hands of our opponents. Don't fly off the handle when you get angry. Instead, try speaking softly when you become annoyed, and see how quickly it softens the anger of others.

TODAY'S POWER POINT

Anger kills both laughter and joy; what greater foe is there than anger?
—Tiruvalluvar

February 22

TODAY IN HISTORY

1630—Indians introduced popcorn to pilgrims

1819—United States acquired Florida from Spain

1860—Organized baseball's first game played in San Francisco

1878—F. W. Woolworth opened first five-and-ten-cent store

1942—President Franklin D. Roosevelt ordered General Douglas MacArthur to leave Philippines

1980—Miracle on Ice: U.S. hockey team upset heavily favored Soviet squad to set up Olympic gold-medal win at Lake Placid, New York

1987—Death of artist Andy Warhol, age fifty-six

1994—CIA agent Aldrich Ames arrested as Soviet double agent

2000—U.S. space crew returned from successful earth-mapping mission

2004—Consumer advocate Ralph Nader announced independent presidential candidacy

2005—Ibrahim al-Jaafari named Iraq's interim prime minister

BORN TODAY

President George Washington. . . . 1732

Composer Frédéric Chopin 1810

Baseball manager Connie Mack . . 1862

Comedian "Chico" Marx 1891

Poet Edna St. Vincent Millay 1892

Senator Edward M. Kennedy 1932

Baseball manager George "Sparky" Anderson 1934

Basketball player Julius "Dr. J" Erving 1950

Naturalist Steve Irwin. 1962

Actress Drew Barrymore. 1975

Actor Miko Hughes 1986

OUR ACCOMPLISHMENTS

When life is over, what will the world remember of your accomplishments? One extraordinary achiever was the French tightrope walker and acrobat Charles Blondin. Although performing countless feats of daring, Blondin is probably best known for his tightrope heroics 160 feet above Niagara Falls. Beginning in 1859 he made the trek across the 1,100-foot cable on at least four occasions. He finally died of natural causes at age seventy-three.

While few of us are likely to be known for great physical achievements, the Bible makes it clear that our accomplishments are duly noted by God. As you go about your daily activities today, realize that God is watching over you. When life seems baffling and your accomplishments few, remember that he sees beyond the challenges of today, well into tomorrow. Need help? Call on God. He's always there. What will you be remembered for today?

TODAY'S POWER POINT

Man is always more than he can know of himself; consequently, his accomplishments, time and again, will come as a surprise to him.—Golo Mann

TODAY IN HISTORY

155—Polycarp arrested and burned at stake
303—Persecution of Christians ordered by Emperor Diocletian
1455—First book, the *Bible*, printed by Johannes Gutenberg (estimated date)
1836—Alamo besieged by Santa Ana
1861—Failed Lincoln assassination attempt
1893—Rudolph Diesel received German patent for diesel engine
1896—Tootsie Roll introduced
1940—Woody Guthrie wrote "This Land Is Your Land"; release of Walt Disney's
      movie *Pinnochio*
1945—U.S. Marines raised flag at Iwo Jima
1954—Salk polio vaccine inoculations started on massive scale
1980—Eric Heiden won all five speed-skating Olympic gold medals in Lake Placid
1991—Start of Allied forces ground attack in Iraq
1997—"Dolly" the sheep announced to be first clone of an adult animal

BORN TODAY

Composer George Frideric Handel
. . . . 1685
African American scholar W. E. B.
  DuBois 1868
Newscaster Sylvia Chase 1938
Actor Peter Fonda. 1939

Football player Ed "Too Tall" Jones;
  actress Patricia Richardson . . . 1951
Musician Howard Jones 1955
Baseball player Bobby Bonilla. . . . 1963
Actress Dakota Fanning 1994

TRUTH AND HONESTY

Some say the traditional values of truth and honesty are no longer relevant in this "enlightened" age. However, God's laws have never changed. Dishonesty is just as wrong today as it was in the Garden of Eden, no matter what society may think.

Years ago, *Liberty* magazine sent out letters containing a one-dollar bill to one hundred randomly selected people throughout the United States. The letter accompanying the dollar stated that the payment was an adjustment of an error the recipient had complained of (a situation which did not really exist). Of the one hundred recipients, only twenty-seven returned the dollar, saying it was a mistake. Years later the magazine repeated the test, with fewer than half as many returning the money.

Although it sometimes seems that honesty doesn't hold the place of importance it once did, God's Word has not changed. Today live your life so that even under the closest scrutiny, you would be known for your honesty.

TODAY'S POWER POINT

To make your children capable of honesty is the beginning of education. —John Ruskin

February 24

TODAY IN HISTORY

1803—U.S. Supreme Court, for first time, ruled a congressional act unconstitutional (*Marbury v. Madison*)

1840—Former president John Quincy Adams began Supreme Court argument of *Amistad* slave-ship case

1868—President Andrew Johnson impeached

1938—Nylon bristle toothbrush patented

1942—Initial broadcast of *Voice of America*

1949—First U.S. rocket reached outer space

1970—Birth of Kienast quintuplets—three girls and two boys

1981—Jean Harris found guilty of murdering Scarsdale diet doctor, Herman Tarnower

1988—Supreme Court upheld right to satirize public figures (*Hustler* parody of Jerry Falwell)

2004—President George W. Bush called for ban on same-sex marriages

BORN TODAY

Fairytale writer Wilhelm Grimm . . 1786
Painter Winslow Homer. 1836
Baseball great Honus Wagner 1874
Admiral Chester Nimitz. 1885
Actor James Farentino 1938
Senator Joe Lieberman 1942

Actor Barry Bostwick 1945
Actor Edward James Olmos 1947
Apple cofounder Steven Jobs 1955
Actor Billy Zane. 1966
Quarterback Jeff Garcia 1970
Boxer Oscar de la Hoya 1973

GAINING SUCCESS

Not everyone who makes it to the top of the heap ends up staying there. One such person was George Train. Although a penniless orphan at the age of three, Train made a fortune in shipping and retired at age thirty. About that time he wrote ten books, took two trips around the world, and was even a candidate for U.S. president in 1872. Then his life began a downward spiral. Train became a recluse, hardly ever speaking to other adults during the last ten years of his life. He died penniless in a $3-a-week New York hotel room.

One Christian businessman stated: "I have made many millions, but they have brought me no happiness. I would barter them all for the days I sat on an office stool in Cleveland and counted myself rich on $3 a week."

Mark 8:36 asks a rhetorical question: "What good is it for a man to gain the whole world, yet forfeit his soul?" Wealth can be a blessing, but only when we keep it in its proper context. Do you recognize God as the source of all your blessings? Ask that he give you no more wealth and prestige than you can handle.

TODAY'S POWER POINT

Success is counted sweetest by those who ne'er succeed.—Emily Dickinson

February 25

TODAY IN HISTORY

1793—First cabinet meeting (at George Washington's home)
1837—Electric printing press patented
1870—First African American member of U.S. Senate (Hiram Revels of Mississippi) sworn in
1908—Opening of first railroad tunnel under the Hudson River to link New York and New Jersey
1913—Sixteenth Amendment (authorizing U.S. income tax) ratified
1919—First gas tax levied (Oregon)
1928—Federal Radio Commission (later to become the FCC) issued first television-station license (Washington DC)
1936—Colt revolver patented
1938—First drive-in movie theater opened (in Miami)
1964—Cassius Clay upset Sonny Liston for heavyweight boxing title
1982—Final episode of *The Lawrence Welk Show*
2004—Mel Gibson's *The Passion of the Christ* opened in U.S. theaters

BORN TODAY

Painter Pierre Auguste Renoir.... 1841
Singer Enrico Caruso 1873
Herbert "Zeppo" Marx 1901
Actor Jim Backus 1913
Author Anthony Burgess 1917
Producer Larry Gelbart......... 1928
Newscaster Bob Schieffer 1937
Beatle George Harrison 1943
Baseball player Cesar Cedeno.... 1951
Actress Tea Leoni 1966

GOD'S PROTECTION

James R. Stuart tells the story of a dramatic railroad trip. It seems a train jumped the tracks just before reaching a high trestle. Sensing danger, the engineer immediately slammed on his brakes—but not before the engine had headed onto the bridge. Finally, after the train had ground to a halt and the engineer inspected the scene, he realized just how close he had come to disaster. He discovered that had the engine gone just six inches farther onto the bridge, the derailed cars would have gone over the side and taken the entire train with it. When asked his reaction, the shaken engineer replied, "I never go on a run without committing my train and my life into the hands of God, and when I saw the danger on that occasion, I put on the emergency brakes, reversed the engine, and turned my face to God and called for help. I believe it was the hand of God that saved us from a most horrible wreck."

God stands ready to carry you through any challenges you may face, if you'll just call upon him.

TODAY'S POWER POINT

With God in charge of our defenses, there will be peace within.—T. T. Faichney

February 26

TODAY IN HISTORY

1815—Napoleon Bonaparte escaped from exile on island of Elba
1870—First subway opened in New York City
1919—Grand Canyon established as a national park
1929—Grand Teton National Park established
1938—Radar first installed on passenger ship
1950—B-50 *Lucky Lady II* flew around the world nonstop in ninety-four hours
1951—Twenty-Second Amendment (limiting president to two terms) ratified
1962—NBA's Wilt Chamberlain scored sixty-seven points in one game
1984—Last U.S. Marine peacekeepers left Beirut
1993—Bomb blast in parking garage beneath New York's World Trade Center: six
    killed, a thousand injured
1998—Oprah Winfrey won lawsuit brought by Texas cattlemen

BORN TODAY

Author Victor Hugo. 1802
Businessman Levi Strauss 1829
Entertainer Buffalo Bill Cody. . . . 1846
Cornflake inventor John Kellogg. . . 1852
Comedian Jackie Gleason. 1916
Actor Tony Randall 1920
Singer Antoine "Fats" Domino. . . 1928
Singer Johnny Cash 1932
Actress Jennifer Grant. 1966
Football player Marshall Faulk . . . 1973

THE FOUNDATION FOR JUSTICE

An example of justice comes from overseas. In the Supreme Court building in Switzerland hangs a huge painting titled, "Justice Instructing the Judges." Various litigants are in the foreground—a wife against a husband, an architect against a builder, and so on, while above these stands a group of judges. How will they judge the various litigants? The artist depicts it this way: justice (typically shown blindfolded with her sword vertical) here is blindfolded with her sword pointing downward to a book on which is written, "The Word of God."

Yes, God's Word is the basis of not only our Western justice system but also of the Judeo-Christian ethic by which we work and live. People may not recognize it as such, but God is the foundation for our entire way of life. Be sure to thank God for the great life and freedoms he has given us.

TODAY'S POWER POINT

Justice is rather the activity of truth than a virtue in itself. Truth tells us what to do to others, and justice renders that due.—Horace Walpole

TODAY IN HISTORY

1860—Matthew Brady photographed beardless presidential candidate Abraham Lincoln

1872—First black woman lawyer (Charlotte Ray) graduated from Harvard

1879—Sugar substitute saccharin discovered

1922—Supreme Court upheld women's right to vote

1960—*Family Circus* comic strip debuted (as *Family Circle*)

1974—First issue of *People* magazine published

1982—Wayne Williams sentenced to two life terms for murdering twenty-eight African American Atlanta-area youths

1991—Just one hundred hours into ground offensive, president George H. W. Bush declared Kuwait liberated

1997—Divorce legalized in Ireland

BORN TODAY

Poet Henry Wadsworth Longfellow 1807

Author John Steinbeck 1902

Actress Joanne Woodward 1930

Actress Elizabeth Taylor 1932

Consumer advocate Ralph Nader . 1934

Actor Howard Hesseman 1940

Actor Adam Baldwin 1962

Singer Josh Groban 1981

PATIENCE AND DILIGENCE

Booker T. Washington described how diligence to detail in little things led to his entry into college. He waited quietly for several hours while others were admitted before him. Glancing down the hall, the headmaster saw Washington still patiently waiting. "Here, take a broom and sweep the recitation room," he was told. So Washington swept it—three times. Then he dusted it—four times, Washington noted: "All the woodwork, around the walls, every bench, table and desk. He moved every piece of furniture and cleaned carefully every closet and corner in the room." At last he reported back to the administrator—a strict woman who knew just where to search for dirt. She took her handkerchief and slowly rubbed it over the woodwork, along the walls and over the tables and benches. Finally, unable to find even a speck of dirt or dust, she quietly remarked, "I guess you will do to enter this institution."

Washington's patience and diligence, even when the situation was unfair, paid off. Not only was he admitted to college; he went on to found the famous Tuskegee Institute.

Today do all you do as if you were doing it for God—because you are.

TODAY'S POWER POINT

Our duty is to be useful, not according to our desires but according to our powers.—Henri Fredreic Amiel

February 28

TODAY IN HISTORY

1646—Roger Scott tried in Massachusetts for sleeping in church
1780—John Wesley chartered first U.S. Methodist church
1803—Congress approved $2,500 for the Lewis and Clark expedition
1827—Baltimore and Ohio Railroad incorporated
1844—President John Tyler narrowly escaped death aboard the USS *Princeton*
1940—First televised basketball game
1979—Death of Mister Ed, TV's talking horse
1982—Puerto Rican nationalist group bombed Wall Street
1983—Final episode of *M*A*S*H* aired
1984—Michael Jackson set new record, winning eight Grammy Awards for *Thriller*
1993—Four killed in initial ATF raid of Branch Davidian compound, Waco, Texas
1998—United States successfully tested unmanned reconnaissance aircraft that can
      stay aloft for forty hours with range of 13,500 nautical miles
2002—European currencies replaced by the euro

BORN TODAY

Chemist Linus Pauling 1901
Actor Zero Mostel 1915
Actor Gavin MacLeod 1930
Racer Mario Andretti 1940
Football player Bubba Smith 1945
Actress Bernadette Peters 1948
Comedian Gilbert Gottfried 1955
Actor Robert Sean Leonard 1969
Hockey player Eric Lindros 1973
Basketball player Jamaal Tinsley . . 1978

LIFE'S DISAGREEMENTS

Have you ever noticed that what often draws couples together is not so much what they have in common but how different (yet complementary) they are? But sometimes this can be carried to an extreme. Such is the tale of the man who applied for a marriage license and then waited eleven years before going back to claim the permit. When asked why he and his fiancée had waited so long to get married, he explained, "We had a few disagreements about details."

Los Angeles police have reported that "80 percent of the morning rush-hour accidents were caused by people who had earlier been involved in arguments with their mates before leaving home."

Though your relationships in life may be marked by many differences, you can still count on an unchanging God to carry you through.

TODAY'S POWER POINT

Quarrels are the dowry which married folk bring one another.—Ovid

TODAY IN HISTORY

1692—Start of Salem witch hunt
1781—Articles of Confederation ratified
1790—First U.S. census began
1803—Seventeenth state, Ohio, admitted to Union
1867—Thirty-seventh state, Nebraska, admitted to Union
1872—Yellowstone National Park established (first national park)
1873—First practical typewriter produced
1932—Lindberg baby kidnapped
1961—Five House members shot at U.S. Capitol by Puerto Rican nationalists; Peace Corps established
1963—First liver transplant
1999—Breitling Orbiter 3 balloon launched from Switzerland on first nonstop balloon trip around the world
2002—Operation Anaconda (targeting Taliban and al Qaeda fighters) began in eastern Afghanistan
2003—Khalid Shaikh Mohammed, mastermind behind 9/11 terrorist attack on U.S., captured in Pakistan

BORN TODAY

Painter Sandro Botticelli. 1445
Composer Frédéric Chopin 1810
Bandleader Glenn Miller 1904
Sportscaster Harry Caray 1914
Israeli prime minister Yitzak Rabin
. . . . 1922
Apollo 18 astronaut Donald "Deke" Slayton 1924
Singer Harry Belafonte;
    Judge Robert Bork 1927
Actor Robert Conrad 1935
Chairman of the Joint Chiefs of Staff
    Richard Myers 1942
Actor Alan Thicke 1947
Actor and director Ron Howard;
    actress Catherine Bach 1954

FAME

Former president Woodrow Wilson was getting his hair cut when famed evangelist D. L. Moody entered the barbershop. Wilson listened to the conversation between the renowned preacher and the barber. Moody talked not about himself but focused, instead, on the barber, on his spiritual condition, and on the Lord. After Moody left, Wilson lingered for a moment to watch the reaction of those in the shop. He later wrote that "something had raised their thoughts . . . I felt that I left that place as I should have left a place of worship."

What a testimony to the influence of God in a life—that people should notice not our achievments but rather God's presence reflected in our behavior.

TODAY'S POWER POINT

Remember, the noisiest drum has nothing in it but air.—English Proverb

March 2

TODAY IN HISTORY

1836—Texas declared independence from Mexico
1877—Rutherford B. Hayes affirmed as president, despite losing popular vote
1917—Czar Nicholas II abdicated; Russian Revolution began
1925—Standardized road signs and highway numbering adopted in U.S.
1949—U.S. Air Force bomber Superfortress *Lucky Lady II* completed first nonstop
flight around the world
1962—Wilt Chamberlain scored one hundred points against New York Knicks
1972—United States launched *Pioneer 10* spacecraft, first outerplanetary probe
1978—Charlie Chaplin's coffin stolen from Swiss graveyard
1985—FDA approved screening test for AIDS
1991—Battle at Rumalla oil field brought Gulf War to an end
2004—NASA announced Mars rover *Opportunity* had discovered evidence that
water once existed on Mars

BORN TODAY

Politician Sam Houston 1793
Children's author Dr. Seuss. 1904
Entertainer Desi Arnaz. 1917
Russian president Mikhail Gorbachev;
    Journalist Tom Wolfe 1931
Author John Irving. 1942
Singer Karen Carpenter 1950
Comedienne Laraine Newman. . . 1952
Singer Jon Bon Jovi 1962
Singer Chris Martin 1977
Quarterback Ben Roethlisberger. . 1982
Actor Robert Iler 1985

REPENTANCE

A nineteen-year-old once held up a bank. He escaped justice when two convicts, incorrectly identified by the bank as the robbers, died in a car accident.

The man struggled to reform on his own, but with little success. One day he read a gospel tract that said, "Repent and be baptized, every one of you, in the name of Jesus Christ for the forgiveness of your sins" (Acts 2:38). He did so, and his whole life became new.

But he was still guilty of a serious crime. The man knew what he had to do. He confessed and promised to repay what he had stolen. But the statute of limitations had run out, so he was allowed to go free. This time he was truly free. Today he is an outstanding Christian—not through reform but through repentance and God's grace.

Is something holding you back from being fully free? Whatever your past, you can be free today. Confess your sins and shortcomings to God, repent, and free yourself from guilt and self-recrimination.

TODAY'S POWER POINT

Remorse is impotence; it will sin again. Only repentance is strong; it can end everything.—Honoré de Balzac

TODAY IN HISTORY

1791—U.S. Mint created by Congress

1845—Florida admitted to Union as twenty-seventh state

1918—Treaty of Brest-Litovsk signed, ending Russia's involvement in World War I

1923—*Time* magazine launched

1931—*Star Spangled Banner* officially adopted as U.S. national anthem

1933—Dedication of Mount Rushmore

1938—Oil discovered in Saudi Arabia

1952—Supreme Court ruled communists could be kept from teaching in schools

1955—Elvis Presley's first TV appearance

1965—Premiere of *The Sound of Music*

1991—Beating of motorist Rodney King by police officers in Los Angeles captured on film by amateur photographer

2005—First nonstop solo flight around the world completed by Steve Fossett, in a single-engine jet

2006—First World Baseball Classic began (in Tokyo, Japan)

BORN TODAY

Inventor Alexander Graham Bell	1847	Actress Julie Bowen	1970
Actress Jean Harlow	1911	Actor David Faustino	1974
Actress Miranda Richardson	1958	Actress Jessica Biel	1982
Football player Herschel Walker	1962	Singer Stacie Orrico	1986
Hockey player Brian Leetch	1968		

IMMORTAL

Immortality is forever—an eternity. But infinity is a difficult concept for most of us to fully comprehend. Mathematicians say, for example, that a googol (a one with one hundred zeroes behind it) represents an inconceivably large number. But then there are googolplexes (ten raised to the power of a googol), which, if written out, would more than cover the entire earth! Mathematicians say that even just a lowly googol would be more than sufficient to count all of the atoms in the universe, while a googolplex is vastly larger. Yet when compared to eternity, even the googolplex is a small number.

Grasping the truth that our souls are immortal and that we will live forever is equally difficult. But the vastness of eternity makes it all the more important that we understand that our souls are immortal. Will you be spending eternity with God? What does the fruit in your life indicate about the eternal destination you've chosen? Don't put off life's most important decision. Trust God today.

TODAY'S POWER POINT

To rest in God eternally is the supreme joy of heaven.—Bede Jarrett

March 4

TODAY IN HISTORY

1681—Pennsylvania chartered

1789—U.S. Constitution became effective

1791—Vermont admitted to Union as fourteenth state

1837—Chicago officially established

1861—Confederate States of America approved Stars and Bars flag

1933—President Franklin D. Roosevelt named Frances Perkins first woman cabinet secretary

1974—Debut of *People* magazine

1980—Robert Mugabe became leader of new African nation of Zimbabwe

1983—While in Nicaragua, Pope John Paul II denounced liberation theology

1986—Former UN ambassador Kurt Waldheim charged with hiding his Nazi background

1994—Four suspects convicted in first World Trade Center bombing

2004—Afghan leaders signed new constitution giving rights to women

BORN TODAY

Composer Antonio Vivaldi. 1678

Football coach Knute Rockne. . . . 1888

Actress Paula Prentiss 1939

Singer/songwriter Gloria Gaither . . .1942

Singer Mary Wilson 1944

Writer Catherine O'Hara 1954

Actress Patricia Heaton. 1959

Actress Patsy Kensit 1968

Actress Margo Harshman 1986

FEAR

A nationwide survey of more than two thousand children, ages seven to eleven, showed that over two-thirds said they were afraid that "something bad" was lurking about their neighborhood. Fully one-fourth were scared they would be attacked when they went outside (and for good reason: more than 40 percent of them said they had been harassed by older kids or adults while playing). The survey concluded that children who watch more than four hours of television a day are twice as likely as other children to be afraid.

But fear affects adults too. Doctors say that stress, caused by fear, greatly influences a person's health.

Do you have fears that stress—or even cripple—you? If you fear (respect) God, you don't have to be afraid. Ask God to help you overcome your fears. He is able and faithful to help. As Psalm 34:4 says, "I sought the LORD, and he answered me; he delivered me from all my fears." Ask the One who can see beyond tomorrow to remove the fear from your life and guide you throughout today.

TODAY'S POWER POINT

Fear the LORD, you his saints, for those who fear him lack nothing.—Psalm 34:9

TODAY IN HISTORY

1770—Boston Massacre
1830—Use of limelight first demonstrated in London (technique later used to illuminate lighthouses and movie-theater screens)
1868—President Andrew Johnson's impeachment moved to Senate; patent of office stapler patented in England
1922—Women's trap-shooting record set by sharpshooter Annie Oakley
1923—Enactment of first pension laws
1933—Four-day "bank holiday" declared by President Franklin D. Roosevelt
1946—Winston Churchill's famous Iron Curtain speech delivered
1953—Death of Soviet premier Josef Stalin, age seventy-four
1982—Death of actor John Belushi, age thirty-two
2004—TV homemaker Martha Stewart found guilty on obstruction-of-justice charges

BORN TODAY

Actor Rex Harrison 1908
Broadcast executive Laurence Tisch . . 1923
Actor Dean Stockwell 1936
Actress Samantha Eggar 1939
Actor Michael Warren 1946
Football player Michael Irvin 1966
Basketball player Brian Grant 1972
Actor Jake Lloyd 1989

UNBELIEF

In this era of increasing doubt, beware of philosophies that deny the existence of God or the deity of Christ. The late self-proclaimed atheist Madalyn Murray O'Hair once spoke on a college campus in Ohio. After a prolonged, scathing attack on believers in God, O'Hair mocked anyone so stupid as to believe in anything religious.

At the conclusion of her address, one young college girl at the back of the room rose to speak. "Mrs. O'Hair, we must always be grateful for your visit, because now and forever we have strengthened our Christian beliefs by listening to you tonight. . . . I thank you because I know you have strengthened my faith in our church and in our religion." The speaker stood silently, perplexed as the crowd burst into thunderous applause.

We are in the middle of a daily battle between the forces of God and the forces of evil. The battle is for our world and for our very souls. It's vital that we're sure of what we believe and why (doctrine) if we are to withstand great onslaughts still to come. Rely on God to give you the strength and wisdom to live his way in the daily spiritual battle for your soul.

TODAY'S POWER POINT

He did not waver through unbelief regarding the promise of God, but was strengthened in his faith and gave glory to God.—Romans 4:20

March 6

TODAY IN HISTORY

1836—Fall of the Alamo to Santa Ana
1857—Slavery upheld in historic *Dred Scott* case
1896—First automobile driven (in Detroit, Michigan)
1930—Packaged frozen food first sold
1969—First astronaut transfer from one orbiting spacecraft to another
1982—Five Muslims sentenced to death for killing Egyptian president Anwar Sadat
1986—Soviet spacecraft sent back hundreds of pictures of Halley's Comet
1994—Start of Biosphere II experiment in self-contained living
2002—Close of *Whitewater* case, ending threat of criminal charges against former
    president Bill Clinton

BORN TODAY

Sculptor and painter Michelangelo . . 1475
Poet Elizabeth Barrett Browning . . 1806
Comedian Lou Costello 1906
Economist Alan Greenspan 1926
Baseball player Willie Stargell 1941

Director Rob Reiner 1945
Actor Tom Arnold 1959
Comedian D. L. Hughley 1963
Basketball player Shaquille O'Neal
    1972

PERSEVERANCE

What does it take to make you give up? Jerry Falwell has said, "You can determine the character of a man by what it takes to make him quit."

For more than fifteen years Robert McCormick worked in his farm's blacksmith's shop to develop the first horse-drawn reaper. Still unsuccessful as the harvest of 1831 began, he finally gave up.

But his twenty-two-year-old son, Cyrus, picked up where his discouraged father left off. Using his father's basic design, Cyrus made several important additions and refinements. By the conclusion of the harvest, Cyrus had successfully demonstrated the "Virginia Reaper," a device that would revolutionize farming and, consequently, American life.

Are you discouraged—close to quitting? Victory may be just ahead—a victory that might be tasted only if you persevere. Are you using all your strength—including God's strength working within you? "Let us throw off everything that hinders and the sin that so easily entangles, and let us run with perseverance the race marked out for us" (Hebrews 12:1). Call upon God for his help and blessing. Ask him to carry you over life's rough spots and on to victory as you persevere.

TODAY POWER POINT

Most of the important things in the world have been accomplished by people who have kept on trying when there seemed to be no hope at all.—Dale Carnegie

March 7

TODAY IN HISTORY

1869—Opening of Suez Canal to shipping
1876—Telephone patented
1897—Introduction for Corn Flakes (in Battle Creek, Michigan)
1911—Patent for coin-operated locker
1916—Formation of BMW (to make aircraft engines)
1926—Start of transatlantic radio-telephone service between New York City and London
1933—Monopoly board game trademarked
1965—Civil rights march in Selma, Alabama, broken up by police
1979—*Voyager I* spacecraft photos showed faint ring around Jupiter
2003—UN pronounced Iraqi documents seeking to buy uranium "forgeries"

BORN TODAY

Botanist Luther Burbank 1849
Musician Maurice Ravel 1875
TV weatherman Willard Scott . . . 1934
Businessman Michael Eisner 1942
Actor John Heard 1945
Football player Franco Harris 1950
Actor Bryan Cranston 1956
Tennis player Ivan Lendl 1960
Baseball player Jeff Kent 1968
Actress Rachel Weisz 1971

GOVERNMENT

God has intended governments to administer the public affairs of mankind, and we should honor them as God commands, even if it costs us something. *The Prairie Overcomer* told of a poor, elderly widow who was sent a tax bill requiring immediate payment. Counting her money, she found she had enough to pay the bill but had no transportation to go and pay it. Determined to fulfill her duty, she set out for the tax office on foot, but he nearest tax office was fourteen miles away.

"We need to take care of our government financially so that it stays democratic," the woman said in explanation of her Herculean effort to pay her taxes promptly. Her dedication was rewarded: the tax office saw to it that the woman got a ride back home.

Romans 13:7 says, "Give everyone what you owe him: If you owe taxes, pay taxes; if revenue, then revenue; if respect, then respect; if honor, then honor." What do you owe to your government? Your family? Your God? How faithful are you in paying your debts to the government or to the Lord?

Ask God to protect and guide our government leaders as they make decisions today and in the days and months ahead. And while you're at it, why not ask him to help you understand what more you could be doing to faithfully support and assist the government.

TODAY'S POWER POINT

I'm proud to pay taxes.—Payne Stewart

March 8

TODAY IN HISTORY

1618—Law of planetary motion proposed by astronomer Johannes Kepler
1894—First dog licensing law passed
1917—Russian Revolution sparked by uprising in Saint Petersburg
1957—Canal reopened following Suez crisis
1971—Joe Frazier defeated Muhammad Ali in world heavyweight fight
1983—Soviet Union called "evil empire" by president Ronald Reagan in speech to
        National Association of Evangelicals
1984—Pentagon smoking ban announced
1996—Dr. Jack Kevorkian acquitted of assisting in suicide of two patients

BORN TODAY

Surgeon Karl Ferdinand von Grafe . . 1787
Actress Claire Trevor. 1910
Actress Susan Clark 1940
Baseball player Jim Rice 1953
Actor Aidan Quinn 1959
Actor Freddie Prinze Jr. 1976
Actor James Van Der Beek 1977
Gymnast Marcia Newby. 1988

CHURCH-STATE SEPARATION

Separation of church and state should never be confused with separation of God from the state, for to do so invites disaster. In 1890 Liberal, Missouri, was established as a community of "free thinkers" so completely separated from God that churches were not even allowed in the town. The community claimed to be "the only town of its size in the United States without a priest, preacher, church, saloon, God, Jesus, hell, or devil."

What happened in this experiment to totally separate the state (and its people) from God? A newspaper reporter said of the town, "There was little else than hell and the devil there." One disgruntled citizen, on leaving the town, noted: "An infidel surrounded by Christians may spout his infidelity and the community may be able to stand it, but it will never do to establish a society with infidelity as its basis."

So much for the effort to separate God from society. When Jesus prayed for believers, he said to the Father, "My prayer is not that you take them out of the world but that you protect them from the evil one" (John 17:15). God has called Christians to be salt and light here on earth. Without such spiritual preservative and enlightenment, society quickly deteriorates.

Have you withdrawn from the world? Or are you indistinguishable from it? God has called you to influence your world for good. Are you acting as salt and light in your world today?

TODAY'S POWER POINT

The legislative powers of government reach actions only, and not opinions . . . thus building a wall of separation between Church and State.—Thomas Jefferson

TODAY IN HISTORY

1074—Married Catholic priests excommunicated from church
1858—Street mailboxes first introduced in United States
1862—Civil War battle of the ironclad ships *Monitor* and *Merrimac*
1938—Bob Hope film debut: *The Big Broadcast of 1938*, in which he sang "Thanks for the Memories"
1945—Assault launched on Tokyo by U.S. bombers
1959—Barbie doll first appeared in stores
1961—Dog launched into space aboard Soviet spacecraft
1996—Death of comedian George Burns, age one hundred
2000—John McCain's withdrawal left George W. Bush the GOP frontrunner for U.S. president

BORN TODAY

Explorer Amerigo Vespucci. 1454
Mystery writer Mickey Spillane . . .1918
Singer Keely Smith. 1932
Russian cosmonaut Yuri Gagarin . .1934
Actor Raul Julia 1940
Chess champ Bobby Fischer. 1943
News anchor Faith Daniels. 1957
Baseball player Terry Mulholland. .1963
Actress Juliette Binoche 1964
Olympic biathlon champion Curt
  Schreiner. 1967
Actor Emmanuel Lewis 1971

PRAYER

Do we really believe God answers prayer? Listen to the words of Joseph Scriven in his hymn "What a Friend": "O what needless pain we bear, all because we do not carry everything to God in prayer!" Yet how often we try to do things all by ourselves.

A man was busy in his study while his young son played nearby. Needing a book he had left upstairs and not wanting to lose his train of thought by going to get it, the man asked the youngster to get it for him. The boy eagerly ran to retrieve it but was gone for a long time. Leaving the office to check on the boy, the father heard crying at the top of the stairs. He found the little boy at the top of the stairs with the large book lying at his feet.

"Daddy," he cried, "I can't carry it. It's too heavy for me." The father lovingly stooped down and carried both the boy and the book down to the study.

That's just what God wants to do for us. He sees us in our weakness and stands ready to help if only we'll ask for his assistance. We need not struggle under our burdens. When we turn them over to God, he will carry us.

TODAY'S POWER POINT

If I could hear Christ praying for me in the next room, I would not fear a million enemies. Yet distance makes no difference. He is praying for me.—Robert Murray McCheyne

March 10

TODAY IN HISTORY

1862—Paper money first issued in United States
1876—Alexander Graham Bell's demonstration of telephone
1880—Salvation Army started U.S. operations
1908—First Mother's Day observed
1922—Mahatma Ghandi first arrested in India (for sedition)
1956—British aviator set new flight speed record (1,132 mph)
1964—First Ford Mustangs produced
1979—Fifteen thousand Iranian women protested Islamic rule
2003—PLO leader Mahmoud Abbas accepted role as new Palestinian prime
   minister

BORN TODAY

Diplomat Clare Boothe Luce 1903
Actress Pamela Mason 1916
Martial-arts master and actor Chuck
   Norris 1940
Actress Sharon Stone 1958

Prince Edward of England;
   actress Jasmine Guy 1964
Olympic gymnast Shannon Miller . . 1977
Singer Carrie Underwood. 1983

HARD WORK

A great orchestra was gathered for rehearsal before the celebrated conductor Sir Michael Costa. Virtually every instrument played during one loud crescendo, but not the piccolo. The piccolo player was tired and felt that his instrument's small voice wouldn't be missed. But the conductor stopped the orchestra suddenly and cried out, "Where's the piccolo?" In the resounding thunder of many loud instruments, one tiny piccolo was missed!

No matter how insignificant you may feel or how hard your task, keep on doing the part to which God has called you. Consider the little titmouse that awakens at 3:00 a.m. and keeps going until nine at night—an eighteen-hour day—feeding its chicks 417 meals.

Then there's the blackbird, whose work schedule is less rigorous—just seventeen hours—during which time it feeds its young up to one hundred times, every day. Suddenly our eight- or nine-hour workday, five days a week (with three meal breaks) doesn't seem so bad after all!

Ask God to teach you the rewards of hard work as you go about your daily activities.

TODAY'S POWER POINT

One machine can do the work of fifty ordinary men. No machine can do the work of one extraordinary man.—Elbert Hubbard

TODAY IN HISTORY

1824—U.S. Bureau of Indian Affairs established

1918—Spanish flu struck the United States (40 million people died worldwide)

1941—Lend-Lease Law signed by Franklin D. Roosevelt to aid Nazi foes in World War II

1942—General Douglas MacArthur assumed top Pacific command

1969—Levi Strauss first sold bell-bottom jeans

1985—Mikhail Gorbachev assumed leadership of Soviet Union following death of Konstanin Chernenko

1990—Lithuania declared independence from USSR

1993—Janet Reno confirmed as first female U.S. attorney general

2004—Madrid commuter train bombing: 1,600 wounded, 202 killed on four trains

2006—Former Yugoslavian president and accused war criminal Slobodan Milošević found in his cell, dead from a heart attack

BORN TODAY

Musician Lawrence Welk 1903

Media mogul Rupert Murdoch. . . 1931

Broadcast journalist Sam Donaldson
. . . . 1934

Supreme Court Justice Antonin Scalia
. . . . 1936

Writer and director Jerry Zucker;
singer Bobby McFerrin 1950

Author Douglas Adams 1952

Basketball player Elton Brand. . . . 1979

Actress Thora Birch 1982

GOD'S LAWS

Which laws should we obey, man's or God's? The Bible makes it clear that civil disobedience is allowed only when human laws run counter to the law established by God.

Benjamin Franklin's autobiography includes a story of a colonial clergyman who was ordered to read the proclamation issued by King Charles I encouraging the people to participate in sports on Sundays. Much to the amazement of his congregation, the preacher complied and read the edict that so many others had refused to read. But the preacher followed the king's edict with these words, "Remember the Sabbath day by keeping it holy" (Exodus 20:8), adding, "Brethren, I have laid before you the commandment of your king and the commandment of your God. I leave it to you to judge which of the two you ought rather to observe."

When in doubt about whether you are obligated to obey a law or resist, check it out—in God's Word, the Bible. When you conscientiously uphold God's laws, you'll always be in the right.

TODAY'S POWER POINT

When a stupid man is doing something he is ashamed of, he always declares that it is his duty.—George Bernard Shaw

March 12

TODAY IN HISTORY

1894—Bottled Coca-Cola first sold
1904—Andrew Carnegie contribution of $5 million established Carnegie Hero Fund
1912—Girl Scouts founded
1933—President Franklin D. Roosevelt's first fireside chat
1938—Nazi invasion of Austria
1945—Death of diarist Anne Frank, age fifteen, in Nazi concentration camp
1966—Indonesian president Sukarno overthrown, Haji Mohammad Suharto installed as acting president
1987—Premiere of *Les Miserables*
1993—Bomb blasts in Bombay kill three hundred people
1994—First woman ordained as priest in Church of England
1999—NATO joined by Hungary, Czech Republic, and Poland
2000—Pope John Paul II asked for God's forgiveness for errors of Catholic Church through the ages

BORN TODAY

British landlord Charles Boycott . . . 1832
Singer Gordon MacRae 1921
Author Jack Kerouac 1922
Playwright Edward Albee 1928
Civil-rights leader Andrew Young. . 1932
Songwriter Al Jarreau 1940
Singer Liza Minelli. 1946
Singer James Taylor 1948
Auto racer John Andretti 1963

CURIOSITY

Have you ever been intrigued about something or wondered why a task is done the way it is? Some of mankind's greatest inventions have been produced through just such curiosity. A department-store janitor, Murray Spangler, grew tired of breathing dust when he swept and knew there must be a better way. His curiosity motivated him to find a way to lift dirt from the floor and into a sealed bag, thus eliminating the dusty broom. The result was a crude but workable vacuum cleaner, which he then encouraged his friend, H. W. Hoover, to finance. The rest is history.

If God has instilled within you a sense of curiosity, be glad. Thank him for his creation and for giving you the ability to tame and understand it. Be careful to channel your curiosity into a greater appreciation of God's creation and his Word.

TODAY'S POWER POINT

It is the object of learning, not only to satisfy the curiosity and perfect the spirits of ordinary men, but also to advance civilization.—Woodrow Wilson

March 13

TODAY IN HISTORY

1868—Impeachment proceedings against President Andrew Johnson launched in U.S. Senate

1884—World time standard adopted

1887—Earmuffs patented

1904—Dedication of statue overlooking Argentina and Chile: Christ of the Andes

1980—Resignation of Ford chairman Henry Ford III left Ford Motor Company without family leadership for first time

1983—Premiere of the *Larry King Show*

2003—Overwhelming congressional approval for ban on "partial birth" abortions (later vetoed by president Bill Clinton); FDA issued recommendation for bar codes on hospital medications to avoid mix-ups, wrong dosages

BORN TODAY

Astronomer Percival Lowell 1855

Publisher Walter Annenberg. 1908

Voice actor Clarence Nash 1936

Singer Neil Sedaka 1939

Actor William Macy. 1950

Actress Dana Delany 1956

Musician Adam Clayton. 1960

Baseball player Will Clark 1964

HUMAN NATURE

Despite the slick appearance mankind often displays, the Bible says, "There is no one righteous, not even one" (Romans 3:10). Game wardens demonstrated their understanding of this darker side of human nature by the way they set up their check-in station on the opening day of hunting season not long ago. They posted a first road sign that informed hunters, "Check Station 1,000 yards ahead."

Five hundred yards beyond the sign was a convenient side road. The wardens correctly assumed that lawful hunters would continue straight ahead, but over-limit and dubious hunters would likely duck down the side road—where wardens had aptly located the real check station.

On our own, humankind has no hope of being righteous. But a loving God has provided a way to escape the limitations of human nature. We can be righteous with God's help. Romans 3:22 says, "This righteousness from God comes through faith in Jesus Christ to all who believe." We no longer have to live according to our human nature. When we believe in Jesus, he replaces that old nature with a new nature like his. He gives us the power we need to act and live in a way consistent with that new nature—in a way that pleases God.

TODAY'S POWER POINT

It is the lying at the top levels of our society that concerns me the most because morality, like water (and unlike money), really does trickle down.—Jim Lehrer

March 14

TODAY IN HISTORY

1794—Cotton gin patented by Eli Whitney
1900—Gold standard ratified by Congress
1913—Rockefeller Foundation given $100 million gift by John D. Rockefeller
1938—First theater built for rear movie projection (New York City)
1939—Nazi Germany dissolved Republic of Czechoslovakia
1950—Publication of first FBI Ten Most Wanted Fugitives list
1954—Braves' Henry Aaron homered in his first exhibition game
1960—First televised courtroom verdict; Wilt Chamberlain (Philadelphia) set NBA playoff record of fifty-three points
1964—Jack Ruby sentenced to death for Lee Harvey Oswald murder
1983—OPEC members agreed to price cuts for first time in cartel's twenty-five-year history
1990—Mikhail Gorbachev made president of Soviet congress
2004—Opposition Socialists scored upset win in Spanish national elections following terrorist bombing of Madrid commuter trains

BORN TODAY

Violinist and composer Johann Strauss 1804
Railroad engineer Casey Jones . . . 1864
Physicist Albert Einstein. 1879
Bandleader Les Brown 1912
Cartoonist Hank Ketcham 1920

Producer and singer Quincy Jones;
    Actor Michael Caine. 1933
Actor Billy Crystal 1947
Actress Tamara Tunie 1959
Musician Taylor Hanson 1983

ACCOUNTING FOR TIME

Studies have shown that during the average lifetime, people spend twenty years sleeping, twenty years working, six years eating, seven years playing, five years dressing, one year on the telephone, two-and-a-half years in bed, three years waiting for someone, a year and a half in church, five months tying their shoes, and a year and a half on other things.

Someday we will all be called upon to account for how we have used our time, including how much we've given in service to the Lord. Take account today of your time and your priorities. Are you doing all you can for God, or are you wasting precious minutes and hours you might spend with or for him?

TODAY'S POWER POINT

Most time is wasted, not in hours, but in minutes. A bucket with a small hole in the bottom gets just as empty as a bucket that is deliberately kicked over.
—Paul Meyer

TODAY IN HISTORY

44 BC—Julius Caesar assassinated
1729—First Catholic nun designated
1820—Twenty-third state, Maine, joined Union
1892—Introduction of voting machine
1906—Rolls Royce introduced
1913—First presidential news conference held (by President Woodrow Wilson)
1917—Last Russian czar, Nicholas II, abdicated throne
1919—American Legion established
1954—Doo-wop born
1966—Watts riots in Los Angeles
1972—Premiere of *The Godfather*
1974—President Richard Nixon named co-conspirator in Watergate scandal
1984—Voluntary silent prayer in public schools rejected by Senate
1998—Death of children's doctor Benjamin Spock, age ninety-four
2005—Bernie Ebbers, former head of WorldCom, found guilty of charges in
      connection with $11 billion loss

BORN TODAY

President Andrew Jackson 1767
Composer Eduard Strauss. 1835
Bandleader Harry James. 1916
Evangelist Jimmy Swaggart;
    actor Judd Hirsch 1935
Beach Boys' singer Mike Love. . . . 1941
Singer Sly Stone 1944
Baseball player Bobby Bonds 1946
Model Fabio. 1961

GUARDING OUR FREEDOM

In Washington DC the statue Lady Freedom stands nearly twenty feet tall atop the capitol's dome. A crest of stars surrounds her head, and in her left hand she holds a shield of stars and stripes. But few know the story of Lady Freedom's shipment from Rome.

Encountering a fierce storm, the ship's captain ordered some cargo to be thrown overboard. Some of the sailors wanted to jettison the heavy statue, but the captain refused. "No! Never!" he shouted above the howling storm. "We'll flounder before we throw Freedom away."

Do you value freedom enough to weather the storm or risk your life in its defense? Or do you sometimes take freedom for granted? If we're not watchful, we might someday find that our freedoms have been taken away. As Edmund Burke said, "The only thing necessary for the triumph of evil is for good men to do nothing." Ask God today for his protection of our country and our freedoms.

TODAY'S POWER POINT

If the Son sets you free, you will be free indeed.—John 8:36

March 16

TODAY IN HISTORY

1521—Philippines discovered by Ferdinand Magellan
1802—Establishment of U.S. Military Academy at West Point
1827—Founding of *Freedom's Journal*, first African American newspaper in the U.S.
1829—First high-school night classes
1915—Federal Trade Commission authorized
1926—First liquid-fueled rocket flight
1945—U.S. victory over Japan in battle of Iwo Jima
1966—Two spacecraft successfully docked by U.S. astronauts
1985—American journalist Terry Anderson kidnapped in Lebanon
2000—Vermont House approved civil unions between same-sex partners

BORN TODAY

President James Madison 1751
Comedian Henny Youngman. . . . 1906
Comedian Jerry Lewis 1925
Filmmaker Bernardo Bertolucci . . 1941
TV host Chuck Woolery 1942
Actor Erik Estrada 1949
Pastor and author Ed Young. 1961

ENCOURAGING ONE ANOTHER

The deep hunger people feel for a word of affirmation and praise is illustrated by a British telephone company's installation of a service called MOR (for morale). The service targeted Britain's neglected housewives who were starved for a kind word and a little reassurance, even when they knew the person on the other end of the phone didn't really know them at all. When family members weren't quite as appreciative as they should be at home, the lonely mum could dial a special number to hear a soothing male voice coo, "You're really quite beautiful, you know," and similar flattering words.

Would those in your family or circle of friends have reason to call MOR? If you're doing your job as an encourager, they shouldn't have to. As Christians and children of God, we should be appreciative and complimentary to our families, our associates, and others God has placed in our sphere of influence. While we should always shun insincere flattery, an honest compliment to those we meet lets them know we value them, and it can help make their day.

Mark Twain once said, "I can live two months on a good compliment." Find something good in everyone you meet—and praise them sincerely every chance you get!

TODAY'S POWER POINT

Hunger is never delicate; they who are seldom gorged to the full with praise may be safely fed with gross compliments, for the appetite must be satisfied before it is disgusted.—Samuel Johnson

TODAY IN HISTORY

1897—First film of a heavyweight championship fight
1910—Founding of Camp Fire Girls
1941—Opening of National Gallery of Art in Washington DC
1949—First Porsche produced in Germany
1966—U.S. sub located missing H-bomb off coast of Spain
1973—Release of navy pilot (and future U.S. senator) John McCain from
          Vietnamese POW camp after five years in captivity
1982—EPA started allowing toxic liquid drums to be buried in landfills
2000—Smith and Wesson agreed to put safety locks on all its handguns
2003—Iraq ultimatum: U.S. President George W. Bush told Iraqi president Saddam
          Hussein to resign within forty-eight hours or face war

BORN TODAY

Frontiersman Jim Bridger 1804
Golfer Bobby Jones 1902
Civil-rights leader Bayard Rustin . . . 1910
Singer Nat King Cole 1919
Actor Patrick Duffy 1949
Actor Kurt Russell 1951
Actor Gary Sinise 1955
Actor Rob Lowe 1964
Olympic soccer player Mia Hamm . . 1972

FORGIVENESS

It is one thing to forgive our friends, but forgiving our enemies—that takes strength that only God can give. During the Revolutionary War a pastor, John Miller, once learned that one of his greatest enemies—a man who had habitually made Miller's life miserable and who was a traitor to his country—was to be hanged for his crimes. Upon hearing this, Miller walked sixty miles to visit General George Washington to plead for the man's life.

After listening to Miller's plea, Washington said, "I'm sorry, but I cannot pardon your friend."

"Friend!" Miller exclaimed. "That man is my worst enemy."

Seeing the preacher's forgiveness and self-sacrificing display of love for his sworn enemy, Washington signed the pardon. Miller then quickly carried the message fifteen miles to the execution site, arriving just as the condemned man was trudging toward the scaffold.

What forgiveness! Yet Christ did that and more for you and all humanity. The Bible states, "While we were still sinners, Christ died for us" (Romans 5:8). Now it is our turn to love and forgive those who have wronged us. Think of those who have wronged you and whom you have not yet forgiven. Seek them out today and tell them you have forgiven them.

TODAY'S POWER POINT

He who forgives ends the quarrel.—African Proverb

March 18

TODAY IN HISTORY

1925—Worst U.S. tornado: nearly seven hundred people killed across Missouri, Illinois, and Indiana

1931—First electric razor introduced by Schick

1949—Organization of North Atlantic Treaty Organization (NATO)

1965—First spacewalk performed by Russian cosmonaut

1995—Michael Jordan returns to the Chicago Bulls after temporary retirement

2000—Opposition leader favoring independence from China elected in Taiwan

BORN TODAY

President Grover Cleveland 1837

Singer Charlie Pride 1932

Singer Wilson Pickett 1941

Actress Vanessa Williams 1963

Olympic speed skater Bonnie Blair . . 1964

Actress Queen Latifah 1970

Figure skater Alexei Yagudin 1980

A FITTING MEMORIAL

Many great figures in history have not been fully appreciated until after they died—like Luíz Vaz de Camões, who died virtually unknown and in poverty but now is recognized as one of Portugal's leading poets. Because it was not known where Camões's body was buried, friends gathered dust from places he visited and put it in an expensive burial vault. They hoped some of the dust might include a particle of his body.

The public is fickle—and often not too observant or discerning. Some downright unworthy characters become celebrities, achieve success, or wield power. And some people who are talented, generous, intelligent, and have integrity live their whole lives in obscurity.

Ecclesiastes 9:11 says, "The race is not to the swift or the battle to the strong." But God will one day sort it all out justly. No matter how well a person's true character has been hidden during life, eventually the substance of each life becomes known. First Timothy 5:24–25 says, "The sins of some men are obvious, reaching the place of judgment ahead of them; the sins of others trail behind them. In the same way, good deeds are obvious, and even those that are not cannot be hidden."

Your deeds, the sum of your life, won't be hidden for long. What will people say about you after you die? What will God say? Rather than worrying about people, be concerned with what God thinks of you. Even if others don't honor you as you deserve, God will. He's preparing a place for you to spend eternity with him.

TODAY'S POWER POINT

I would rather have a memorial of one I dearly loved, than the noblest artist's work ever produced.—Elizabeth Barrett Browning

TODAY IN HISTORY

1931—Gambling legalized in Nevada

1953—First televised Academy Awards

1954—Newspaper vending machine introduced

1974—Oil embargo lifted, resulting in end to ban on Sunday gas sales and other restrictions

1977—Study reported the number of single adults living alone more than doubled since 1970

2003—Unleashing of U.S. "shock and awe" aerial attack on Iraqi targets; Senate defeated measure to allow oil drilling in Arctic National Wildlife Refuge

BORN TODAY

Puritan leader William Bradford. . 1589

Missionary David Livingstone . . . 1813

Marshal Wyatt Earp 1848

Orator William Jennings Bryan . . 1860

Author Philip Roth 1933

Actress Glen Close 1947

Actor Bruce Willis 1955

Basketball player Hedo Turkoglu. . . 1979

HOPE

Six navy pilots left their aircraft carrier on a scouting mission during World War II. They courageously did their part in dangerous enemy territory, discovering the enemy was closer than previously known, and then were eager to head back to the safe refuge of their ship.

But when the pilots returned, they couldn't locate their ship. While they had been gone, the captain had felt it necessary to order a total blackout on the ship to keep it from being detected by the enemy. The frantic pilots radioed, pleading for help—for just one small light—so they could see to land. But their desperate pleas were met with stony silence and endless blackness. The blackout and radio silence was maintained so that the lives of hundreds on the carrier might be safeguarded. The pilots were forced to ditch in the cold Atlantic, hopelessly lost just a short distance from their dark, silent ship.

What darkened ship have you been counting on? investments? retirement savings? good health? good friends? respect in the community, a good reputation, or an honorable vocation? Nothing is worthy of our hope and trust. People, institutions, even life itself, will eventually fail us. But God never will. Put your hope in him, and with the psalmist you can say, "In you, O LORD, I have taken refuge; let me never be put to shame. Rescue me and deliver me in your righteousness; turn your ear to me and save me. Be my rock of refuge, to which I can always go" (Psalm 71:1–3).

TODAY'S POWER POINT

Life with Christ is an endless hope, without him a hopeless end.—Source Unknown

March 20

TODAY IN HISTORY

1852—*Uncle Tom's Cabin* first published

1976—Kidnapped Patty Hearst found guilty of armed robbery

1985—Libby Riddles, age twenty-eight, became first woman to win the Iditarod

1987—Resignation of Jim and Tammy Bakker from PTL ministry; leadership temporarily given to Jerry Falwell

1997—Chesterfield cigarettes admitted targeting teenagers with their smoking ads, agreed to put addiction warning on every pack

1999—Aviators Bertrand Piccard and Brian Jones were first to fly nonstop around the world in hot-air balloon

BORN TODAY

Playwright Henrik Ibsen. 1828

Psychologist B. F. Skinner. 1904

Actor Carl Reiner. 1922

TV host Fred Rogers 1928

Actor Hal Linden. 1931

Singer Jerry Reed 1937

Basketball coach Pat Riley 1945

Director Spike Lee;

    actress Theresa Russell. 1957

Actress Holly Hunter 1958

GOD'S PROVISION

A story is told of August Francke, famed German preacher of the 1600s, who established a home for needy children. Francke was often concerned about raising the funds to continue his work, and during one of these low points a distraught widow came to him, pleading for one small coin. Faced with diminished resources and scores of children needing his help, Francke sadly turned her away.

The woman, having nowhere else to turn, began to weep. Francke asked her to wait one moment while he took time to pray. After calling on God for guidance and for the resources to meet the children's needs, Francke returned to the widow and gave her what he had: one small coin.

Several days later Francke received a thank-you letter from the widow. She explained that because of his kindness in meeting her need, she had called upon God to shower his blessings on Francke's orphanage.

Later that day Francke received fourteen coins from donors he did not even know. But God was not done with his blessing. A messenger came and explained that the estate of a wealthy prince had been settled, and the orphanage was being given five hundred gold coins to help carry out its work.

Overwhelmed at the outpouring of God's provision, Francke broke down in tears of gratitude. For in giving generously what he could not afford, God had multiplied his humble gift hundreds of times over. Do you have a need today? Ask God to supply it: he is always faithful.

TODAY'S POWER POINT

Giving is the thermometer of our love.—Source Unknown

March 21

TODAY IN HISTORY

1617—Death of Pocahontas on trip to England

1851—Yosemite Valley, California, discovered

1939—First foreign-language course broadcast on radio; Kate Smith recorded "God Bless America"

1963—Alcatraz prison ceased operation

1965—Civil-rights march from Selma to Montgomery, Alabama, led by Martin Luther King Jr.

1980—U.S. boycott of Moscow Olympics announced

2001—Russian diplomats expelled from United States (in follow-up to earlier arrest of FBI agent)

2005—Ten dead in shooting rampage at Minnesota's Red Lake High School

BORN TODAY

Composer Johann Sebastian Bach . . 1685
Poet Phyllis McGinley 1905
Industrialist John D. Rockefeller III. . 1906
Director Peter Brook 1925
Actor Timothy Dalton 1944
Actor Gary Oldman 1958
Talk-show host Rosie O'Donnell;
   actor Matthew Broderick 1962

POWER TO CHANGE

God's Word has the power to bring revolutionary changes to our lives. Henry Bosch told of a traveling salesman who had been stealing money from his company and was growing increasingly concerned that he would be caught. He became a workaholic—always keeping busy to avoid his nagging conscience. While shaving at a Chicago hotel in preparation for a business appointment, he looked for a piece of paper to wipe the blade of his old-fashioned razor. Finding none, he reached for the nearby Gideon Bible and tore a page from it. When he smoothed it out, his gaze fell on these words: "The wages of sin is death; but the gift of God is eternal life in Christ Jesus our Lord" (Romans 6:23).

The startled salesman began reading through the Bible in earnest, and before long accepted Christ as his Savior. Later he confessed his theft to his employer, who allowed him to make full restitution through deductions from his salary.

God's Word is powerful: "The word of God is living and active. Sharper than any double-edged sword, it penetrates even to dividing soul and spirit, joints and marrow; it judges the thoughts and attitudes of the heart" (Hebrews 4:12). It penetrated the salesman's heart, revolutionized his life, and led him to the Savior and freedom from the bondage of sin.

What is God's Word saying to you? Take a look in the Book today and see.

TODAY'S POWER POINT

The Bible is alive, it speaks to me; it has feet, it runs after me; it has hands, it lays hold on me.—Martin Luther

March 22

TODAY IN HISTORY

1765—Passage of the Stamp Act
1882—Polygamy prohibited in United States
1907—Meters installed in London cabs
1941—Grand Coulee Dam began operation
1945—Arab League established
1946—Jordan granted independence from Britain
1960—Laser patented
1972—Equal Rights Amendment passed by U.S. Senate
1994—Death of cartoonist Walter Lantz, age ninety-three
1997—Seventeen-year-old Tara Lipinski crowned youngest world figure-skating
        champion
2004—Israeli missile killed militant Hamas leader in Gaza City
2005—Federal judge refused to order Terri Schiavo's feeding tube to be reinserted

BORN TODAY

Actor Karl Malden 1914
TV evangelist Pat Robertson;
    composer Stephen Sondheim . 1930
Actor William Shatner 1931
Singer George Benson 1943

Producer Andrew Lloyd Webber. . 1948
Sportscaster Bob Costas 1952
Olympic skater Elvis Stojko 1971
Actress Reese Witherspoon. 1976

NOT IN A HURRY

A kindly pastor was being honored by hundreds of people upon his retirement after forty years of ministry. One by one, great and eloquent speakers came to the platform to extol his many virtues. Then, at the following reception in his honor, one gentleman came up to his beloved pastor and said that his fondest memory of him was that in all the time he knew him, he was never in a hurry.

Later, reflecting on the day's events, the pastor told his wife that of all the many kind words spoken in his honor that day, the remark he cherished most was the one given in private by that parishioner.

Sometimes, with all our obligations and responsibilities, life feels rushed. But even when the world seems to be rapidly spinning out of control, believers can gain strength from simply waiting upon the Lord.

Martin Luther once said that he was so busy that he couldn't possibly get everything done until he had spent at least three hours in prayer. If you're stressed and pressured today, concerned about how you can possibly complete every task, take a lesson from the wise Reformer. In every situation learn to keep your eyes fixed upon the Lord, and you can be calm in the midst of the fiercest storm.

TODAY'S POWER POINT

Never take on more work than you have time to pray about.—Richard DeHaan

TODAY IN HISTORY

1775—Patrick Henry's famed "Give me liberty or give me death" speech delivered
1857—World's first passenger elevator installed in New York by Elisha Otis
1858—First cable car introduced
1925—Tennessee outlawed teaching of evolution in public schools and universities
1933—German legislature granted Nazis sweeping powers
1950—Premiere of TV game show *Beat the Clock*
1956—Pakistan became a republic in British Commonwealth
1957—U.S. Army's last homing pigeons sold
2000—Pope John Paul II paid respect at Israel's Holocaust memorial; Chicago priest Daniel Coughlin named first Roman Catholic chaplain of U.S. House

BORN TODAY

Actress Joan Crawford 1904
Scientist Wernher von Braun 1912
Musician Doc Watson 1923
Runner Roger Bannister 1929
Basketball player Moses Malone . . 1954
Actress Amanda Plummer 1957
Basketball player Jason Kidd. 1973
Actress Keri Russell 1976

ON GUARD!

A sentry stood guard against a suprise attack at the entrance to a fort in colonial America. His strict orders were to fire on any suspicious target. He heard a rustling in the leaves, cocked his gun, and just before shooting realized that the intruder was a wild hog. Not long afterward, more rustling brought a similar response—and likewise proved to be a hog rooting in the leaves. Then, from another direction, came movement in the underbrush. The man raised his gun to fire, then recognized the typical colorings of another wild hog—but this one stayed hidden. The sentry quickly reasoned, "Yes, this could be another hog; on the other hand, it could be an enemy wrapping himself in hog skin."

He made his decision, aimed, and fired. The sentry saved the fort, felling a scout sent to discover the fort's weaknesses.

Evil seldom presents itself openly. Rather, it comes disguised as something harmless—maybe even something good. But its disguised appearance doesn't make it less dangerous but more so. Being vigilant against evil is increasingly important in this day and age.

How can we survive in this dark and threatening age? How can we keep from being surprised and overwhelmed by the enemy? By being vigilant and not letting down our guard. First Thessalonians 5:6 says, "Let us not be like others, who are asleep, but let us be alert and self-controlled." On guard!

TODAY'S POWER POINT

It is one thing to recognize evil as a fact. It is another thing to take evil to one's breast and call it good.—John Foster Dulles

March 24

TODAY IN HISTORY

1882—Tuberculosis bacillus discovered

1900—Construction began on first successful New York City subway

1934—Philippine Islands gained independence from United States

1949—First father-and-son Oscar winners (Walter and John Huston, for *Treasure of Sierra Madre*)

1972—Equal Employment Opportunity Act made law in United States

1989—Supertanker *Exxon Valdez* ran aground off coast of Alaska, spilling millions of gallons of crude oil in worst U.S. oil spill

2000—Judge awarded newspaperman Terry Anderson $341 million from frozen Iranian assets after Anderson was held hostage for seven years by Iranian agents in Lebanon

BORN TODAY

Hymn writer Fannie Crosby 1820

Magician and escape artist Harry Houdini 1874

Actor Fatty Arbuckle 1887

Cartoonist Joseph Barbera 1911

Poet Lawrence Ferlinghetti 1919

Actor Steve McQueen 1930

Designer Bob Mackie 1940

Actress Lara Flynn Boyle 1970

Football player Peyton Manning . . 1976

IN NONESSENTIALS, LIBERTY

Throughout the ages, hundreds of the world's rulers have tried to limit or restrict their citizens' right to worship as they please. One such ruler was France's Charles V, who eventually abdicated his throne after failing to compel his subjects to conform to his own thinking about religion. Weary from a long reign, Charles retired to a monastery, where he amused himself by trying to synchronize a dozen clocks. Failing in this, he exclaimed, "How foolish I have been to think that I could make all men believe alike about religion when I cannot even make twelve clocks run together."

The great church father Augustine is often quoted as saying, "In essentials unity, in nonessentials liberty, in all things charity." This is an excellent motto for those who follow Christ and encounter those who do things just a little bit differently. Some things are foundational to the faith, but others are a matter of preference or interpretation. They matter little in the long run and should not be allowed to threaten the unity and brotherhood of believers. Be thankful for the freedom to worship God in the manner you wish, but be careful to recognize that you don't have a corner on God's truth.

TODAY'S POWER POINT

In the future days . . . we look forward to a world founded upon four essential human freedoms . . . [including the] freedom of every person to worship God in his own way—everywhere in the world.—Franklin D. Roosevelt

TODAY IN HISTORY

1634—Landing of British colonists in Maryland

1857—First photo of a solar eclipse

1958—Sugar Ray Robinson became first five-time world middleweight boxing champ

1997—Former President George H. W. Bush, age seventy-three, parachuted from a plane

2000—Vladimir Putin elected president of Russia

2004—Meeting of British and Libyan leaders to plan joint fight against terrorism; U.S. Senate outlawed harming a fetus while committing a federal crime against a pregnant woman

BORN TODAY

Sportscaster Howard Cosell 1920
Feminist Gloria Steinem. 1935
Singer Aretha Franklin 1942
Actress Bonnie Bedelia 1946
Singer Elton John. 1947
Actress Sarah Jessica Parker. 1965
Baseball player Tom Glavin 1966
Basketball player Sheryl Swoopes . . .1971

TRUE WISDOM

Mortimer Adler, former University of Chicago professor, recalls that if, when he entered the classroom and said, "Good morning," the students responded, "Good morning," he knew they were undergraduates. But if they took out their notebooks and wrote down his greetings, he knew they were graduate students.

Having education and having wisdom are not necessarily the same thing. Some people would say wisdom involves common sense. It's often a product of experience, being able to apply what you've seen and learned. But perhaps the greatest hallmark of wisdom is knowing when a problem or situation is bigger than you—and knowing where to go for answers. James 1:5 says, "If any of you lacks wisdom, he should ask God, who gives generously to all without finding fault, and it will be given to him."

Abraham Lincoln had such wisdom. On the eve of the crucial Battle of Gettysburg, someone asked him why he was so calm and assured in such a dark hour of peril. Lincoln replied, "I spent last night in prayer before the Lord, and he has given me the assurance that our cause will triumph and that the nation will be preserved."

Are you facing your own internal civil war? Wish you had wisdom to know what is best or right? Remember, God is the source of all wisdom, and he'll gladly share that wisdom with you if you'll just ask.

TODAY'S POWER POINT

Knowledge is the small part of ignorance that we arrange and classify.—Ambrose Bierce

March 26

TODAY IN HISTORY

1790—First U.S. naturalization law passed by Congress

1827—Death of composer Ludwig van Beethoven, age fifty-seven

1885—First motion-picture film stock (blank movie film) produced by Kodak, enabling professional movies to be made

1953—Polio vaccine first introduced by Jonas Salk

1971—Independence from Pakistan declared by Bangladesh

1979—Thirty years of hostilities between Egypt and Israel ended with Camp David accord

1992—Russian cosmonaut returned to earth after 313 days in space aboard the Mir space station

1999—Dr. Jack Kevorkian convicted of giving lethal injection to patient

BORN TODAY

Poet Robert Frost 1874

Actor Leonard Nimoy 1931

Actor James Caan 1940

Singer Diana Ross 1944

Actress Vicki Lawrence 1949

Singer Teddy Pendergrass;

    actor Martin Short 1950

Football player Marcus Allen 1960

Country singer Kenny Chesney . . 1968

Actor Josh Lucas. 1972

POLISHING PROBLEMS

A young man worked hard to establish himself as a fruit grower. Finally, after years of tedious preliminary work, his crop blossomed beautifully, and the harvest looked promising. But then an unseasonable frost wiped it out. Noting that the man had stopped coming to church soon after, his pastor paid him a visit.

"I'm not going to church any more," the young man said. "How can I worship a God who allows my entire crop to be destroyed?"

The preacher said, "Don't you see, God loves you more than he loves your peaches. While he knows that peaches grow better without frosts, he also knows it is impossible to grow the best men without frosts. God's desire is to grow people, not peaches."

The troubles we encounter in life help us blossom into what God wants us to become. The apostle Paul recognized the value of trials. He told the Corinthian believers, "This happened that we might not rely on ourselves but on God. . . . On him we have set our hope" (2 Corinthians 1:9–10).

While we can see only our immediate problems, God focuses on the eternal results. After all, it's the work of the abrasive that makes a gem glisten. You should be glad when God starts polishing!

TODAY'S POWER POINT

All growth is a leap in the dark, a spontaneous, unpremeditated act without benefit of experience.—Rebecca West

TODAY IN HISTORY

1794—U.S. Navy established
1884—First long-distance call in United States (between Boston and New York City)
1899—Guglielmo Marconi sent first radio signals across English Channel
1905—Fingerprints first used as murder evidence
1912—Japanese cherry trees planted in Washington DC
1964—Major earthquake rocked Alaska, killing more than one hundred people
1981—Poland's Solidarity trade union called nationwide strike in Poland
1998—Viagra, first male impotency drug, approved by FDA

BORN TODAY

Automobile pioneer Henry Royce . . . 1863
Photographer Edward Steichen . . . 1879
Actress Gloria Swanson 1899
Singer Sarah Vaughan 1924
Author Anthony Lewis 1927
Actor Michael York 1942
Actress Maria Schneider 1952
Director Quentin Tarantino 1963
Singer Mariah Carey 1970

SERVING GOD

Evangelist John R. Rice tells of a building contractor who made a commitment to Christ in one of his revival campaigns. The contractor was building several houses and had a sizeable crew working for him. The local church had revival meetings scheduled midmorning, and the contractor announced to his crew that they were all going to go hear the guest preacher.

When one man said he planned to remain working that hour, the builder told him that all employees would receive their normal pay and would go to church on his time. So the crew attended church each day, and a number committed their lives to God. This astute contractor had invested in the lives of his employees—giving them an opportunity to accept something mere wages could never provide—everlasting life.

Whether we realize it or not, all believers are in full-time Christian service. Being a Christian involves a total commitment. It also involves being alert to opportunities to share the most valuable treasure imaginable with those around us—and loving them enough to follow through. Imagine the change in America today if every business owner were to take his or her employees to hear the gospel. Imagine the possibilities if every believer were committed to finding and utilizing opportunities to serve God every day and in every way. Ask God to give you opportunities to tell others about him, either on the job or among your daily contacts.

TODAY'S POWER POINT

Your brother needs your help, but you meanwhile mumble your little prayers to God, pretending not to see your brother's need.—Desiderius Erasmus

TODAY IN HISTORY

1797—Washing machine patent issued to Nathaniel Briggs

1848—First child-labor law passed (in Pennsylvania)

1977—Worst aviation disaster in world history: collision of two 747s on runway in Canary Islands, 574 dead

1979—Worst nuclear accident in U.S. history at Three Mile Island, Pennsylvania, yet no one killed or injured

1980—Start of eruptions on Mount St. Helens (Washington) after 123 years of silence

2002—Arab League approved peace plan with Israel

2003—Japanese spy satellites deployed over North Korea

2005—Indonesian island of Java struck by earthquake, hundreds killed while fleeing, fearing tsunami

BORN TODAY

Novelist Maxim Gorky 1868

Pianist Rudolf Serkin 1903

Singer and songwriter Bill Gaither . . . 1936

Actor Ken Howard 1944

Actress Dianne Wiest 1948

Singer Reba McEntire 1954

Soccer player Earnie Stewart 1969

Hockey player Keith Tkachuk . . . 1972

Actress Julia Stiles 1981

A HEART IN THE RIGHT PLACE

Robert DeVincenzo, a tough Argentine golfer, won a major tournament and was awarded a sizeable check. After the ceremonies DeVincenzo met a sad-eyed young woman who said, "It's a happy day for you, but the doctors say my baby is dying of an incurable blood disease."

Immediately the champion took out a pen, signed over his check, and urged the woman to "Make some good days for the baby."

Later he was told the woman had no sick baby: he had been tricked out of his winnings. DeVincenzo responded, "Do you mean there's no baby dying without hope? Why, that's the best news I've heard all week!"

How do you respond when you've been wronged? What's more important to you, your money or other people? Are you more careful of your financial investments or your Christian witness? If your treasure is in the right place, so will your heart be.

In Luke 12:33–34 Jesus challenged his followers: "Provide purses for yourselves that will not wear out, a treasure in heaven that will not be exhausted, where no thief comes near and no moth destroys. For where your treasure is, there your heart will be also."

TODAY'S POWER POINT

Character is long-standing habit.—Plutarch

TODAY IN HISTORY

1848—Flow of Niagara Falls stopped for several hours due to upstream ice jam

1885—First batch of Coca-Cola brewed

1927—Automobile first broke 200-mph speed barrier

1932—Debut of Jack Benny on Ed Sullivan's radio broadcast

1935—Color film introduced

1961—Washington DC residents first allowed to vote

1993—Five suspects arrested for bombing at World Trade Center

1999—Dow-Jones Industrial Average reached new high of ten thousand points

2004—Massachusetts legislators approved state constitutional amendment to permit civil unions between same-sex partners

2005—UN secretary general Kofi Annan cleared of wrongdoing in Iraq's oil-for-food progam

BORN TODAY

President John Tyler 1790
Baseball pitcher Cy Young 1867
Businessman Sam Walton;
    singer Pearl Bailey 1918
Actor Bud Cort 1950

Football player Earl Campbell . . . 1955
Gymnast Kurt Thomas 1956
Actor Christopher Lambert 1957
Model Elle Macpherson 1964
Tennis player Jennifer Capriati . . . 1976

LIFTING THE LAMP

We are uniquely blessed in America with many freedoms that few others in the world enjoy. One day a young girl was taken to see the Statue of Liberty standing tall in New York Harbor. She was amazed at seeing Lady Liberty standing aloft with her upraised torch. That night as the little girl was tucked into bed, she murmured, "I'm thinking of that lady out there in the dark, holding up her light. Shouldn't we be helping Miss Liberty hold up her lamp?"

What could you be doing today to hold up a lamp of hope and freedom?

YEARNING TO BE FREE

Years ago many Scotsmen were imprisoned during the border wars with England. Their prison cells were scarred with long grooves worn in the stone from prisoners frantically clawing at the walls in a vain effort to be free.

How much do you value your freedom? Jesus said, "I tell you the truth, everyone who sins is a slave to sin" (John 8:34). What's keeping you from being truly free?

TODAY'S POWER POINT

Give me your tired, your poor, your huddled masses yearning to breathe free.—Emma Lazarus

March 30

TODAY IN HISTORY

1840—Death of men's fashion leader Beau Brummell, age sixty-one

1842—First surgery performed using anesthesia

1858—Lead pencil patented

1867—Alaska territory acquired

1909—Opening of double-decker Queensboro Bridge linking Long Island City and Manhattan

1943—Opening of Rodgers and Hammerstein's first musical, *Oklahoma*

1981—Death of *Reader's Digest* founder DeWitt Wallace, age ninety-one; assassination attempt on president Ronald Reagan

2001—Scientists announced they believe stem cells could repair damaged heart tissue

BORN TODAY

Artist Vincent van Gogh 1853

Singer Frankie Laine. 1913

Restaurateur Bob Evans 1918

TV host Peter Marshall 1927

Actor John Astin 1930

Actor Warren Beatty. 1938

Musician Eric Clapton 1945

Actor Robbie Coltrane 1950

Actor Paul Reiser 1957

Rapper MC Hammer. 1963

Singer Celine Dion. 1968

SEEING BEYOND THE TREES

The teacher was using a visual aid to get her point across. Using a marking pen, she drew a two-inch-diameter black dot in the middle of a large sheet of paper and asked the class to tell her what they saw. Most students noted the dot, so the teacher asked what else they saw. After several minutes and a number of failed guesses, the students admitted they didn't know the answer.

The teacher then pointed out what she felt was most important—the paper itself. She explained that many times our lives are like that illustration. While we're focusing on the single black dot, something that seems troubling at the time, we're overlooking the much bigger picture. In a spiritual sense, while we're concentrating on our problems, we often lose sight of God's many blessings to us each day.

Rather than focusing on our problems, let us rather look at the big picture— God's many blessings that we too often overlook. The Psalmist David said, "Blessed be the Lord, who daily loads us with benefits" (Psalms 68:19 NKJV).

TODAY'S POWER POINT

As you ramble on through life, whatever be your goal, keep your eye upon the doughnut and not upon the hole.—Source Unknown

TODAY IN HISTORY

1820—Arrival of first missionaries in Hawaii
1840—Ten-hour workday established for government employees
1850—U.S. population exceeded 23 million for first time
1854—Treaty signed opening Japanese ports to U.S. ships
1889—Eiffel Tower, world's tallest structure, dedicated
1900—First magazine car ad printed
1918—Introduction of daylight saving time
1970—First U.S. satellite, *Explorer I,* burned up reentering Earth's atmosphere (after orbiting for more than twelve years)
1975—Fall of Hue and Da Nang as North Vietnamese troops swept toward Saigon
1979—Leaders of Israel and Egypt signed historic joint peace agreement (after which eighteen Arab states severed ties with Egypt); Three Mile Island nuclear mishap brought under control
2002—Euthanasia legalized in the Netherlands, first nation to do so

BORN TODAY

Labor organizer César Chávez . . . 1927
Designer Liz Claiborne. 1929
Singer and actress Shirley Jones . . 1934
Richard Chamberlain. 1935
Actor Christopher Walken 1943
Actress Rhea Perlman 1948
Actor Ewan McGregor;
    hockey player Pavel Bure. 1971

EXPOSURE TO THE LIGHT

One of the inventors of photography, Frenchman Louis Daguerre, discovered that by exposing a metal plate to light, he could take a faint picture. But as soon as the plate was removed from the camera, the image quickly faded away. Daguerre experimented with countless procedures to preserve the image, but try as he might, none of them succeeded. Discouraged, he put away his exposed plates, storing them beside chemicals and other supplies in a closet.

Then one day Daugerre rediscovered his forgotten plates. Much to his surprise, when he took the plates from the closet, the images remained bright and sharp. Vapor from some mercury that had spilled in the closet had fixed the pictures' images on the plates. The result was the long-lasting Daguerreotype—the clear images of which can still be seen in archives around the world more than one hundred years later.

Much like the mercury on photo plates, the Holy Spirit serves as the "fixer" of Christ's impression on your heart. As you follow the Spirit's leading, you'll discover that Christ remains "in focus" in your life.

TODAY'S POWER POINT

Either Christ is God and Savior and Lord, or he isn't; and if he is, then he has to have all my time, all my devotion, all my life.—Mark Hatfield

April 1

TODAY IN HISTORY

1789—First U.S. House of Representatives elected speaker
1826—Internal combustion engine patented
1863—First wartime draft established in United States
1918—British Royal Air Force founded
1927—First nighttime air passenger flight
1930—First live teleconference
1954—U.S. Air Force Academy established
1970—President Richard Nixon signed legislation banning cigarette ads on radio
    and television
1995—Ukraine started dismantling nuclear missiles
1998—Arkansas judge dismissed sexual harassment case against president Bill
    Clinton

BORN TODAY

Composer Sergei Rachmaninov . . 1873
Psychologist Abraham Maslow . . . 1908
Actress Jane Powell; football coach Bo
    Schembechler 1929
Actress Debbie Reynolds 1932
Actress Ali McGraw 1939
Author and presidential grandson David
    Eisenhower 1947
Director Barry Sonnenfeld 1953
Actress Annette O'Toole. 1954

KINDNESS

A simple act of kindness is often remembered long after the fact. Years ago, an inexperienced young preacher in Missouri walked twenty miles to preach to a small congregation. His delivery was not polished. His halting style and lack of confidence did little to capture people's interest. They grew restless with the novice's floundering presentation, and many left before the service even concluded. Following the sermon, not one person stopped to offer the preacher a meal or lodging. Dejectedly, he headed toward the long road home. As he was leaving, the janitor offered to share his humble meal with the preacher.

Years passed, and the young preacher became the world-renowned Bishop Marvin. Once more he was invited to speak at the dedication of a church near the site of his first floundering sermon. People came from miles around to hear the famous man speak. After the service, many offered him lavish hospitality, but the bishop waved them all aside in favor of the old janitor, saying, "When I was here before, I was none too good for you, and I am none too good for you today."

We never can tell to whom we are rendering kindness.

TODAY'S POWER POINT

Today we are afraid of simple words like *goodness* and *mercy* and *kindness*. We don't believe in the good old words because we don't believe in good old values anymore. And that's why the world is sick.—Lu Yutang

TODAY IN HISTORY

1513—Ponce de Leon claimed Florida for Spain
1792—U.S. Mint established
1827—First pencils manufactured by Joseph Dixon
1870—First woman nominated for U.S. president (Victoria Woodhull)
1917—President Woodrow Wilson asked Congress to declare war on Germany
1921—Einstein lectured in New York City on new theory of relativity
1931—Teenaged girl struck out Babe Ruth and Lou Gehrig in exhibition game
1956—Premieres of soaps *As the World Turns* and *The Edge of Night*
1978—Premiere of *Dallas*; Velcro fasteners first marketed
1982—Argentine troops seized Falkland Islands
2001—Census Bureau announced that population increase of 32.7 million in 1990s
　　　is highest of any ten-year period in U.S. history
2005—Death of Pope John Paul II, age eighty-four

BORN TODAY

First Holy Roman Emperor,
　Charlemagne 742
Fairy-tale author Hans Christian
　Andersen. 1805
Actor Buddy Ebsen 1908
Actor Alec Guinness. 1914
Actor Jack Webb. 1920
Singer Marvin Gaye 1939
Musician Leon Russell 1941

Baseball pitcher Don Sutton. 1945
Singer Emmylou Harris 1947
Actress Pamela Reed. 1953
Actor Ron Palillo 1954
Comedian Victoria Jackson 1959
Actor Christopher Meloni 1961
Rodney King (black motorist beaten by
　L.A. police). 1965

BECOMING A SPIRITUALLY FIT CHAMPION

It's inspiring to read of the physical conditioning undertaken by Olympic athletes. They train constantly, often much of the day, for years on end so they'll be fit for the challenge of world championship competition.

Just as the victorious athlete blocks out hours a day for his or her fitness routine, so the mature believer will develop a daily regimen to keep spiritually fit. Besides daily studying the Bible, such a program will include setting aside time for prayer. Some people keep a journal of prayers answered or other activities they undertake to develop that will lead to a stronger spiritual life.

Spiritual conditioning will equip you to overcome temptation and will strengthen you for training others in godly disciplines. Are you growing spiritually stronger and becoming more godly day by day?

TODAY'S POWER POINT

I rise superior to my pain; when I am weak, then I am strong.—Charles Wesley

April 3

TODAY IN HISTORY

1837—First state school for the blind established in Ohio

1860—Pony Express mail service launched

1936—Bruno Hauptman executed for kidnap and murder of Charles Lindbergh Jr.

1948—Marshall Plan enacted, giving billions of dollars for European recovery

1988—Arizona governor Evan Mecham convicted and removed from office; federal judge ruled Microsoft violated antitrust laws and proposed restrictions, breakup

1996—Suspected "Unabomber" arrested

2004—Madrid train-bombing suspect killed in police raid

BORN TODAY

Author Washington Irving 1783

Actor Marlon Brando;
   actress Doris Day 1924

Journalist Max Frankel 1930

Anthropologist Jane Goodall 1934

Actress Marsha Mason;
   singer Wayne Newton 1942

Singer Tony Orlando 1944

Actor Alec Baldwin 1958

Actor David Hyde Pierce 1959

Comedian Eddie Murphy 1961

Actress Jennie Garth 1972

WORK VERSUS LEISURE

Over the past sixty years, leisure time has increased around the world; but what we've seen thus far may be only the beginning. While it may yet be a ways off, social scientists predict that eventually a twenty-hour workweek or a six-month work year will be able to sustain the average American's current standard of living. France has already established a thirty-five-hour workweek, and the Netherlands appear to have the world's shortest workweek at just under thirty hours.

Even those working longer hours have it much easier today than their parents did years ago. Author R. F. Norden even predicts the establishment of a "Department of Leisure" to balance the present U.S. Department of Labor, since, he says, 2 percent of the population can accomplish the work necessary to provide food and goods for the rest of us.

Yet God has not promised us a life of leisure. Rather, believers are to be busy doing the Lord's work. But keep faithfully doing your Father's business today, and you can enjoy an eternity of leisure in heaven.

TODAY'S POWER POINT

Employ thy time well, if thou meanest to get leisure.—Benjamin Franklin

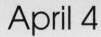

TODAY IN HISTORY

1800—First bankruptcy law passed

1841—Death of president William Henry Harrison after only thirty-one days in office

1886—First woman elected mayor in United States

1902—Cecil Rhodes willed $10 million for American scholarship for graduate study in England

1949—North Atlantic Treaty Organization (NATO) established

1968—Civil rights leader Martin Luther King Jr. gunned down in Memphis

1969—Controversial *Smothers Brothers* comedy show cancelled

2006—Saddam Hussein charged with attempting to annihilate Iraq's Kurdish population

BORN TODAY

Inventor Linus Yale 1821

Newsman John Cameron Swayze . 1906

Composer Elmer Bernstein 1922

Poet Maya Angelou 1928

Actor Tony Perkins. 1932

Actor Craig T. Nelson. 1946

Actress Christine Lahti. 1950

Actor Robert Downey Jr. 1965

Magician David Blaine. 1973

Baseball player Scott Rolen. 1975

Actress Jamie Lee Spears 1991

THE SHEPHERD'S VOICE

An American traveler in Syria watched as three native shepherds brought their flocks to the same brook. After a while, one shepherd called out, "Men-ah, Men-ah" (Arabic for "follow me"), and his sheep followed where he led them. The next shepherd did the same, and his flock went off after him.

The traveler asked the remaining shepherd if he could try to get the sheep to follow his voice. Taking the shepherd's staff and turban, he called out to the flock, "Men-ah, Men-ah." Not a sheep moved. "Will your flock follow no one but you?" the traveler asked.

"Oh yes," the seasoned shepherd replied, "but sometimes a sheep gets sick, and then he will follow anyone."

How many times have you observed the spiritually weak follow strange voices that have led them away from God? How closely are you following the Good Shepherd? How can you keep yourself spiritually strong and in tune with God so you'll never weakly follow the wrong voice?

TODAY'S POWER POINT

I am more and more convinced that our happiness or unhappiness depends far more on the way we meet the events of life than on the nature of those events themselves.—Wilhelm von Humboldt

April 5

TODAY IN HISTORY

1792—First presidential veto (George Washington)
1923—First balloon tires produced by Firestone
1933—First successful lung-removal surgery
1940—First bonded-plastic plane approved for flight
1963—Soviets OK'd direct "hot line" connection with United States
1975—Death of nationalist Chinese leader Chiang Kai-shek, age eighty-seven
1976—James Callaghan elected Britain's prime minister; death of billionaire
        Howard Hughes, age seventy
1979—Former Pakistani prime minister Ali Bhutto reportedly executed
1986—Terrorist bombing of Berlin military club, fifty-five American servicepeople
        killed
1999—Two suspects in Pan Am jet bombing extradited by Libya; UN sanctions
        against Libya suspended
2003—U.S. troops entered Baghdad

BORN TODAY

Physician Joseph Lister 1827
Educator Booker T. Washington . . 1856
Actor Spencer Tracy 1900
Actor Gregory Peck 1916
Author Arthur Hailey 1920
Actress Gale Storm 1922
General Colin Powell 1937
Actor Michael Moriarty 1942
Football player Tony Banks 1973
Baseball player Ryan Drese 1976

THE GIFT OF TIME

When your children leave home, how will they remember you? A successful young attorney recalled the greatest gift he ever received: "It occurred one Christmas, when my dad gave me a small box. Inside was a note saying, 'Son, this year I will give you 365 hours, an hour every day after dinner. It's yours. We'll talk about what you want to talk about, we'll go where you want to go, play what you want to play. It will be your hour.'"

The attorney said, "My dad not only kept his promise, but every year he renewed it—it's the greatest gift I ever had in my life. I'm the result of his time."

How much time do you share with your family or those who mean most to you? Nothing we can give will show others how much we love them more than the gift of our time and attention. Why not share quality time with someone you love today—and every day?

TODAY'S POWER POINT

Time is a created thing. To say, "I don't have time" is like saying, "I don't want to."—Lao Tzu

TODAY IN HISTORY

1837—George Müeller's orphanage opened in England
1896—United States won ten gold medals at first modern Olympic games
1906—First animated film copyrighted
1909—North Pole discovered
1917—America entered World War I (against Germany)
1930—Twinkies snack cake invented
1938—Teflon invented
1965—First commercial communications satellite, *Early Bird,* launched
1987—Dow Jones Average closed above 2,400 for first time
1992—Premiere of *Barney and Friends* on PBS
1994—Genocide of 800,000 Rwandans
2000—UN concluded that up to two-thirds of world's blood supply could be tainted
2001—Major tax reduction bill passed by U.S. Senate

BORN TODAY

Painter Raphael 1483
Newsman Lowell Thomas. 1896
DNA codiscoverer James Watson . 1928
Composer Andre Previn 1929
Singer Merle Haggard 1937
Actor Billy Dee Williams 1937

Producer Barry Levinson 1942
Actor John Ratzenberger 1947
Actress Marilu Henner 1952
Baseball player Brett Boone 1969
Actress Candace Cameron 1976
Actor Matthew Thomas Carey . . . 1980

TOO BUSY

It's not just the complicated forms that confuse taxpayers today. Sometimes even top government officials have failed to pay their taxes. Such was the case of one former director of the Securities and Exchange Commission. Upon being charged with failure to file his income-tax return on time for four years, he was quoted as saying he had been "so engrossed with public matters" that he neglected personal affairs, including paying his taxes.

May this never be said of us when it comes to taking care of business with God. Imagine having to admit to God someday that we were so busy, we just didn't make time to regularly read his Word and pray.

If you haven't already established a daily habit of Bible reading and prayer—getting alone with God and his Word—do so today. Encourage your family to do the same. In fact, consider leading your family in daily devotions.

TODAY'S POWER POINT

The family that prays together, stays together.—Al Scalpone

April 7

TODAY IN HISTORY

1877—Matches invented

1917—Coast-to-coast commercial telephone service launched (at $6.75 per minute); U.S. Navy fired first American shot in World War I

1927—First telecast (with both picture and sound) aired in United States

1933—First open-mesh highway bridge (in Seattle)

1948—World Health Organization (WHO) founded

1953—Dag Hammarskjöld elected UN Secretary General

1978—Neutron bomb production stopped in United States; Gutenberg Bible sold for $2 million, highest price ever paid for a book

1985—Sudan's president ousted during visit to the United States

2003—Cuban crackdown on democratic reformers

BORN TODAY

Poet William Wordsworth 1770

Musician Percy Faith 1908

Jazz singer Billie Holiday 1915

Actor James Garner 1928

Actor Wayne Rogers. 1933

British broadcaster David Frost;
  director Francis Ford Coppola 1939

Singer John Oates. 1949

Singer Janis Ian. 1951

Actor Jackie Chan;
  football player Tony Dorsett . . 1954

Actor Russell Crowe 1964

ACCOUNTABILITY

The Bible tells of disastrous results during the time of the judges of people feeling no accountability, since they had no king. Apparently feeling exempt from the law, "Everyone did as he saw fit" (Judges 21:25)—which included idol worship, sexual misconduct, and violence.

Unfortunately, setting our own standards—doing as we see fit—seems to be a growing trend today, even in government, where one would expect officials to be particularly supportive of the law. During a recent six-year period, according to statistics, more than one thousand key government officials, ranging from county sheriff up to high-ranking federal officials, have faced serious criminal charges.

Of course, wrongdoing is not exclusive to any social class or strata but is found at all levels of society. This again proves God's Word true when it says, "The heart is deceitful above all things and beyond cure" (Jeremiah 17:9). When we see dishonesty and corruption all around us, it becomes even more important to be sure we don't fall into the same trap. How? By staying close to God and living according to his Word.

TODAY'S POWER POINT

Good people do not need laws to tell them to act responsibly, while bad people will find a way around the laws.—Plato

TODAY IN HISTORY

1730—First Jewish congregation established in United States
1873—Margarine patented
1913—Seventeenth Amendment ratified (requiring direct election of U.S. senators)
1974—Hank Aaron's 714th home run broke Babe Ruth's longstanding record
1997—Appeals court upheld California ban on affirmative action
2005—Pope John Paul II buried at the Vatican; Britain's Prince Charles married
     Camilla Parker Bowles

BORN TODAY

Pathologist William Henry Welch 1850
Actress Mary Pickford 1893
Singer Carmen McRae 1920
Actress Connie Stevens 1938
Basketball player John Havlicek . . 1940

Baseball pitcher Jim "Catfish" Hunter
. . . . 1946
Actor John Schneider 1960
Singer Julian Lennon 1963
Actress Patricia Arquette 1969

DOING NOTHING

Anyone who has visited a school classroom knows the chaos that quickly takes over when students are left on their own. The same can be said of society. In this age of moral relativism and "do your own thing" attitudes, one should not be surprised at the chaos and moral degradation clearly visible in the world today. But does it concern you enough to do something about it? Or have you, perhaps feeling overwhelmed and outmatched, simply ignored the world's problems, hoping they might just go away?

If developments at Johns Hopkins University are any indication, it would seem that reporting dishonesty is on the decline. Apparently the school decided to drop its student honor code of more than sixty years and replace it with a policy of the administration's policing students. Dishonesty was said to have risen to the point where the school felt the honor system was no longer effective for deterring cheating. While more students were cheating, the real problem was that so many people were doing nothing about it.

Other institutions face similar problems with increased wrongdoing and an accompanying unwillingness of good people to do something about it. What about the political leader who is promoting actions counter to those taught in the Bible? Or that local referendum that would expand immoral influences in your community? Stand up, speak out, and do your part to ensure that evil will not triumph where you live.

TODAY'S POWER POINT

The only thing necessary for the triumph of evil is for good men to do nothing.
—Edmund Burke

April 9

TODAY IN HISTORY

1816—African Methodist Episcopal Church organized
1865—Confederate surrender at Appomattox ended Civil War
1940—Nazi invasion of Norway and Denmark
1877—Dry milk patented
1953—First *TV Guide* published
1959—First seven U.S. astronauts named (all military officers)
1963—Winston Churchill made honorary U.S. citizen
1965—Houston Astrodome opened
1975—FCC designated 7:00–9:00 p.m. TV "family viewing time"
1992—Former Panamanian dictator Noriega convicted in U.S. court
1996—President Bill Clinton signed line-item veto into law
1998—Stampede at Mecca killed 150 Muslims
2003—Saddam Hussein ousted from power by U.S. forces in Baghdad

BORN TODAY

German scientist Charles Steinmetz
. . . . 1865
Cartoonist Frank King 1883
Singer Paul Robeson. 1898
Songwriter Tom Lehrer. 1928
Editor Paul Krassner. 1932

Actor Jean-Paul Belmondo 1933
Actress Michael Learned. 1939
Actor Dennis Quaid. 1954
Golfer Seve Ballesteros 1957
Actress Keshia Knight Pulliam . . . 1979
Singer Jesse McCartney 1987

PERSISTENCE

It's human nature to want to give up when things get difficult, yet this is exactly the time we most need to redouble our efforts and push forward. James Birdseye McPherson, General Ulysses S. Grant's chief engineer at the battle of Shiloh, was discouraged after the first hard day of fighting. McPherson reported, "Things look bad, General. We have lost half our artillery and a third of the infantry. Our line is broken, and we are pushed back nearly to the river."

Grant made no reply, and McPherson asked impatiently what he intended to do. General Grant barked back, "Do? Why, re-form the lines and attack at daybreak. Won't they be surprised?"

Indeed the enemy was surprised, and the Confederate forces were routed before eight o'clock the next morning.

How many victories have been within your grasp, only to be lost when you quit at the eleventh hour? Never give up the good fight!

TODAY'S POWER POINT

Nothing in the world can take the place of persistence. . . . The slogan "Press On" has solved, and always will solve, the problems of the human race.—Calvin Coolidge

April 10

TODAY IN HISTORY

1790—First U.S. patent law
1866—First animal humane society (ASPCA) established
1916—First pro-golf tournament
1945—Allies liberated Buchenwald Nazi concentration camp
1963—Sinking of Navy nuclear submarine *Thresher* (129 crew members dead)
1978—First Volkswagen made in America
1996—President Bill Clinton vetoed bill to ban partial-birth abortions
1998—Historic peace accord reached in Northern Ireland
2003—National AMBER Alert established to notify public of child kidnappings

BORN TODAY

Salvation Army founder William Booth 1829
Publisher Joseph Pulitzer 1847
Actor Chuck Connors 1921
Actor Omar Sharif 1932
Sportscaster John Madden 1936
Commentator Don Meredith 1938
Actor Haley Joel Osment 1988

TIME-MANAGEMENT PLAN

Finding it hard to fit in everything you *need* to do—to say nothing of the things you *should* do? Here's a time-management plan that, if followed, guarantees you'll take time for the most important priorities. Shortly after his conversion, evangelist Billy Sunday was advised to follow this simple, but effective, plan: "Take fifteen minutes each day to listen to God; take fifteen minutes each day to talk to God; and take fifteen minutes each day to talk to others about God."

Have you ever heard of anyone who died from hard work? Too often the opposite is true—people seek a life of ease and so waste their lives on pursuits with little intrinsic value or purpose.

A hard-working young lawyer was struggling with the direction his life was taking. One day, upon awakening, he asked himself what he would do when he finished law school. *Make a lot of money,* he thought in reply. He then considered what he would do after he became rich. *I'll retire,* he thought. *What will happen then?* he wondered. His conclusion? *I guess I'll just die.*

As a result of his unsatisfying reflections, the young Charles Finney quit law school, surrendered himself fully to God, and became a person God used greatly to further his kingdom.

Are you working as hard for God as you are for gold? Do you need to reorder your priorities? What will you do today that has eternal importance?

TODAY'S POWER POINT

There are no secrets to success. It is the result of preparation, hard work, and learning from failure.—Colin Powell

April 11

TODAY IN HISTORY

1876—Stenographic typewriter invented
1900—First U.S. submarine, USS *Holland*
1921—First international underwater cable telephone service (linking U.S. and Cuba)
1947—Jackie Robinson became first African American major-league baseball player
1951—General Douglas MacArthur relieved of Korean command
1965—President Lyndon Johnson approved pioneering school-aid program for underprivileged children in U.S. schools.
1981—President Ronald Reagan released from hospital twelve days after being shot
1996—Seven-year-old pilot killed in plane crash, thus ending goal to become youngest person ever to fly cross-country
2006—Iran admitted to processing nuclear fuel

BORN TODAY

Chief Justice Charles E. Hughes . . 1862
Judge Jane Bolin 1908
Designer Oleg Cassini 1913
Journalist Tony Brown 1933
Actress Louise Lasser 1939

Actor Meshach Taylor 1947
Columnist Ellen Goodman 1948
Actor Bill Irwin 1950
Pitcher Bret Saberhagen 1964
Singer Joss Stone 1987

ENDURING LOVE

A young woman once brought her work to a New York magazine and informed the editor that she had some poems she wanted published. "What's the subject?" the editor asked.

"Love," she answered.

"Oh, what kind of love?"

"Love as in gazing upon a moonlit lake with an attractive companion," she replied.

"Stop, stop" he pleaded. "I'll tell you what love is. Love is getting out of a warm bed at two o'clock in the morning to feed sick children. That's real love. I'm sorry, I don't think we can use your poems."

While there's a place for sincere, romantic love for another, it seems society too often shows a highly distorted view of love—all pleasure, and no pain. But that isn't the way life—or love—really is. While poetry has its place, we need to be more concerned about helping others than we are about reading someone's romantic ideas of love. Read 1 Corinthians 13:1-7, and in that light consider the way you show love to others. How do you measure up?

TODAY'S POWER POINT

Love is the thing that enables a woman to sing while she mops up the floor after her husband has walked across it in his barn boots.—Hoosier Farmer

April 12

TODAY IN HISTORY

1631—Massachusetts Bay Colony established first militia
1776—North Carolina urged colonies to set up autonomous governments
1861—Civil war launched when Confederates fired on Fort Sumter, South Carolina
1892—Portable typewriter patented
1955—Salk polio vaccine approved
1961—Soviet Yuri Gagarin first to orbit earth
1981—Space shuttle *Columbia* launched (first reusable spacecraft)
1982—British navy established blockade of Falkland Islands
1985—Jake Garn became first U.S. senator to fly in space
1987—Texaco declared bankruptcy in wake of $5 billion debt to Pennzoil
2003—SARS genome decoded, paving the way for developing test and vaccine for the disease
2005—Three Britons indicted on charges of plan to attack U.S. financial institutions

BORN TODAY

Statesman Henry Clay 1777
Musician Herbie Hancock 1940
Actor Ed O'Neill 1946
Author Tom Clancy; actor Dan Lauria; comedian David Letterman . . 1947
Actor David Cassidy. 1950
Actor Andy Garcia 1956
Singer Vince Gill 1957
Actress Shannen Doherty 1971
Actress Claire Danes. 1979

LOYALTY

An unusual sculpture stands outside a mansion in Yorkshire, England. It shows a two-faced butler. On one side of the statue is a man's face that is pleasant and smiling, but the other side shows a face that looks disrespectful and rude. The sculpture represents a butler who once worked at the estate who was the height of politeness and good humor when his employer was looking. But when he thought no one was watching, his true nature was revealed as he grumbled, mocked his employer, and was even seen sticking out his tongue at her. When the man's disloyalty was eventually discovered, he was fired, and the statue was created and erected on a prominent spot as a warning to any other servants who might be tempted to imitate the butler's rebellious behavior.

It's easy to put on a good face in front of an audience, an employer, a customer, or anyone you're trying to impress. But what are you like when they turn around? Your true face shows when no one can see you. Are you loyal to your employer, your church, your nation, and your God? If a statue were made of you, how many faces would it have?

TODAY'S POWER POINT

Greater love has no one than this, that he lay down his life for his friends.—John 15:13

April 13

TODAY IN HISTORY

1742—First performance of Handel's *Messiah*
1870—Metropolitan Museum of Art established in New York City
1902—Opening of first J. C. Penney store (in Wyoming)
1943—Jefferson Memorial dedicated
1952—UHF band created, allowing hundreds of new TV stations
1970—*Apollo 13* flight temporarily crippled when oxygen tank exploded
1971—Patience Latting sworn in as first woman mayor of a major U.S. city
     (Oklahoma City)
1983—Harold Washington elected first African American mayor of Chicago
1997—Golfer Tiger Woods shattered records with Masters tournament win
1998—NationsBank and Bank of America merger formed first coast-to-coast bank

BORN TODAY

President Thomas Jefferson. 1743
Author Samuel Beckett. 1906
Actor Howard Keel. 1919
Actor Lyle Waggoner 1935
Actor Paul Sorvino 1939
Composer Bill Conti 1942
Musician Jack Casady. 1944
Actor Tony Dow. 1945
Singer Al Green 1946
Actor Ron Perlman. 1950
Chess player Garry Kasparov 1963
Actor Rick Schroder. 1970

FREEDOM

The United States of America was founded on the principle of freedom for all. But true freedom is less a political state than a state of mind.

One man who illustrated this truth is Rabinovitch, who lived in Moscow during the height of the Cold War. While traveling through Europe, he sent home to his family postcards from the various cities he visited, with the message dearest to his heart: "Greetings from a free Warsaw," "Greetings from a free Prague," and so on. Finally he was on his way home. Just outside the Iron Curtain, he stopped again and sent one last card with this penciled note: "Greetings from a free Rabinovitch."

America's greatness lies less in its political freedoms than in its spiritual freedom. Psalm 33:12 says, "Blessed is the nation whose God is the Lord." The United States has been mightily blessed of God and will continue to be blessed as long as it honors him. As long as you're living in America, you can live free. As long as you're living for God, your heart can be truly free as well.

TODAY'S POWER POINT

The things that will destroy America are prosperity at any price, peace at any price, safety first instead of duty first, the love of soft living, and the get-rich-quick theory of life.—Theodore Roosevelt

TODAY IN HISTORY

1865—President Abraham Lincoln gunned down at Ford's Theater
1912—*Titanic* hit Atlantic iceberg on initial voyage
1984—Texas stopped requiring that textbooks refer to evolution as a theory
1995—UN eased sanctions on Iraq
1997—Fire killed three hundred pilgrims outside Mecca
2000—Russian parliament OK'd START II arms reduction treaty
2001—Defibrillators placed on airlines to revive heart-attack victims

BORN TODAY

Historian Arnold Toynbee 1889
Actor John Gielgud 1904
Singer Loretta Lynn 1935
Actress Julie Christie. 1940
Baseball player Pete Rose 1941
Actress Emma Thompson. 1959
Baseball player Greg Maddux 1966
Actress Sarah Michelle Gellar 1977

MONEY AND HAPPINESS

Does having lots of money bring true happiness? To find out, researchers studied two dozen people who had won at least fifty thousand dollars in the lottery: "The lottery winners proved no happier than the nonwinners. Neither did they expect greater future happiness. While the winners gained a moment of exhilaration," the researchers discovered, "they lost some of their ability to enjoy commonplace pleasures."

But what about the megarich? John Jacob Astor, who left $5 million at his death, claimed he was "the most miserable man on earth." John D. Rockefeller stated, "I have made many millions, but they have brought me no happiness. I would barter them all for the days I . . . counted myself rich on three dollars a week." W. H. Vanderbilt observed, "The care of $200 million is too great . . . to bear. There is no pleasure in it." Industrialist Henry Ford observed that he "was happier doing a mechanic's job," and multimillionaire Andrew Carnegie noted that "millionaires seldom smile."

The Bible often speaks of money. Matthew 6:19–21 says, "Do not store up for yourselves treasures on earth, where moth and rust destroy, and where thieves break in and steal. But store up for yourselves treasures in heaven, where moth and rust do not destroy, and where thieves do not break in and steal. For where your treasure is, there your heart will be also."

Regardless of how much—or how little—you own, it's important to keep a proper perspective. Manage your money; don't ever let it manage you.

TODAY'S POWER POINT

It's good to have money and the things that money can buy, but it's good, too, to . . . make sure that you haven't lost the things that money can't buy.—George H. Lorimer

TODAY IN HISTORY

1865—Death of president Abraham Lincoln

1878—Ivory soap developed as first floating soap bar

1912—*Titanic* sank after hitting iceberg, more than 1,500 dead

1955—First McDonald's restaurant opened by Ray Kroc in Chicago suburb

1974—San Francisco bank robbed by group including kidnap victim Patty Hearst

1981—*Washington Post* reporter returned Pulitzer Prize for fictitious story of eight-year-old heroin addict

1986—U.S. planes swept across Libya in widespread raids (in retaliation for Libyan terrorism)

2002—Pope John Paul II summoned cardinals to discuss clergy sex-abuse scandals

2003—South Africa pledged $85 million for victims of apartheid

2004—EPA said thirty-one states failed to meet clean-air standards

BORN TODAY

Artist Leonardo da Vinci 1452

Author Henry James. 1843

Actress Elizabeth Montgomery;
    Singer Roy Clark 1933

Actress Claudia Cardinale. 1938

Columnist Heloise Cruse Evans . . 1951

Olympic athlete Evelyn Ashford . . 1957

Football player Jason Sehorn 1971

Actress Emma Watson 1990

FEEDING THE GOVERNMENT

Taxes are the lifeblood that keeps all of government functioning. But understanding the need for taxes doesn't mean you won't have an occasional fantasy about the Internal Revenue Service forgetting all about you. Believe it or not, that has actually happened. Shortly after the IRS opened its new computer complex in Louisiana, without warning, part of the gigantic computer's memory suddenly went blank. Tax officials soon discovered the cause: their building was in the flight path of the New Orleans airport, and stray radar signals from the control tower had erased certain tax records stored on magnetic tape. (Presumably they were retrieved from backup tapes.)

The need for people to pay taxes to "feed" the government is nothing new—Even Jesus paid taxes (Matthew 17:24–27). He taught that it is good and right to give the government what it is due: "Give to Caesar what is Caesar's, and to God what is God's" (Luke 20:25). When tax money is used well, it maximizes government efficiency, keeping it alive and strong to defend our freedom to worship God as we please.

TODAY'S POWER POINT

You can't blame the IRS for being worried. How would you feel if you had billions of dollars owed to you—all coming by mail.—Source Unknown

TODAY IN HISTORY

1787—First American play performed (in New York City)

1900—U.S. Post Office issued first book of stamps

1926—First Book-of-the-Month Club selection made

1940—First major-league-baseball opening day no-hitter as Indians beat White Sox

1947—More than five hundred people killed in Texas harbor explosion

1972—*Apollo 16* launched historic moon-walk flight

1977—West Point began admitting female cadets

1979—Runner Bill Rogers set new record (2:09:27) in winning Boston Marathon

1991—Supreme Court set limits on death-row appeals

2003—European Union expanded to ten nations

BORN TODAY

Aviator Wilbur Wright 1867

Actor Charlie Chaplin 1889

Actor Peter Ustinov 1921

Composer Henry Mancini 1924

Actress Edie Adams 1931

Singer Bobby Vinton 1935

Basketball's Kareem Abdul-Jabbar 1947

Singer Selena 1971

Actor Lukas Haas 1976

WAR

Writing in the *Calgary Herald*, Jamie Portman reported that a research team, in an effort to find out the causes of war, once fed all the data pertaining to World War I into a computer. The result? The computer calculated that the First World War was "an impossibility—that it never really happened. Blunders and casualties of such magnitude" could only be imagined and not reality. Of course, World War I did occur—costing more than $100 billion and an estimated ten million lives, changing the world forever.

Time published a statistician's calculation that "over the 5,560 years of recorded human history, there have been 14,531 wars, or, as the computer pointed out, (over) 2.6 wars a year."

British Air Marshall Arthur Harris predicted, "War will go on until there is a change in the human heart, and I see no signs of that." And the Bible tells us, "You will hear of wars and rumors of wars, but see to it that you are not alarmed. Such things must happen, but the end is still to come" (Matthew 24:6).

War is frightening, horrible, and cruel, but we don't have to be afraid. Jesus told us that the story will have a happy ending: "When these things begin to take place, stand up and lift up your heads, because your redemption is drawing near" (Luke 21:28).

TODAY'S POWER POINT

It is well that war is so terrible, or we should grow too fond of it.—Robert E. Lee

April 17

TODAY IN HISTORY

1961—Invasion of Fidel Castro's Cuba at Bay of Pigs ended in failure
1964—Debut of Ford Mustang
1969—Sirhan Sirhan convicted of murdering Senator Robert Kennedy
1975—Former Texas governor John Connolly acquitted of bribery charges
1975—Communist-led forces seized control of Phnom Penh, Cambodia, ending
    five-year civil war
1998—U.S. trade deficit highest in a decade
2004—Opposition Hamas leader killed by Israelis

BORN TODAY

Supreme Court Justice Samuel Chase
.... 1741
Actor William Holden 1918
Actor Rod Steiger 1920
Actress Olivia Hussey 1951

Sportscaster Boomer Esiason 1961
Actress Lela Rochon 1966
Singer Liz Phair 1967
Actress Jennifer Garner 1972
Singer Victoria Adams Beckham. . 1975

SUPERNATURAL GIVING

Many people seem willing to trust God for the hereafter yet are hesitant to rely on him for their needs in the here and now. But this certainly wasn't true of the late Dr. Bill Bright, who related how God had richly blessed him and his wife when they turned over their ownership of everything to him.

Dr. Bright recalled that early in his marriage, "my wife, Vonette, and I made a total commitment of our lives to Christ, including the giving of our finances and all material possessions to him. Since that time," Bright related, "we have experienced the faithfulness of God to meet our every need, 'superabundantly' above and beyond our fondest hopes and desires."

He explained that because of their decision to put giving to God first, although "we own(ed) very little of this world's goods, we have always enjoyed the 'best of everything' without having to ask for it." Our homes, said Bright, are "as nice or nicer than anything we might have chosen had I been a millionaire. Yet we have never sought to live luxuriously." What evidence of just the material blessings of putting God first!

If we expect God to be generous in giving back to us, we need to be generous first in our giving to him. Ask the Lord where you can be generous with your time, treasure, and talent this week—and then do it.

TODAY'S POWER POINT

Don't be afraid of outgiving God. It is impossible to do that. He will keep every one of his promises related to generosity. Try him and see!—Chuck Swindoll

April 18

TODAY IN HISTORY

1775—Paul Revere's midnight ride
1796—First opera by an American composer opened in New York City
1906—San Francisco devastated by earthquake and subsequent fire
1924—First crossword-puzzle book published
1930—First women state police officers appointed, in Massachusetts
1934—First coin laundry (in Ft. Worth, Texas)
1942—Initial U.S. bombing raid on Japan
1945—War correspondent Ernie Pyle killed by Japanese sniper
1949—Republic of Ireland established
1955—"Walk" and "Don't Walk" signs first appeared on U.S. street corners
1960—First pacemaker successfully implanted
1978—Senate ratified treaty that would give Panama Canal back to Panama in 1999
1980—African nation of Rhodesia renamed Zimbabwe
1983—Forty people killed in terrorist bombing of U.S. embassy in Beirut

BORN TODAY

Lawyer Clarence Darrow 1857
Conductor Leopold Stokowski . . . 1882
Actress Hayley Mills 1946
Director Dorothy Lyman 1947
Actor Rick Moranis 1954
Actor Eric Roberts 1956
TV host Conan O'Brien 1963
Actress Melissa Joan Hart 1976

A WITNESS FOR GOD

A little boy was sitting in church one Sunday as he heard the preacher explain all the beauties of heaven: no night, no death, no labor, streets of gold, joy and happiness forever. So he nudged his mom and whispered, "If heaven is so wonderful, why don't we just go there now?" Later his mother explained that God leaves his children here on earth to share their faith in God with others and thus bring them with them to heaven.

The famed D. L. Moody once gave an account of witnessing to a man who barked at Moody, "Mind your own business." Moody responded gently, "This is my business" and, unfazed by the rebuke, went on his way. Time passed, and the stranger again approached Moody—this time to apologize for his harshness and to ask how he could become a Christian. Later the man went on to become a faithful worker in the church.

Only eternity will reveal the true impact of your life on others as they observe Christianity in action day by day. Be encouraged. You're God's ambassador here on earth!

TODAY'S POWER POINT

Pray also for me, that whenever I open my mouth, words may be given me so that I will fearlessly make known the mystery of the gospel.—Ephesians 6:19

April 19

TODAY IN HISTORY

1775—Beginning of the American Revolution

1933—End of gold standard in United States

1951—General Douglas MacArthur's farewell address to Congress ("Old soldiers never die")

1956—Wedding of Grace Kelly and Prince Rainier of Monaco

1982—United States prohibits travel to Cuba

1989—Pro-democracy student rally in China's Tiananmen Square

1993—Branch Davidian compound burned after fifty-one-day standoff in Waco, Texas, cult leader David Koresh and eighty-six others dead

1994—Motorist Rodney King awarded $3.8 million for beating by police in Los Angeles

1995—Bombing of Alfred Murrah Federal Building in Oklahoma City, 168 dead

1999—Supreme Court ruled that free-speech rights are not violated by law limiting e-mail pornography

BORN TODAY

Declaration of Independence signer Thomas McKean 1721

Actor Don Adams 1927

Actor Hugh O'Brian 1930

Actor Dudley Moore 1935

Race-car driver Al Unser Jr. 1962

Actress Kate Hudson 1979

Actor Hayden Christensen 1981

OLD AGE

You're as old as you feel—or so they say. Here's how General Douglas MacArthur described old age: "Nobody grows old by merely living a number of years. People grow old only by deserting their ideals. Years may wrinkle the skin, but to give up interest wrinkles the soul. Worry, doubt, self-distrust, fear and despair . . . these are the long, long years that bow the head and turn the growing spirit back to dust. . . . You are as young as your faith, as old as your doubt; as young as your self-confidence, as old as your fear; as young as your hope, as old as your despair."

Later life can be a time of exciting accomplishment and new ventures. We're never too old to learn something new—or to allow God to accomplish something new through us. Sarah was around ninety years old when she gave birth to the child of promise, Isaac (see Genesis 21:1–7). Grandma Moses only started painting in her seventies, when her arthritis made it difficult to embroider. Texas oil baron T. Boone Pickens became a billionaire after he was seventy. Even the difficulties associated with aging can actually be springboards to great accomplishments and the best time of our lives. With God's help, you can bear fruit no matter what your age.

TODAY'S POWER POINT

About the only thing that comes to us without effort is old age.—Gloria Pitzer

TODAY IN HISTORY

1902—Radium first identified by Marie and Pierre Curie

1953—U.S. POWs freed at end of Korean War

1971—Supreme Court upheld busing to achieve racial desegregation

1976—Barbara Walters became first woman TV network news anchor

1986—Pianist Vladimir Horowitz performed in Soviet Union after sixty-one years in the West

1999—Twelve students and one teacher shot to death at Columbine High School in Colorado

2000—Petrified dinosaur heart recovered in South Dakota

2004—*USA Today* editor resigned over fabrications by reporter

2006—In dramatic reversal, FDA dismissed the value of marijuana in medical uses

BORN TODAY

Emperor Napoleon	1808	Football player Steve Spurier	1945
Sculptor Daniel Chester	1850	Actress Jessica Lange	1949
Nazi dictator Adolf Hitler	1889	Singer Luther Vandross	1951
Musician Lionel Hampton	1908	Baseball player Don Mattingly	1962
Actress Nina Foch	1924	Actress Carmen Electra	1973
Actor Ryan O'Neal	1941	Actor Joey Lawrence	1976

THANKS TO THE PASTOR

Most audiences appreciate a speaker who can state his or her point simply and briefly and then be done with it. Poet James Whitcomb Riley once responded to a fellow writer who asked Riley why his speeches were such a success when his own usually fell flat: "Well Jim, the big reason as I see it: I talk until I get tired, while you talk until the audience gets tired."

The Bible tells the story of one preacher who spoke so long that a man actually died. The apostle Paul preached well into the night, and a man named Eutychus fell asleep and then tumbled from a third-story window to his death. But the story had a miraculous ending, as Paul prayed and Eutychus was brought back to life.

So maybe your pastor hasn't raised anyone from the dead lately (he or she probably hasn't talked anyone to death either), but you know he or she has done some pretty noteworthy things—raising money for the big missions drive, raising the moral climate in your community, maybe even raising the spiritually dead. When was the last time you thanked your pastor for his or her ministry and the way he or she communicates God's miraculous nature week after week? Why not do so today?

TODAY'S POWER POINT

Speeches are for the younger men who are going places.—Dwight D. Eisenhower

TODAY IN HISTORY

1836—Sam Houston defeated Mexican forces at San Jacinto, Texas
1878—First firehouse pole
1895—First motion picture projected on a screen (in New York City)
1910—Death of author Mark Twain, age seventy-five
1945—Russian forces entered Berlin
1960—Brasilia named new capital of Brazil
1962—World's Fair opened in Seattle (first ever financially successful)
1967—Daughter of Soviet leader Joseph Stalin arrived in United States
1986—American air strikes on Libyan leader Muammar Qadhafi's headquarters
    drew bipartisan support in Congress
1995—Timothy McVeigh arrested for Oklahoma City bombing
2000—Russian parliament voted to end nuclear testing

BORN TODAY

Educator Friedrich Froebel 1782
Novelist Charlotte Brontë 1816
Naturalist John Muir 1838
Actor Anthony Quinn 1915
Britain's Queen Elizabeth II 1926
Actress Elaine May 1932

Actor Charles Grodin 1935
Actress Patti LuPone 1949
Actor Tony Danza 1951
Hockey player Ed Belfour 1965
Comedian Nicole Sullivan 1970

IMMIGRANTS

A vast percentage of citizens in the United States are—or are descended from—immigrants. The excitement of coming to America was beautifully captured many years ago by Polish immigrant Janina Atkins, who wrote: "Just six years ago I came with my husband to this country with $2.60 in my purse, some clothes, a few books, a bundle of old letters, and a little pillow. I was an immigrant girl hoping for a new life and happiness in a strange new country. There is something in America that filled my soul with a feeling of freedom and independence, which gave me strength. There is no one here to lead you by the hand and order you about. We believed in the future, and the future did not disappoint us. Today my husband is studying for his doctorate. We live in a comfortable apartment."

Just as Janina expressed gratitude for her newly adopted homeland, so believers should give thanks to God for adopting them into his family and making them citizens of his kingdom. Christians are no longer aliens without a home, but full-fledged citizens of a heavenly kingdom—and children of the King too!

TODAY'S POWER POINT

As Americans, we go forward, in the service of our country, by the will of God.
—Franklin D. Roosevelt

TODAY IN HISTORY

1864—Congress ordered U.S. coins to be stamped with "In God We Trust"
1889—Start of Oklahoma land rush
1954—Senator Joseph McCarthy hearings began
2000—Elian Gonzalez reunited with his Cuban father
2001—Canadian astronauts attached robot arm to International Space Station
2002—Actor Robert Blake pled not guilty to murdering his wife
2003—Alan Greenspan appointed to fifth term as Federal Reserve Board chairman
2005—Terror suspect Zacharias Moussaoui pled guilty to planning attack on White House; top army officers cleared in Abu Ghraib prison scandal in Iraq

BORN TODAY

Spain's Queen Isabella I 1451
Revolutionary Vladimir Lenin . . . 1870
Actor Eddie Albert 1908
Evangelist Jack Wyrtzen 1913
Violinist Yehudi Menuhin 1916
Actress Charlotte Rae 1926
Producer Aaron Spelling. 1928
Singer Glen Campbell 1935
Actor Jack Nicholson 1936
Singer Peter Frampton 1950

GOLDEN OPPORTUNITY

One of the most notorious criminals of the 1930s, John Dillinger, was put on probation as a young teenager and began attending Sunday school with his parents. Other parents, disturbed that a youth with a court record was attending the class, threatened to keep their children home. When told of the parents' concerns, young Dillinger never returned to church again. Within twenty years this former Sunday-school boy became the most dangerous criminal in the country.

In contrast is the story of young Dwight L. Moody. A visit from his Sunday-school teacher resulted in Moody's making the most important decision of his life. He recalled, "My teacher . . . put his hand upon my shoulder and talked to me about Christ and my soul. I had not felt that I had a soul till then. . . . I don't remember what he said, but I can feel the power of that man's hand on my shoulder [and I know] that I was brought into the Kingdom of God."

His teacher, known only as Mr. Kimball, also recalled that day clearly: "I made what I afterward thought was a very weak plea for Christ. I don't know just what words I used. . . . I simply told him of Christ's love for him and the love Christ wanted in return."

What if Mr. Kimball had simply gone on his way and not taken the time to share the love of God? With whom can you share God's love today?

TODAY'S POWER POINT

The number one cause of atheism today is Christians. Those who proclaim God with their mouths and deny him with their lifestyles are what an unbelieving world finds simply unbelievable.—Karl Rahner

April 23

TODAY IN HISTORY

1616—Death of playwright William Shakespeare, age fifty-two

1635—Opening of first U.S. public school (in Boston)

1789—First Catholic magazine published

1867—First animated picture machine (Zoetrope, the "wheel of life") patented

1896—Edison's "Vitascope" method of projecting movies demonstrated to first paying audience in New York City

1897—Opening of first state hospital for disabled children (in St. Paul, Minnesota)

1977—Ethiopia ousted 330 U.S. government officials and missionaries (likely in response to U.S. foreign-aid cutoff for human rights violations)

1981—First transplant of artificial skin completed in Boston

1985—Coca-Cola replaced original formula with "new" Coke

1988—First smoking ban enforced on U.S. airline flights

2004—Trade ban against Libya dropped after they agreed to disarm

BORN TODAY

Writer William Shakespeare	1564	Actress Sandra Dee	1942
President James Buchanan	1791	Actor Herve Villechaize	1943
Composer Sergei Prokofiev	1891	Filmmaker Michael Moore	1954
Actress Shirley Temple Black	1928	Actress Valerie Bertinelli	1960
Actor David Birney	1940	Baseball player Andrew Jones	1977

PLANNING AHEAD

Many books have been written recently on the importance of planning and time management. Yet this is not a new concept. It seems people have always understood the value of making the most of their time. George Knox wrote with admiration that Napoleon "once plotted an entire campaign between the acts, while at the theater. . . . Napoleon conquered all of Europe because he fully utilized the time that the rest of the world was letting go to waste."

But Napoleon was not alone. Others have used their time productively. Historian and author Thomas Macaulay, for example, was said to have learned German during a long voyage. Robert Fulton and Samuel Morse worked out the finer details of the steamboat and the telegraph in their spare time. In just thirty years, the apostle Paul preached the gospel and planted churches all across the known world.

How well do you use your time? Do you plan ahead and organize your activities to fully utilize your time for God?

TODAY'S POWER POINT

If anything is certain, it is that change is certain. The world we are planning for today will not exist in this form tomorrow.—Philip Crosby

April 24

TODAY IN HISTORY

1790—Washington College (in Washington College, Tennessee) chartered as first school named after president George Washington

1800—Library of Congress established

1898—Spain declared war on United States

1913—Woolworth Building opened in New York City (At 791 feet, it was the tallest edifice in the world at the time. Only the 986-foot Eiffel Tower in Paris stood higher.)

1979—China launched its first satellite into space; U.S.-educated Abel Muzorewa became first black prime minister of Rhodesia

2003—North Korea announced possession of nuclear bomb

2005—Pope Benedict XVI installed in St. Peter's Square

BORN TODAY

Artist Willem de Kooning 1904
Poet Robert Penn Warren 1905
Actress Shirley MacLaine 1934
Author Sue Grafton 1940
Singer Barbra Streisand 1942

Politician Richard M. Daley 1942
Playwright Eric Bogosian 1953
Actor Michael O'Keefe 1955
Baseball player Chipper Jones 1972
Singer Kelly Clarkson 1982

GOD'S PERFECT BOOK

The Library of Congress in Washington DC houses millions of books, yet perhaps the most beautiful is a rare Bible hand-copied by a sixteenth-century monk. Even the world's best printer could not surpass its matchless perfection. In this thousand-page Bible, the German text is written in black ink. Each letter is perfect, without a scratch or blot. There are two columns to a page, and even under a magnifying glass, not the slightest irregularity of line, space, or letter formation is detectable. At the beginning of each chapter is a large initial letter, colorfully illustrated in red and blue ink with a scene from the chapter.

It's hard to imagine the painstaking years of toil, devotion, and even love that went into such a work of art. Yet the real value of this priceless book (which took a lifetime to copy) lies in its contents, not its form. This book should be admired more for its God-inspired contents than for the beauty of its appearance. Even the most perfect work of humans is hopelessly flawed in comparison with the perfection of God and his Word, which is perfect and eternal. The best part is knowing that each of us has access to this matchless Word of God. Don't neglect this gift of incomparable value, given to you by God himself. Think of God's perfection every time you read his book, the Bible.

TODAY'S POWER POINT

It's not those parts of the Bible that I can't understand that bother me, it's the parts that I do understand.—Mark Twain

April 25

TODAY IN HISTORY

1876—First baseball shutout (between Chicago White Stockings and Louisville)
1898—United States declared war on Spain
1901—First license plates issued for vehicles
1935—First around-the-world telephone conversation (from and to AT&T headquarters in New York City)
1940—First televised circus
1945—Conference convened to establish a "united nations" organization
1967—Colorado became first state to legalize abortion as a medical procedure
1982—Last Israeli soldiers left Sinai as area reverted to Egypt
1990—Hubble space telescope launched
1995—Death of actress Ginger Rogers, age eighty-three
2000—Snowmobiles banned from national parks
2003—Judge ruled that two file-swapping services did not violate copyright laws

BORN TODAY

Statesman Oliver Cromwell 1599
Inventor Guglielmo Marconi 1874
Journalist Edward R. Murrow . . . 1908
Singer Ella Fitzgerald 1918
Director Paul Mazursky 1930
Globetrotter Meadowlark Lemon . 1935
Actor Al Pacino 1940
Actor Hank Azaria 1964
Actress Renee Zellweger 1969
Basketball player Tim Duncan . . . 1976

HEALTH AND SECURITY

Many things in life can be either helpful or harmful, depending on their use. Ordinary table salt, for example, is a blend of two substances harmful to humans (sodium and chloride), yet salt is essential to human health. Additionally, as a preservative, salt protects us from harmful disease organisms.

Likewise the cobalt bomb. Cobalt, put into radioactive cylinders, is a versatile substance that has proven to be more powerful than radium in treating various cancers. Yet when combined with an explosive powder in a bomb, the cobalt becomes a source of death and destruction as its radioactive fallout contaminates a vast area. Still, cobalt (or any bomb) can provide people a sense of security if it functions as a strong deterrent to an enemy's aggression.

The Bible provides spiritual food and gives spiritual nourishment. It contains great wisdom, tremendous stories, and truths that can change lives. As we gain a better understanding of Jesus, we can even obtain a peace that passes understanding.

TODAY'S POWER POINT

Health consists of having the same diseases as your neighbors.—Quentin Crisp

TODAY IN HISTORY

1819—Initial Odd Fellows lodge established (in Baltimore)
1929—First exhibition of fluorescent minerals opened in Philadelphia
1954—National Salk polio-vaccine testing began
1986—Chernobyl, Ukraine, nuclear accident
2000—Vermont governor Howard Dean signed nation's first bill allowing same-sex couples to form civil unions
2005—Syrians completed withdrawal of troops from Lebanon after twenty-nine years

BORN TODAY

Naturalist and artist John James
    Audubon 1785
Korean president Syngman Rhee . 1875
Architect I. M. Pei 1917
Entertainer Carol Burnett. 1936
Guitarist Duane Eddy 1938

Singer Bobby Rydell. 1942
Musician Gary Wright 1943
TV host Boyd Matson 1947
Actress Joan Chen 1961
Actor Michael Damian. 1962
Actor Tom Welling. 1977

GOOD READING

Dr. Howard Pope tells a story of a young woman who, after reading a certain book, remarked that it was certainly one of the dullest she had ever read. Soon after that she met and fell in love with a young man, and they became engaged.

One day the woman remarked of a strange coincidence. She noted that in her collection was a book by a man whose name and initials were the same as her fiancé. "There's no coincidence," he said. "I wrote that book." Motivated anew, the young woman was said to have gone home and reread the book straight through, but with a deeper interest because now she knew the author.

In the same way, believers treasure the Bible because they know its author personally. How much do you get out of reading God's Word? What does that say about your relationship with the Author?

AVID READERS

History records some voracious readers of the Bible. It was said that Tertullian devoted both day and night to Bible reading and had committed much of it to memory, including the punctuation. One man, Dr. Gouge, was said to read fifteen chapters of the Bible every day, and at age eighty Theodore Beza could quote all of Paul's epistles.

How devoted are you to reading God's Word?

TODAY'S POWER POINT

There is no mistaking a real book when one meets it. It is like falling in love.
—Christopher Morley

April 27

TODAY IN HISTORY

1816—Congress passed first protective tariff

1817—Rush-Bagot treaty established an unfortified border between the United States and Canada

1865—Almost fifteen hundred Union prisoners killed in steamship explosion on the Mississippi

1875—John McCloskey became first U.S. Catholic priest to be named a cardinal

1880—Patent issued for first electric hearing aid

1937—First Social Security checks issued

1938—First baseball game played with a yellow ball (between Columbia and Fordham Universities)

1970—First "automated bank" (precursor to today's automatic teller machines) opened in Los Angeles

1972—Eleven-day *Apollo 16* space mission ended (two hundred pounds of moon rocks collected)

1994—First criminal convicted based on DNA evidence

2000—First successful gene therapy reported

2005—House of Representatives passed bill requiring parental consent for underage girls to cross state lines for abortions

BORN TODAY

Historian Edward Gibbon 1737
Inventor Samuel Morse 1791
President Ulysses S. Grant 1822
Animator Walter Lantz. 1900
Actor Jack Klugman 1922
Author Tim LaHaye. 1926
Civil-rights activist Coretta Scott King 1927
Radio host Casey Kasem 1932
Singer Sheena Easton 1959

BIG SHOES

Who hasn't smiled at the youngster who idolizes someone much bigger than he is, and says proudly, "When I grow up, I want to be just like you." How great you feel if the person he says it to is you. Even as adults we want to be like those we admire.

Who is it you admire and want to be like? As followers of Christ, we should want to be more like him. But although Jesus had the power to heal the sick and raise the dead, what truly distinguished him was the way he served others. Jesus told his disciples: "I am among you as one who serves" (Luke 22:27). He washed their feet, a dirty and lowly job reserved for servants. He broke bread with and touched outcasts—even gave his life that we might live.

Do you admire Christ enough to want to be like him? Enough to follow his example of serving? To what acts of service is he leading you today?

TODAY'S POWER POINT

If your children look up to you, you've made a success of life's biggest job. —Source Unknown

TODAY IN HISTORY

1788—U.S. Constitution ratified by seventh state, Maryland
1789—Mutineers took the HMS *Bounty* from Captain Bligh
1890—First state employment service established in Ohio
1932—First yellow-fever vaccine announced
1937—First animated electric sign on Broadway: four-minute show (which required two thousand bulbs) featured a dancing horse and ball-tossing cats
1980—U.S. hostage-rescue attempt failed: Secretary of State Cyrus Vance resigned
2001—First space tourist, private citizen Dennis Tito, blasted into space for $20 million visit to International Space Station
2003—Iraqis met to elect transitional government

BORN TODAY

President James Monroe 1758
Actor Lionel Barrymore 1878
Author Harper Lee 1926
Actress Carolyn Jones 1932
Dictator Saddam Hussein 1937
Actor Bruno Kirby 1940
Actress Ann-Margret 1941
Actress Marcia Strassman 1948
TV host Jay Leno 1950
Baseball player Barry Larkin 1964
Actress Penelope Cruz 1974
Actress Jessica Alba 1981

MAKING WAY FOR PEACE

King Solomon was the wisest, richest, and most powerful man of his era. He had at his command every sort of pleasure and privilege imaginable. Did his unsurpassed riches or power provide him lasting peace? No. Here's what Solomon said of his restless search for what can only be described as inner peace: "I devoted myself to study and to explore by wisdom all that is done under heaven. What a heavy burden God has laid on men! I have seen all the things that are done under the sun; all of them are meaningless, a chasing after the wind" (Ecclesiastes 1:13–14).

By the end of Ecclesiastes, Solomon had reached some important conclusions that finally seemed to bring him a measure of peace: "Now all has been heard; here is the conclusion of the matter: Fear God and keep his commandments, for this is the whole duty of man" (Ecclesiastes 12:13).

Like Solomon, our search for peace and happiness will only end when we finally recognize that true peace and fulfillment come only from knowing and living for God. We can experience this enduring peace today if we'll trust in God and keep his commandments. Only in him will we find the peace we seek.

TODAY'S POWER POINT

I do not want the peace which passeth understanding. I want the understanding which bringeth peace.—Helen Keller

April 29

TODAY IN HISTORY

1749—Benjamin Franklin experimented with electric cooking

1851—First college to ban racial and religious discrimination chartered in New York City

1879—Electric street lights, employing the carbon arc lamp, introduced

1900—Fabled railroad engineer Casey Jones rode the Cannonball Express to his death in Mississippi

1913—Zipper fastener patented

1945—Dachau concentration camp liberated by U.S. forces in Germany

1953—First 3-D telecast

1992—Riots in Los Angeles caused fifty-four deaths and $1 billion in damages following acquittal of four police officers on charges of beating motorist Rodney King

1994—First interracial national elections in South Africa

1997—First joint United States–Russian spacewalk

2001—U.S. census reported whites a minority in nearly half of the nation's one hundred largest cities

BORN TODAY

Publisher William Randolph Hearst 1863
Bandleader Duke Ellington 1899
Actress Celeste Holm 1919
Poet Rod McKuen 1933
Conductor Zubin Mehta 1936

Race-car driver Dale Earnhardt . . 1952
Comedian Jerry Seinfeld 1954
Actor Daniel Day-Lewis 1957
Actress Michelle Pfeiffer 1958
Actress Uma Thurman;
    tennis player Andre Agassi . . . 1970

COST OF WAR

War is not cheap. Some time ago *Moody Monthly* calculated that for the cost of the first atomic bomb (about $2 billion), ten thousand missionaries could have been sent and supported for one hundred years each.

The money spent by the United States alone in World War II would have kept 1.5 million missionaries on the field. The cost of vigilance is high indeed.

Christians are constantly at war. In 2 Corinthians 10:3–4 Paul said, "We do not wage war as the world does. The weapons we fight with are not the weapons of the world. On the contrary, they have divine power to demolish strongholds."

We have great power to wage war when we use the spiritual weapons God has given us (see Ephesians 6:10–18). But there is a cost to this sort of war too. We must "take captive every thought to make it obedient to Christ" (2 Corinthians 10:5). Controlling our thoughts is a daily struggle. We may not win all the skirmishes, but with God's help, we can win the battle.

TODAY'S POWER POINT

The quickest way of ending a war is to lose it.—George Orwell

TODAY IN HISTORY

1789—George Washington sworn in as first U.S. president

1796—Samuel Lee Jr. granted patent for "Lee's New London Bilious Pills" (first tablets to be patented)

1798—Navy purchased New Hampshire land for first naval base (in Portsmouth)

1812—Eighteenth state, Louisiana, admitted to Union

1889—First national holiday (centennial of president George Washington's inauguration)

1939—First presidential appearance on television (Franklin D. Roosevelt)

1945—Suicide of Adolf Hitler and mistress Eva Braun as Russian troops approached their bunker

1973—Four top Nixon aides resigned in the wake of growing Watergate scandal

1975—Saigon surrendered to Communists as last Americans left Vietnam

1984—President Ronald Reagan signed cultural, trade agreements with China

2003—President George W. Bush outlined road map to peace in the Middle East

BORN TODAY

Composer Franz Lehar	1870	Actress Jill Clayburgh	1944
Actress Eve Arden	1908	Film director Jane Campion	1954
Actress Cloris Leachman	1930	Basketball player Isiah Thomas	1961
Singer Willie Nelson	1933	Singer Carolyn Dawn Johnson	1971
Actor Gary Collins	1938	Actress Kirsten Dunst	1982

HELPING OTHERS

These days it seems there's a growing resistance to charitable organizations collecting funds for the needy. In fact, the familiar red kettles and bell ringers of the Salvation Army have even been banned by some major store chains. Yet so much good can be done when everyone does a little. Recognizing this fact, many utilities now encourage their customers to donate a dollar or two to a fund that helps the needy keep the lights and heat on during the cold winter months. While one dollar doesn't seem like much, when added to what thousands of others have done, it really adds up.

In today's Scripture reading we learn that the widow's tiny gift, amounting to less than a penny, was of greater value, in God's eyes, than the much larger donations of others because it was all she had. As the Bible points out, it's not so much the amount we give but our purpose and what we are willing to forgo in order to give that count. So when given the opportunity to help others, give as God has given to you. To God, even a small gift, when given from a sacrificial heart, amounts to more than a large gift given for the recognition or praise of others.

TODAY'S POWER POINT

Little is much when God is in it.—Kittie L. Suffield

May 1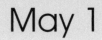

TODAY IN HISTORY

1704—First U.S. newspaper ad published
1884—Start of construction on first U.S. skyscraper (in Chicago)
1906—Nighttime banking introduced
1931—Opening of Empire State Building, then world's tallest building
1960—U.S. spy plane shot down over USSR
1961—First U.S. plane hijacked, to Cuba
1981—Senator Harrison Williams convicted in Abscam bribery case
1995—Linking of U.S. space shuttle and Russian space station
2003—President George W. Bush's "Mission accomplished" in Iraq speech; House
        passed $15 billion global AIDS package
2004—Ten new member nations brought total number in European Union to
        twenty-five

BORN TODAY

Engineer Benjamin Latrobe 1764
Singer Kate Smith 1909
Actor Glenn Ford 1916
Writer Terry Southern 1924
Singer Judy Collins. 1939
Actor Stephen Macht 1942
Singer Rita Coolidge 1945
Singer Tim McGraw. 1967
Football player Curtis Martin. . . . 1973
Actor Darius McCrary 1976

MAN'S LAWS

Have you ever considered just how many laws are on the books? If you were to take time to familiarize yourself with just two laws each day, it would take you six thousand years! And too many laws isn't a new problem. When Emperor Justinian ordered all Roman laws to be compiled, it took sixteen assistants three years to collect them into a total of two thousand volumes.

By comparison, all of God's laws for mankind are contained in just one volume, consisting of sixty-six books: the Bible. Many people read through the Bible at least once a year. If you've never done this, consider reading the entire Bible this year. No matter how many times you've read God's Word, it's time to read it again. How else will you know and be able to obey God's laws?

TODAY'S POWER POINT

Good laws make it easier to do right and harder to do wrong.—William Gladstone

TODAY IN HISTORY

1670—Hudson Bay Company chartered
1876—First home runs hit in baseball
1936—Premiere of *Peter and the Wolf* in Moscow
1941—First commercial TV station licenses issued
1945—Berlin yielded to Russians
1954—Stan Musial slammed five home runs in one day (in two games)
1970—First woman jockey to compete in Kentucky Derby (Diane Crump)
1972—Death of FBI Director J. Edgar Hoover, age seventy-seven
1977—First protest of nuclear power plant (in Seabrook, New Hampshire)

BORN TODAY

World War I German flying ace "Red
   Baron" Manfred Von Richthofen
   1892
Pediatrician Benjamin Spock 1903
Kids' TV host Pinky Lee. 1907
Singer and actor Theodore Bikel. . 1924

Singer Englebert Humperdinck . . 1936
Singer Larry Gatlin. 1949
Actress Elizabeth Berridge 1962
Soccer player David Beckham . . . 1975
Actress Jenna Von Oy. 1977
Olympic skater Sarah Hughes . . . 1985

TAKING THE CONSEQUENCES

Marshall Cummings likely has a better appreciation of laws (and lawyers) since his conviction on robbery charges. The accused purse snatcher chose to serve as his own counsel. But his case took a turn for the worse when he absentmindedly asked his accuser, "Did you get a good look at my face when I took your purse?"

Cummings was sentenced to ten years in prison, which should provide plenty of time for him to think about how he might have done things differently. Sometimes it takes a direct confrontation with the law before we gain a healthy respect for the fact that our actions all have consequences. When it comes to God's laws as found in the Bible, we're told that relatively few will heed them. Yet that in no way reduces the power of God's law or cancels his coming judgment. Not only does God promise to forgive all those who trust in him but also to forget—forever—that the violations ever occurred.

Death is the natural consequence of sin. But because of Jesus, we don't have to suffer it. When we go to God with a repentant heart, he wipes the slate clean. "The wages of sin is death, but the gift of God is eternal life in Christ Jesus our Lord" (Romans 6:23).

TODAY'S POWER POINT

First rule of life—all actions have consequences. . . . And the second rule is this—you are the only one responsible for your own actions.—Source Unknown

TODAY IN HISTORY

1765—First U.S. medical school established

1919—First air passenger service, between New York and Atlantic City, New Jersey

1948—Premiere of *CBS Evening News* (fifteen-minute daily TV newscast, Douglas Edwards, anchor)

1971—Antiwar protestors tried to shut down U.S. capital; National Public Radio's first broadcast

1979—Margaret Thatcher elected Britain's first woman prime minister

1983—U.S. Catholic bishops called for elimination of nuclear weapons

1998—Euro adopted as common currency for European Union

2000—Death of New York cardinal John O'Connor, age eighty

2003—Syria promised to crack down on terrorists

2004—Israeli proposal to withdraw settlers and soldiers from Gaza strip rejected by ruling party

2005—New Iraqi cabinet sworn in

BORN TODAY

Philosopher Niccolo Machiavelli . 1469
Israeli prime minister Golda Meir 1898
Singer Bing Crosby 1903
Songwriter Pete Seeger 1919
Boxer Sugar Ray Robinson 1921
Singer James Brown 1933
Singer Frankie Valli 1937
NBA coach Pat Williams 1940
Magician Doug Henning 1947
Singer Christopher Cross 1951
Actor Dulé Hill 1975

THE SUPREME COURT

A justice on the Supreme Court more than a century ago, Judge Horace Gray, once told a man he was setting free on a legal technicality, "Both you and I know you are guilty, but remember that one day you will stand before a better and wiser Judge, and there you will be dealt with according to Justice and not according to law."

Dependent as it is on the implementation of imperfect human beings, earthly justice will always be flawed. But a time of perfect justice will come eventually. Someday every individual—great or small, rich or poor, powerful or weak, good or bad—will stand before God to be judged. Those who have acknowledged Jesus Christ as their Lord will have no need to fear when they stand before the Judgment Seat. He will be their advocate—the ultimate lawyer, who never loses a case.

TODAY'S POWER POINT

Our constitution works. Our great republic is a government of laws, not of men.—Gerald R. Ford

TODAY IN HISTORY

1884—First photograph of lightning
1932—Start of Al Capone's prison sentence
1964—Premiere of soap opera *Another World*
1970—Four students killed by National Guard troops during Vietnam War protest at Kent State University (Ohio)
1973—Sears Tower in Chicago set record as first U.S. skyscraper taller than 1,400 feet
1983—President Ronald Reagan sought support for "Freedom Fighters" seeking aid for rebel forces in Nicaragua
1989—Oliver North convicted in Iran Contra affair
1998—"Unabomber" sentenced to four life terms

BORN TODAY

Educator Horace Mann 1796
Scientist Thomas Huxley 1825
Household-hints guru Heloise . . . 1919
Actress Audrey Hepburn 1929
Columnist George Will 1941

Dancer Pia Zadora 1956
Singer Randy Travis 1959
Basketball player Dawn Staley . . . 1970
Baseball player Ben Grieve 1976
Singer Lance Bass 1979

TRUE HAPPINESS

Have you ever observed teenagers anxious to get away from home in order to find "true happiness"? They just can't wait to be free from Mom and Dad's restrictions. Yet often, much to their amazement, they discover that getting away from the rules makes them miserable. And given a few years' perspective, they begin to see the wisdom in the guidelines their parents had carefully laid down.

Some years ago a young man, growing tired of "all the rules" at his Christian school, decided to join the U.S. Marines. Imagine the shock he must have felt upon meeting the "friendly" drill sergeants at Parris Island.

We all need rules to live by. For just as a train requires rails to direct it safely to its destination, so we need the guidelines established in God's Word to lead us safely home. Most likely, the longer you live, the more you'll discover that living by God's rules is the only course to lasting happiness.

Want true happiness? Do things God's way.

TODAY'S POWER POINT

Blessed are those who hunger and thirst for righteousness, for they will be filled.
—Matthew 5:6

May 5

TODAY IN HISTORY

1847—First U.S. medical society founded
1862—Mexico defeated the French in the battle of Puebla, which Cinco de Mayo
    festivals commemorate to this day
1891—Opening of Carnegie Hall in New York City
1936—First bottle with a screw-on cap introduced
1955—Germany regained independence
1961—Fifteen-minute flight made Alan Shepard first American in space
1973—University of Miami offered first athletic scholarships to women
2002—French president Jacque Chirac reelected in landslide; *Spiderman* set box-
    office record—$114 million in first three days
2004—Picasso painting brought a record $104 million at auction

BORN TODAY

Philosopher Sören Kierkegaard. . . 1813
Philosopher and revolutionary
    Karl Marx. 1818
Actress Pat Carroll 1927
Actor Michael Murphy. 1938
Actor Lance Henriksen. 1940

Singer Tammy Wynette 1942
Actor Roger Rees 1944
Actor Richard Grant. 1957
Hockey player Ziggy Palffy. 1972
Actress Tina Yothers 1973
Actress Danielle Fishel 1980

THE PRINCE OF PEACE

High atop a mountain, straddling the border between Argentina and Chile, stands a massive statue called, "Christ of the Andes." The statue commemorates the signing of a peace treaty in 1903 that ended a long-smoldering border dispute. In fact, the military cannons which had terrorized the Chileans were melted down and molded to form the 125-foot-tall bronze statue of Christ with a cross in his left hand and his right hand extended in blessing over the two countries.

This figure, towering over both nations, serves as a reminder of Christ, the Prince of Peace—the hope of the world. Engraved in Spanish at the base of the monument are these words: "He is our peace who has made us one. Sooner shall these mountains crumble into dust than Argentines and Chileans break the peace sworn at the foot of Christ the Redeemer."

In human experience peace is transitory. Treaties are broken, wars rage, uncertainties chase away our fleeting sense of peace. But the peace that comes from God is eternal. We think of mountains as a good symbol of permanence, but compared with God's peace, they are momentary. Fix your attention on God, and don't be troubled by the temporary struggles of this world.

TODAY'S POWER POINT

I could not live in peace if I put the shadow of a willful sin between myself and God.—George Eliot

TODAY IN HISTORY

1840—First postage stamps (issued by England)
1851—Patent issued for first mechanical freezer
1916—First ship-to-shore radiophone conversation
1935—Launch of Franklin D. Roosevelt's Works Progress Administration (to provide jobs for the unemployed)
1937—Explosion of hydrogen-filled German dirigible *Hindenburg*, thirty-six killed
1954—First four-minute mile (run by Roger Bannister—3:59.4)
2000—Vladimir Putin inaugurated as new Russian president
2003—Paul Bremer named to manage transition government in Iraq

BORN TODAY

Explorer Robert E. Peary;
   psychiatrist Sigmund Freud. . . 1856
Actor Orson Welles 1915
Baseball player Willie May 1931
Musician Bob Seger 1931
British prime minister Tony Blair . 1953
TV host Tom Bergeron. 1955
Actor George Clooney 1961
Actress Roma Downey 1964
Hockey player Martin Brodeur. . . 1972

STURDY TREES

Some years ago woodsmen cut down a giant sequoia and studied its growth rings. They learned that the tree had been a seedling 271 years before Christ was born. When it was 516 years old, the tree sustained damage in the first of several fires it had endured through the years. Drought, bitter cold, and blistering heat were frequently evident in the tree's growth record.

How could any tree survive such assaults to stand tall and strong for so many years? Credit goes to a tree's complex root system. Perhaps you've heard that the roots of a tree stretch as far as the spread of its branches; but depending on the environment, they can stretch four to seven times farther than the tree's drip line. The roots, with a combined length of as much as one hundred miles in a large oak, are what give the tree strength and stability—power to withstand the fearsome storms, periodic droughts, and other stresses.

Are you rooted in the Word of God? Reading, meditating on, and following the instructions in the Bible are how we send our roots deep into the life-giving water of God's blessing. When we root ourselves in God's Word, not only do we anchor ourselves against the storms to come, but we also ensure that we're connected to the Living Water that nourishes and sustains the soul. We can be "like a tree planted by streams of water, which yields its fruit in season and whose leaf does not wither" (Psalm 1:3). Like a giant tree, we too can withstand the tests of time.

TODAY'S POWER POINT

The greatest oak was once a little nut that held its ground.—Source Unknown

May 7

TODAY IN HISTORY

1789—First presidential inaugural ball (for George Washington)
1907—First postage stamp featuring a Native American issued
1912—First machine gun installed on an aircraft
1915—Passenger ocean liner *Lusitania* sunk by German sub
1945—Nazi forces surrendered unconditionally
1947—First regularly scheduled dramatic program on TV (*Kraft Television Theater*)
1951—Premiere of TV game show *Strike it Rich*
2004—Defense Secretary Donald Rumsfeld apologized to Iraqi prisoners reportedly abused at Abu Ghraib prison

BORN TODAY

Poet Robert Browning 1812
Composer Johannes Brahms. 1833
Composer Peter Tchaikovsky 1840
Actor George "Gabby" Hayes. . . . 1885
Actor Gary Cooper. 1901
Actor Darren McGavin 1922
Singer Theresa Brewer 1931
Football player Johnny Unitas . . . 1933
Political analyst Tim Russert. 1950
Actor Peter Reckell. 1955
Basketball player Marko Milic . . . 1977
Football player Alex Smith 1984

BLOOMING WHERE YOU'RE PLANTED

Years ago a church congregation gave special recognition to its members who had entered full-time Christian service. While it's commendable to honor those who serve in the ministry, evangelism, or missionary work, in reality all believers are in full-time Christian service, regardless of who provides their paychecks.

As *Our Daily Bread* writer Paul Van Gorder notes, whether you're employed by a secular organization or a Christian ministry, "Any employment not prohibited by God's Word can be done for his glory. The important consideration is not the job itself but the attitude of the Christian in the place God has called him to fill."

So do your work as unto the Lord, even if you have what some might consider to be a menial job. A maintenance supervisor at a Christian university once remarked, "It's not unusual for graduate students to be cleaning toilets" as they worked their way through school. That job may not be the one they want to have for the rest of their lives, but if they're doing it to the glory of God, even that is a Christian service.

We all need to bloom where we're planted. The apostle Paul wrote, "Whatever you do, work at it with all your heart, as working for the Lord, not for men" (Colossians 3:23). Wherever you're employed, do your work as unto God—for you truly are in full-time Christian service.

TODAY'S POWER POINT

The simplest thing we learn to do well—even if it is only to sweep a room in a beautiful spirit of service—makes life infinitely worthwhile.—Helen Keller

TODAY IN HISTORY

1541—Mississippi River discovered by Spanish explorer Hernando DeSoto
1816—American Bible Society founded
1945—VE Day—Victory in Europe (World War II)
1973—Militant Native Americans surrendered after ten-week siege at Wounded Knee
1980—First nonstop U.S. transcontinental balloon flight launched (four-day flight)
1984—National Olympic Committee of the Soviet Union announced its team would withdraw from upcoming Los Angeles Summer Olympics (in retaliation for U.S. boycott of 1980 summer games in Moscow)
2000—Hundreds of homes burned in forest fire near Los Alamos, New Mexico— 25,000 people evacuated
2003—Congress overwhelmingly approved antiterrorist Patriot Act for two-year trial

BORN TODAY

President Harry Truman 1884
Comedian Don Rickles 1926
Author Peter Benchley 1940
Singer Toni Tennille 1943
Football player Ronnie Lott 1959
Race-car driver Bobby LaBonte; actress Melissa Gilbert 1964
Singer Enrique Iglesias 1975

THE DOMINO EFFECT

Remember playing with dominoes as a child? For many the fun was not so much in matching the dots as it was in standing rows of dominoes on end, then knocking one over and watching them all tumble in sequence. Even in diplomacy the term "domino effect" describes how the fall of one nation can trigger the collapse of neighboring countries, one by one.

We see this effect in the Christian life as well, for no one lives in a vacuum. What one person does affects all. As Paul reminded the Romans, "None of us lives to himself alone and none of us dies to himself alone" (Romans 14:7). He went on to caution mature believers not to offend, by inattention or insensitivity, those who were newer in the faith and so cause them to stumble in their walk with Christ. Unfortunately, the negative behavior of just one believer can extend even beyond the Christian community, affecting our neighbors, coworkers, and others who might then reject God.

With God's help, determine to remain solid and upright in your faith and daily living. Don't become the domino that triggers the downfall of others.

TODAY'S POWER POINT

No man is an island, entire of itself; every man is a piece of the continent, a part of the main. . . . Any man's death diminishes me, because I am involved in mankind.—John Donne

May 9

TODAY IN HISTORY

1926—Richard E. Byrd and Floyd Bennett become first aviators to fly over North Pole

1960—First eye bank opened; FDA approved sale of first birth control pill

1994—Nelson Mandela elected first black president of South Africa

1995—First Cuban refugees returned to homeland under new U.S. policy

2004—Chechen president Akhmed-Hadji Kadyrov killed in bomb blast in Grozny, Russia

2005—U.S. Marines launched major assault against insurgents in Iraq

BORN TODAY

Abolitionist John Brown. 1800
TV journalist Mike Wallace 1918
Tennis champ Pancho Gonzalez . . 1928
Actor Albert Finney 1936
Producer James Brooks. 1940

Actress Candice Bergen 1946
Singer Billy Joel 1949
Actress Alley Mills 1951
Baseball player Tony Gwynn 1960
Actress Rosario Dawson 1979

FLEEING TEMPTATION

If you find yourself struggling with temptation, you're not alone. It's a problem common to all of us. Victorian-era playwright Oscar Wilde was quoted as saying "I can resist everything except temptation." Perhaps that describes your experience. But with God's help, it doesn't have to.

Christian author Charles Swindoll, in *Three Steps Forward Two Steps Back*, urged total avoidance of temptation: "Do not try to coexist peacefully with temptation. . . . If you're weakened by certain . . . pictures that bring before your eyes things that build desires within you that you can't handle, then you're not counteracting sin and temptation. You're tolerating it. You're fertilizing it. You're prompting it. . . . There's a name for folks who linger and try to reason with lust—victim."

One man told of the pressures of temptation he was facing, remarking that he no longer would enter a convenience store that displayed suggestive literature. Instead, following Paul's advice in 2 Timothy 2:22, "Flee also youthful lusts; but pursue righteousness, faith, love, peace" (NKJV), he would flee (run from—totally avoid) temptation by paying at the pump or, better yet, making his purchases at a store that did not sell pornography.

Just as Joseph ran from the advances of Potiphar's wife, as recorded in Genesis 39, so we need to flee temptation the moment it is encountered. That means avoiding places where we know temptation can be found. With God's help we can flee temptation and not become its victims.

TODAY'S POWER POINT

You can't keep the devil from coming down your street, but you can keep him from stopping at your house.—David Egner

TODAY IN HISTORY

1869—U.S. transcontienental railroad linked at Promontory Summit, Utah
1908—First Mother's Day observed (unofficially)
1923—J. Edgar Hoover became head of FBI
1927—First radio receiver installed in a hotel (in Boston)
1930—Opening of first U.S. planetarium (in Chicago)
1940—Winston Churchill became Britain's prime minister
1968—United States and North Vietnam began peace talks
1975—Federal judge ordered school busing in Boston to correct racial imbalance
1976—Premiere of Paul Harvey's radio program *The Rest of the Story*
1977—Oklahoma became first state to authorize execution by lethal injection
1981—François Mitterrand became first socialist president of France
2001—Record tax cut (largest in twenty years) approved by Congress
2005—Senate approved $82 billion emergency spending bill

BORN TODAY

Dancer Fred Astaire 1899
Producer David O. Selznick 1902
Actress Nancy Walker. 1921
Football coach Ara Parseghian . . . 1923
Sportscaster Pat Summerall. 1930

Actor Gary Owens 1936
Musician Dave Mason 1946
Singer Bono 1960
Actor Jason Brooks 1966

COURAGE

Henry Ward Beecher once preached a series of sermons on drunkenness and gambling that upset some members of the community who profited from these vices. On one occasion he was accosted by an assailant who threatened to shoot Beecher if he didn't promise to retract what he'd been saying.

"Shoot away," Beecher said as he calmly walked away. "I don't believe you can hit the mark as well as I did."

Are your convictions strong enough that you can stand in the face of such opposition and danger? What makes someone like Beecher—or like you—courageously stand for what is right under threat of great personal harm? It all boils down to what a person fears most—physical harm, even death, or dishonoring God.

The Westminster Abbey memorial for Lord John Laird Lawrence, governor general and viceroy of India, consists simply of his name and these words: "He feared man so little because he feared God so much."

Whom do you fear more, God or men? John Wesley once said, "Give me a hundred men who fear nothing but sin, and desire nothing but God, and I will shake the world." Will you be one of those who desire nothing but God?

TODAY'S POWER POINT

Courage is resistance to fear, mastery of fear—not absence of fear.—Mark Twain

May 11

TODAY IN HISTORY

1858—Minnesota admitted to Union as thirty-second state
1928—First regularly scheduled TV programs (on WGY Schenectady, New York)
1940—First ship-to-shore telecast
1947—B. F. Goodrich introduced tubeless tires
1996—ValuJet crashed in the Florida Everglades, killing all 110 aboard
2001—United States pledged $200 million to battle AIDS worldwide
2004—United States placed economic sanctions on Syria for not reigning in terrorists
2006—*USA Today* reported government had accessed phone records of millions of
    Americans in search for terror suspects

BORN TODAY

Composer Irving Berlin 1888
Choreographer Martha Graham . . 1894
Artist Salvador Dali 1904
Entertainer Phil Silvers 1912

Physician Robert Jarvik 1946
Actress Natasha Richardson 1963
Actor Jonathan Jackson 1982
Singer Holly Valance 1983

THINKING STILL REQUIRED

When God created humans, he gave them unique and powerful brains. In this current age of technology, the computer, with its artificial intelligence, has taken over many routine tasks—often with somewhat amusing results. One such instance involves a bank official, years ago, who objected to purchasing a new data-processing system, calling it a "needless expense." Finally he gave in, and soon the massive mainframe arrived. Only then did the delivery crew discover that the unit was too big to fit into the bank's elevator.

"How are we going to get this thing up to the third floor?" one complained.

The skeptical bank official wisecracked, "Since it's so smart, why don't you just plug it in and let it figure it out for itself?"

Sometimes computers can solve problems that might otherwise leave us stumped; but their usefulness only goes so far. Even with the amazing advances in technology, no computer—and no person—can do your thinking for you. The important questions in our lives must be answered by us alone—such as where we will spend eternity. God has left that choice up to us. How will you respond to his offer to spend it with him?

TODAY'S POWER POINT

To err is human, but to really foul things up requires a computer.—*Farmer's Almanac*

TODAY IN HISTORY

1860—First woman news reporter at a political convention
1871—Previously segregated streetcars integrated in Louisville, Kentucky
1890—Louisiana became first state to ban prizefighting
1928—Mussolini ended women's rights in Italy
1932—Kidnapped Lindbergh baby found dead
1949—Soviets ended Berlin blockade after eleven months
1969—First Pacific sailboat crossing by a woman
1993—Last broadcast of *Cheers*

BORN TODAY

Nurse Florence Nightingale 1820
Actress Katherine Hepburn 1907
Baseball manager Yogi Berra. 1925
Composer Burt Bacharach 1929
TV host Tom Snyder 1936
Comedian George Carlin 1937
Actor Emilio Estevez 1962
Actor Stephen Baldwin. 1966
Skateboarder Tony Hawk 1969
Actor Jason Biggs 1978

GOD'S ANSWERS

On December 24, 1814, John Quincy Adams and an American delegation, along with their British counterparts, signed the Treaty of Ghent to end the War of 1812. The prayers of many Americans and Britons had finally been answered after a costly war. Then, some two weeks later, on January 8, 1815, British and American forces clashed in the famous Battle of New Orleans, resulting in the tragic loss of more than two thousand men from both sides, needlessly killed, wounded, or captured. They had been unaware of the treaty, as word had not yet arrived from peacemaking officials in the Netherlands (where the treaty was signed).

God, our Commander in Chief, has already settled our conflicts for us. The outcome is no longer in doubt. He has won! When we follow him, victory will be ours as well. No matter what dangerous foe we may face, when we cry out to God for help, he hears and answers us: "How gracious he will be when you cry for help! As soon as he hears, he will answer you" (Isaiah 30:19).

We don't have to wait for a courier with news that brings peace. In Isaiah 65:24 God said: "Before they call I will answer; while they are still speaking I will hear." We never have to face any struggle alone. What a great God we have—one who knows the thoughts and intents of our hearts and who grants our requests, sometimes even before we ask.

TODAY'S POWER POINT

The time to pray is not when we are in a tight spot but just as soon as we get out of it.—Josh Billings

May 13

TODAY IN HISTORY

1607—First English-speaking settlement in North America established (in Jamestown, Virginia)

1867—Noonday prayer meetings begun by D. L. Moody in London

1908—U.S. Navy nurse corps established

1918—First airmail stamps issued

1981—Pope John Paul II wounded in assassination attempt in St. Peter's Square

2002—U. S. and Russia agreed to two-thirds cutback in both nations' nuclear arsenals

2003—Treasury department unveiled new, colorful twenty-dollar bills to help thwart counterfeiting

BORN TODAY

Composer Arthur Sullivan 1842
Boxer Joe Lewis 1914
Actress Beatrice Arthur 1926
Critic Clive Barnes 1927

Singer Stevie Wonder;
   sportscaster Bobby Valentine. . 1950
Basketball player Dennis Rodman 1961
Singer Darius Rucker 1966

SEEING POSSIBILITIES

Notice posted in a Chicago store in 1858: "The store will be open from 6 a.m. to 9 p.m. the year 'round. On arrival each morning store must be swept, counters, shelves, and showcases dusted. Lamps must be trimmed, pens made, a pail of water and bucket of coal brought in before breakfast. After fifteen hours of work, leisure hours should be spent in reading."

Today's employees could learn much about hard work from wage earners of long ago. Too many people try to scrape by doing just enough—the bare minimum of what's expected. How refreshing to find a person who understands his or her job is more than a list of duties that *must* be done and sees the opportunities of what *might* be accomplished.

Jesus was aware of opportunities that few others saw. He urged his followers, "Open your eyes and look at the fields! They are ripe for harvest" (John 4:35). Jesus recognized the importance of working hard, being united with other workers, and not procrastinating when it comes to working for an eternal harvest. He understood that the job is great, and the time shorter than any of us realize. "As long as it is day, we must do the work of him who sent me. Night is coming, when no one can work" (John 9:4).

Are you a good worker at your job? For God? Do you do only what you're told, or can you see beyond the mundane tasks to the possibilities of what might be accomplished? Work, for the night is coming.

TODAY'S POWER POINT

Work relieves us from three great evils: boredom, vice, and want.—French Proverb

TODAY IN HISTORY

1796—Smallpox vaccine first tested
1804—Lewis and Clark expedition launched from St. Louis, Missouri
1853—Gail Borden applied for patent for condensed milk
1874—Appearance of first football goalpost
1897—First performance of "The Stars and Stripes Forever"
1942—Act of Congress established the Women's Army Auxiliary Corp (later the WAC), the female branch of the U.S. Army
1973—Skylab launched
1985—The first McDonald's (in Des Plaines, Illinois) was made the first fast-food museum
1998—Final episode of *Seinfeld* televised
2005—First helicopter to land atop Mount Everest

BORN TODAY

Painter Thomas Gainsborough . . . 1727
Filmmaker George Lucas 1944
Conductor Otto Klemperer 1885
Actor Tim Roth 1961
Singer Bobby Darin 1936
Actress Cate Blanchett 1969
Baseball player Tony Perez 1942
Actress Amber Tamblyn 1983

DA VINCI'S ANGER

The story has been told that while Leonardo da Vinci was painting his masterpiece *The Lord's Supper*, he became angry with a certain man. The turbulent emotions were affecting his work. Try as he might, da Vinci could not block out his anger as he prepared to paint the face of Jesus. Finally he became so distraught that he sought out the man and asked for forgiveness.

Returning to the canvas, da Vinci was immediately able to give the Master's face the tender, peaceful expression we're familiar with today.

FORGIVENESS AND PEACE

The Eskimo word for forgiveness is literally translated, "not-being-able-to-think-about-it-anymore." This gives us a glimpse into the expansive, merciful forgiveness of God. Have you forgiven others like this? Such forgiveness is the only way to true peace—with others, within ourselves, and with God. "Forgive as the Lord forgave you" (Colossians 3:13).

TODAY'S POWER POINT

God pardons like a mother, who kisses the offense into everlasting forgiveness. Forgiveness ought to be like a canceled note—torn in two, and burned up, so that it never can be shown against anyone.—Henry Ward Beecher

May 15

TODAY IN HISTORY

1718—World's first machine gun patented
1862—First enclosed U.S. ballpark opened (Union Grounds in Brooklyn)
1869—National Woman Suffrage Association founded by Elizabeth Cady Stanton
    and Susan B. Anthony
1940—Nylon stockings introduced
1941—First British jet flown
1953—Rocky Marciano scored forty-fourth win by knocking out heavyweight Joe
    Walcott
1958—Premiere of movie musical *Gigi*
2006—Saddam Hussein charged with crimes against humanity in connection with
    execution slayings of 150 Iraqi Shiites in 1982

BORN TODAY

Author Frank Baum	1856	Actor Trini Lopez	1937
Actor Joseph Cotton	1905	Baseball player George Brett	1953
Singer Eddy Arnold	1918	Sportscaster Dan Patrick	1956
Photographer Richard Avedon	1923	Football player Emmitt Smith	1969

BEING RICH

A newly married woman was watching a television show that followed a young couple as they shopped for a new home. She gasped at the huge houses, resplendent with amenities and features that made her own little apartment seem shabby and inadequate. How could a couple not much older than she afford such opulence? As her husband came and sat beside her on the couch, she remarked wistfully, "Someday we'll be rich."

Taking her hand, the husband gently replied, "Darling, we are rich. Someday we'll have money."

Are you chasing after money and the wealth this world values, or are you pouring your effort into becoming truly rich? Jesus warned, "Watch out! Be on your guard against all kinds of greed; a man's life does not consist in the abundance of his possessions" (Luke 12:15).

Wealth is fleeting, and security is an illusion. Jesus said, "The pagan world runs after all such things, and your Father knows that you need them. But seek his kingdom, and these things will be given to you as well" (Luke 12:30–31). You can't go wrong when you seek to know and obey God. It's the only way to be truly rich.

TODAY'S POWER POINT

Unquestionably there is progress. The average American now pays out twice as much in taxes as he formerly got in wages.—H. L. Mencken

TODAY IN HISTORY

1866—Congress authorized minting of first five-cent coin

1868—Senate failed (by one vote) to impeach president Andrew Johnson

1888—First phonograph record demonstrated

1893—Patent granted for first typewriter to produce visible printing (while being typed)

1929—First Academy Awards presentation

1959—Sam Snead became first golfer to break sixty (in eighteen-hole tournament play)

1965—SpaghettiOs first sold

1975—First woman to scale Mount Everest (Japan's Junko Tabei)

1985—Michael Jordan named NBA Rookie of the Year

2000—Hillary Clinton nominated to run for U.S. Senate (first U.S. first lady to run for public office)

2005—Kuwaiti women gained right to vote, hold office

BORN TODAY

Actor Henry Fonda 1905
Gymnast Olga Korbut 1955

Pianist Liberace 1919
Singer Janet Jackson 1966

Radio host Bob Edwards 1947
Tennis player Gabriela Sabatini . . 1970

Actor Pierce Brosnan 1952
Actress Tori Spelling 1973

UNDER ORDERS

A dynamic missionary leader in India once dined with several naval officers. During the course of the meal, one of the officers asked, "Why don't missionaries just stay home and mind their own business?"

The missionary answered, "Suppose your commanding officer ordered you to set sail tomorrow; would you choose to obey?"

An officer quickly replied, "If we're ordered to go, we must go, even if the prospect meant that every ship would be sunk and every sailor killed."

"Exactly," the missionary agreed. "And I have orders from my Commander, God, to: 'Go and make disciples of all nations'" (Matthew 28:19).

Whose marching orders do you follow—society's, your own, or those of the eternal God in heaven? Remember, nothing is truly lost that is given up for God, and nothing that is gained apart from him will stand the test of time. When we walk with God in answer to his call, we will accomplish great things of eternal significance. And never fear having to go it alone. Jesus promised, "Surely I am with you always, to the very end of the age" (Matthew 28:20).

TODAY'S POWER POINT

Submission to God's will is the softest pillow on which to rest.—Source Unknown

May 17

TODAY IN HISTORY

1792—New York Stock Exchange founded
1848—Seagulls ate crop-destroying locusts, saving Utah Mormons from starvation
1877—First interstate phone call
1954—Racial segregation in U.S. public schools ruled unconstitutional
1955—First U.S. nuclear reactor patent issued
1973—Start of Senate Watergate hearings
1983—Hockey's Stanley Cup won for fourth straight year by New York Islanders
2000—Two suspects arrested in connection with 1963 deaths of four black girls in Birmingham, Alabama, church
2004—Scores of same-sex couples lined up to get married in Massachusetts, first U.S. state to legalize such unions

BORN TODAY

Physician Edward Jenner 1749
Actress Maureen O'Sullivan 1911
Actor Dennis Hopper. 1936
Actor Bill Paxton 1955
Actor and TV host Bob Saget;
    boxer Sugar Ray Leonard 1956
Singer Jordan Knight 1970
Basketball player Tony Parker. . . . 1982

HIGHER LEARNING

Who said education doesn't make you stand a little taller? The Help Wanted ad read, "Wanted: State Troopers. Applicants must be six feet tall with a high school education, or 5' 11" with two years of college."

While education should better the mind, it doesn't necessarily better the person. Neither do a host of other physical or social benchmarks.

Bigger is not always better. Less is sometimes more. All that glitters is not gold. We have a lot of sayings that remind us that traditional ways of judging value are inadequate and often just plain wrong. James 2:8–9 says, "If you really keep the royal law found in Scripture, 'Love your neighbor as yourself,' you are doing right. But if you show favoritism, you sin."

So how good are you at keeping the "royal law"? Do you love your neighbor as yourself—no matter what his or her education? Do you treat everyone with respect and kindness regardless of how tall he is, what she looks like, how popular he is, what kind of car she drives, or whatever his position and status? You know you're more interesting—more worthy of love and respect—than you may look on paper. Just remember, so is the person next door.

TODAY'S POWER POINT

Education is what survives when what has been learned has been forgotten.
—B. F. Skinner

TODAY IN HISTORY

1804—Start of Napoleon's rule of France
1852—First U.S. mandatory-education law enacted (in Massachusetts)
1951—UN headquarters moved to New York City
1974—India tested nuclear device, the sixth nation to do so
1980—Mount St. Helens (in Washington) exploded, first major eruption since
    1857
1994—First genetically altered food (a tomato) authorized for sale
2001—Premiere of animated movie *Shrek*
2004—Alan Greenspan nominated for fifth four-year term to head Federal Reserve

BORN TODAY

Philosopher Bertrand Russell 1872
Director Frank Capra 1897
Composer Meredith Willson 1902
Singer Perry Como 1913
Actor Robert Morse 1931
Baseball player Reggie Jackson . . . 1946
Singer George Strait 1952
Comedy writer Tina Fey 1970

STAYING PROTECTED

The world's greatest enemy, Satan, is roaming constantly—on the lookout for another victim to devour (see 1 Peter 5:8).

Paul Harvey told the story of how Eskimos kill an unsuspecting wolf: the hunter first coats his knife blade with blood and lets it freeze. He then repeats the process again and again until the blade is hidden deeply inside the coating of frozen blood. Finally he buries the knife with the blade sticking up, in the frozen tundra. The wolf, catching the scent of fresh blood, springs to lick it. He licks feverishly, the cold deadening the pain even as the sharpened blade cuts into his tongue. Eventually the wolf bleeds to death.

Satan's traps are just as subtle and just as lethal. Popular movies, television programs, books, video games, and other pleasures may seem like harmless fun. But we must be aware of how the violence, attitudes toward sex, and messages about ethics, morality, and God can subtly take hold in our minds and affect the way we think and behave. Be sure you're protected by God's armor—the belt of truth, the breastplate of righteousness, and the shield of faith. Then you need not fear even the most deadly and clever of Satan's attacks.

TODAY'S POWER POINT

Most people would like to be delivered from temptation but would like it to keep in touch.—Robert Orben

May 19

TODAY IN HISTORY

1536—Execution of Anne Boleyn, mother of Queen Elizabeth I
1780—Near-total darkness descended on New England in midday, cause unknown
1848—Mexico ceded Texas to the United States
1857—Electric fire alarm patented
1921—First opera broadcast on radio
1962—Marilyn Monroe's famed birthday serenade for President John F. Kennedy at Madison Square Garden
1971—Death of American poet Ogden Nash, age sixty-eight
1978—U.S. planes dispatched to Zaire to rescue three thousand foreigners trapped by Communist rebels
2005—New Iraqi government blamed Saddam Hussein for provoking eight-year war with Iran, called for him to be tried for war crimes

BORN TODAY

Philanthropist Johns Hopkins . . . 1795
Activist Malcolm X. 1925
TV journalist James Lehrer. 1934
Actor David Hartman 1937
Writer Nora Ephron. 1941
Musician Peter Townshend. 1945
Wrestler Andre the Giant 1946
Model, and actress Grace Jones. . . 1948
Basketball player Kevin Garnett . . 1976
Actress Rachel Appleton 1992

CASTING YOUR VOTE

Being "for" a candidate for office means little if you don't stand up and take some action—give your money, volunteer—but most importantly, you have to get out and actually cast your vote. Are you actively casting your vote for God by giving him your time, your resources, and your worship? Are you obedient to him, even when it's painful? Even when those around you refuse to be?

General William Booth, founder of the Salvation Army, was once asked the secret of his success. He answered, "I'll tell you the secret; God has had all of me there was to have. There may have been men with greater opportunities, but from the day I got the poor on my heart and a vision of what Christ could do, I made up my mind that God would have all there was of William Booth. . . . God has all the adoration of my heart, all the power of my will, and all the influence of my life."

As Booth concluded, "The greatness of man's power is the measure of his surrender. Don't be satisfied with second best." Cast your vote for God and his kingdom today!

TODAY'S POWER POINT

Democracy is the recurrent suspicion that more than half of the people are right more than half the time.—E. B. White

TODAY IN HISTORY

1895—First motion picture shown publicly
1899—First driver arrested for speeding (in New York City)
1927—Start of Charles Lindbergh's (and the first ever) solo flight across Atlantic
1930—First aircraft launched from a ship
1939—Start of transatlantic air passenger and mail service
1955—First offshore radar station established
1964—First atomic-powered lighthouse
1993—British lawmakers approved European Unity agreement
2002—FBI issued warnings of possible future terrorist attacks against U.S. high-rise buildings
2006—Barry Bonds hit home run 714, tying Babe Ruth for second place in the record books (behind Hank Aaron's record of 755 homers)

BORN TODAY

First Lady Dolly Madison. 1768
Writer Honoré de Balzac 1799
Actor Jimmy Stewart 1908
Actor George Gobel 1919
Hockey player Stan Mikita. 1940

Singer Joe Cocker. 1944
Singer Cher 1946
Actor Bronson Pinchot. 1959
Actor Tony Goldwyn 1960
Rapper Busta Rhymes 1972

SELF-DEFENSE

A young man who found himself in the middle of many fights got tired of the physical and emotional toll it was taking on him. He thought perhaps if he were tougher, stronger, and better able to defend himself, the attacks would stop. So he asked his pastor if he felt it would be wrong for him to study self-defense.

"Certainly not," said the preacher. "In fact, I've learned it myself and found it to be of great value."

"Oh, really," responded the surprised young man. "Which system did you learn?"

"Solomon's system," the pastor said knowingly. "You'll find it in Proverbs 15:1. 'A gentle answer turns away wrath.' It's the most effective system of self-defense I know."

Sometimes, even when we don't intend to, we bring a lot of our troubles on ourselves. No matter how we control our appetites and discipline our bodies, the tongue is a difficult thing to tame. With it we can antagonize others and stir up anger, gush folly, or crush someone's spirit if we're not careful. Or we can bring healing. How will you use your tongue today?

TODAY'S POWER POINT

People grow through experience if they meet life honestly and courageously. This is how character is built.—Eleanor Roosevelt

May 21

TODAY IN HISTORY

1881—Clara Barton launched the American Red Cross
1901—First automobile speeding law enacted by a state (Connecticut)
1927—First solo transatlantic flight completed: Charles Lindbergh landed in Paris
1932—First telecast received in an airplane
1934—Oskaloosa, Iowa, became first U.S. community to fingerprint citizens
1956—United States conducted first airborne test of hydrogen bomb
1985—Frustaci septuplets born: first septuplets born in America (three survived)
2000—Scientists announced thalidomide showed promise in treating AIDS, leprosy, and certain cancers
2001—Firestone stopped selling tires to Ford following Explorer accidents
2003—House and Senate agreed on a $350 billion ten-year tax cut; massive Algerian earthquake killed more than 2,250 people
2005—Thousands of Sunni Arabs formed pact to give them a voice in new Iraqi government

BORN TODAY

Author Alexander Pope	1688	Comedy writer and political satirist	
Aviation pioneer Glenn Curtiss	1878	Al Franken	1951
Financier Armand Hammer	1898	Actor Mr. T	1952
Actor Raymond Burr	1917	Actor Judge Reinhold	1957
Actress Peggy Cass	1924	Actress Ashlie Brillault	1987

ACT TWO

A tale is told of the heroic rescue of the oldest son of Abraham Lincoln. According to the story, Robert Lincoln was about to board a train in New Jersey when he lost his balance just as the train began pulling away. Sensing Robert's plight, a man reached out from the crowded station platform and pulled him to safety.

Later this hero received a personal thank you from a grateful father in the White House. But it was years after the death of the president that the true identity of Robert's rescuer became known. He was the famed Shakespearean actor, Edwin Booth, whose talents were later recognized in the American Hall of Fame. But less than a year after the rescue, Booth went into hiding, ashamed of the actions of his younger brother, John Wilkes Booth, who had assassinated the president.

These two young men were from the same family, but what a contrast in character and deed! May we raise our children to become godly men and women, walking examples of Christ at work in their lives.

TODAY'S POWER POINT

Having a child ends forever a man's boyhood.—Victoria Secunda

TODAY IN HISTORY

1761—First life-insurance policy sold in United States
1841—Reclining chair patented
1947—Launch of the Truman Doctrine
1961—First revolving restaurant opened (in Seattle)
1972—First U.S. president to visit Soviet Union (Richard Nixon)
1993—First movie broadcast on the Internet
2002—Former Klansman Bobby Cherry sentenced to life in prison for the murder of four black girls in 1963 Birmingham church bombing

BORN TODAY

Composer Richard Wagner 1813
Writer Sir Arthur Conan Doyle . . 1859
Actor Laurence Olivier 1907
Author Garry Wills 1934

Actress Susan Strasberg;
    actor Richard Benjamin 1938
Actor Paul Winfield 1941
Actress Naomi Campbell 1970

BEYOND THE GLASS

Whatever your lot in life—whether you're a king or a beggar—it's nothing compared with what your life can be like in heaven. The very best of this earth is but a poor reflection, a pale shadow of the joys that are to come.

A poor youngster in London was left in the care of a cruel, drunken woman who forced him to beg. When he didn't bring home enough coins, she beat and mistreated him. The youngster's greatest joy in life was to look at the many beautiful things displayed in the store windows, especially the toy store. Always the window stood between the child and the toy soldiers that so drew his interest. He knew they could never be his—the glass kept them within sight, but always out of reach.

One day the unfortunate boy was struck by a passing car and was rushed to the hospital. After several days in a coma, the boy awoke to find other children recovering nearby. Looking around, he could scarcely believe his eyes as he discovered a box of toy soldiers by his bed just for him. He took out the soldiers one by one, exclaiming in joyful amazement, "There's no glass between!"

Imagine the joy you will experience in heaven, when you will no longer "see through a glass, darkly" (1 Corinthians 13:12 KJV). Then our greatest joys and dearest hopes will be real, for we will see God face to face.

TODAY'S POWER POINT

What can you say about a society that says that God is dead and Elvis is alive?
—Irv Kupcinet

May 23

TODAY IN HISTORY

1788—Eighth state, South Carolina, admitted to the Union
1903—First transcontinental trip by car
1911—Opening of New York Public Library
1960—Nazi leader Adolf Eichmann captured by Israeli agents
1984—Surgeon General linked lung damage to secondhand smoke
1988—First statewide ban on handguns enacted (Maryland)
2002—Researchers identified hormone believed related to obesity
2005—President George W. Bush met with Afghani president Hamid Karzai about combating terrorism and eradicating opium trade in Afghanistan

BORN TODAY

Actor Douglas Fairbanks Sr. 1883
Musician Artie Shaw 1910
Singer Helen O'Connell. 1920
Singer Rosemary Clooney 1928
Actress Joan Collins 1933
Boxer Marvin Hagler 1954
Actor Drew Carey;
    author Mitch Albom. 1958
Jeopardy winner Ken Jennings. . . . 1974
Actress Kelly Monaco 1976

FEEDING THE HUNGRY

A story was told of New York City's legendary mayor, Fiorello LaGuardia. Earlier in his career, LaGuardia presided over a police court where, one day, they brought in a troubled old man. The distraught soul was charged with stealing a loaf of bread to feed his starving family. After hearing the case, La Guardia found the man guilty and reluctantly fined him ten dollars. Then, reaching down into his own pocket, LaGuardia pulled out a ten-dollar bill saying, "And I hereby pay the fine in full."

But LaGuardia still was not done. The mayor then ordered the bailiff to "fine" everyone in the courtroom fifty cents for living in a town where a man had to steal in order to survive. After the hat was passed, LaGuardia ordered the bailiff to give the collection to the poor old man, who left the courtroom with $47.50—more than a week's wage in those days.

How sensitive are you to those less fortunate? Do you do what you can to share your food with the hungry and to provide the poor wanderer with shelter? Never forget that it was with the poor that Jesus spent most of his days on earth. Should you love the poor any less?

TODAY'S POWER POINT

He who is dying of hunger must be fed rather than taught.—Thomas Aquinas

TODAY IN HISTORY

1844—First telegraph message sent
1883—Brooklyn Bridge opened, linking Manhattan and Brooklyn
1931—First air-conditioned train put into service
1935—Cincinnati hosted first nighttime baseball game
1941—Germans sank HMS *Hood*, world's largest battleship
1985—West Germany launched joint investigation with Israel to locate Nazi war
    criminal Josef Mengele
1995—Premiere of movie *Braveheart*
2000—U.S. House approved normalized trade with China
2001—Sherpa Temba Tsheri, age fifteen, became youngest person to reach the
    summit of Mount Everest
2006—Taylor Hicks chosen new *American Idol* winner

BORN TODAY

Publisher Samuel Newhouse 1895
Actor Tommy Chong 1938
Singer Bob Dylan 1941
Actress Patti LaBelle 1944
Actress Priscilla Presley 1945
Singer Rosanne Cash 1955
Basketball player Joe Dumar 1963
Singer Billy Gilman 1988

SHARING YOUR FAITH

Have you ever noticed how God often uses a setback to carry out his will? One such story involves a young woman who had just graduated college and was packing her car to leave for home the next day. But when she awoke the next morning she discovered, to her horror, that her car and all its contents were nowhere to be found. Although police located her vehicle a few days later, it had been vandalized, and anything of value was gone.

But the story doesn't end there. What for most of us would have been an emotionally draining, frustrating experience, God used for good. The police officer who was taking the young woman's report noticed a serenity in her that puzzled him. This led to a conversation in which the officer acknowledged that although he was a regular church attendee, he had not found the tranquility and assurance that this woman displayed. Thus the young graduate, who might have been concentrating on her losses, instead shared her faith and led the officer to a closer walk with God.

Remember, people are watching you each day, looking to see evidence of God's love in your life. Let your life reflect the difference that can lead them to the Savior.

TODAY'S POWER POINT

When you have nothing left but God, then for the first time you become aware that God is enough.—Maude Royden

May 25

TODAY IN HISTORY

1790—First U.S. copyright law enacted
1793—First U.S. Catholic priest ordained
1829—First letter written on a typewriter
1935—Babe Ruth hit his last home run
1950—Brooklyn Battery Tunnel opened
1963—Organization of African States founded
1969—Premiere of movie *Midnight Cowboy*
1982—Supreme Court upheld mandatory sex education in New Jersey
1992—Jay Leno became regular host of the *Tonight Show*
2002—Pakistan's missile tests sparked international outcry, tensions with India grew

BORN TODAY

Poet Ralph W. Emerson 1803
Trumpeter Miles Davis. 1926
Novelist Robert Ludlum. 1927
Singer Beverly Sills 1929
Actor Ian McKellen 1939
Puppeteer Frank Oz 1944

Actress Connie Sellecca 1955
Comedian Mike Myers. 1963
Actor Jamie Kennedy 1970
Singer Lauryn Hill 1975
Football player Brian Urlacher . . . 1978

FIRST THINGS FIRST

Have you ever put in a long day of driving only to spot a "No Vacancy" sign just as you'd hoped to turn in for the night? With today's online reservations and multiple accommodations at nearly every highway exit, that may not be the problem it once was. Yet a similar thing can happen in life when we let other things interfere with our relationship with God, leaving little room in our lives for him.

With the hustle of daily living, family members going every which way, and the stresses of ever-increasing outside activities all vying for our attention and time, it's all too easy to let spiritual matters slide. Few believers intend to forget God; but that's exactly what can happen over time. Hopefully we'll wake up in time and get our priorities right before God gives a "wake up" call of his own to help us recognize our daily need for him.

Have you made room (and time) for God in your life today? If not, make seeking God a priority today and every day.

TODAY'S POWER POINT

If Christ is kept outside, something must be wrong inside.—Richard DeHaan

May 26

TODAY IN HISTORY

1538—Religious reformer John Calvin expelled from Geneva
1830—Indian Removal Act passed
1913—First comprehensive college senior exams introduced
1934—First train to complete one-thousand-mile nonstop trip
1956—First bank branch to open in a trailer
1977—George Willig successfully scaled 110-story World Trade Center (1,350 feet)
2004—Following federal court conviction, Oklahoma state court found Terry
       Nichols guilty on 161 first-degree murder counts

BORN TODAY

Singer Al Jolson 1886
Actor John Wayne 1907
Singer Peggy Lee. 1920
Actor James Arness. 1923
Sportscaster Brent Musburger. . . . 1939

Singer Hank Williams Jr.;
    actor Philip Michael Thomas . 1949
Astronaut Sally Ride. 1951
Actress Genie Francis 1962
Singer Lenny Kravitz 1964

VICTORY

The first time most people in America heard of Monty Hall was when he hosted the popular game show *Let's Make a Deal*. His seemed like a classic story of rising from obscurity to success overnight. But Hall set the record straight: "Actually, I'm an overnight success, but it took twenty years." Success is like that. A moment of victory is won only after endless days or years of preparation, faithful plodding, and perseverance.

The Bible relates that when Jesus told the discouraged fishermen to cast their nets again, it was in the same place where they'd already been fishing but had caught nothing? Have you ever thought, *If only I could get away to some other place, winning would be so much easier. . . . If only I could be someone else, go somewhere else, or do something else, it might not be so difficult to have courage and faith?*

For most of us, today will bring the same old difficulties we faced yesterday, and the day before. But remember, it is God who gives us strength to face them and to gain victory in the end.

Are you facing a difficult situation? Don't give up! No matter how long you've languished without seeing victory, regardless of how pointless your struggle feels, never give up the fight. No enemy can separate us from Christ's love. "We are more than conquerors through him who loved us" (Romans 8:37).

TODAY'S POWER POINT

Victory belongs to the most persevering.—Napoleon Bonaparte

May 27

TODAY IN HISTORY

1647—First U.S. execution for witchcraft
1703—St. Petersburg founded by Tsar Peter the Great
1896—First intercollegiate bicycle race
1911—New motorboat speed record set (42 mph)
1937—Cellophane tape patented
2001—Largest tax cut in twenty years negotiated by House-Senate committee
2004—U.S. appeals court in San Francisco ruled that federal government cannot
punish assisted-suicide doctors in states allowing the practice; Surgeon
General expanded list of smoking-related illnesses to include pancreatic,
stomach, kidney, and cervical cancers

BORN TODAY

Writer Julia Ward Howe. 1819
Writer Rachel Carson. 1907
Novelist Herman Wouk 1915
Statesman Henry Kissinger. 1923
Actress Lee Meriwether;
    musician Ramsey Lewis 1935

Actor Lou Gossett Jr. 1936
Actor Todd Bridges. 1965
Baseball player Jeff Bagwell. 1968
Actor Joseph Fiennes 1970
Chef Jamie Oliver. 1975

TAKING A PASS

A certain race-car driver was world renowned for being the best. He'd won all the
great races of Europe with his aggressive jockeying and heavy foot, and yet he was
a complete gentleman on the highway. Upon recognizing him, young men would
often drive up alongside him, rev their engines, and try to lure him into a race,
but he never gave in. In fact, if he noticed someone edging around him to pass—
perhaps just to brag that he had passed the great racer—he would deliberately ease
below the speed limit and let the other driver go by, sacrificing his pride to be a
good example. This master speedster could have passed them all in a flash, yet he
held his talents in check so he wouldn't break the law or take part in something in
which someone who was not as skilled a driver might get hurt.

Will you do the same? Are you willing to sacrifice your prestige, your freedom,
or your fun for something better? All believers enjoy Christian liberty—they are
free to do as they choose but are bound by a love for God to do only those things
that are pleasing to him. What are some things you should voluntarily give up in
order to please God or set an example for others?

TODAY'S POWER POINT

Be wary of the man who urges an action in which he himself incurs no risk.
—Joaquin Setanti

TODAY IN HISTORY

1796—United States banned prison terms for debtors

1929—First color-and-sound motion picture premiered

1934—First surviving quintuplets born (Dionne quintuplets)

1940—More than 300,000 Allied troops began evacuation from France to England

1967—First solo sail around the world, completed by Francis Chichester (age sixty-five) in 220 days

1978—First casino outside Nevada opened (in Atlantic City, New Jersey)

2002—Russia accepted as junior NATO member

2003—President George W. Bush signed third largest tax cut in U.S. history

BORN TODAY

Naturalist Jean Louis Agassiz 1807

Athlete Jim Thorpe. 1888

Writer Ian Fleming. 1908

Actress Carroll Baker 1931

Singer Gladys Knight 1944

Singer John Fogerty 1945

Basketball player Glen Rice 1967

Actor Jesse Bradford 1979

BALANCE

Shortly after the death of Howard Hughes, someone asked a reporter how much money the multimillionaire had left behind. The prompt reply: "Why, he left it all."

Since we can't take money with us, there seems little point in devoting much time and effort pursuing it. As Charles H. Spurgeon thoughtfully noted, "Life is not sufficiently long to enable a man to get rich and do his duty to his fellow man at the same time."

Money is necessary, but we must keep a well-balanced attitude that keeps money in its proper place. Money is certainly not the most important thing and, if we're not wise about its use, can even become a snare. Ecclesiastes 7:11–12 says, "Wisdom, like an inheritance, is a good thing. . . . Wisdom is a shelter as money is a shelter, but the advantage of knowledge is this: that wisdom preserves the life of its possessor."

Remember, all that we have—or ever will have—comes from God, who owns all things. We are merely stewards, temporary managers, of the things God has allowed us to accumulate here on earth.

TODAY'S POWER POINT

Money has never made man happy, nor will it. There is nothing in its nature to produce happiness. The more of it one has, the more one wants.—Benjamin Franklin

May 29

TODAY IN HISTORY

1790—Thirteenth state, Rhode Island, added to Union
1848—Thirtieth state, Wisconsin, added to Union
1909—First domestic-relations court established
1919—Pop-up toaster introduced
1953—Edmund Hillary and Tensing Norgay became first climbers to reach the peak of Mount Everest
1977—A. J. Foyt won record fourth Indianapolis 500 race
1989—Student protesters in China made Statue of Liberty replica
1990—Boris Yeltsin elected president of Russian Republic
2000—*Atlantis* space shuttle made safe night landing at Cape Canaveral after mission to International Space Station
2003—Researchers successfully cloned mule in Idaho
2004—National World War II memorial dedicated in Washington DC

BORN TODAY

Patriot Patrick Henry 1736
Actor Bob Hope. 1903
President John F. Kennedy 1917
Auto racer Al Unser 1939
Actor Anthony Geary. 1948
Singer LaToya Jackson 1956
Actress Annette Bening. 1958
Baseball player Eric Davis. 1962
Actress and author Lisa Whelchel. 1963
Singer Melanie Janine Brown 1975

ETERNITY

Said to be the oldest comedy in literature, *The Acharnians* centers on the plight of an honest citizen who, disgusted at the wars going on around him, makes peace with the enemy. This leaves him in a position to enjoy the blessings of peace while war rages all around him.

Those who follow God are like that citizen. While violence, wars, and troubles rage in our world, we need not be afraid. We've made our peace with the King, so we can enjoy serenity and all the blessings of God here on earth while we wait to spend eternity in blessed fellowship with him. Jesus said, "Do not let your hearts be troubled. Trust in God; trust also in me. . . . And if I go and prepare a place for you, I will come back and take you to be with me that you also may be where I am" (John 14:1, 3).

Now that's a treasure that will last for eternity.

TODAY'S POWER POINT

Our Lord has written the promise of the resurrection, not in books alone, but in every leaf in springtime.—Martin Luther

TODAY IN HISTORY

1431—Joan of Arc burned at the stake
1848—Ice-cream freezer patented
1959—Roger Ward won record $100,000 in Indianapolis 500
1960—Nigeria granted independence by Great Britain
1974—President Richard Nixon was warned that refusal to turn over tapes of White House conversations could be grounds for impeachment
1998—Nuclear tests launched by Pakistan
2000—Northern Ireland parliament restored after Sinn Fein's promise to disarm
2002—FBI emphasis shifted from domestic crimes to counterterrorism
2003—Premiere of *Finding Nemo*

BORN TODAY

Czar Peter the Great 1672
Jeweler Carl Fabergé 1846
Voice actor Mel Blanc 1908
Musician Benny Goodman 1909
Restaurateur Bob Evans 1918
Actor Michael Pollard 1939
Football player Gale Sayers 1943
Actress Meredith MacRae 1945
Actor Colm Meaney 1953
Actor Ted McGinley 1958
Singer Wynonna Judd 1964
Baseball player Manny Ramirez . . 1972
Actor Blake Bashoff 1981

KEEPING GOING

A young man once volunteered to teach a boys' Sunday-school class. The boys enjoyed their teacher's kindness and friendship, but it wasn't long before the youthful teacher grew tired of the responsibility and decided to give it up. As he neared the classroom before his last class, however, he overheard a conversation between two of his students.

The first boy said he planned to stop coming to Sunday school because the teacher was going to quit soon anyway. The other youth spoke up, "He won't quit the class. He told us that God had sent him to teach us and that God was his boss and he had to do his will—he won't give it up."

Humbled, the young man could not go through with his plan to quit.

How often are you tempted to give up, even though you know that God has called you to serve him? Hold on! Tell God you're tired or discouraged, and ask him to help you. He'll give you the ability and the strength you need to do his will. Fully surrender yourself and your will to God, and he will carry you through.

TODAY'S POWER POINT

I know God is alive. I spoke with him this morning.—Source Unknown

May 31

TODAY IN HISTORY

1821—First U.S. cathedral dedicated (in Baltimore)
1853—First Arctic expedition by a U.S. explorer
1889—Johnstown, Pennsylvania, flood: two-thousand people drowned
1919—First wedding on an airplane
1938—First televised movie
1962—Nazi leader Adolph Eichmann executed by Israel
1982—Argentine forces' final stand in the Falkland Islands
1985—British soccer schedule cancelled due to excessive fan violence
1990—Premiere of *Seinfeld*
2003—Atlanta Olympics bombing suspect Eric Rudolph arrested in North Carolina
2006—Katie Couric's final broadcast on *Today*

BORN TODAY

Poet Walt Whitman 1819
Author Norman Vincent Peale . . . 1898
Actor Clint Eastwood. 1930
Singer Peter Yarrow 1938
Author Theodore Baehr 1946
Actress Lea Thompson 1961
Actress Brooke Shields 1965
Baseball player Kenny Lofton. . . . 1967
Musician Christian McBride 1972
Actor Colin Farrell 1976

GOOD COMPANY

The famed German banker Baron Louis von Rothschild was once given a letter of introduction from a young man who was visiting London. The famed banker stated that he regretted not having a position of employment to offer and walked the chap to the door. But the youth was determined to get hired. Later that day he returned and asked the personnel director for a job.

"Aren't you the young man I saw walking with the baron this morning?" the director asked.

When the youth acknowledged that he was, the banker replied, "Well then, you were in very good company. I consider that sufficient recommendation." He hired the young man on the spot.

Are you walking with God? If so, you, too, are in good company. Walking with God wins you more than a job—it brings adoption into God's family as a son or daughter. "The Spirit himself testifies with our spirit that we are God's children. Now if we are children, then we are heirs—heirs of God and co-heirs with Christ" (Romans 8:16–17).

TODAY'S POWER POINT

God gives every bird its food, but he does not throw it into its nest.—J. G. Holland

TODAY IN HISTORY

1638—First recorded earthquake in the United States (in Massachusetts)
1792—Fifteenth and sixteenth states, Kentucky and Tennessee, admitted to Union
1938—Superman comic first published
1980—Premiere of CNN; death of Charles Nielsen, age eighty-three, inventor of
     TV ratings
2003—President George W. Bush met with G-7 leaders
2004—Newly formed Iraqi cabinet took over in Baghdad; Partial Birth Abortion
     Ban Act ruled unconstitutional by San Francisco judge

BORN TODAY

Explorer Pere Marquette. 1637
Mormon leader Brigham Young . . 1801
Actor Andy Griffith;
   actress Marilyn Monroe 1926
Singer Pat Boone 1934
Actor Morgan Freeman 1940
Actor Jonathan Pryce 1947
Singer Alanis Morissette 1974

LATER THAN EVER

Have you heard the story of the little boy who loved to visit his grandma? He was especially impressed with the chiming grandfather clock prominently displayed in her living room. As noon approached, the boy watched the clock, anxiously awaiting the chimes. When the gongs sounded, he patiently counted them aloud: ". . . four, five, six, seven . . ."

But then a strange thing happened. After chiming for the twelfth time, it kept going. Thirteen, fourteen, fifteen. The bells rang on and on, much to the youth's amazement.

"Grandma, Grandma," he shouted, running into the kitchen. "It's later than it has ever been before."

What hour is the clock tolling for you? Is it still in the early morning of youth, the long afternoon of middle age, or in the twilight of old age? No matter what the clock says, or how much time we think remains for us, we would be wise to remember that tomorrow is never certain. All we have is today to take care of what's important in life. It truly is later than it has ever been before. Are you ready for what comes next?

TODAY'S POWER POINT

People who never have any time on their hands are those who do the least.
—Georg Lichtenberg

June 2

TODAY IN HISTORY

1857—Chain-stitch sewing machine patented
1886—First president married in the White House (Grover Cleveland)
1896—Marconi wireless radio patented
1930—Opening of first maritime museum
1933—Franklin D. Roosevelt had swimming pool installed in White House
1953—Coronation of Britain's Queen Elizabeth II
1979—Final report of assassination commission backed JFK plot theory
1987—Alan Greenspan named to head Federal Reserve Board
1997—Timothy McVeigh convicted of Oklahoma City bombing
2003—FCC eased rules restricting media ownership by large corporations

BORN TODAY

Author Thomas Hardy 1840
Composer Edward Elgar. 1857
Astronaut Charles Conrad Jr. 1930
Actress Sally Kellerman. 1936
Musician Charlie Watts 1941
Composer Marvin Hamlisch 1944
Actor Jerry Mathers 1948
Comedian Dana Carvey. 1955
Race-car driver Kyle Petty. 1960

GOING HOME

Though many young men and women have ventured out on their own in search of the good life, for most the pull of home is strong, and memories of home are among their fondest. Ironically, the writer of the song "Home Sweet Home," John Howard Payne, was homeless most of his life, losing both parents while yet in his teens. He once told how the words came to him while walking through the exclusive neighborhoods of London, a drifter. Occasionally he would hear the words of his song wafting from a luxurious townhouse window while he, cold and lonely, had no place to call his home.

Scientists tell us that it's not just humans who are attracted to home. A bee, taken from its hive, finds its way home. A salmon swims upstream to the waters where it was spawned to reproduce or die in the effort to get home. Migrating birds instinctively return to their homelands each year. Likewise dogs and cats, though taken far from their homes, will often return—sometimes making difficult journeys of many months and hundreds of miles.

God has placed within each of us a special homing instinct that calls us back to family and home. Have you felt that homing instinct drawing you to God? He lovingly calls you to follow him to a special place where you are loved, where you belong, and where you are always welcome. Follow God's leading, and you'll soon be home.

TODAY'S POWER POINT

Be it ever so humble, there's no place like home.—John Howard Payne

June 3

TODAY IN HISTORY

1621—First settlers arrived in what is now New York
1916—Congress established Reserve Officers' Training Corps (ROTC)
1942—U.S. victory over Japanese in battle of Midway
1972—First woman rabbi ordained, by the Reformed movement
1975—U.S. ruling established equal educational opportunities for men and women
2003—Leaders of five Arab nations—Saudi Arabia, Egypt, Jordan, Bahrain, and
    Palestine—agreed to reduce Middle East violence
2004—Army announced plans to withdraw two divisions from Germany

BORN TODAY

Author William Hone 1780
Confederate president Jefferson Davis
. . . . 1808
Actor Tony Curtis. 1925
Poet Allen Ginsberg 1926
Producer Chuck Barris 1929
Composer Charles Hart 1961
Tennis player Jan-Michael Gambill
. . . . 1977

LIFE'S TRIALS

Often God lets us exhaust all human resources before he comes to our aid. Captain Eddie Rickenbacker's experience illustrates this truth. In October 1942 Rickenbacker and seven other men were on a B-17 that ran out of gas and crashed into the Pacific. Adrift at sea in a small raft under a blazing sun, perilously close to enemy territory, the situation was dire. Their only food was four small oranges. By the eighth day the men's condition was critical. Rickenbacker rallied the crew to turn to God for comfort and aid. Since they could do nothing to help themselves, they prayed and sought God's help.

Then a strange thing happened—a seagull landed on Rickenbacker's head. Carefully he caught the bird and divided it up for dinner. Fashioning crude fishhooks and bait from the gull's remains, the survivors were able to catch a few fish. Later they caught rainwater that provided two sips of water per man per day. Finally, after more than three grueling weeks adrift, a passing airplane spotted and rescued the stranded airmen.

Why would God send a miracle of a seagull rather than sending an early rescue—or even keeping the plane from crashing? We may never know. But according to Rickenbacker, every person on the raft turned to God through that experience. Not one left the sea an atheist. The trials in our lives often drive us into God's loving arms. That's reason enough to embrace them.

TODAY'S POWER POINT

When Heaven is about to confer a great office on any man, it first exercises his mind with suffering, and his sinews and bones with toil.—Mencius

June 4

TODAY IN HISTORY

1825—Gaslight first demonstrated
1917—Initial Pulitzer Prizes awarded
1934—USS *Ranger* commissioned as first U.S. Navy aircraft carrier
1942—Start of battle of Midway
1944—Rome freed from Nazi occupation
1985—Supreme Court ruled against "moment of silence" in U.S. public schools
1989—Chinese troops opened fire on student protestors in Tiananmen Square
1998—Terry Nichols sentenced to life in prison for his part in Oklahoma City bombing
2000—U.S. president Bill Clinton and Russian president Vladimir Putin agreed to dispose of thirty-four tons of weapons-grade plutonium
2002—Britons celebrated Queen Elizabeth's fifty-year reign
2003—House of Representatives voted to ban D&C abortions; TV homemaker Martha Stewart indicted on various charges over 2001 stock sale

BORN TODAY

Britain's King George III 1738
Singer Robert Merrill 1917
Actor Dennis Weaver 1924
Singer Michelle Phillips 1944
Actor Parker Stevenson 1953
Tennis player Andrea Jaeger 1965
Actor Noah Wyle 1971
Actress Angelina Jolie 1975

DEDICATION

A little boy had a problem—he kept falling out of bed. No matter what his parents tried, the little fellow would roll out onto the floor in the middle of the night. When an uncle came to visit, he asked the youngster why he fell out so frequently. The lad thought a moment and then replied, "I don't know—unless it's that I stay too close to where I get in."

That sounds like the problem with some Christians. Yes, they believe in God, but they're staying so close to where they "got in" that they're doing little for God. Engineer and inventor Charles F. Kettering once said: "I don't want anyone who just 'has a job' working for me." Rather, Kettering sought a worker "whom a job has." The distinction is important, especially when it comes to working for God. Rather than being content to simply put in your time as a Christian, wouldn't it be better to be so enthusiastic about doing something for God that it becomes the driving force in your life day after day?

TODAY'S POWER POINT

I do the very best I know how—the very best I can; and I mean to keep on doing so until the end.—Abraham Lincoln

TODAY IN HISTORY

1783—First hot-air balloon flight
1947—President Truman unveiled Marshall Plan for rebuilding Europe
1968—Senator Robert F. Kennedy shot by Sirhan Sirhan
1975—Suez canal reopened for first time since 1967 Arab-Israeli war
1981—AIDS first identified
1991—Apartheid laws repealed in South Africa
2002—Space shuttle *Endeavor* launched, carrying new crew to International Space
        Station
2003—Two top *New York Times* officials resign in wake of plagiarism scandal

BORN TODAY

Philosopher Adam Smith 1723
Economist John Maynard Keynes. 1883
Actor William Boyd (Hopalong Cassidy)
. . . . 1895
Journalist Bill Moyers. 1934
Novelist Ken Follett 1949
Actor Mark Wahlberg. 1971
Actor Chad Allen 1974

STEADFAST DETERMINATION

In politics, as in religion, it's important to state what we believe and stand firm on that belief despite any opposition. A traveler was once walking a lonely jungle path in the gloom of night when he encountered a man coming from the opposite direction.

"Did you know the bridge is gone?" the man asked.

"No," the traveler answered. "What makes you think it's so?"

"I heard a report to that effect this afternoon, though I'm not really sure it's true," the man admitted.

Unconvinced, the traveler proceeded on toward the gorge and the rushing river below. As he neared the canyon, he encountered a second man who exclaimed, "Sir, the bridge is out. I was just there and barely escaped with my life!"

Convinced by the urgency of his cry and his earnest gestures, the traveler turned back and was safe. What had made the difference? The steadfast determination of the second man, certain of his own personal experience, convinced the traveler of the danger he would face at the missing bridge. When you speak about God, which traveler best matches your level of determination to warn others and the believability of your personal experience? Based on your testimony, would someone heed the warning and turn from danger or continue on toward certain disaster, unconvinced?

TODAY'S POWER POINT

The difference between the impossible and the possible lies in determination.
—Tommy Lasorda

June 6

TODAY IN HISTORY

1844—Founding of Young Men's Christian Association (YMCA)
1892—Elevated trains start operation in Chicago
1918—United States scored its first World War I victory (at Belleau Wood, France)
1933—Opening of first drive-in theatre (in Camden, New Jersey)
1934—Securities and Exchange Commission (SEC) instituted by Congress
1944—D-Day invasion launched on Normandy beach
1968—Senator Robert Kennedy died one day after being shot by assassin
1976—Death of billionaire J. Paul Getty, age eighty-three
1978—Premiere of television news program *20/20*
2000—Australian telescope created first space map
2001—Jury awarded record $3 billion damages to forty-year smoker
2002—Department of Homeland Security proposed
2004—Leaders of seven Western industrial nations met to observe sixtieth anniversary of D-Day invasion

BORN TODAY

Artist Diego Velazquez 1599
Patriot Nathan Hale 1755
Explorer Robert F. Scott 1868
Physician Paul Dudley White 1896

Tennis player Bjorn Borg;
    musician Kenny G 1956
Actor Paul Giamatti 1967
Newscaster Natalie Morales 1972

OUR INVISIBLE SHIELD

God protects us from harm, and often we don't even know the full extent of his protection. An offering had just been taken at a church when a robber came forward and grabbed it. Church ushers raced after the man, and a scuffle ensued. Angered, the robber pulled a gun on his pursuers and pulled the trigger. Miraculously the weapon did not fire. Checking the gun later, police discovered it was indeed loaded: they could find no reason for it not to fire. Perhaps it was God's "invisible shield" serving as a barrier to protect his people from harm.

That brings to mind the Bible story of Daniel in the lion's den. He had been faithful to God, so God surrounded him in his hour of need with an "invisible shield," and the lions' mouths remained shut.

God hasn't changed. He is still able—and willing—to protect and rescue from danger and harm. He stands ready to meet your needs and carry you through today's trials when you trust in him.

TODAY'S POWER POINT

Trust God in the dark. He will change your midnight into music.—Paul Van Gorder

TODAY IN HISTORY

1769—Daniel Boone launched Kentucky exploration
1942—Japanese took control of three Alaskan islands: Attu, Agattu, and Kiska
1955—Premiere of *$64,000 Question* quiz show
1975—Ban on contraception overturned by Supreme Court; VCR introduced
1983—Philadelphia Phillies pitcher Steve Carlton set record with 3,526th career strikeout
2002—U.S. missionary Martin Burnham killed in guerrilla firefight in Philippines
2004—Nine Iraqi militia groups agreed to disband
2006—Leader of al Qaeda in Iraq, Abu Musab al Zarqawi, killed in U.S. airstrike

BORN TODAY

Fashion trendsetter Beau Brummell 1778
Artist Paul Gauguin 1848
Conductor George Szell 1897
Singer and actor Dean Martin . . . 1917
Singer Tom Jones 1940

Poet Nikki Giovanni 1943
Talk-show host Jenny Jones 1946
Actor Liam Neeson 1952
Basketball player Allen Iverson . . . 1975
Tennis player Anna Kournikova . . 1981

A SERVANT OF GOD

A visitor once asked how he might recognize George Washington at a meeting of the Continental Congress. The gentleman was told, "General Washington is the man who kneels when the Continental Congress stops for prayer." What a fine way to be remembered—as the person who kneels to pray. History records how God honored the prayers of General Washington and blessed his steadfast leadership in winning the American colonies their freedom.

Another man of humble spirit was missionary Hudson Taylor, who was once introduced at a crowded meeting as "our illustrious guest." After the applause subsided, Taylor slowly rose, the light of Christ shining in his face, and said, "Dear friends, I am only the little servant of an illustrious Master." Taylor had his priorities right.

It often does us well to consider our humble roots, lest pride overtake us. Visitors to the famed Thomas Road Baptist Church are often amazed to learn that the congregation, now numbering in the tens of thousands, began with just thirty-five people meeting in a defunct bottling plant. So that no one would forget the church's humble beginnings, a plaque was placed on the tiny building, marking the unassuming setting in which this great church began.

Lest we become proud, let us simply recall where we were when God rescued us.

TODAY'S POWER POINT

Prayer is the key of the morning and the bolt of the evening.—Mahatma Gandhi

TODAY IN HISTORY

1786—First ice cream sold commercially in United States
1869—Vacuum cleaner patented
1872—First mail-fraud law passed by Congress
1939—George VI became first British monarch to visit United States
1965—U.S. forces committed to combat Vietcong in South Vietnam
1968—James Earl Ray charged with murder of Dr. Martin Luther King Jr.
1982—Ronald Reagan gave first U.S. presidential address to British parliament
1998—Actor Charlton Heston elected head of National Rifle Association
2003—Poland voters approved plan to join European Union
2004—UN Security Council approved transfer of power to Iraqis
2006—First-ever cancer vaccine (for cervical cancer) approved by FDA

BORN TODAY

Composer Robert Schumann 1810
Architect Frank Lloyd Wright 1867
Supreme Court Justice Byron White
. . . . 1917
First Lady Barbara Bush 1925
Singer James Darren 1936

Comedienne Joan Rivers 1937
Musician Boz Scaggs 1944
World Wide Web inventor Tim
Berners-Lee 1955
Tennis player Kim Clijsters 1983

SELF-CONTROL

Just as in a maturing democracy power is transferred to local authorities, so maturing individuals rely more and more on internal control (self-control) and less on outside authority. This is especially true in spiritual matters.

A missionary asked a young man who had recently been converted to describe how he felt. The man, tapping himself on the chest, replied: "Two dogs are always fighting inside there. The one is a good dog; the other is a bad dog, and they fight all the time."

The missionary went on to explain that believers still have their old sinful nature to deal with after they become Christians, so he asked the convert, "Which dog wins when they fight?"

The young convert replied, "The one I say 'Sic 'em' to."

That young man had it right. Believers can be victorious over daily temptations, but we must first realize that we still have to grapple with our old nature. However, with God's help, we can gain the victory. Which nature will dominate is up to us. We are the ones who determine which side will triumph.

To which nature are you saying. "Sic 'em"?

TODAY'S POWER POINT

Self-respect is the fruit of discipline; the sense of dignity grows with the ability to say no to oneself.—Abraham Heschel

TODAY IN HISTORY

1934—Donald Duck introduced by Walt Disney
1959—U.S. Navy launched first ballistic missile submarine, USS *George Washington*
1969—Warren Burger confirmed as Supreme Court Chief Justice
1978—Mormons first allowed African American men into the priesthood
1986—Report confirmed *Challenger* disaster was caused by failure of an O-ring seal on the solid rocket, causing the explosion that killed the entire crew
1999—Serbian forces agreed to withdraw from Kosovo
2003—Britain rejected euro as currency
2004—New Iraqi president, Ghazi al-Yawar, greeted by world leaders at G-8 summit

BORN TODAY

Composer Cole Porter 1891
Conductor Fred Waring 1900
Actor Robert Cummings 1908
Guitarist Les Paul. 1915
Comedian Jackie Mason. 1934
Sportscaster Dick Vitale 1939
Actor Michael J. Fox 1961
Actor Johnny Depp 1963
Actress Gloria Reuben 1964
Basketball player Peja Stojakovic. . 1977

GODLY LOVE

Once there was a poor young farmer who had little of this world's wealth yet truly experienced godly love. The man had little education and was not likely to extend his influence much beyond his local community, yet he was blessed with a godly, loving wife "radiant in face and beautiful in form . . . who loved her husband with a great outpouring of service, admiration, and delight."

Telling the story, John R. Rice continued, "I thought to myself how blessed he is. No king on the throne could have healthier, happier, more beautiful children, nor be better taught or better mannered. That young farmer was not poor. He was rich beyond expression. God had flooded his life with 'loving-kindness and tender mercies.'"

What a blessing from God—to love and be loved tenderly, wholly, and unconditionally. If you are blessed with family and friends who love you like this, you are rich beyond measure. But even those not blessed with such true earthly love can experience and understand pure godly love at its best. Think of how much Christ loves you and how his sacrificial death demonstrated the ultimate height and depth of love. No matter what your upbringing or childhood experience, it's still true that God loves you. Regardless of who you are or what you've done, God's love for you is greater than you could possibly fathom. He loves you totally. He'll love you forever.

TODAY'S POWER POINT

God proved his love on the cross . . . it was God saying to the world, I love you.—Billy Graham

TODAY IN HISTORY

323 BC—Death of Alexander the Great, age thirty-three
1935—Alcoholics Anonymous founded
1943—Ballpoint pen patented
1944—At age fifteen, pitcher Joe Nuxhall became youngest major-league baseball player
1948—Test pilot Chuck Yeager broke sound barrier
1977—First Apple II computer shipped
1979—First directly elected European parliament; Pope John Paul II said mass for more than one million Poles in his former homeland
1985—Israelis began withdrawing from Lebanon after three years of destroying guerrilla bases
2000—Syrian president Hafez al-Assad died suddenly, dampening hopes for renewed peace talks with Israel

BORN TODAY

Actress Hattie McDaniel 1889
England's Prince Philip. 1921
Singer and actress Judy Garland . . 1922
Author Nat Hentoff. 1925
Lawyer F. Lee Bailey. 1933
Author Jeff Greenfield 1943
Politician John Edwards 1953
Actress Elizabeth Hurley. 1965
Olympic figure-skating gold medalist
    Tara Lipinski. 1982

SILENT WITNESS

An American was hired to teach in a Japanese school. As part of the agreement, the man, a Christian, had to promise not to mention Christ or his faith at all during the school day. The man was careful to keep his word. However, his life and Christlike example were so consistent that, unknown to him, forty of his students publicly denounced their false beliefs.

You never know who may be influenced by observing your life. Scottish evangelist Robert Murray McCheyne received a letter from one of his converts that read, "It was nothing you said which made me wish to be a Christian; rather it was the beauty of holiness I saw in your face." McCheyne had achieved the goal: his conduct was consistent with his creed. His face and his life reflected the love of Christ in every action, every attitude, every word.

When people see you—at work, at home, or relaxing and having fun—what do they see? Do they see an ambitious striver, a selfish spouse, a poor sport? Or do they see Jesus?

TODAY'S POWER POINT

He is a Christian indeed who is neither ashamed of the gospel nor a shame to the gospel.—Richard DeHaan

June 11

TODAY IN HISTORY

1859—Claim for Comstock Lode filed in Nevada (mine eventually produced $300 million in silver)
1895—First U.S. auto race
1927—Distinguished Flying Cross awarded to pilot Charles Lindbergh
1947—World War II–era sugar rationing ended in United States
1950—Ben Hogan won U.S. Open golf championship after recovering from crippling auto accident
1979—Death of actor John Wayne, age seventy-two
2001—Convicted Oklahoma City bomber Timothy McVeigh executed
2002—Delegates met to form new government in Afghanistan; premiere of television's *American Idol*
2003—More than one hundred killed or wounded in suicide bomb attack on Jerusalem bus

BORN TODAY

Artist John Constable 1776
Composer Richard Strauss 1864
Explorer Jacques Cousteau 1910
Football great Vince Lombardi . . . 1913
Author William Styron . . . . : . . 1925
Actor Gene Wilder 1935
Actor Chad Everett 1936
Actress Adrienne Barbeau 1945
Actor Peter Bergman 1953
Quarterback Joe Montana 1956
Actor Joshua Jackson 1978

PROSPERITY

In what do you put your trust? The mansion of Henry Ford in Dearborn, Michigan, built in 1917 at a cost of over $1 million, stands as a monument to the great industrialist's prosperity. It had fifty-three rooms and 31,000 square feet of space on three floors overlooking the meandering Rouge River. The home was powered by its own generators, providing current to 550 lights.

The generators operated continuously from the time the home was completed until one rainy night in April 1947. Torrential rains had caused the nearby river to flood, extinguishing the fire in the boilers and causing the steam-powered generators to stop. In the mansion, Henry Ford lay dying. Surrounded by engineering marvels, he left this life in the same manner he had entered it nearly ninety years before—in a cold, dark house lighted only by candles.

Where is your prosperity? Are you wealthy in the goods this life offers—technology, stock options, property? Never forget that such wealth is only temporary. Seek instead spiritual wealth that will last for eternity.

TODAY'S POWER POINT

God judges what we give by what we keep.—George Müeller

June 12

TODAY IN HISTORY

1880—Worcester's John Richmond pitched baseball's first perfect game
1898—Philippine Islands granted independence from Spain
1930—Max Schneling won heavyweight boxing championship
1939—Opening of Baseball Hall of Fame in Cooperstown, New York
1978—Supreme Court ruled Nazis should be allowed to demonstrate in heavily
        Jewish Skokie, Illinois
1987—Margaret Thatcher won third term as Britain's prime minister
1991—Boris Yeltsin chosen first freely elected president of Russia
2000—Justice Department agreed to $18-million settlement to estate of Richard
        Nixon for papers confiscated following his resignation as president
2001—President George W. Bush made first overseas trip (to Europe)
2003—Iraqi cleric Muqtada al-Sadr announced plans to form political party and
        vote in 2005 election

BORN TODAY

Bridge builder John Roebling. . . . 1806   President George H. W. Bush. . . . 1924
Author Charles Kingsley. 1819   Singer Vic Damone 1928
Statesman Anthony Eden 1897   Singer and actor Jim Nabors. 1932
Banker David Rockefeller. 1915   Sportscaster Marv Albert 1941

YOUR NEW LOCATION

Writing in *Our Daily Bread*, Bible teacher Richard DeHaan related the story of a bank that "had some flowers sent to a competitor who had recently moved into a new building. However, there was a mix-up at the flower shop, and the card sent with the arrangement read, 'With our deepest sympathy.' The florist, who was greatly embarrassed, apologized. But he was even more embarrassed when he realized that the card intended for the bank was attached to a floral arrangement sent to a funeral home in honor of a deceased person. That card read, 'Congratulations on your new location.'"

While such a mix-up might be regrettable, the story illustrates an important truth—believers will be moving to a wonderful new location when they die. They will go to be with Christ, and the sorrows and heartaches of this earthly existence will be gone forever. When loved ones die in Christ, we are sad, of course; but Christians do not grieve as those who have no hope. Instead, like Paul, you can say, "I desire to depart and be with Christ, which is better by far" (Philippians 1:23).

TODAY'S POWER POINT

To be absent from the body . . . [is] to be present with the Lord.—2 Corinthians 5:8 (KJV)

TODAY IN HISTORY

1944—Missile age launched as Germans fired "flying bombs" at England

1966—Supreme Court's Miranda decision mandated police inform suspects of their rights before taking their statements

1967—Thurgood Marshall first African American nominated for Supreme Court

1971—Pentagon Papers published by *New York Times*

1986—Death of bandleader Benny Goodman, age seventy-seven

1994—Jury awarded $15 billion to claimants in *Exxon Valdez* tanker-spill case

2001—Italian authorities dropped charges against Turk suspected of attempting to assassinate Pope John Paul II, paving the way for trial in Turkey

2002—United States let ABM treaty lapse (after thirty years) so Star Wars missile defense shield program could move forward

2002—Pakistan's interim leader, General Prevez Musharraf, overwhelmingly chosen to serve as president until 2004 elections

2003—Maine extended low-cost health-care coverage to all residents

BORN TODAY

Poet William Butler Yeats 1865
Football player "Red" Grange 1903
Actor Malcolm McDowell 1943
Actor Richard Thomas 1951
Comedian Tim Allen 1953
Actresses Mary Kate and Ashley Olsen
. . . . 1986

FIXED WAGES

Some of the greatest heroes in God's eyes have been some whose earthly wages have been the lowest. A medical missionary who had performed critical surgery on a penniless indigenous person was asked what he would have earned had he performed the operation in the United States.

"Several thousand dollars," he replied.

"And what will you receive for doing the surgery here?" his questioner pressed.

The missionary quickly responded, "My payment will simply be the gratitude of this man, for there can be no greater payment than that."

The Bible gives no indication that when Jesus walked on earth he was paid for any work he did—and he's God's own Son! He healed multitudes, fed crowds, taught, showed the Father's love, and even raised the dead; but the percentage of those who even gave him thanks was small.

Have you ever thanked the Lord for paying the price to forgive your sins? Take a moment and do so today.

TODAY'S POWER POINT

Whatever you do, do it all for the glory of God.—1 Corinthians 10:31

June 14

TODAY IN HISTORY

1775—Army established as first U.S. military service
1922—President Warren Harding first U.S. president to deliver a radio broadcast
1940—German Nazis took control of Paris
1951—World's first commercial computer, Univac, unveiled in Philadelphia
1974—Introduction of Heimlich maneuver
1982—Argentina surrendered to Britain, ending seventy-four-day Falkland Island war
1986—Death of librettist Alan Lerner, age sixty-seven
1993—Justice Ruth Bader Ginsburg nominated to U.S. Supreme Court
2000—General John Gordon named first director of Nuclear Security Administration
2002—New planet discovered, similar to Jupiter
2004—Explosions at Iraqi oil terminals shut down two pipelines, causing estimated $1 billion loss of oil revenue

BORN TODAY

Author Harriet Beecher Stowe . . . 1811
Editor John Bartlett 1820
Pathologist Alois Alzheimer 1864
Actor Burl Ives 1909
Actor Gene Barry 1921
Businessman Donald Trump 1946
Actor Will Patton 1954
Olympic speed-skating gold medalist
    Eric Heiden 1958
Tennis player Steffi Graf 1969

THE FLAG

The title for the world's oldest national flag goes to Denmark. Its banner, *Dannebrog*—red with a white cross—has not changed since the thirteenth century. According to legend, as the greatest Danish king of medieval times, Waldemar II, led his troops into battle against the Estonians on June 15, 1219, the banner fell miraculously from the sky. Convinced the flag demonstrated God's favor and blessing, Waldemar and his troops fought valiantly and were victorious. For almost eight hundred years Danes have looked to this flag as a source of inspiration, pride, identity, and courage in the face of any threat.

We honor and salute our country's flag. It inspires us and rallies us to courage and patriotism. But never forget that only by looking to the banner of Christ and his sacrifice for us can we truly be saved.

TODAY'S POWER POINT

There is hopeful symbolism in the fact that flags do not wave in a vacuum.
—Arthur C. Clarke

TODAY IN HISTORY

1752—Ben Franklin's kite experiment proved lightning contains electricity
1836—Twenty-fifth state, Arkansas, added to Union
1938—Cincinnati Reds pitcher Johnny Vander Meer pitched second no hitter in a row
1977—Spain held first free elections in forty-one years
1986—High-level Chernobyl officials fired after nuclear disaster
1996—Death of singer Ella Fitzgerald, age seventy-eight
2004—Plans for national "No Spam" list dropped by Federal Trade Commission

BORN TODAY

Composer Edvard Grieg	1843	Actress Helen Hunt	1963
Singer Waylon Jennings	1937	Actress Courteney Cox Arquette	1964
Songwriter Harry Nilsson	1941	Actress Leah Remini	1970
Actor Jim Varney	1949	Golfer Justin Leonard	1972
Actor Jim Belushi	1954	Actor Neil Patrick Harris	1973

THE LAW OF GOD

Besides Christ himself, there has never lived a perfect person—one who has not broken God's law. It appeared, however, that one had been located in a western state some years ago. Testifying in court, the man said he neither smoked nor chewed, drank nor swore. Attempting to clarify the point, the lawyer then asked the witness, "You claim, then, that you are a perfect man?"

The man responded, "I do—as perfect as one can be."

Of course the witness lost any presumption of perfection when he qualified his testimony with the words "as perfect as one can be," for there's no such thing as partial perfection. In the same way, we either comply fully with God's laws or we fall short of the whole Law. The Bible says, "There is no one righteous, not even one. . . . All have sinned and fall short of the glory of God" (Romans 3:10, 23).

But the situation is far from hopeless. God, in his mercy, provides just what we need to bridge the gap between our shortcomings and the perfection needed to fulfill the law. We can be "justified freely by his grace through the redemption that came by Christ Jesus" (Romans 3:24). Under the law we fail miserably because we can't be perfect. But under God's grace, he "justifies those who have faith in Jesus" (Romans 3:26). It just makes sense to trust in Jesus rather than our own "perfection."

TODAY'S POWER POINT

It is not so desirable to cultivate a respect for law, so much as a respect for right.
—Henry David Thoreau

June 16

TODAY IN HISTORY

1941—National Airport opened in Washington DC

1977—Death of rocket scientist Wernher von Braun, age eighty-five

1980—Supreme Court ruling allowed new life forms from synthetic biology to be patented

1995—Salt Lake City chosen to host 2002 Winter Olympics

1997—European Union called for standardized currency

1999—Nelson Mandela resigned as South African president; U.S. vice president Al Gore announced candidacy for president

BORN TODAY

Comedian Stan Laurel	1895	Golfer Phil Mickelson	1950
Publisher Katherine Graham	1917	Boxer Roberto Duran	1951
Author Erich Segal	1937	Actress Laurie Metcalf	1955
Author Joyce Carol Oates	1938	Rapper Tupac Shakur	1971
Actress Joan Van Ark	1943	Baseball player Kerry Wood	1977

STRENGTH TO WIN

Irish evangelist W. P. Nicholson used to tell of a radiation treatment he had received from his doctor. After some preliminaries, Nicholson reclined in a chair while the doctor sat at his desk reading a newspaper. After a while Nicholson asked the doctor when the treatment would begin. "Why, you're being treated right now," the doctor replied, holding a fluorescent bulb next to him that glowed from the strength of the electrical field.

Relating the incident later, Nicholson said, Christian, "you have all the power of God within you, though you may not feel it now. But when a special need arises, the power will become evident, for it is there."

A wonderful true story is told of the famed pianist Ignacy Paderewski, who was playing in concert at New York's Carnegie Hall. During the intermission a mother, noticing her young son was missing, turned in horror to see the lad onstage playing "Chopsticks" on the magnificent concert grand. Unperturbed by the incursion, Paderewski silently slipped behind the youth and, placing his skilled hands upon the boys', began playing a beautiful, harmonious melody from the familiar, simple tune.

In the same way, God stands ready to make beautiful music with your life if you simply do your part and leave the rest to him.

TODAY'S POWER POINT

God's work, done in God's way, will never lack God's supplies.—Hudson Taylor

TODAY IN HISTORY

1928—Start of Amelia Earhart's transatlantic flight, first by a woman

1947—Start of first commercial worldwide airline service

1963—Prayer and Bible reading banned from public schools by U.S. Supreme Court

1967—China launched successful H-bomb test

1972—Five arrested in connection with break-in at Democratic Party headquarters in Watergate scandal

1974—Eleven injured in IRA bombing of British parliament

1982—President Ronald Reagan delivered "Evil empire" speech about USSR

1986—Death of singer Kate Smith, age eighty-six

2000—U.S. Appeals Court in Miami rejected request by relatives of six-year-old Cuban Elian Gonzalez to keep him in United States

BORN TODAY

Methodist leader John Wesley . . . 1703

Composer Igor Stravinsky 1882

Actor Ralph Bellamy 1904

Author John Hersey 1914

General Tommy Franks 1945

Singer and songwriter Barry Manilow 1946

Comedian Joe Piscopo 1951

Football player Dermontti Dawson 1965

Tennis player Venus Williams. . . . 1980

BLESSINGS OF LIBERTY

Hanging near the platform at Boston's historic Fanueuil Hall is a dramatic painting of U.S. senator Daniel Webster fiercely debating Robert Hayne on the nature of America's Union. It bears the following inscription, a quote from Webster's powerful rebuttal: "Union and Liberty, now and forever, one and inseparable." When at Fanneuil Hall to make an address, Salvation Army founder William Boothe spotted the imposing painting and noted the parallels between Webster's speech and the Christian walk: "Union and Liberty—union with Christ and liberty from sin, one and inseparable now and forever. . . . There is no spiritual liberty apart from this union."

As great as the freedoms we may enjoy here on earth, much greater is the eternal freedom we can enjoy as believers. Recall these ringing words of the apostle Paul describing spiritual freedom: "There is now no condemnation for those who are in Christ Jesus, because through Christ Jesus the law of the Spirit of life set me free from the law of sin and death" (Romans 8:1–2). And this ironclad guarantee: "If the Son sets you free, you will be free indeed" (John 8:36).

TODAY'S POWER POINT

The condition upon which God has given liberty to man is eternal vigilance.
—John P. Curran

June 18

TODAY IN HISTORY

1940—Winston Churchill's "Finest hour" speech before House of Commons united Britons against marauding Nazis

1979—President Jimmy Carter and Soviet leader Leonid Brezhnev signed SALT II agreement limiting spread of nuclear arms

1994—O. J. Simpson arrested in connection with the deaths of his ex-wife Nicole and her friend

2001—Russia threatened arms buildup if United States pursued Star Wars (Strategic Defense Initiative)

2002—Jury awarded flight attendant $5.5 million in secondhand-smoke case

2003—United States warned Iran not to build nuclear weapon

BORN TODAY

Actor E. G. Marshall 1910
Journalist Sylvia Porter 1913
Educator Donald Keene 1922
Columnist Tom Wicker 1926

Baseball player Lou Brock 1939
Musician Paul McCartney;
    movie critic Roger Ebert 1942
Actor Eddie Cibrian 1973

THE JOY OF GIVING

A little girl once told her friend that she was going to give her dad a pair of slippers for his birthday. "Where will you get the money?" the friend asked.

"Why, from Dad, of course," the girl replied.

We have nothing to give God apart from what we have first received from him.

Many years ago the finance committee of a small church called on its members for donations. Eventually they visited a widow's humble home. The poor woman had to work two jobs just to make ends meet, and the visitors were embarrassed even to ask her to give. However, the woman surprised the group by going into another room and bringing back a fifty-dollar bill, a larger gift than many wealthier church members had given. The leader of the committee tried to return the gift to the woman, saying kindly, "You can't afford to give so much. We couldn't take that money!"

But the woman adamantly refused to take back her gift. "Don't take away my blessing," she said firmly. "I love the Lord and my church as much as the rest of you, and I want to do my part. Please don't take away my joy."

Humbled by the woman's sincerity, the group left with her gift.

Do you view giving to God as an obligation or an opportunity? The size of your gifts matter far less to God than the attitude of your heart.

TODAY'S POWER POINT

One must be poor to enjoy the luxury of giving!—George Eliot

TODAY IN HISTORY

1855—Arrival of Statue of Liberty in New York
1905—First nickelodeon opened
1952—Television premiere of *I've Got a Secret*
1953—Two convicted spies, Julius and Ethel Rosenberg, executed for wartime espionage
1984—PG-13 classification adopted by Motion Picture Association
1986—College basketball standout Len Bias died of cocaine overdose
1999—Marriage of Britain's Prince Edward and Sophie Rhys-Jones
2001—Syria withdrew six thousand troops from Beirut, Lebanon, area; Germans awarded $4.5 billion in Nazi-era settlement to thousands of wartime prisoners
2002—National Security Agency revealed overhearing September 10, 2001, conversation among al Qaeda terrorists; Morocco captured senior al Qaeda official Abu Zubaydar
2003—Justice Department reported al Qaeda supporter Iyman Faris pled guilty (in May) to plotting to destroy Brooklyn Bridge
2004—United States launched air strikes in Fallujah against terrorist leader Abu Musab al-Zaraqawi

BORN TODAY

Mathematician and philosopher Blaise Pascal 1623
Bandleader Guy Lombardo 1902
Baseball player Lou Gehrig. 1903
Supreme Court Justice Abe Fortas. . 1910
Architect Charles Gwathmey 1938
Actress Phylicia Rashad 1948
Actress Kathleen Turner 1954
Basketball player Dirk Nowitzki. . 1978

UNITED AT HOME

To really want to get to know people, visit them in their homes. Bible teacher C. I. Schofield once wrote to a friend: "I like to be able to picture people who deeply interest me, in their homes. Downtown we are all pretty much alike, but at home we are just ourselves . . . at home we are at ease; we throw off care; we are understood, and loved, and welcome."

Our outlook on the world is, in large part, determined by what we've learned at home. Such basic concepts as sharing, politeness, and putting others' interests ahead of our own should be learned first at home. Many disputes, wars, and grievances could be prevented simply by remembering the fundamental principles we learned at home as children.

TODAY'S POWER POINT

Nobody shoulders a rifle in defense of a boarding house.—Bret Harte

June 20

TODAY IN HISTORY

1819—First transatlantic steamship voyage
1863—Thirty-fifth state, West Virginia, admitted to Union
1893—Lizzie Borden acquitted of murdering her father and stepmother
1977—Transalaskan pipeline opened across eight hundred miles of Alaskan wilderness
1985—Four off-duty Marines killed in blast of gunfire at outdoor café in San Salvador
2000—Bashar al-Assad nominated to succeed his father as president of Syria
2002—New Homeland Security director Tom Ridge briefed Congress on agency's mission
2003—Search for Saddam Hussein stepped up after captured Iraqi official said Saddam and his two sons survived initial U.S. attack

BORN TODAY

Composer Jacques Offenbach. . . . 1819
Actress Olympia Dukakis 1931
Songwriter Brian Wilson 1942
Singer Anne Murray 1945
Home improvement guru Bob Vila. . 1946
Singer Lionel Richie 1949
Director, writer, and actor Michael Landon Jr.. 1964
Actress Nicole Kidman 1967

ONE IN CHRIST

The *Sunday-School Times* once reported on a new convert living overseas who announced he would no longer worship his ancestors since becoming a Christian. Later, learning that the missionary who had witnessed to him would be beaten with a thousand stripes for his faith, the new believer called on the head of the local tribe to plead for mercy for his friend. "As a Christian, this man is the same as my brother. I cannot stand by and do nothing while he is beaten," he said, and asked that the believers from nearby tribes "be allowed to join in sharing the stripes with him."

Fearing there would be trouble if members of another tribe were stricken by "outsiders," the leader sent his apologies, saying he did not understand the oneness of the Christian religion. Thus, noted the *Times*, the "unity of the Christians was stronger than the tribal powers, and God was glorified."

The Bible says that when we become Christians, we're adopted into God's family along with countless "brothers and sisters." Do you need the support of your Christian brothers and sisters? God will send someone to stand with you at just the right time. Is there something you can do to help and encourage someone in need? Don't keep your brother or sister waiting. Step up to help bear their burdens. In Christ we're one big happy family, and families stand together in times of need or joy.

TODAY'S POWER POINT

Jesus found time to forgive between the blows of the hammer.—Source Unkown

TODAY IN HISTORY

1788—U.S. Constitution became effective when ninth state, New Hampshire, ratified it

1948—Demonstration of first long-playing record

1956—First service at Jerry Falwell's Thomas Road Baptist Church

1973—Supreme Court ruled that states should set obscenity standards

1982—John Hinkley Jr. judged not guilty by reason of insanity of attempting to assassinate President Ronald Reagan

2000—NASA reported finding evidence of possible ancient water on Mars

2003—President George W. Bush warned of Hussein supporters trying to "kill and intimidate" U.S. forces; fifth Harry Potter book, *Harry Potter and the Order of the Phoenix,* set record sales

2004—Civilian Michael Melvil piloted first private aircraft to enter space

BORN TODAY

Illustrator Al Hirschfield. 1903

Actress Jane Russell. 1921

Actor Bernie Kopell 1933

Actress Meredith Baxter 1947

Baseball player Rick Sutcliffe 1956

Cartoonist Berke Breathed 1957

Britain's Prince William 1982

SAFE

A story is told of a Christian army sergeant serving as a train engineer in the Middle East, in charge of a run between Haifa and Cairo. Each time the train headed out, the soldier-engineer would bow his head and ask for God's protection for the trip. One dark night, for no apparent reason, the engine suddenly stopped. Stranded on a desolate track on a rainy night, he and several others tried to get the engine started once again, but to no avail.

As daylight broke, several messengers, approaching the train from the other direction, reported that the track ahead had washed away in the storm, leaving a gap large enough to engulf the entire train. Upon hearing the report, the passengers remarked about how "lucky" they had been. Sensing an opportunity to share his faith, the soldier told of his prayer before their departure and that he believed it was God who had protected them. Many hours later, when the track had been repaired, the soldier again tried to start the engine. Quickly it sprang to life, and the train continued on its way.

Isn't it great to know that God protects us? He holds you firmly and safely in his arms.

TODAY'S POWER POINT

Christians are the Lord's property—dearly bought, lawfully acquired, and carefully preserved.—Henry Bosch

June 22

TODAY IN HISTORY

1872—First fire-alarm call boxes installed

1873—Evangelist D. L. Moody preached first service in England

1937—Joe Louis won heavyweight boxing championship

1939—First U.S. beauty pageant televised

1941—Germany marched into Soviet Union

1960—First multiple satellite launch

1964—Three civil-rights workers disappeared in Philadelphia, Mississippi

1969—Death of entertainer Judy Garland, age forty-seven

1970—American eighteen-year-olds given right to vote

1985—Sikhs blamed for Air India 747 crash off England killing all 329 aboard

2003—Missile near Syrian border struck convoy believed to include Saddam Hussein

2004—South Korean interpreter killed in Iraq; Bill Clinton memoir sold record-setting 500,000 copies first day

BORN TODAY

Director Billy Wilder 1906

Singer Kris Kristofferson 1936

TV journalist Ed Bradley 1941

Singer Todd Rungren 1948

Actress Meryl Streep 1949

Football player Kurt Warner 1971

Singer Cyndi Lauper 1953

TV host Carson Daly 1973

UNSPOTTED

Bible teacher Paul Van Gorder once told the story of a pristine white flower that was found blooming in the midst of a fallen, rotted tree. All around the blossom was darkness and decay, yet the little flower bloomed immaculately unspotted there on the forest floor.

In the same way, believers are called to shed forth the light of God's Word in the midst of a dark and dying world. Imagine the Christians who served in Caesar's household. What would it have been like to shine God's light under the rule of Nero, who was notorious for being a ruthless emperor, who presided over a palace full of lust, indulgence, and unspeakable depravity?

If you think you're experiencing pressure living the Christian life today, consider what it would have been like to be a believer in ancient Rome. Surely if God could sustain and protect his saints living there in Nero's court, he can sustain you today. Determine that with God's help you will bloom, unspotted by the sin around you, showing his glory to a darkened world.

TODAY'S POWER POINT

All truth passes through three stages. First, it is ridiculed. Second, it is violently opposed. Third, it is accepted as being self-evident.—Arthur Schopenhauer

TODAY IN HISTORY

1775—First book published in United States (*Bay Psalm Book*)
1860—U.S. Secret Service established
1868—Typewriter patented
1886—First hospital chartered exclusively for infants
1938—First flight instructor's license issued
1969—Warren Burger sworn in as U.S. Chief Justice
1980—President Jimmy Carter met with heads of other industrialized nations to discuss ways to reduce Western oil dependence
2004—United States offered North Korea fuel oil in exchange for taking steps to dismantle its nuclear program

BORN TODAY

Author Irvin S. Cobb 1876
Edward VIII, Duke of Windsor . . 1894
Conductor James Levine 1943
Sprinter Wilma Rudolph 1940
Singer June Carter Cash 1929
Actor Bryan Brown 1947
Supreme Court Justice Clarence Thomas
. . . . 1948
Musician and *American Idol* judge
Randy Jackson 1956

SMALL THINGS

Several promising young employees were being considered for promotion in a large bank's trust department. The board of directors reviewed each candidate's qualifications and selected the one whose achievement and potential they judged to be greatest.

One applicant was full of confidence as he went to the cafeteria that noon for lunch. As the young man went through the line, he put two pats of butter on his plate, then deftly flipped some slices of bread on top so the cashier wouldn't see the butter and charge him.

That afternoon he was summoned to the boardroom. But instead of receiving the promotion he expected, he was dismissed. A member of the bank's board of directors had been in line a few places behind the butter thief. The bank officers said they would not tolerate someone working in their trust department who was dishonest in even the smallest things.

Honesty—in both earthly as well as spiritual things—is not just the best policy; it's the only policy that wins God's approval. In small things as well as large things, live your life in a manner that will win the Master's commendation: "Well done, good and faithful servant! You have been faithful with a few things; I will put you in charge of many things. Come and share your master's happiness!" (Matthew 25:23).

TODAY'S POWER POINT

God may entrust us with a little to see what we'll do with a lot.—M. R. DeHaan

June 24

TODAY IN HISTORY

1947—First flying saucers reported in United States (near Mt. Rainier, Washington)

1948—Soviets cut off all land and water access to Berlin

1981—Israel announced it had capability of making atomic bombs

1983—First U.S. woman in space, physicist Sally Ride, returned from six-day *Challenger* mission

2002—United States vowed not to recognize Palestinian state while Yasser Arafat was in authority; not-guilty plea entered by judge in trial of "twentieth hijacker" Zacarias Moussaoui

2003—United States promised billions in aid to Pakistan, but no fighter jets

BORN TODAY

Orator Henry Ward Beecher 1813
Boxer Jack Dempsey. 1895
Author John Ciardi 1916
Musician Mick Fleetwood 1942
Actress Nancy Allen 1950
Actress Sherry Stringfield 1967

OUR RIGHTS

Although the U.S. Constitution guarantees citizens certain rights, the Bible indicates that, spiritually, as Christians, we are to give up our rights: we are to be controlled by God. Rather than expecting to have more privileges than other people, believers need to realize they have more responsibilities.

Two young men were caught red-handed in a holdup attempt. One, from a wealthy family, had attended the finest schools and was represented by several high-powered lawyers. The other, who had spent two years in prison, had a court-appointed attorney.

It was no surprise when the judge found them both guilty. What was surprising was the dissimilar sentences they received: the repeat offender was sentenced to three years in prison, while the wealthy man got ten. The judge reasoned that the wealthy youth had been given tremendous opportunities, but he had squandered them. The privileged young man had greater responsibilities to society, yet he had turned against the code of ethics of his community, his school, and his country. In the judge's opinion, this made the youth deserving of a greater punishment.

Whatever our feelings on the matter, the judgment follows God's standard. The Bible states: "From everyone who has been given much, much will be demanded; and from the one who has been entrusted with much, much more will be asked" (Luke 12:48).

TODAY'S POWER POINT

Consider the rights of others before your own feelings, and the feelings of others before your own rights.—John Wooden

June 25

TODAY IN HISTORY

1788—Tenth state, Virginia, ratified U.S. Constitution

1876—General George Custer defeated in battle of Little Big Horn

1950—Korean War triggered when North Korea invaded South Korea

1962—U.S. Supreme Court ruled group prayer in New York public schools unconstitutional

1973—Former White House counsel John Dean described to the Watergate Committee an eight-month cover-up of certain activities as a "cancer on the presidency"

1982—George Shultz replaced Alexander Haig as secretary of state

1986—In major policy shift, Congress approved $100 million aid package for Nicaraguan Contras

1987—Russian president Mikhail Gorbachev proposed reforms and restructuring of the Soviet economy

1996—Nineteen killed in truck bomb blast at U.S. base in Saudi Arabia

2000—Philip Morris agreed to buy Nabisco for $14.9 billion

2002—WorldCom admitted it inflated cash flow by nearly $4 billion over past fifteen months

2004—Taliban claimed responsibility for killing of fourteen Afghan voters

BORN TODAY

Author George Orwell 1903
Director Sidney Lumet 1924
Actress June Lockhart 1925
Basketball player Willis Reed 1942
Singer Carly Simon 1945
Baseball player Carlos Delgado . . . 1972

A WORD TO HUSBANDS

One of the reasons many marriages fall apart is because husbands are not following the directive of Scripture: "Husbands, love your wives, just as Christ loved the church and gave himself up for her" (Ephesians 5:25).

If you're a husband, do you love your wife as much as Christ loves the church? Do you sacrifice yourself—your wants, your comforts, your pleasures—for her? Do you live to please your wife more than yourself? Does your wife feel that you respect and value her? Do you tell your wife that she's beautiful? (It won't make her vain.) Do you remember your anniversary and other dates that matter to her? How often do you tell her you love her?

Your love bestows well-deserved dignity to a faithful wife and mother. Remember how you treated your wife on your honeymoon? When you give yourself for your wife in service and sacrifice, the honeymoon never ends.

TODAY'S POWER POINT

Chains do not hold a marriage together. It is the threads, hundreds of tiny threads, which sew people together through the years.—Simone Signoret

June 26

TODAY IN HISTORY

1917—U.S. troops landed in France
1919—*New York Daily News* began publication
1945—United Nations chartered
1948—Start of Berlin airlift
1950—Premiere of television's *The Garry Moore Show*
1974—UPC bar code first used
1975—250,000 mental patients released following Supreme Court ruling
1976—World's tallest freestanding structure (CN Tower) opened in Toronto
1979—Heavyweight boxing champion Muhammad Ali announced retirement
2000—Human genome genetic code successfully mapped by scientists

BORN TODAY

Baseball inventor Major-General
   Abner Doubleday 1819
Author Pearl S. Buck 1892
Athlete Babe Didrikson Zaharias . 1911
Author Charlotte Zolotow 1915
Actress Eleanor Parker 1922
Cyclist Greg Lemond 1961
Actor Sean Hayes 1970
Baseball player Derek Jeter 1974

MONEY

For anyone who's ever experienced more month at the end of the money, it's reassuring to realize we needn't fret over how to pay the bills. God already knows our needs and has everything under control. The apostle Paul noted: "God will meet all your needs according his glorious riches in Christ Jesus" (Philippians 4:19).

The Bible speaks of money on many occasions. Jesus spoke of money in his historic Sermon on the Mount (Matthew 6:25–34). One way God supplies our needs is through returns on our prudent, long-term investments.

A story is told about Benjamin Franklin, who set aside $5 thousand in his will for the city of Boston in 1791, instructing that the money be invested for three hundred years. One hundred years later, his original sum had grown to $92,000 and was reinvested. At last report the Boston trust fund established by Franklin had climbed to $1.5 million. As Franklin noted, "Money begets money, and its offspring begets more."

Have money problems? Handle your finances wisely, and realize that God is your source—and that he has promised to meet the needs of every one of his children.

TODAY'S POWER POINT

Money isn't everything, but it ranks right up there with oxygen.—Rita Davenport

TODAY IN HISTORY

1844—Mormon leader Joseph Smith killed by Illinois mob

1859—World's most-sung song, "Happy Birthday to You," composed

1942—FBI announced capture of eight Nazi terrorists attempting to invade United States

1950—U.S. Air Force shot down three North Korean planes in first U.S. support of South Korean forces

1974—President Richard Nixon and Soviet leader Brezhnev began third summit session in Moscow

2001—United Nations outlined plans for combating worldwide AIDS crisis

2002—Congress increased national debt limit to a record $6.4 trillion

BORN TODAY

Writer and speaker Helen Keller. . 1880
Poet Paul Lawrence Dunbar 1872
Television's Captain Kangaroo (Bob Keeshan). 1927

Billionaire H. Ross Perot 1930
Opera singer Anna Moffo. 1934
Actress Julia Duffey 1951
Actor Toby Maguire 1975

LOOKING IN THE BOOK

How often do you turn to other sources to meet your needs rather than turning to God's Word? A number of years ago the telephone company, hoping to increase the use of its business directory, started using the slogan "Look in the book." That advice is even more important for believers: we would be wise to look in God's book, the Bible.

One person who "looked in the book" was twelve-year-old Helen Cadbury. She had become a believer in Bible school and began carrying a large family Bible wherever she went so she might share her newfound faith with others. Realizing how difficult it was for the young girl to carry such a large volume from place to place, her father presented her with a New Testament small enough to carry in her pocket. The idea caught on, and soon a number of Helen's young friends began carrying the Word and reading it every day. Before long the group became known as the Pocket Testament League and began handing out small New Testaments to anyone who promised to read it. Over the years thousands have found Christ as a result. Today the Pocket Testament League has grown into a dynamic organization of more than 100,000 members who carry God's Word with them every day—all because of one young girl who was determined to "look in the book" whenever and wherever she went.

TODAY'S POWER POINT

Other books were given for our information. The Bible was given for our transformation.—Walter B. Knight

June 28

TODAY IN HISTORY

1902—United States purchased rights from France to unfinished Panama Canal

1914—Archduke Ferdinand assassinated in Sarajevo, triggering World War I

1919—Treaty of Versailles signed, ending World War I

1965—First commercial telephone link established between the United States and Europe via satellite

1976—Female cadets first enrolled at U.S. Air Force Academy

1978—Supreme Court approved affirmative action for college admission

1988—Russian president Mikhail Gorbachev proposed new policies to boost Soviet economy

1992—Supreme Court reaffirmed abortion rights

2000—Proposal for elected senate rejected by Russian parliament

2004—NATO agreed to train Iraqi troops (but refused to send troops to Iraq)

BORN TODAY

England's King Henry VIII 1491
Author Esther Forbes 1891
Composer Richard Rodgers 1902
Musician Lester Flatt 1914
Director and actor Mel Brooks . . . 1928
Comedienne Gilda Radner 1946
Actress Alice Krige 1954
Quarterback John Elway 1960
Actor John Cusack 1966

ONE FOR ALL

How God must grieve for the masses of people who have never heard of his saving love. How large is this population? According to figures cited by *Christian Victory*, missionaries throughout the world are reaching about two million unchurched people each year. That sounds great until you realize that world population is increasing at a rate of sixty-five million each year. The U.S. Census Bureau has estimated that the world population increases by more than 205,000 people every day. With these figures in mind, we may begin to see how important the development of the Internet, mass media, and satellite communication may be in reaching these vast masses of humanity with the gospel.

How great is God! His timing is perfect. Today's media makes it possible for one person or ministry to reach millions down the street or around the world. Yet nothing can take the place of a personal word from a flesh-and-blood person with a warm handshake and friendly smile. God still commands each individual believer to go into the world in which God has placed him or her and share the gospel with those who need to hear. When was the last time you shared your faith? Do so today!

TODAY'S POWER POINT

If Christ is the way, why waste time traveling some other way?—Source Unknown

TODAY IN HISTORY

1767—Britain's Townshend Revenue Act passed, increasing tensions that eventually led to the American Revolution

1928—Al Smith became first Catholic nominee for president

1967—Israelis named to oversee united Jewish and Arab Jerusalem

1972—Supreme Court ruled that the death penalty, as the existing laws were written, was unconstitutional

1984—New figures showed average price for a new home in the United States was over $100,000 for the first time

2001—Kofi Annan reelected secretary general of United Nations

2003—Hamas, Al Fatah, and Islamic Jihad called for cease-fire against Israel

2004—Paul Martin reelected Canadian prime minister

BORN TODAY

Artist Peter Paul Rubens 1577
Engineer George Geothals 1858
Physician William James Mayo . . . 1861
Singer Nelson Eddy 1901
Composer Leroy Anderson 1909
Author Jill Briscoe 1935
Baseball player Harmon Killebrew
. . . . 1936
Actor Gary Busey 1944
Hockey player Theo Fleury 1968

A CHRISTIAN BIRTHRIGHT

The doctor of a young man with serious injuries was delighted with his patient's unexpectedly rapid progress. When he admitted that God deserved much more of the credit than the doctor did himself, the patient quickly dismissed the notion.

"Don't be too modest, Doc," the young man waved his hand dismissively. "My family is religious, but I don't put much stock in that sort of thing myself."

The physician saw an opportunity to make his point. "You have inherited stock in it, young man," he replied. "Do you know why you are recovering so rapidly from your accident? It is because your family and your ancestors before them have given you a strong physical makeup. You have also been given a strong spiritual heritage. It's your responsibility to pass that on to your children."

This kind of heritage may be thought of as our Christian "birthright." Many people see clearly the value of both inheriting and passing on such a spiritual legacy. One young mother held her baby in her lap while reading aloud from the Bible. When asked whether she thought her baby understood what she was reading, the mother replied, "I'm sure she doesn't understand yet, but I want her earliest memories to be of hearing God's Word."

What have your children learned about God from watching and listening to you?

TODAY'S POWER POINT

Men are what their mothers make of them.—Ralph Waldo Emerson

June 30

TODAY IN HISTORY

1936—*Gone with the Wind* published
1966—National Organization for Women (NOW) founded
1971—Ratification of Twenty-Sixth Amendment officially gave eighteen-year-old
    U.S. citizens right to vote
1974—Soviet dancer Mikhail Baryshnikov defected to Canada
1994—Supreme Court limited abortion protests
2000—Iraq resumed testing of short-range missiles
2002—Brazil won record fifth World Soccer Cup
2004—United States transferred custody of Saddam Hussein and Iraq's former
    leaders to Iraqis while retaining physical custody

BORN TODAY

Singer Lena Horne 1917
Actress Nancy Dussault 1936
Actor David Alan Grier 1955
Actor Vincent D'Onofrio 1959
Basketball player Mitch Richmond
. . . . 1965
Boxer Mike Tyson 1966

BROTHERLY LOVE

Have you heard it said, "You can judge someone's character by his love for his fellow man"? Two brothers were fighting side by side in a battle in France when one of them went down. The other requested permission to go out and rescue his brother from the field of fire.

"He's probably already dead," his commanding officer told him. "Why risk losing your own life to bring back a body?" But the soldier persisted and finally was given permission to go to his brother's side.

When the soldier returned with his brother over his shoulder, the officer saw that the brother was indeed dead, and the surviving soldier had received several minor wounds.

"You see," his officer said gruffly, "you risked your life for nothing!"

"No," the brave soldier replied unflinchingly. "I did what I had to do, and I have my reward. When I reached him, he was still alive for just a moment. He looked me in the eye, and I could see his relief . . . and peace. He told me, 'I knew you would come for me. I knew you would come.'"

Proverbs 18:24 describes this kind of brotherly love: "There is a friend who sticks closer than a brother." Have you found that friend in God? He'll come for you. You know he will.

TODAY'S POWER POINT

Where there is hatred, let me sow love. Where there is injury, pardon. Where there is doubt, faith.—Francis of Assisi

TODAY IN HISTORY

1800—First Methodist camp meeting conducted in Kentucky
1847—Postage stamps first issued in United States
1848—First photographs printed in a newspaper
1862—First income-tax law passed in United States
1874—First zoo opened in United States (in Philadelphia)
1946—U.S. atom bomb testing resumed
1941—U.S. television broadcasting began
1963—Zip codes introduced in United States
1966—Start of Medicare
1979—Sony Walkman introduced
1991—Premiere of Court TV
1992—Bill Clinton and Al Gore nominated for Democratic presidential ticket
1997—Hong Kong returned to Chinese rule
2000—Vermont became first state to recognize same-sex unions
2003—Seán O'Malley appointed Archbishop of Boston, replacing controversial
　　　Bernard Law
2004—Saddam Hussein and eleven other Iraqis arraigned for crimes against humanity

BORN TODAY

Actor Charles Laughton . . . . 1899　Actor Dan Akroyd 1952
Cosmetics developer Estee Lauder 1908　Britain's Princess Diana 1961
Actress Olivia de Havilland . . . . . 1916　Actress Pamela Anderson 1967
Actor Jamie Farr . . . . 1934　Actress Liv Tyler 1977

SERENITY

Bible teacher M. R. DeHaan told of two artists who determined to paint pictures depicting "perfect peace." The first artist painted a young boy rowing across a peaceful lake. Not so much as a ripple disturbed the water's surface.

The second artist took a different approach. He painted a raging waterfall with winds whipping the spray violently about. Overlooking the raging torrent was a bird's nest built on a branch overhanging the cascade. The mother bird sat peacefully far above the roaring falls.

Real peace is not in the absence of turmoil but in rising above it. Turning to God in the midst of trial is the surest way to confidence, peace, and rest, no matter what storms may rage.

Have you experienced God's peace in the midst of a storm? You can trust him today.

TODAY'S POWER POINT

Peace I leave with you; my peace I give you. . . . Do not let your hearts be troubled and do not be afraid.—John 14:27

July 2

TODAY IN HISTORY

1776—Continental Congress decreed that colonies should become states
1881—President James Garfield shot in Washington DC
1937—Pilot Amelia Earhart disappeared in Pacific Ocean
1964—President Lyndon B. Johnson approved Civil Rights Act
1979—Supreme Court ruled minors could have abortions without parental consent
1980—President Jimmy Carter signed law requiring all males to register for the draft at age eighteen
2001—First successful implant of self-contained artificial heart
2002—Steve Fossett traveled around the world in fourteen days aboard a hot-air balloon

BORN TODAY

Novelist Hermann Hesse	1877	Actor and director Ron Silver	1946
TV host Dan Rowan	1922	Baseball player Jose Canseco	1964
Race-car driver Richard Petty	1937	Baseball player Sean Casey	1974
Mexican leader Vicente Fox	1942	Actress Lindsay Lohan	1986

GOD'S FORGIVENESS

In the late 1800s Dr. A. J. Gordon was pastoring in Boston when he met a young boy carrying a birdcage near his church. The rusty cage contained two small birds fluttering around in distress and alarm, perhaps sensing that their lives were in danger. Dr. Gordon questioned what the boy planned to do with the birds.

"I just want to take them home and play with them," was the boy's response.

"Then what?" asked the pastor.

"I guess I'll just feed them to our old cat," said the boy.

Shocked, Dr. Gordon asked how much the boy wanted for the birds. "Oh, mister, you don't want these birds," said the young man. "They're old field birds. They can't sing very well."

"I'll give you two dollars for the whole thing," said pastor Gordon.

"Sold," said the boy, "although you're making a bad bargain."

The preacher released the birds, who went off into the blue, singing.

The next Sunday he brought the empty cage to the pulpit, where he told his congregation, "That little boy said the birds couldn't sing very well. But when I released them from the cage, they flew off singing. And it seems to me they were singing, 'Redeemed, redeemed, redeemed.'" What joy there is in the song of the soul set free!

TODAY'S POWER POINT

To err is human, to forgive divine.—Alexander Pope

TODAY IN HISTORY

1775—George Washington took command of the Continental Army

1890—Forty-third state, Idaho, admitted to Union

1898—United States suffered one death in its victory in the battle of Santiago (Spanish American War)

1950—First U.S. battle with North Korea

1988—Almost three hundred people killed when U.S. Navy ship mistakenly shot down Iranian passenger plane

1996—Boris Yeltsin re-elected Russian president

2003—United States announced $25 million reward for capture of Saddam Hussein

BORN TODAY

Composer George M. Cohan 1878

Musician Pete Fountain 1930

Playwright Tom Stoppard 1937

Humorist Dave Barry 1947

Talk-show host Montel Williams . 1956

Actor Tom Cruise 1962

Baseball player Moises Alou 1966

Hockey player Teemu Selanne . . . 1970

KEEPING IT SIMPLE

Folks at a food-processing company once thought they had a great time-saving idea people were sure to love—a cake mix so simple, all you had to do was add water. The mix produced a creamy batter and a fine cake, but there was just one problem: it didn't sell. Company leaders were amazed and hired researchers to find out what the public didn't like about the product.

What did the study show? The mix was just too simple! The public expected a good cake to require something more from them. So the company changed the formula to require adding an egg plus the water. The cake mix quickly became a success.

Could it be that people reject God's free gift of salvation for the same reason, that it sounds too simple—too good to be true? They want to go to heaven but feel they must do something to earn their way in—good works, self-sacrifice, doing something for the good of mankind, being somehow "worthy." But salvation can't be earned. It's a free gift—it's that simple. All we have to do is acknowledge our need and God's gift—and accept it. How tragic that people spend their lives working to earn something they might still miss because it's so simple and basic. "The gift of God is eternal life in Christ Jesus our Lord" (Romans 6:23). Could it be any simpler? Could there be any acceptable reason for not simply accepting this gift?

TODAY'S POWER POINT

Everything should be made as simple as possible, but not one bit simpler.—Albert Einstein

TODAY IN HISTORY

1817—Construction began on Erie Canal

1826—Thomas Jefferson and John Adams died, on the fiftieth anniversary of the signing of the Declaration of Indepencence

1884—France presented Statue of Liberty to United States

1942—Premiere of Irving Berlin's *This Is the Army*

1976—United States celebrated its bicentennial

1986—Restored Statue of Liberty reopened with massive show and fireworks extravaganza in New York Harbor

1997—U.S. spacecraft began exploring Mars

2004—Cornerstone for new Freedom Tower laid on former World Trade Center site in New York

BORN TODAY

Songwriter Stephen Foster 1826

President Calvin Coolidge 1872

Twin advice columnists Ann Landers and Abigail Van Buren 1918

Actress Eva Marie Saint 1924

Playwright Neil Simon 1927

TV personality Geraldo Rivera . . . 1943

Basketball player Horace Grant . . 1965

ONE NATION, UNDER GOD

Delegates gathered in the old statehouse in Philadelphia undoubtedly were seized by many conflicting but strong emotions—anticipation, anxiety, excitement, fear, uncertainty, and dread. They had come from the thirteen colonies to discuss and act upon the increasingly troubled relations between America and Mother England. Clearly something had to be done. To this distinguished group fell much of the burden of decision: was their best hope in ironing out their differences with England, or was it time to break free and become a new, self-determining nation?

After much discussion and disagreement, American patriot and elder statesman Benjamin Franklin spoke: "I have lived, Sir, a long time, and the longer I live, the more convincing proofs I see of this truth—that God governs in the affairs of men. And if a sparrow cannot fall to the ground without his notice, is it probable that an empire can rise without his aid?"

This statement was followed by a time of prayer—and then a singleness of purpose that gave birth to the United States of America on July 4, 1776. Truly America is a nation founded upon prayer.

TODAY'S POWER POINT

The longer I live, the more convincing proofs I see of this truth—that God governs in the affairs of men.—Benjamin Franklin

TODAY IN HISTORY

1946—The first two-piece "bikini" swimsuit appeared
1948—Start of free health care in Britain
2002—Death of baseball's Ted Williams, age eighty-three
2003—SARS outbreak said to be controlled
2004—Portland, Oregon, Catholic archdiocese declared bankruptcy in wake of sexual-abuse lawsuits involving priests and children
2006—North Korea fired six test missiles over Sea of Japan

BORN TODAY

Showman P. T. Barnum 1810
Playwright Jean Cocteau. 1889
Actor Warren Oates 1928
Musician Robbie Robertson 1944
Baseball player Goose Gossage . . . 1951
Actress Edie Falco. 1963
Hockey player Chris Gratton 1975
Singer Shane Filan 1979

POSITIVE IMPRESSIONS

A country boy was hoping to attract the attention of a young woman at his church. She was lovely in form, face, and character. After the first date, he invited her out again, but she said she was busy. Repeated requests were met with the same response.

Finally he got her to tell why she wasn't willing to see him again. "Your fingernails were dirty, you slurped your soup, and you didn't even open the car door for me," she replied.

"Please, just give me a chance," he pleaded. "I don't know good manners, but I'll learn if you'll just be patient with me."

Reluctantly, she agreed to give him another chance.

Emphatically the young man devoted himself to learning how to please the girl. The more time he spent in her presence, the easier it became to adopt her tasteful ways. Two years later they were married. In learning better how to please her, he found he really was bettering himself. With time and determination he became the kind of companion she wanted—and the sort of man he was glad to have become.

Everyone who starts a relationship with God does so with inadequacies similar to this young man's. God is gracious, holy, and perfect. Our human nature is brutish, profane, and flawed. Those who want to grow more like God should read the Bible to discover what he requires. The more time spent in God's presence, the easier and more complete the transformation will become. Little by little, the rough edges will be smoothed away, and we'll become more like Christ.

TODAY'S POWER POINT

When you are courting a nice girl, an hour seems like a second.—Albert Einstein

July 6

TODAY IN HISTORY

1854—Republican Party founded
1885—Introduction of first successful anti-rabies shot
1933—Baseball's first All-Star Game
1944—Circus tent fire in Hartford, Connecticut, killed 169 people
1981—Former Argentine leader Isabel Perón freed after five-year house arrest
1982—President Reagan ordered U.S. peacekeeping troops to Beirut
2002—Afghani vice president Haji Abdul Qadeer assassinated in Kabul
2003—Israeli cabinet agreed to release three hundred Palestinian prisoners
2004—Democratic presidential candidate John Kerry selected North Carolina
      senator John Edwards as running mate
2006—New York appeals court ruled same-sex couples not allowed to marry

BORN TODAY

Navy hero John Paul Jones 1747
Mexican emperor Maximilian. . . . 1832
First Lady Nancy Reagan 1921
TV host Merv Griffin. 1925
Actress Janet Leigh 1927
Singer and actress Della Reese . . . 1932
President George W. Bush; actor
    Sylvester Stallone 1946
Actor Geoffrey Rush. 1951
Basketball player Paul Gasol 1980

PEACE ON EARTH

The weather was uncomfortable and the mud deep in the trenches that day in November 1918. Weary citizen-soldiers, recruited to fight for a just cause and uprooted from their families and jobs to fight a long and bloody war, longed to be through with it all and to go home.

Then news reached the soldiers: "Peace is at hand! Today is Armistice Day!" What excitement gripped their hearts! The long, bloody war that had spanned half the globe had at last come to an end. Bells rang from church towers, celebratory gunshots sounded, soldiers shouted and sang in joy and triumph. It was a time of rejoicing. Justice had triumphed, and the soldiers would soon be coming home!

The soldiers' rejoicing that day was epic, yet it was nothing compared with a night long before it when angels brought the good news of peace on earth to shepherds in the rolling fields outside Bethlehem. The angels led the humble shepherds in joyous praise at the birth of the newborn Savior, Jesus Christ, God's own Son come to earth! Have you discovered God's true peace?

TODAY'S POWER POINT

Our cause is just. Our union is perfect.—John Dickinson

July 7

TODAY IN HISTORY

1898—United States annexed Hawaiian Islands

1941—U.S. forces established base in Iceland

1981—First solar-powered plane crossed English Channel; Sandra Day O'Connor first woman nominated for Supreme Court justice

2004—Military tribunal ruled to allow six hundred terrorist suspects imprisoned at Guantanamo Bay to pursue release; former Enron CEO, Ken Lay, indicted for conspiracy and fraud

BORN TODAY

Artist Marc Chagall 1887

Baseball legend Satchel Paige 1906

Author Robert A. Heinlein. 1907

Designer Pierre Cardin. 1922

Musician Doc Severinsen 1927

Musician Ringo Starr 1940

Actress Shelley Duvall. 1949

Actress Jorja Fox. 1968

Singer Cree Summer 1969

Figure skater Michelle Kwan. 1980

THE WILL TO WIN

It takes determination to win—whether a sporting event, a personal challenge, or a war. When determination is strong enough, we can sometimes achieve the "impossible."

It's said that inventor Charles Kettering once challenged an associate to tackle a tough assignment just so he might observe the young man's "will to win." He gave the assistant only one stipulation—he must not consult any reference materials for information on the subject. Kettering knew that past studies had published many reasons why the task couldn't possibly be accomplished. But in his ignorance, the associate attacked the project with confidence that he would succeed. And he did! Not knowing the thing was impossible, he found a way to do it.

Have well-intentioned people ever told you of something you set out to accomplish, "It can't be done"? You're making a mistake if you listen to them rather than to God's promise: "Everything is possible for him who believes" (Mark 9:23).

Do you have the will to win? With God's help you can!

TODAY'S POWER POINT

If one has determination, then things will get done.—Chinese proverb

July 8

TODAY IN HISTORY

1775—Continental Congress adopted Olive Branch Petition appealing to King George III for redress for Colonial grievances

1776—Liberty Bell rung to call Philadelphians to a reading of the Declaration of Independence

1835—Liberty Bell cracked in Philadelphia

1889—First publication of the *Wall Street Journal*

1986—"Classic" Coca-Cola relaunched after sales of "New" Coke drop

1997—Last use of electric chair for capital punishment in Florida

2000—Episcopalians voted to approve ecumenical tie with Lutherans; critical U.S. missile-shield test failed

BORN TODAY

Inventor Ferdinand von Zeppelin 1838
Politician Nelson Rockefeller 1908
Bandleader Billy Eckstine 1914
TV executive Roone Arledge 1931
Singer Steve Lawrence 1935

Actress Anjelica Huston; author Marianne Williamson . 1952
Actor Kevin Bacon 1958
Singer Toby Keith 1961
Actress Kathleen Robertson 1973

IMPRINTED

A story is told of when Woodrow Wilson, then president of Princeton University, addressed a group of visiting parents about the real reason for their children's success—or lack of it. He told them:

> I get many letters from you parents about your children. You want to know why we people here at Princeton can't make more out of them and do more for them. Let me tell you the reason we can't. It may shock you just a little, but I am not trying to be rude. The reason is that they are your sons, reared in your homes, blood of your blood, bone of your bone. They have absorbed the ideals of your homes. You have formed and fashioned them. They are your sons. In those malleable, moldable years of their lives you have forever left your imprint upon them.

Take an honest look at your own life. Whose influence does it reflect? Does your life show God's imprint, or does it mirror the values of this world? If your life doesn't measure up, maybe it's time to make changes. Don't know how? "If any of you lacks wisdom, he should ask God . . . and it will be given to him" (James 1:5).

TODAY'S POWER POINT

It is our responsibilities, not ourselves, that we should take seriously.—Peter Ustinov

TODAY IN HISTORY

1816—Argentina gained independence
1850—Death of President Zachary Taylor
1893—First successful open-heart surgery performed
1974—Death of former Chief Justice Earl Warren, age eighty-three
1982—Britain's Queen Elizabeth found intruder in her bedroom
1983—Convicted attacker of Pope John Paul II claimed Soviet secret police took part in plot against pope's life
2001—Chile's court declared elderly dictator Pinochet too ill for trial
2002—Yucca Mountain approved as nuclear waste site; hormone replacement therapy linked to breast cancer and other serious illnesses in women
2003—U.S. government reported Iraqi war costing $3.9 billion a month
2004—World Court told Israel to remove fence separating occupied West Bank areas

BORN TODAY

Inventor Elias Howe. 1819
Actor Vince Edwards 1928
Secretary of Defense Donald Rumsfeld
. . . . 1932
Actor Brian Dennehy 1938

Musician and TV host John Tesh . 1952
Actor Jimmy Smits. 1955
Actor Tom Hanks. 1956
Actress Kelly McGillis 1957
Actor Fred Savage. 1976

DIVINE SERVICE

Have you ever seen a plaque hanging over a kitchen sink that reads: "Divine service conducted here three times daily"? We may not wash the dishes by hand anymore, but we all have small, repetitive tasks that feel pointless and thankless. The sentiments on the plaque remind us that all our duties, no matter how small or unimportant they may seem to us, are honorable and important when done well and to honor God. Luke 16:10 says, "Whoever can be trusted with very little can also be trusted with much." Based on how you do the inconvenient, unpleasant, small things in daily life, how much should you be trusted with the big things? How can you improve and show yourself worthy of greater things?

Psychologist and philosopher William James recommended performing an unpleasant task each day just to "keep in moral trim." He wisely understood that our moral "muscles" grow with exercise and use. Therefore, we should help to strengthen them by using them to resist life's ever-recurring "small" temptations—even the temptation to put off, shortchange, or let up on the little things in life.

TODAY'S POWER POINT

You should do your duty in all things. You can never do more. You should never wish to do less.—Robert E. Lee

July 10

TODAY IN HISTORY

1890—Forty-fourth state, Wyoming, admitted to Union
1929—New U.S. paper money first put into circulation
1980—President Jimmy Carter met with Chinese leaders to solidify stand against Soviet threat
1991—Boris Yeltsin elected president in first free Russian elections in a thousand years
1992—Captain of *Exxon Valdez* cleared of charges in connection with oil spill off Alaska's coast
1999—U.S. soccer team won Women's World Cup
2002—Airline pilots authorized to carry guns in cockpit
2006—Four three-ton ceiling slabs fell from Boston tunnel (the Big Dig project), killing one woman and revealing widespread vulnerabilities in the structure

BORN TODAY

Theologian John Calvin 1509
Painter James Whistler 1834
Author Saul Bellow 1915
Newscaster David Brinkley. 1920
Author Jean Kerr 1923
Actor Fred Gwynne 1926
Actor Lawrence Pressman. 1939
Tennis player Arthur Ashe 1943
Singer Arlo Guthrie 1947
Singer Jessica Simpson 1980

FINALLY HOME

What are the most exclusive privileges you have? Are you a member of an elite social or golf club? Is the best table reserved just for you at the finest restaurant in town? Are you a founding member of your fraternity or sorority? Are you a rising star on the corporate or political ladder, with all the privileges of power? Whatever your advantages, it's good to remember that all earthly perks quickly fade in comparison with the exclusive privilege of being adopted into God's family and living with him forever in heaven.

Famed evangelist Dwight L. Moody said: "Someday you will read in the papers that D. L. Moody of East Northfield is dead. Don't you believe a word of it! At that moment I shall be more alive than I am now. I shall have gone higher, that is all—out of this old clay tenement into a house that is immortal. . . . That which is born of the Spirit will live forever."

Death for those who are right with God is somewhat like exchanging money at the bank. For as we bring a crumpled paper note to the bank to obtain a crisp new bill in exchange, so it is that when we depart this life, we will exchange a frail body for an eternal one—plus God's treasures, liberty, victory, and knowledge—forever! Benefits like that make joining God's family the best decision you could ever make.

TODAY'S POWER POINT

To get to heaven, turn right and keep straight.—Source Unknown

TODAY IN HISTORY

1936—Opening of Triborough Bridge in New York City

1955—Opening of U.S. Air Force Academy

1975—Chinese uncovered remarkable burial mound with six thousand statues of warriors believed to be several thousand years old

2000—First woman elected to lead African Methodist Episcopal Church

2001—Quahtani septuplets—third known set of septuplets in the world—born in Washington DC (five boys and two girls)

2004—International AIDS conference convened in Bangkok

2006—Multiple terrorist bombs on commuter trains in Mumbai, India, kill hundreds

BORN TODAY

President John Quincy Adams . . . 1767

Author E. B. White 1899

Actor Yul Brynner 1920

Designer Giorgio Armani. 1936

Boxer Leon Spinks 1953

Actress Sela Ward 1956

Actress Lisa Rinna 1965

TV host John Henson 1967

Actor Michael Rosenbaum 1972

Rapper Lil' Kim 1975

THE TROUBLE WITH LAZINESS

It has been said that doing nothing is about the most tiresome work in the world because you can't stop and rest. A Chinese story tells of a merchant with a son who loved to sleep late. Despite repeated warnings from his father against laziness, the youth continued his habit of sleeping until midday.

In desperation the father thought of an idea to try to motivate his son to rise earlier. "Want to make some money?" he asked. "You know the saying, 'Get up early in the morning, pick up a pot of lost gold!'"

"In that case," his son answered, "the one who lost the gold must have gotten up even earlier."

It seems, considering his clever answer, that the son continued his lazy ways. But we can also surmise the course of his life if he failed to learn the value of discipline and hard work. Few things of lasting value get done without real effort. One day such a son might find his house falling down around him, his fields overgrown with weeds, and his cupboards and coffers empty. Even if laziness doesn't lead immediately and directly to failure, laziness is, in itself, a kind of failure. While life has no guarantee of monetary success if we work hard, we can be sure that success never comes from being lazy.

TODAY'S POWER POINT

Laziness is nothing more than the habit of resting before you get tired.—Jules Renard

July 12

TODAY IN HISTORY

1862—U.S. Congressional Medal of Honor authorized
1933—Minimum wage set (forty cents per hour)
1970—Television premiere of *Evening at Pops*
1984—First woman vice-presidential candidate, Geraldine Ferraro, chosen
2001—Campaign finance reform bill died in House of Representatives
2004—Ban restricting development in national forests lifted; U.S. standards for
        LDL cholesterol lowered by about 30 percent

BORN TODAY

Author Henry David Thoreau . . . 1817
Photography pioneer George Eastman
        1854
Educator and agricultural researcher
        George Washington Carver. . . 1861
Lyricist Oscar Hammerstein II . . . 1895
Pianist Van Cliburn 1934
Actor Bill Cosby. 1938
Actress Cheryl Ladd 1951
Actress Lisa Nicole Carson 1969
Olympic skater Kristi Yamaguchi . 1971
Wrestler Brock Lesnar 1977

GETTING THE WORD OUT

How motivated are Christians to proclaim God's Word? Here are some interesting comparisons: Fuller Brush Company sales representatives were said to get into one of every seven homes called on, with a sale made in one of every six homes entered. In contrast, it's been reported that Mormon missionaries succeed in entering only one in seven homes visited and spend five hundred hours dealing with an individual before he or she is converted. Even so, the Mormons reportedly start one new church every three days!

Famed evangelist Vance Havner once told of a young preacher who stood on a street corner in Indianapolis and preached. Soon such a huge crowd had gathered that the meeting had to be moved into a large auditorium nearby. The crowd followed the preacher and soon completely filled the main floor. His fervent preaching brought the crowd to tears and repentance. But their service was cut short. The great hall had already been reserved for a convention, and the gathered crowd would have to leave. The subject of the convention that halted the impromptu evangelistic service? "How to Reach the Masses." As Havner pointed out, "While the convention was discussing how to reach the masses, D. L. Moody was out there doing it!"

Are you a "discusser" or a doer of God's command to "preach the good news to all creation" (Mark 16:15)?

TODAY'S POWER POINT

Do not merely listen to the word. . . . Do what it says.—James 1:22

TODAY IN HISTORY

1787—Northwest Territory claimed by United States
1863—Civil War draft riots in New York City
1930—First World Cup soccer competition
1960—John F. Kennedy nominated for president
1965—Death of politician Adlai Stevenson, age sixty-five
1985—Live Aid benefit concerts raised $100 million for famine relief; President Ronald Reagan underwent surgery to remove cancerous colon polyp
2000—United States and Vietnam signed trade agreement
2003—Iraqi leaders met to begin forming interim government
2004—Al Qaeda suspect arrested for scouting various U.S. buildings
2006—Hezbollah rockets rained down on northern Israeli cities, killing two and injuring dozens

BORN TODAY

Socialist and economist Sidney Webb 1859
Actor Bob Crane 1928
Politician Jack Kemp 1935
Actor Patrick Stewart 1940
Actor Harrison Ford. 1942

Inventor Erno Rubik 1944
Singer Louise Mandrell 1954
Boxer Michael Spinks. 1956
Writer Cameron Crowe 1957
Basketball player Spud Webb 1963

KEEPING IT CLEAN

An army corporal, writing in *Moody Monthly*, told of his experience some years ago on a train en route to New York. As he was riding along, an army officer came and sat beside him. They struck up a conversation and soon learned of each other's faith in Christ. The soldier asked the officer if he'd had many opportunities to witness to his fellow soldiers.

The officer replied, "The first night in the tent most of the troops were swearing and telling filthy stories. Finally, having had enough of the filth, I told the soldiers: 'I've heard your rough talk, but now I am going to talk to God and, out of respect for him, I ask you to please be quiet.' The tent grew suddenly silent as I prayed, and I never again had to contend with immoral talk."

It's amazing how the world will respect a Christian who unashamedly takes a stand for what's right!

TODAY'S POWER POINT

A life of peace, purity, and refinement leads to a calm and untroubled old age.
—Cicero

TODAY IN HISTORY

1789—Bastille Day first observed in France

1958—Iraq monarchy overthrown

1974—Gallup poll showed Americans more concerned about inflation than anything else (including energy crisis)

1986—Death of industrial designer Raymond Loewy, age ninety-three

2000—Jury awarded record $144.8 billion in damages to 500,000 Florida smokers

2002—Unsuccessful assassination attempt on French president Jacques Chirac

2003—North Korea announced plans to build six nuclear bombs; *Columbia* Accident Investigation Board warned more NASA accidents possible due to inconsistent shuttle-parts tests

BORN TODAY

Cartoonist William Hanna 1910

Folksinger Woody Guthrie 1912

President Gerald Ford 1913

Director Ingmar Bergman 1918

Actress Polly Bergen 1930

Football player Rosie Greer 1932

Sportscaster Steve Stone 1947

Music executive Tommy Mottola . 1949

Actor Matthew Fox 1966

Baseball player Robin Ventura . . . 1967

Actress Missy Gold 1970

ENEMIES

The late Texas preacher R. C. Campbell told of two men with farms on opposite sides of a river. One day the first farmer's cows got away, crossed the narrow riverbed, and damaged half an acre of his neighbor's corn before the second farmer corralled and locked them securely in his barn. Rather than return the herd, the aggrieved farmer demanded a significant ransom.

Later, the second farmer's hogs escaped and began rooting up the first farmer's potatoes. But this farmer simply rounded up the hogs and herded them safely back where they belonged.

When the hogs' owner saw that his neighbor had returned the wayward herd, he shook his head with amazement and newfound respect. To the man he had treated as an enemy he admitted: "You have something that I don't have."

When we do good to those who mistreat us, not only does God promise to reward us, but people will truly see that we're children of God. Titus 2:7 instructs: "In everything set them an example by doing what is good." Do others see something in you that they don't have—the love of Christ?

TODAY'S POWER POINT

Observe your enemies, for they first find out your faults.—Antisthenes

TODAY IN HISTORY

1968—Television premiere of *One Life to Live*

1971—China visit announced by President Richard M. Nixon

1976—Former governor Jimmy Carter and Senator Walter Mondale headed Democratic ticket

1979—President Jimmy Carter proposed energy plan to save 4.5 billion gallons of oil daily by 1990

1982—Marriage of 4,150 followers of Reverend Sun Myung Moon in New York's Madison Square Garden

2002—Pakistani court convicted four in death of *Wall Street Journal* reporter Daniel Pearl; in wake of Enron scandal, U.S. Senate unanimously approved tough new law against business fraud, including jail sentences for executives who juggle figures

2004—UN report said life expectancy in Africa was forty years, poverty rising in seven countries; obesity declared an illness to be covered by Medicaid

BORN TODAY

Artist Rembrandt 1606
Author Clement Moore 1779
Guitarist Julian Bream 1933
Football player Alex Karras;
    actor Ken Kercheval 1935
Singer Linda Ronstadt 1946

Wrestler and politician Jesse Ventura
    1951
Actor Willie Aames. 1960
Actor Forest Whitaker 1961
Actor Scott Foley 1972
Actor Brian Austin Green. 1973

CONSISTENCY

One of the benefits of a Christian education, publicized by the Christian-school movement, is consistency of message at church, at home, and at school. The importance of such uniformity is illustrated by the following tale.

A group of fish was trying to teach some young crabs how to move forward rather than in the sideways manner normal for crabs. Although the fish had some success in their one-day practice session, they found that a week later, despite their encouragement, the crabs had gone back to their familiar gait. It was then the fish realized that while they could influence the crabs for one day a week, when they returned to their homes, the influence of the adult crabs had more than offset the lessons taught by the fish.

To influence others, especially our children, we need to maintain consistency in all we say and do, not just on Sunday morning but throughout the week.

TODAY'S POWER POINT

It is easier to build boys than to repair men.—Source Unknown

TODAY IN HISTORY

1790—District of Columbia recognized

1945—United States conducted first atom-bomb test

1969—*Apollo II* astronauts began voyage to land on moon

1985—Seven teenage computer hackers accused of accessing confidential data

1999—John F. Kennedy Jr., his wife, Carolyn Bissett, and Carolyn's sister killed in small plane crash off Massachusetts coast; first woman named to head space-shuttle mission

2001—China signed twenty-year friendship pact with Russia

2002—IRA apologized to relatives of 650 civilians killed in three decades of violence in Northern Ireland

2003—Drive to investigate handling of intelligence on Iraq narrowly defeated in U.S. Senate

2004—Martha Stewart given five-month jail term and a $30,000 fine for lying to investigators over ImClone stock trade

BORN TODAY

Journalist Ida Wells 1862

Explorer Roald Amundsen 1872

Actress Barbara Stanwyck 1907

Actress Ginger Rogers. 1911

TV panelist Bess Myerson 1924

Singer Ruben Blades. 1948

Dancer Michael Flatley. 1958

Actor Will Farrell 1967

Football player Barry Sanders 1968

Actor Corey Feldman 1971

A GODLY MOTHER

What is the value of a godly mother—one who models godly behavior daily before her children and who trains them in the eternal principles of God's Word? The Bible describes a godly woman (and mother) this way:

> A wife of noble character who can find? She is worth far more than rubies. Her husband has full confidence in her and lacks nothing of value. She brings him good, not harm, all the days of her life. . . . She gets up while it is still dark; she provides food for her family. . . . Her children arise and call her blessed; her husband also, and he praises her: "Many women do noble things, but you surpass them all." Charm is deceptive, and beauty is fleeting; but a woman who fears the LORD is to be praised. Give her the reward she has earned, and let her works bring her praise at the city gate. (Proverbs 31:10–12, 15, 28–31)

TODAY'S POWER POINT

All that I am, or hope to be, I owe to my angel mother.—Abraham Lincoln

TODAY IN HISTORY

1945—Start of Potsdam summit conference of Allied leaders
1948—Korea founded
1955—Opening of Disneyland in Anaheim, California
1980—Methodist minister Marjorie Matthews became first woman bishop of an American church; presidential candidate Ronald Reagan chose rival George H. W. Bush as vice-presidential running mate
1988—Democrats selected Michael Dukakis and Lloyd Bentsen to head their presidential ticket
1996—Two hundred thirty people killed in plane crash off Long Island
2000—Germany agreed to pay $5 billion to victims of Nazi-era atrocities
2003—United States records 147th combat death in Iraq, matching losses in 1990 Gulf War; British prime minister Tony Blair told U.S. Congress that Iraq war was justified even without finding weapons of mass destruction
2006—Death of "Mike Hammer" mystery writer, Mickey Spillane, age eighty-eight

BORN TODAY

Merchant John Jacob Astor 1763
Writer Erle Stanley Gardner 1889
Actor James Cagney 1904
Radio and TV host Art Linkletter. 1912
Actress Phyllis Diller. 1917

Actor Donald Sutherland;
   singer Diahann Carroll 1935
Actor David Hasselhoff 1952
Baseball player Jason Jennings . . . 1978

WHEN GOD IS FOR YOU

Who hasn't had the crushing experience of getting turned down for a job, being rejected by someone who matters, or losing the big sale? It's times like these, when everything seems to be going sour, that we can take comfort in knowing that God is for us, no matter what!

In biblical times, when the people of Israel were taken prisoner and led into exile by powerful Babylon, and the mighty capital, Jerusalem, lay in ruins, all seemed lost. But the story didn't end there. Even though those captives would not live to see the day, God promised to raise up their nation once again. And he did.

If you're discouraged by the events of your day or by the way things seem to be going in the world, take heart. All your troubles are known to God, and he has told us: "In this world you will have trouble. But take heart! I have overcome the world" (John 16:33).

TODAY'S POWER POINT

If God is for us, who can be against us?—Romans 8:31

TODAY IN HISTORY

1534—Authority of pope declared void in England
1925—Adolph Hitler manifesto *Mein Kampf* published
1940—Franklin D. Roosevelt nominated for unprecedented third term as U.S. president
1969—Start of Senator Edward Kennedy's Chappaquiddick scandal
1976—Gymnast Nadia Comaneci earned first perfect score in Olympic history
2000—United States pledged $1 billion a year to fight AIDS in Africa; Senate cut taxes for most married taxpayers

BORN TODAY

Author William Thackeray 1811
Semanticist S. I. Hayakawa 1906
Comedian Red Skelton 1913
Astronaut John Glenn 1921
Writer Hunter S. Thompson 1937
Singer Dion 1939
Baseball player and manager Joe Torre
. . . . 1940
Actor James Brolin 1941
Singer Ricky Skaggs 1954
Actor Vin Diesel. 1967
Basketball player Penny Hardaway 1972

STRONG LOVE

According to *The Truth for Youth*, a group in Africa once wrote to David Livingstone asking, "Have you found a good road to where you are? If so, we want to know how to send other men to join you."

Livingstone replied, "If you have men who will come only if they know there is a good road, I don't want them. I want men who will come if there is no road at all!" Livingstone wanted those whose drive for success would not be derailed by hostile terrain or difficult circumstances. If something is important to us—if we love someone or are passionate about something—we'll be willing to spend our energy and ourselves for it, no matter how difficult that may be.

Consider your own commitments in life. Based on where you expend the most effort, what do you value most? Do you love your God and your family with all your strength? Don't let difficulties or obstacles keep you from doing what's important.

TODAY'S POWER POINT

As a general rule the most successful man in life is the man who has the best information.—Benjamin Disraeli

TODAY IN HISTORY

1848—First women's rights convention
1881—Sitting Bull surrendered to U.S. troops at Fort Burford, Dakota
1941—Winston Churchill introduced "V for Victory"
1954—Elvis Presley released first record; J. R. R. Tolkien's *Lord of the Rings* published
1975—U.S. *Apollo* spacecraft undocked with Soviet counterpart, *Soyuz*, after two-day international space mission
1980—Boycotted Summer Olympics opened in Moscow with no U.S. or West German teams
1984—Democrats chose Walter Mondale and Geraldine Ferraro to head their presidential ticket
1993—Saddam Hussein agreed to UN weapons inspections
2006—President George W. Bush cast his first veto, to block expansion of stem-cell research

BORN TODAY

Inventor Samuel Colt 1814
Artist Edgar Degas 1834
Politician George McGovern 1922
Singer Vikki Carr 1941
Tennis player Ilie Nastase 1946
Musician Alan Collins 1952
Actor Anthony Edwards 1962
Actor Topher Grace 1978

NO WAITING

A man once had an open sore on his face. The sore didn't heal but rather grew larger. His friends warned that it might be cancer and urged him to seek treatment immediately. But the man read a newspaper ad for a salve that promised to cure cancer, and rather than seek medical help, he bought the salve and applied it, pleased with himself for saving the cost of the doctor's visit and the pain of surgery. For a while the sore did seem to be healing, but underneath it a deadly cancer still grew, spreading until it eventually claimed the man's life.

Too many people ignore the deadly nature of their spiritual affliction, salving their consciences through their own ineffective efforts to cure or at least cover up what ails them. But their effectiveness is only skin deep, and no amount of diligence or effort is sufficient to reach to the roots of the deadly affliction that threatens our souls. Only God can effect a real cure—one from the inside out. Without delay, we must go to God and allow him to cut away the diseased, defective parts to make us whole throughout.

TODAY'S POWER POINT

Destiny . . . is not a matter of chance, it is a matter of choice; it is not a thing to be waited for, it is a thing to be achieved.—William Jennings Bryan

July 20

TODAY IN HISTORY

1715—"Riot Act" in England made gatherings of twelve or more people illegal

1944—Bomb intended for Adolf Hitler misfired; U.S. forces invaded Guam

1968—First Special Olympics held; *Apollo 11* became first manned spacecraft to land on moon

1969—U.S. astronaut Neil Armstrong became first human to walk on moon

1976—After eleven-month journey, *Viking I* spacecraft sent detailed photos of Mars

1990—Appeals court overturned conviction of Oliver North

2004—Kidnapped Filipino hostage released in Iraq following withdrawal of Philippine troops; Microsoft declared record-setting dividend (of three dollars per share, at a total cost of $32 billion)

2006—U.S. Marines entered embattled Lebanon to evacuate American citizens

BORN TODAY

Actress Thea Bera 1890
Explorer Edmund Hillary 1919
Basketball coach Chuck Daly 1930
Actress Natalie Wood;
   actress Diana Rigg 1938
Singer Kim Carnes 1946
Musician Carlos Santana 1947
Singer Chris Cornell 1964
Hockey player Peter Forsberg 1973
Basketball player Ray Allen 1975

ONE SMALL STEP

Few who saw it will ever forget the sight of Neil Armstrong setting foot on the moon—a small but historic step. Sometimes the steps we take in this life seem small—maybe inconsequential. But God can use all of our steps—everything we do and say, perhaps even unintentionally, to accomplish his will.

Some time ago the British Press Association reported the story of a submarine that lay disabled on the ocean floor. After frantic attempts to raise the vessel failed, all hope of rescue was lost, and the effort was abandoned. The sub's commanding officer admitted to the crew that they didn't have long to live and led them in singing "Abide with Me." Following the song, the sailors took sedatives to calm them as they waited for the end to come.

One of the sedated men collapsed and fell against a control panel, forcing forward the sub's jammed surfacing mechanism. The craft slowly began to rise and eventually made it safely back to port. Some might call this a freak accident or a stroke of luck, but the sailors were convinced God had been at work on their behalf. They learned firsthand that with God, there are no accidents.

In what difficult situation do you find yourself? Can't even fathom a way of escape? Don't give up. God knows where you are—and he knows what he's doing. Trust him.

TODAY'S POWER POINT

That's one small step for a man, one giant leap for mankind.—Neil Armstrong

July 21

TODAY IN HISTORY

1930—Veterans Administration organized

1944—Democrats nominated President Franklin D. Roosevelt for unprecedented fourth term

1959—First nuclear-powered cargo ship launched

2000—Government officials cleared in Waco deaths of Branch Davidian cult members

2002—EPA agreed to fund cleanup of eleven toxic waste sites; WorldCom filed for bankruptcy—largest in U.S. history

2004—Scientist Stephen Hawking said information may be gained from black holes in space

BORN TODAY

Author Ernest Hemingway 1899
Author Marshall McLuhan 1911
Violinist Isaac Stern 1920
Actor Don Knotts 1924
Producer Norman Jewison 1926
Cartoonist Garry Trudeau 1949
Actor Robin Williams 1952
Actor Jon Lovitz 1957
Actor Josh Hartnett 1978

WASTED YEARS

Have you ever heard someone say, "Had I known I was going to live this long, I would have taken better care of myself"? None of us knows how long God will allow us to remain here on earth. That's why it's so important to make every day count in his service.

A preacher was talking with a mother who was discouraged. All of her children had grown up and left home, and she was wondering if she had really accomplished anything of importance over the years. Knowing her family, the pastor told her, "Why ma'am, two of your children are out serving the Lord on the mission field, the third is now in training for the ministry. I would think that your heavenly reward will be great because of how you faithfully served the Lord by ministering to your family."

That mother's faithful example day by day helped her children grow up to be vital, giving, loving adults eager to serve God and all humanity. Because this parent had done her job well, her children would accomplish things far beyond her own reach or ability to serve. By her faithful service all through the years, she paved the way for their successes and shared in them fully.

Your efforts are never wasted if you're doing what God has asked you to do.

TODAY'S POWER POINT

Short as life is, we make it still shorter by the careless waste of time.—Victor Hugo

July 22

TODAY IN HISTORY

1620—Pilgrims boarded the *Mayflower* heading for the New World
1796—Cleveland, Ohio, chartered
1916—Mysterious explosion at parade in San Francisco killed ten
1934—Fugitive John Dillinger gunned down
1944—International Monetary Fund established
1999—Chinese government banned radical Falun Gong sect
2001—U.S. and Russian leaders agreed to reduce stockpiles of nuclear weapons
2003—Saddam Hussein's sons Uday and Qusay killed in Iraq shootout; former POW Jessica Lynch returned home to hero's welcome
2004—Panel recommended major overhaul of U.S. intelligence agencies and appointment of a cabinet-level intelligence chief; army inspector general called prison abuse at Abu Ghraib an isolated incident

BORN TODAY

Botanist Gregor Mendel 1822
Psychiatrist Karl Menninger 1893
Sculptor Alexander Calder 1898
Politician Bob Dole 1923
Singer Margaret Whiting 1924
Actress Louise Fletcher 1934
Game-show host Alex Trebek 1940
Singer Bobby Sherman 1945
Actor Danny Glover 1947
Actor Rob Estes 1963
Comedian David Spade 1965
Singer Daniel Jones 1973

UNRECOGNIZED BLESSINGS

Our Daily Bread relayed the story of a mother with a brain-injured child. She wrote that her daughter's handicap could have become the greatest tragedy of their lives were it not for their coming to know the Lord better. "How disappointed we were when our little girl failed to experience normal mental development—perhaps like the Savior feels when his children do not spiritually mature."

God knows that trials and heartaches can enrich your life in such ways that would not otherwise happen. Herb Vander Lugt described a friend who "walks with difficulty and can't use his arms very well, but he believes he knows God better than if he had been healed."

Are you going through difficult times? Recognize that God's ways are not your ways. Once you do, you'll be taking the first step to a stronger faith in him. If you've ever come face to face with your human limitations, why not admit your weakness to God and ask him to carry you over the rough spots in life?

TODAY'S POWER POINT

Knowing what you cannot do is more important than knowing what you can do.—Lucille Ball

TODAY IN HISTORY

1827—Opening of first swimming school in United States
1904—Ice-cream cone reportedly invented in St. Louis, Missouri
1956—Site of Statue of Liberty named Liberty Island
1986—Marriage of England's Prince Andrew and Sarah Ferguson
2002—Israelis launch raid against militant Hamas leaders, killing fifteen; homosexual advocate named new Archbishop of Canterbury
2003—New York City councilman James Davis gunned down by rival in City Hall shooting; government investigation reported nearly eight hundred children in Boston archdiocese had been abused by Catholic priests and church officials over a sixty-year period

BORN TODAY

Psychiatrist Karl Menninger 1893
Baseball player Pee Wee Reese . . . 1918
TV host Bert Convy 1933
Sportscaster Don Drysdale 1936
Talk-show host Don Imus 1940
Actor Woody Harrelson 1961
Actor Eriq LaSalle 1962
Basketball player Gary Wayne Payton 1968
Actor Daniel Radcliffe 1989

STEP BY STEP

Have you ever gone on a hike after dark? If you were fortunate enough to have a flashlight, you undoubtedly were grateful to have its light to guide your way. Radio teacher Richard DeHaan observed, "He who carries a lantern on a dark road at night sees only one step ahead. When he takes that step, the lamp moves forward, and another step is made plain. He finally reaches his destination in safety without once walking in darkness. All the way is lighted, but only a single step at a time. This is the method of God's guidance."

When we follow God, our destination is sure. But every person's path is filled with obstacles and challenges. To overcome these bumps along the way and reach your heavenly destination, you need the light from the lamp of God's Word. By daily searching the Scriptures and calling out to God for assistance, you'll find enough light to guide you through that day. As DeHaan noted, "It isn't necessary to see beyond what the Lord reveals. By daily following his leading, there's always enough light for each step of the way."

TODAY'S POWER POINT

Your word is a lamp to my feet and a light for my path.—Psalm 119:105

TODAY IN HISTORY

1874—Pioneer Day marked Mormon settlement of Salt Lake City, Utah

1959—U.S. vice president Richard Nixon and Soviet premier Nikita Khrushchev conduct "kitchen" debate

1967—Furor created by French president Charles de Gaulle's sympathy for Quebec separatists led to abrupt end to his visit

1978—*New York Times* reporter jailed for refusing to turn over notes

1980—Tennis player Bjorn Borg scored record fifth win at Wimbledon

1983—Iraq charged United States with giving weapons to Iranians in Iran-Iraq war

2002—Stock market gained 488 points, biggest one-day increase in fifteen years

2003—Congressional committee blamed CIA and FBI for not taking warnings of terrorist attacks against the United States more seriously

2005—Lance Armstrong won historic seventh straight Tour de France

BORN TODAY

South American revolutionary Simón
  Bolívar 1783
Aviator Amelia Earhart. 1897
Cartoonist Pat Oliphant. 1935
Musician Peter Serkin. 1947

Actor Michael Richards;
  actress Lynda Carter 1951
Basketball player Karl Malone . . . 1963
Baseball player Barry Bonds 1964
Actress Jennifer Lopez 1970

LENDING A HAND

"This isn't a man's job," the husband vainly protested as he dried the dishes.

But his wife would hear none of it. "Oh, yes it is," she shot back. "Second Kings 21:13 says, 'I will wipe out Jerusalem as one wipes a dish, wiping it and turning it upside down.'"

No matter how boring the task may be, the believer who is serving God will find it a blessing to participate as part of God's family. As the English poet and clergyman John Donne wrote some four hundred years ago, "No man is an island, entire of itself; every man is a piece of the continent, a part of the main; any man's death diminishes me, because I am involved in mankind; and therefore never send to know for whom the bell tolls; it tolls for thee."

When asked to do a job you feel is beneath your abilities, rejoice that you may serve God in yet another way. Keep a good attitude in the little things, then watch God bless you with increasingly greater responsibilities for him.

TODAY'S POWER POINT

Look up and not down; out and not in; forward and not back; and lend a hand.
—Edward Everett Hale

TODAY IN HISTORY

1909—First successful flight across English Channel

1952—Puerto Rico became self-governing

1978—World's first "test-tube baby" born (Louise Brown)

1994—Israel and Jordan signed Washington Agreement, formally ending state of war between the two nations that had started in 1948

1996—Bomb exploded at Atlanta Summer Olympics

1997—Strongman Pol Pot underwent trial by Khmer Rouge

1999—Lance Armstrong won his first Tour de France

2000—Presidential candidate George W. Bush chose Dick Cheney as his running mate; Air France *Concorde* crashed on takeoff from Paris, killing all aboard

2002—Former Yugoslav president Slobodan Milošević diagnosed with serious heart disease, likely to delay his trial for war crimes; bankruptcy bill passed that would require debtors to pay back debt

BORN TODAY

Illustrator Maxfield Parrish 1870

Actor Walter Brennan 1894

Producer Blake Edwards 1922

Actress Estelle Getty 1924

Actress Barbara Harris 1935

Football player Walter Payton 1954

Actress Illeana Douglas 1965

Actor Matt LeBlanc 1967

Actor Brad Renfro 1982

BEING CONSISTENT

Family Weekly reported that a man from Brooklyn had his name changed from Kelly to Feinberg, then a year later from Feinberg to Garibaldi. When the man appeared in court, the judge asked why he was changing his name yet again. The man replied, "My neighborhood keeps changing."

Consistency sometimes seems to be a thing of the past, but not with the U.S. government. For seven months in a row, the Veterans Administration sent Ronald Vest's check to Candy Postlethwaite. Despite her valiant efforts to correct the delivery error, the checks keep turning up in her mailbox month after month. To make matters worse, Candy can't simply destroy the unwanted checks, since they're government property. Thus she is forced to expend time and energy trying to get the checks to the intended recipient.

While it's usually a good thing to be consistent, it's possible to be consistently wrong. Thank God that not only is he perfect, but he also is consistently so, in spite of our ever-changing world.

TODAY'S POWER POINT

Let your character be kept up to the very end, just as it began, and so be consistent.—Horace

July 26

TODAY IN HISTORY

1788—New York eleventh state to ratify U.S. Constitution
1908—FBI established
1947—Defense Department formed (comprised of U.S. Army, Navy, and Air Force)
1953—Fidel Castro led futile attack on army barracks at Santiago, Cuba, starting
    his revolution
1956—Egypt nationalized Suez Canal
1981—Reverend Sun Myung Moon under investigation for tax evasion
1990—Public facilities became accessible to handicapped in the United States
2000—U.S. judge approved award of $1.25 billion to settle claims by Holocaust
    survivors

BORN TODAY

Playwright George Bernard Shaw . 1856
Psychologist Carl Jung 1875
Author Aldous Huxley 1894
Comedienne Gracie Allen 1902
Actress Vivian Vance. 1912

Producer Stanley Kubrick. 1928
Musician Mick Jagger. 1943
Actress Susan George 1950
Actor Kevin Spacey 1959
Actress Sandra Bullock 1964

NO PAIN, NO GAIN

Though God's gift of salvation is priceless, it's not cheap. A preacher was having a hard time getting through to a grizzled old miner the truth that God's salvation is a free gift. The preacher asked the miner what he thought of the plan of salvation, and he replied, "It's just too cheap. I can't believe in a religion such as that. If there's no pain, then there can be no gain."

The preacher asked the miner how he had gotten back out of the mine at the end of the day. "In an elevator, of course," came the response.

"Well," said the preacher, "that sounds too simple to me. Isn't there something you have to do to help raise yourself?"

"No, of course not," the miner responded.

"What about the work needed to drill the 1,800-foot elevator shaft? Was it expensive?"

"Why, yes, it was very costly, but it was necessary. Otherwise we could never get out of the mine."

"The same is true of salvation," explained the minister. "The work of Christ on the cross has already been completed at a tremendous cost, sacrificing the best that heaven had so that all who come to Christ might be saved. All you need to do is to believe."

"How shall we escape if we ignore such a great salvation?" (Hebrews 2:3).

TODAY'S POWER POINT

You must pay the price if you wish to secure the blessing.—Andrew Jackson

TODAY IN HISTORY

1789—U.S. State Department established
1866—England and U.S. sent first telegraph messages over new cable link
1944—U.S. Army training camps desegregated
1953—End of Korean War
1984—Death of pollster George Gallup Sr., age eighty-two
2001—Nathaniel Brazill, fourteen-year-old Florida youth, sentenced to twenty-eight years in prison for killing his teacher
2004—Former officials of Islamic charity Holy Land Foundation charged with donating more than $12 million to Palestinian terrorists

BORN TODAY

Novelist Alexandre Dumas 1824
Baseball manager Leo Durocher . . 1905
Producer Norman Lear 1922
Actor Jerry Van Dyke 1931
Songwriter Bobby Gentry 1942

Figure skater Peggy Fleming;
director Betty Thomas 1948
Singer Maureen McGovern 1949
Baseball player Alex Rodriguez . . . 1975

BIGGER THAN IT SEEMS

We should be mindful of the little things of life, for the power they wield can be tremendous. A single comparatively small rudder controls the movement of a massive ocean liner. And a single life dedicated to God can impact a multitude.

Long ago a woman was preparing a box to send to missionaries when a little girl came to her door with a penny to send along. With this one penny the woman bought a gospel tract, which she included in the box. The tract was read by a tribal chief, who accepted Christ as his Savior. He was then influential in reaching many of his people with the gospel. As a result of one little girl's small gift, more than 1,500 faraway people who had never before heard the good news eventually became Christians—freed from everlasting hopelessness. As Richard DeHaan noted: "It is later than it's ever been before in the history of this world, in the days allotted to man and on God's calendar of events."

With each passing hour the words of James 5:8 take on added significance: "Be patient and stand firm, because the Lord's coming is near." Never underestimate the little things of life, for the Bible reminds us that God uses the little things to confound the wise (see 1 Corinthians 1:27).

TODAY'S POWER POINT

Enjoy the little things, for one day you may look back and realize they were the big things.—Robert Brault

July 28

TODAY IN HISTORY

1821—Peru gained independence

1914—Austria and Hungary declared war on Serbia, launching World War I

1932—"Bonus Army" of World War I veterans dispersed in Washington DC

1945—Army bomber crashed into fog-shrouded Empire State Building, killing thirteen people

2002—Nine Pennsylvania miners rescued after being trapped for more than three days in Quecreek mine

2003—U.S. prison population reported to have grown to nearly 2.2 million

2004—After twenty-five years of service, Doctors Without Borders left Afghanistan due to dangerous conditions

BORN TODAY

Author Beatrix Potter 1866

Singer Rudy Vallee 1866

First Lady Jacqueline Kennedy Onassis 1929

Actor Darryl Hickman 1931

Basketball player and politician Bill Bradley 1943

Cartoonist Jim Davis 1945

Actress Sally Struthers 1948

Actress Lori Laughlin 1964

MIGHTY WEAPONS

Professor Haddon Robinson noted: "As you page through the pages of your Bible, you may be surprised by how little God seems to care for the ease and comfort of his saints." That doesn't mean he's not concerned for them. Rather, Robinson said, God "cares more about what happens in you so that he can accomplish his purposes through you."

In the twenty-first century, nations seem to rely more on weapons of mass destruction than on God for their strength. This confidence is misplaced. A news story told of a remarkable catch made some time ago by fishermen aboard a French trawler. After reporting an "enormous pulling" on its nets, the ship's crew discovered they had snagged a 382-foot submarine, the USS *Robert E. Lee*. It took five hours to untangle the submarine (which suffered no major damage) from the trawler's nets. All the might of a state-of-the-art naval submarine—sixteen Polaris missiles and a crew of highly skilled sailors—was rendered useless as the vessel lay hopelessly trapped by a simple fishing net!

In what do you place your trust? In the "big stick" of weapons and defenses, or in the almighty power of God?

TODAY'S POWER POINT

The most powerful weapon on earth is the human soul on fire.—Ferdinand Poch

TODAY IN HISTORY

1588—Spanish Armada defeated by British
1890—Death of artist Vincent van Gogh, age thirty-seven
1935—Thomas Dewey appointed by New York governor to investigate organized crime
1958—NASA established
1981—Britain's Prince Charles married Lady Diana Spencer in lavish London wedding; U.S. House and Senate approved President Reagan's 25 percent tax cut request
1994—Stephen Breyer confirmed to Supreme Court
2003—United States stepped up efforts to find Saddam Hussein, rounded up 174 suspected Hussein backers
2004—Increased kidnappings forced postponement of Iraqi national congress

BORN TODAY

Writer Booth Tarkington 1869
Actor William Powell 1892
Attorney Melvin Belli 1907
Choreographer Paul Taylor 1930
Politician Elizabeth Dole 1936
Broadcast journalist Peter Jennings 1938
Filmmaker Ken Burns 1953
Singer Martina McBride 1966
Actor Wil Wheaton 1972
Singer Wanya Morris 1973

DOING YOUR DUTY

According to one source, federal agencies require more than one billion reports each year—nearly five reports for every man, woman, and child in the United States!

One U.S. company was expected to handle 2,700 individual reports to meet federal, state, and local requirements. "Getting something done in government," said one consultant, "is like pushing one end of a wet noodle—no one knows where the noodle is connected, where it goes in the mass, and what, if anything, will move." It makes one wonder just how effective our public servants can be at fulfilling their public duty.

How diligent are you at doing your job? Do you realize that by doing your job well you are also serving the Lord? Ask God to help you work in a way that honors him today.

TODAY'S POWER POINT

No eulogy is due to him who simply does his duty and nothing more.
—Saint Augustine

July 30

TODAY IN HISTORY

1619—Virginia General Assembly met for first time in Jamestown, Virginia

1942—Women's U.S. Navy section established: Women Appointed for Volunteer Emergency Service (WAVES)

1973—H. R. Haldeman said secret White House tapes failed to show his or President Richard Nixon's involvement in Watergate crisis

1974—Supreme Court ruled Nixon must turn over all tapes sought by special prosecutor; House committee voted 27-11 for Nixon's impeachment

1994—Supreme Court limited abortion clinic protests

2002—Rwanda and Congo signed peace accord, ending war that caused three million deaths

2004—UN demanded Sudan disarm radical groups in Darfur; White House estimated record $445 billion deficit for fiscal year

BORN TODAY

Novelist Emily Brontë 1818
Businessman Henry Ford 1863
Baseball coach Casey Stengel 1891
Actor Ed "Kookie" Byrnes 1933
Producer Peter Bogdanovich. 1939
Singer Paul Anka 1941
Actor and politician Arnold
    Schwarzenegger. 1947
Actress Delta Burke 1956
Actress Lisa Kudrow. 1963
Actress Hilary Swank 1974

POVERTY

All priests take a vow of poverty upon being accepted into the clergy. However, this policy was recently challenged by two priests on the law-school faculty of a Catholic institution in the Washington DC area. The two, whose pay was as little as half what others in their field were making, filed separate suits against their administration, seeking parity with other law professors. The priests contended that the university had promised to end their "discounted" salaries but that nothing was ever done.

What sacrifices have you made in the service of something (or Someone) in whom you truly believe? Was the sacrifice worth it? Although we all need to make a living, often there's a wide gulf between what we want and what we actually need. It's easy to forget the true value of the eternal. Gaining something of eternal value is worth any sacrifice we could make.

TODAY'S POWER POINT

You can't get rid of poverty by giving people money.—P. J. O'Rourke

TODAY IN HISTORY

1790—First U.S. patent granted (for potash process)

1979—Chrysler asked for record $1 billion in loan guarantees

1985—South Africa declared state of emergency, banning mass funerals for victims of racial unrest

1991—U.S. and Russian leaders agreed to arms reduction treaty

2001—House bipartisan vote barred human cloning

2002—Bombing at Jerusalem cafeteria killed five Americans; Senate reported the United States could successfully oust Saddam Hussein, but it would require large troop commitment and might mean increases in oil prices and future terrorist attacks; two former WorldCom officials charged with inflating revenues by more than $3.8 billion

BORN TODAY

Engineer John Ericsson 1803	Actor Wesley Snipes 1962
Economist Milton Friedman 1912	Author J. K. Rowling 1965
Sportscaster Curt Gowdy 1919	Actor Dean Cain 1966
Tennis player Evonne Goolagong . 1951	Football player Jonathan Ogden . . 1974
Producer Sherry Lansing 1944	Actor Eric Lively 1981

AFRAID TO DIE

Alfred Krupp, the German industrialist who specialized in producing cannons and other weapons of war, was sometimes called the "manufacturer of death." Yet he was said to be so afraid of death that he never forgave anyone who talked about death around him. His employees were strictly barred from speaking of death in his presence, under threat of losing their jobs. Once a relative who was visiting him suddenly died, driving Krupp out of the house in terror. Later, when his wife chided him for his cowardice, Krupp forsook her and never lived with her again. Finally, nearing death himself, Krupp offered his physician the equivalent of $1 million if he would prolong his life ten years more. The doctor was, of course, unable to do this, and eventually Krupp died.

The Bible says, "Man is destined to die once" (Hebrew 9:27). But no one need live his or her life in fear of dying, as Alfred Krupp did. Because of the work of Jesus Christ, we have nothing to fear from death. Death is merely a doorway to eternity with our Maker. First Corinthians 15:54–55 exults in the ultimate triumph over death: "Death has been swallowed up in victory. Where, O death, is your victory? Where, O death, is your sting?" With Christ living within, the believer has no need to fear death.

TODAY'S POWER POINT

Life is to live in such a way that we are not afraid to die.—Teresa of Ávila

August 1

TODAY IN HISTORY

1790—First U.S. census began
1791—Virginia plantation owner released five hundred slaves—largest such emancipation in United States
1873—San Francisco cable cars began operation
1876—Thirty-eighth state, Colorado, admitted to the Union
1946—Atomic Energy Commission created
1958—U.S. postage increased to four cents (after twenty-six years at three cents)
1981—MTV premiered on cable TV
1988—*Rush Limbaugh Show* premiered on radio
1994—Lisa Marie Presley and Michael Jackson announced their secret wedding
2002—Iraq took steps to reauthorize UN weapons inspections
2004—Twelve killed in bombings of Christian churches in Mosul and Baghdad, Iraq

BORN TODAY

Explorer William Clark 1770
Composer Francis Scott Key. 1779
Author Herman Melville 1819
Actor Arthur Hill 1922
Comedian Dom DeLuise 1933
Designer Yves St. Laurent. 1936
Songwriter Robert Cray 1953
Actress Tempestt Bledsoe 1973

FORGETTING WHAT IS BEHIND

Many years ago the manager of Baltimore's largest hotel refused lodging to a man dressed as a humble farmer. His hotel was for a better clientele, he rationalized. It would harm the hotel's reputation to cater to such a lowly man.

But before long the manager discovered much to his horror, that he had just turned away the vice president of the United States, Thomas Jefferson. The man tried to remedy his mistake by sending an urgent message to the famed patriot, inviting him to be a guest at his hotel. But Jefferson replied: "Tell him I have already engaged a room elsewhere. If he has no room for a dirty American farmer, he also has none for the vice president of the United States."

Clearly the innkeeper would have liked to go back and change what he had done, but the past is past and cannot be redone. If he were wise, he would put the past behind him (without forgetting the important lesson learned) and focus on the future. Part of the Christian experience is in the journey, the learning and growing. "Forgetting what is behind and straining toward what is ahead, I press on toward the goal to win the prize" (Philippians 3:13–14). No matter how you've failed in the past, you can still win the prize. Forget the mistakes of the past and strain to do better tomorrow—and today. With God's help, you can do it!

TODAY'S POWER POINT

The smallest courtesies sweeten life; the greater enoble it.—Christian Bovee

TODAY IN HISTORY

1909—Wilbur and Orville Wright sold first military plane to U.S. War Department

1923—President Warren Harding died in San Francisco, succeeded in office by Vice President Calvin Coolidge

1934—Adolf Hitler proclaimed himself leader of Germany

1937—Franklin D. Roosevelt signed first law banning possession and sale of marijuana

1946—First use of nuclear elements for peaceful purposes (as medical radiation treatment)

1964—Firing on two U.S. destroyers (in Gulf of Tonkin) led to U.S. troops' involvement in Vietnam

1990—East and West Germany officially reunited; Persian Gulf War launched as Iraq invaded neighboring Kuwait

1996—Minimum wage raised to $5.15 per hour

2000—George W. Bush and Dick Cheney chosen to head GOP presidential ticket

2002—Leader of Taiwan stated that his country was separate from China

2004—President George W. Bush supported naming a Director of National Intelligence

BORN TODAY

Architect Pierre L'Enfant 1754
Movie-studio chief Jack Warner . . 1892
Actress Myrna Loy 1905
Actor Carroll O'Connor. 1924
Sports executive Lamar Hunt 1932

Actor Peter O'Toole 1933
Writer Wes Craven. 1949
Actress Victoria Jackson 1959
Actress Mary Louise Parker. 1964
Actress Hallie Eisenberg 1992

FREEDOM

One of the greatest blessings of being born again is independence forever from the bondage of sin. Someone has likened the bonds of sin to a chain around the neck of a dog. Of course, while he's sleeping in the cool breeze of a summer day, the dog isn't aware of the chain. Later, when he eats from his dish near his kennel, he still feels free enough. But when his master calls and he runs the length of the chain, he abruptly realizes his plight.

That is the way it is with sin—for a time it gives us the feeling that we're free and in control; then suddenly something reminds us that we're actually trapped, with no way out. But God brings true freedom. He proclaims freedom for sin's captives; the brokenhearted can receive healing, and the chained can be released from darkness.

Are you truly free, or are you still on sin's leash? You can be free today. Ask God to make you truly free, and he will.

TODAY'S POWER POINT

Freedom is not the right to do what we want, but what we ought.—Abraham Lincoln

August 3

TODAY IN HISTORY

1492—Christopher Columbus set sail from Spain, heading for India
1882—First immigration ban passed by Congress (barring convicts and paupers)
1927—First broadcast drama, *The Wolf,* on WGY radio (Schenectady, New York)
1958—First underwater crossing of the North Pole (submarine USS *Nautilus*)
1979—First African American female to occupy a cabinet position, Patricia Harris, named Department of Health, Education, and Welfare (HEW) secretary
1989—Television premiere of *Primetime Live*
2004—Voters in Missouri passed amendment to state constitution, barring same-sex marriages (first state to do so); for the first time since the 9/11 attacks, Statue of Liberty reopened to tourists

BORN TODAY

Journalist Ernie Pyle. 1900
Composer Richard Adler 1921
Singer Tony Bennett. 1926
Director Steven Berkhoff 1937
Actor Martin Sheen 1940
Home-living guru Martha Stewart . . 1941
Director John Landis 1950
Actor Jay North 1952
Gymnast Blaine Wilson 1974
Football player Tom Brady 1977

A FAMILY RESEMBLANCE

The story is told of a newly married man who was asked to work extra hours on the job. With the long workday finally over, he got in his car and headed for home—but not to the home where his new bride was waiting. Instead, he absentmindedly drove to his mother's house.

Something similar sometime happens with a new believer. Although the Bible clearly teaches that "if anyone is in Christ, he is a new creation; the old has gone, the new has come" (2 Corinthians 5:17), sometimes we still find ourselves sliding back into the habit of hanging out with the old gang or frequenting places we know we shouldn't.

The great nineteenth-century evangelist D. L. Moody described those moments immediately after his conversion: "I thought the old sun shown a good deal brighter than it ever had before. I thought that it was just smiling upon me. As I walked out upon Boston Common and heard the birds singing in the trees I thought they were all singing a song to me. . . . I fell in love with the birds (I had never cared for them before) and with all creation. I had not a bitter feeling against any man, and I was ready to take all men to my heart."

You're a child of the King. Go out today and live like it!

TODAY'S POWER POINT

Since we are born into God's family, we should bear a family resemblance.
—Source Unknown

August 4

TODAY IN HISTORY

1790—U.S. Coast Guard founded

1830—Survey completed for new City of Chicago

1892—Lizzie Borden's parents found murdered in Massachusetts

1930—Work began on first international bobsled run, (1.5 miles long, in North Elba, New York)

1956—First motorcycle to exceed 200 mph (at salt flats in Wendover, Utah)

2000—Britain's Queen Mother celebrated her one-hundredth birthday

2004—Three banks robbed in Davenport, Iowa, during presidential campaign appearances there by George W. Bush and John Kerry

BORN TODAY

Poet Percy Bysshe Shelley 1792

Britain's Queen Mother Elizabeth;
    singer Louis Armstrong. 1900

Journalist Helen Thomas 1920

Writer Leon Uris 1924

Comedian Richard Belzer. 1944

Actor Billy Bob Thornton. 1955

Politician Barack Obama 1961

Baseball player Roger Clemens . . . 1962

Race-car driver Jeff Gordon 1971

DEFENDING THE CAUSE

Shortly after the time of the Napoleonic Wars, the farmers of a certain area of England grew tired of huntsmen galloping over their fields, so they locked the gates and posted a boy at each one to stand guard. To one such guarded gate the Duke of Wellington arrived with his hunting party and asked the lad to open the gate. "I must not," said the boy, faithful to his charge.

The Duke asked him sternly, "Do you know who I am?"

Nervous but resolute, the boy replied, "I believe you are the Duke of Wellington, sir."

"Won't you open the gate for me?"

"My master told me not to open the gate to anyone," said the lad.

The Duke was so pleased at the youth's faithfulness that he handed him a reward, the equivalent of a five-dollar bill. The lad was thrilled and sat on the gatepost waving his cap in victory at the departing huntsmen. He had done what Napoleon and his army could not do—hold back the advance of the Duke of Wellington.

What is important enough for you to defend—no matter the danger or cost? Are you willing to stick your neck out to obey the instructions of your Lord and Master? What does that say about who you are as a person? As a Christian? Call upon God for strength and courage to be true and faithful.

TODAY'S POWER POINT

Faith in Christ makes both the uplook good and the outlook bright.—Herb Vander Lugt

■ 216 ■

August 5

TODAY IN HISTORY

1780—Benedict Arnold took command of fort at West Point, New York

1862—First U.S. income tax collected (to support Civil War)

1884—Cornerstone for Statue of Liberty laid at Bedloe's Island, New York

1914—First traffic lights installed (in Cleveland)

1924—*Little Orphan Annie* cartoon first appeared

1957—Television premiere of *American Bandstand*

1986—Artist Andrew Wyeth sold 240 paintings and drawings never before seen by the public

2003—Episcopal Church confirmed first openly gay bishop

BORN TODAY

Bible translator John Eliot 1604

Director John Huston 1906

Astronaut Neil Armstrong 1930

Actor John Saxon 1936

Actress Ja'net DuBois 1938

Actress Loni Anderson 1946

Basketball player Patrick Ewing . . 1962

Soccer player Lorrie Fair 1978

FOREVER FORGIVEN

Have you ever been caught doing something you knew was wrong and immediately wanted to "take back" your behavior? Such is the story of a young accountant who was seen taking money from his boss, a Christian. Called to the front office to face the music, the youth expected to be roundly chastised and fired—at best. What's worse, he fretted, his boss could even turn him over to the police, as he had committed a felony. The more the young man pondered the consequences of his behavior, the more nervous he got.

Once inside the boss's office, he was asked his name and if he had stolen the funds. With bowed head, the man ashamedly admitted doing wrong. But what came next was totally unexpected. His boss said, "If I take you back, can I trust you never to steal again?"

Suddenly the bookkeeper's face brightened, and sincerely sorry for what he did, he assured his boss that he could be trusted from that day on.

The manager continued: "You see, you're the second man who has fallen and been pardoned in this company. . . . I was the first! I'm forgiving you today because I have experienced God's mercy myself."

Chastised, the young man went back to work with a renewed bounce in his step, determined never to disappoint his boss again.

Whatever you may have done, God will forgive you. Then you, too, can offer God's kind of reforming forgiveness to others.

TODAY'S POWER POINT

All religions say, "Be good." Christianity says, "It is forgiven and finished."
—Source Unknown

TODAY IN HISTORY

1819—First military school established in the United States (in Norwich, Vermont)

1890—First execution by electrocution

1926—Gertrude Ederle became first U.S. woman to swim English Channel; era of talking pictures began with premiere of Vitaphone films

1945—U.S. bombed Hiroshima, Japan, launching nuclear age

1965—Voting Rights Act struck down discrimination at the polls

1981—President Ronald Reagan fired twelve thousand federal air-traffic controllers following illegal strike

1986—Longest-surviving artificial heart recipient to date, William Schroeder, died after 620 days

2000—Drive to allow free press blocked by Iranian leader

2002—UN set prerequisites for weapons inspectors in Iraq

2003—Arnold Schwarzenegger announced plans to run for governor of California

BORN TODAY

Poet Alfred Lord Tennyson 1808

Penicillin discoverer Alexander Fleming 1881

Actress Lucille Ball 1911

Actor Robert Mitchum 1917

Artist Andy Warhol 1928

Actor and director Peter Bonerz . . 1938

Actress Michelle Yeoh 1962

Basketball player David Robinson . . 1965

Singer Geri Estelle Halliwell 1972

Actress Soleil Moon Frye 1976

ALMIGHTY FORCE

New York's Wall Street is known as the financial center of the world, but it was also the place where evangelist D. L. Moody was empowered by God's irresistible force. One time, when Moody was on Wall Street to raise funds for one of his schools, God's power swept down upon him in a mighty way, so much so that Moody begged God to stop, "or I will die."

Afterward, although Moody used the same scriptures, the same outlines, and the same sermons as before, he began to see hundreds of people making decisions to follow Christ rather than the few that had responded earlier. The difference was God's anointing power. Moody learned that God "is able to do immeasurably more than all we ask or imagine, according to his power that is at work within us" (Ephesians 3:20).

That same power from God's Holy Spirit is present in all who have believed on the Lord Jesus Christ and put their trust in him. Do you have this irresistible force in your life? Be faithful in prayer, and then stand back and watch God go to work!

TODAY'S POWER POINT

If God is for us, who can be against us?—Romans 8:31

August 7

TODAY IN HISTORY

1794—President George Washington mobilized troops to quell Whiskey Rebellion

1919—U.S. stages closed by actors' strike

1959—*Explorer 6* transmitted first photographs of earth by satellite (over Pacific)

1970—Judge Harold Haley, kidnapped at gunpoint from his courtroom, was killed—with three others—in California

1974—First tightrope walker to cross between two skyscrapers (Frenchman Philippe Petit between Twin Towers of World Trade Center, New York City)

1978—Families began to leave Love Canal area of Niagara Falls, New York, due to seepage from abandoned chemical dump

1985—Cable TV's Ted Turner abandoned plans to buy CBS (instead, he bought film company MGM/UA for $1.5 billion cash)

1998—Terrorists attacked U.S. embassies in Kenya and Tanzania, killing 224 people, twelve of them Americans

2001—President Bill Clinton accepted $10 million advance for his autobiography, a record for a nonfiction book

2002—Fourteen killed in Bogota explosions during swearing in of Columbian president

BORN TODAY

Animator Rudolf Ising 1903

Statesman Ralph Bunche 1904

Satirist Stan Freburg 1926

Humorist Garrison Keillor 1942

Actress Lana Cantrell 1943

Marathon runner Alberto Salazar . 1957

Actor David Duchovny 1960

Actress Charlize Theron 1975

CHRIST OVER ALL

Have you ever considered the question, where does Jesus live? It brings to mind the story of the man who, coming home from a long day on the job, asked his wife if anything had happened that day.

"Why yes," his wife replied. "The new pastor came by. He wanted to know if Jesus lives here."

"Did you tell him we were good people?" the husband asked. "You did tell him that we go to church and read our Bible, didn't you?"

"No, he didn't ask me that," said the woman. "He only asked if Christ lived here."

Sensing the true meaning and intent behind the pastor's inquiry, the couple soon invited Christ into their hearts—and their home.

Does Christ live in your home? If not, invite him in today.

TODAY'S POWER POINT

Christ is not valued at all unless he his valued above all.—Saint Augustine

TODAY IN HISTORY

1797—First medical journal, *The Medical Repository*, published (in New York City)

1876—Thomas A. Edison patented the mimeograph machine

1900—First Davis Cup tennis match played

1933—United States chartered first Savings and Loan Association (in Miami, Florida)

1940—Germany launched air attacks on Britain

1963—Thieves stole a record $7 million from a train near London

1974—President Richard Nixon resigned from office—first ever to do so

1997—Mars space probe sent back thousand of pictures

2000—Leaders closed last rebel newspaper in Iran

2001—Iranian leader Mohammad Khatami inaugurated for second term, promised reforms

2002—U.S. and Palestinian leaders discussed future of Yasser Arafat and Palestinian statehood

BORN TODAY

Explorer Matthew Henson 1866
Producer Dino DeLaurentis 1919
Designer Rudi Gernreich 1922
Swimmer and actress Esther Williams
. . . . 1923
Singer Mel Tillis 1932
Actor Dustin Hoffman 1937

Actress and singer Connie Stevens
. . . . 1938
Actor Keith Carradine 1950
Actor Donny Most 1953
TV host Deborah Norville 1958
Tennis player Roger Federer 1981

A THANKFUL HEART

Have you ever stopped to consider that thinking precedes thanking? Somewhere in our thoughts should be thoughts of God. When the apostle Paul charted the downward course of mankind, he began by highlighting humanity's disregard of their creator: "Although they knew God, they neither glorified him as God, nor gave thanks to him" (Romans 1:21). Imagine, people were not thankful that they had received a message from God.

Why are we not more thankful? Perhaps because we don't stop to think. Thankfulness is really the result of careful cultivation. It's the fruit of a deliberate resolve to think about God, ourselves, and our privileges and responsibilities. In giving thanks we demonstrate that our lives are not dictated by the material things of life. Give gratitude where it is due—to God, for the blessings he has generously provided.

TODAY'S POWER POINT

If a fellow isn't thankful for what he's got, he isn't likely to be thankful for what he's going to get.—Frank Clark

August 9

TODAY IN HISTORY

1607—English settlers and American Indians held a thanksgiving feast and prayer
service in the New World (in what is now Phippsburg, Maine)

1936—Track star Jesse Owens became the first American to win four gold medals,
in the track-and-field events, in a single Olympics

1939—First tennis tournament televised in United States (from Rye, New York)

1945—U.S. dropped second atomic bomb (on Nagasaki, Japan)

1969—Actress Sharon Tate and four others found murdered (Charles Manson later
convicted of the crimes)

1974—Vice President Gerald Ford became president after Richard Nixon resigned

1975—Superdome opened in New Orleans

1989—Colin Powell became first African American chairman of Joint Chiefs of Staff

2000—Bridgestone/Firestone recalled 6.5 million tires for suspected defects

2002—Leaders of Iraqi opposition agreed to work with United States once Saddam
Hussein was out of power

BORN TODAY

Actor Robert Shaw 1927
Basketball player Bob Cousy 1928
Actor Sam Elliott 1944
Boxer Ken Norton Sr. 1945
Actress Melanie Griffith 1957

Singer Whitney Houston 1963
Hockey player Brett Hull 1964
Football player Deon Sanders 1967
Actress Gillian Anderson 1968
Journalist Christopher Cuomo . . . 1970

TRUE REST

What a difference God's free salvation makes in a life! Evangelist John R. Rice
tells of a man who came to him searching for life's answers. That morning he had
tried to take his own life but was rescued just in time. That evening he came to the
preacher, distraught at the many problems in his life: his wife had left him, he had
no home and no job, and he was suffering from an incurable disease.

With the evangelist's guidance, the man knelt and trusted Christ as Savior.
When he got up, he said, "Isn't that strange. A moment ago I was so worried I
thought I wouldn't live—couldn't face another day. Now all that is gone, and I feel
so peaceful and happy. I haven't a care in the world—isn't that strange?"

Dr. Rice replied, "No, that isn't strange. For Jesus said, 'Come to me, all you
who are weary and burdened, and I will give you rest. Take my yoke upon you and
learn from me, for I am gentle and humble in heart, and you will find rest for your
souls' [Matthew 11:28–29]. Friend, you have found rest for your soul."

If you haven't done so, accept God's priceless—yet free—salvation today.

TODAY'S POWER POINT

Nothing gives rest but the sincere search for truth.—Blaise Pascal

TODAY IN HISTORY

1821—Twenty-fourth state, Missouri, admitted to Union (first state west of the Mississippi)

1833—Chicago incorporated as a village

1846—Smithsonian Institution organized

1869—Movie projector patented (by O. B. Brown of Malden, Massachusetts)

1948—Television premiere of *Candid Camera*

1954—Elvis Presley made first professional appearance in his hometown of Memphis, TN

1981—Pete Rose beat Stan Musial's record of 3,630 career hits

1985—Singer Michael Jackson bought rights to 251 Beatles songs for $47.5 million

1995—Norma McCorvey (the Roe in Roe v. Wade case legalizing abortion) sided with antiabortion group

2004—U.S. border patrol agents given power to deport suspected illegal aliens without a hearing; Congressman Porter Goss chosen to head the CIA

BORN TODAY

President Herbert Hoover	1874	Actress Rosanna Arquette	1959
Actress Rhonda Fleming	1923	Antonio Banderas	1960
Singer Jimmy Dean	1928	Boxer Riddick Bowe	1967
Designer Betsy Johnson	1942	Actress Angie Harmon	1972

OUT OF MANY, ONE

The motto on the U.S. Great Seal, *E pluribus unum* ("out of many, one"), describes America's simultaneous diversity and unity. But this concept can be seen outside of government as well. Consider, for example, the 130 artists who worked together, not to exhibit their own accomplishments, but to complete a single, monumental, painting. It happened in France in the early 1900s, when a team of talented craftsmen took four years to create a gigantic, panoramic scene of World War I. By working together, the artists were able to complete the mural, which featured life-size portraits of some six thousand war heroes and the leaders of fifteen countries. The combined efforts of these painters produced a massive mural that towered 45 feet high and stretched 402 feet long.

While such an enormous endeavor was a remarkable accomplishment, it pales beside what Christ singlehandedly did for humankind on the cross. There, he, the God-man, willingly sacrificed himself to pay the penalty for the sins of all mankind. As the perfect Son of God, Christ paid in full and forever the debt of sin for all who trust in him. What a mysterious yet glorious truth—from the death of one comes forgiveness for all who believe!

TODAY'S POWER POINT

Christians are not perfect, just forgiven.—Source unknown

August 11

TODAY IN HISTORY

1909—First radioed SOS sent by ship

1924—First newsreel of presidential candidates filmed (Calvin Coolidge and opponents)

1972—First female sailor assigned to U.S. Navy ship (hospital ship USS *Sanctuary*)

1997—President Bill Clinton used line-item veto for first time

2002—Former government biodefense scientist Steven Hatfill denied role in anthrax attacks; sixth largest airline, U.S. Airways, filed for bankruptcy protection

2003—All peacekeeping forces in Afghanistan consolidated under NATO (first NATO action outside Europe)

BORN TODAY

Educator Charles Fowler 1837

Author Alex Haley 1921

TV host Mike Douglas. 1925

Pastor Jerry Falwell 1933

Columnist Marilyn vos Savant . . . 1946

Apple Computer cofounder
   Stephen Wozniak 1950

Wrestler Hulk Hogan 1953

POVERTY

Historians tell us that in the entire history of man, there have been only about 100,000 truly great achievers. Of that number, an estimated 80,000 or more have come from humble backgrounds. While no one wishes to live in poverty, those who have experienced it are not excluded from accomplishing something remarkable and important.

J. H. Bomberger has compiled a list of some of these achievers:

- Christopher Columbus begged for bread as a boy and died in poverty but discovered a new continent.
- Preacher Jonathan Edwards's wife and daughters helped support the family while he produced some of the most profound works written on this continent.
- Industrialist Andrew Carnegie was not much better paid at $3 a week to start, but eventually he was able to give away more than $350 million to philanthropic endeavors.
- Abraham Lincoln was a miserably poor farmer's son but became one of the greatest American presidents.
- But the greatest man of all time, Jesus Christ, had neither gold nor silver in this life. He suffered and died between two thieves, yet his words still ring with priceless truth today.

Never be ashamed of your roots; rather, work to become all God intends you to be.

TODAY'S POWER POINT

Being poor is no shame, but being ashamed of it is.—Benjamin Franklin

■ 223 ■

August 12

TODAY IN HISTORY

1851—Isaac Singer invented sewing machine

1898—Spanish-American War ended; Hawaii annexed by United States

1918—Regular U.S. airmail service established between Washington DC and New York

1960—First communications satellite, *Echo I*, launched by United States

1961—Construction started on wall to seal off East Berlin from West Berlin

1981—IBM introduced first personal computer

2000—Sinking of Russian nuclear sub *Kursk*, entire crew perished

2001—Chinese turned down U.S. offer of compensation for collision between U.S. spy plane and Chinese jet

2002—Record floods affected more than seventy thousand Europeans

2004—California Supreme Court overruled four thousand gay marriages performed in February and March 2004

BORN TODAY

Poet Katharine Lee Bates 1859
Director Cecil B. DeMille 1881
Singer Buck Owens 1929
Writer William Goldman 1931

Actor George Hamilton 1939
Author Ann Martin 1955
Tennis player Pete Sampras. 1971
Actress Dominique Swain. 1980

GOD'S RICHES

You needn't be a believer for long before God's riches become evident in your life. Scarcely, however, does God respond as quickly as he did to a Baptist pastor years ago. During his morning devotions, the preacher asked the Lord to provide ten dollars to pay for license plates so he could drive to the prison the following Sunday to preach. He told God that if he wanted him to preach, he would have to supply the money for the plates.

While the pastor was still praying, his wife, who was cleaning downstairs, called up the steps, "Are you praying for ten dollars?"

"Yes," the preacher responded.

"Well you can quit praying now," she said. "Someone has just shoved a ten dollar bill through the mail slot in the door."

Even when God's answer or provision doesn't seem as timely or providential as that, never forget that all good gifts come from God. He is the source of all your blessings. Don't take credit for what he has done for you or enabled you to do for yourself or others. God is a great philanthropist, even when he does his giving quietly.

TODAY'S POWER POINT

Real riches are the riches possessed inside.—B. C. Forbes

August 13

TODAY IN HISTORY

1889—Pay telephone patented (by William Gray of Hartford, Connecticut)
1907—Motorized taxis started running in New York City
1961—Berlin wall completed
1969—*Apollo II* astronauts honored in three cities (New York, Chicago, and Los Angeles)
1970—First no-fault car-insurance law passed (in Massachusetts)
1972—According to Israeli report, Russians agreed to let fifteen thousand Jews emigrate to Israel annually
1985—Japanese Airlines plane crash killed 517 (second major air disaster in a month)
1994—Strike called by major-league baseball players
2002—High-speed trains halted by Amtrak until design flaws could be fixed
2004—Summer Olympics opened in Athens

BORN TODAY

Sharpshooter Annie Oakley 1860
Actor Bert Lahr 1895
Director Alfred Hitchcock 1899
Golfer Ben Hogan 1912
Evangelist Rex Humbard;
    pianist George Shearing 1919
Cuban dictator Fidel Castro 1927
Singer Don Ho. 1930
Actor Kevin Tighe 1944
Musician Dan Fogelberg. 1951
Actor Danny Bonaduce 1959
Actress Quinn Cummings 1967

A GOOD EDUCATION

Someone has wisely said, "You cannot lift your children to a higher level than that on which you live yourself." Along that vein, professor Sidney Hook has said both intelligence and courage are essential outcomes of education. Stated Hook, "There are human beings who have intelligence but who do not have the moral courage to act on it. On the other hand, moral courage without intelligence is dangerous, for it leads to fanaticism."

"Intelligence alone," noted Hook, "is not enough." God has given us our "gray matter," but what we do to develop it, he leaves up to us.

When you are asked to give account of what you have done with your talents, what will be your report? Seek God's wisdom and guidance as you consider what he would have you do with your abilities.

TODAY'S POWER POINT

There are two educations. One should teach us how to make a living and the other how to live.—John Adams

TODAY IN HISTORY

1924—First two-way radio broadcast from a plane (aired by WJZ in New York City)
1935—U.S. Social Security Law enacted
1945—Japan surrendered, ending World War II
1959—First televised view of earth from space (via *Explorer 6* satellite)
1985—Vice President George H. W. Bush called for strong military in speech marking fortieth anniversary of World War II end
1997—Oklahoma City bomber, Timothy McVeigh, sentenced to death
2003—Nation's largest power failure affected fifty million people in eight states

BORN TODAY

Novelist John Galsworthy 1867
Musician Buddy Greco 1926
Actor Steve Martin 1945
Actress Susan Saint James 1946
Author Danielle Steel 1947
Cartoonist Gary Larson 1950
Race-car driver Rusty Wallace 1956
Basketball player Earvin "Magic" Johnson Jr. 1959
Actress Halle Berry 1968

NOT LOST

A mother and her daughter once attended a church service in a large auditorium. Somehow the little girl slipped away from the mother, who then frantically tried to locate her but failed. Anxious, the woman finally sent a note up to the podium. It read, "A little girl in the audience is lost. Will she please raise her hand so her mother can find her?" No hands were raised.

When mother and daughter were finally reunited, the mother sternly asked, "Didn't you hear the message read? Why didn't you raise your hand?"

"Mother," the girl protested, "that announcement couldn't have been for me: I wasn't lost!"

While we may smile at this story, it's a far more serious matter that some people feel God's message is not for them. To their eternal sorrow they go on their way, ignorant of their true condition and their great need until life is over and it's too late to turn to God.

We can't talk people into recognizing their need for God (although we have a responsibility to tell them). Jesus said, "No one can come to me unless the Father who sent me draws him" (John 6:44). So it is God's task to draw people. Still, it is our task to share the gospel and to pray fervently for God to work in people's hearts. Someone you know needs to hear that he or she is lost—but that Jesus is the Way.

TODAY'S POWER POINT

A genuine Christian is the best evidence of the genuineness of Christianity.
—Source Unknown

August 15

TODAY IN HISTORY

1635—First U.S. hurricane recorded (in Plymouth Colony, Massachusetts)

1848—Waldo Hanchett patented first adjustable dental chair (in Syracuse, New York)

1870—U.S. transcontinental railway link completed

1935—Deaths of Will Rogers and Wiley Post in Alaskan plane crash

1947—Passengers placed first telephone calls from aboard a train

1969—Massive crowd of 400,000 showed up for outdoor concert at Woodstock, New York

1971—President Richard Nixon put ninety-day freeze on wages and prices due to inflation

1984—Wreckage of the luxury liner *Titanic* believed found in twelve-thousand feet of water off coast of Newfoundland

2003—Libya agreed to $2.7 billion settlement with victims' families for the 1988 terrorist attack on an airliner over Lockerbie, Scotland, opening door to end of UN sanctions

BORN TODAY

Emperor Napoleon Bonaparte . . . 1769
Actress Ethel Barrymore 1879
Writer Edna Ferber 1887
Chef Julia Child 1912
Author Phyllis Schlafly 1924
Actress Rose Marie 1925
Civil-rights leader Vernon Jordan . 1935
Journalist Linda Ellerbee 1944
Actress Debra Messing 1968
Actor Ben Affleck 1972

ALWAYS PRESENT

Theologian Dr. A. J. Gordon was preparing a sermon one time when he fell fast asleep. He dreamed he was in his pulpit preaching when a compelling stranger walked in and sat down. The stranger's manner was so commanding and attentive that Dr. Gordon resolved to speak with him after the service.

As the congregation filed out, the pastor searched in vain for the stranger. "Do you know who he was?" Dr. Gordon asked a deacon.

"Why, yes," said the deacon. "He's Jesus Christ."

The deacon continued, "It's alright pastor, he'll be back next Sunday."

Dr. Gordon awoke with a new realization that Christ is always present, hearing our every word. That dream revived both the pastor and his church.

Remember that an all-knowing God is observing everything you do and goes with you everywhere you go. As your unseen companion in all you do and the unseen guest at every meal, will he be pleased with you or ashamed to be seen with you?

TODAY'S POWER POINT

You see things and you say "Why?" But I dream of things that never were, and I say: "Why Not?"—George Bernard Shaw

TODAY IN HISTORY

1829—First "Siamese" twins, Chang and Eng, arrived in Boston (later married sisters and fathered a total of nineteen children)

1896—Gold discovered in Alaska

1898—First roller coaster with a 360-degree loop patented (later opened as Boynton's Centrifugal Railway at Coney Island, New York)

1920—Raymond Chapman first player to be killed in a major-league baseball game (accidentally hit in the head by a pitch from Willie Mays)

1977—Death of Elvis Presley, age forty-two

2002—Pope John Paul II embarked on last visit to his home country, Poland

2003—Motorcyclist accidentally killed by South Dakota congressman Bill Janklow, who failed to stop at an intersection

2004—Iraqi group selected commission to oversee national elections

BORN TODAY

Labor leader George Meany 1894
Actor Fess Parker 1927
Sportscaster Frank Gifford 1930
Singer Eydie Gorme 1932
Actress Julie Newmar 1935

TV personality Kathie Lee Gifford
. . . . 1953
Director James Cameron 1954
Singer Madonna. 1958
Actor Timothy Hutton. 1960

SUCCESS

One must be more than just a good thinker to get through school. Consider these brilliant men who nearly didn't make it.

At the age of six, Thomas Alva Edison brought home a note from his teacher. She suggested he be taken out of school, as he was just "too stupid to learn."

Sir Isaac Newton was next to the lowest in his class and failed geometry because he didn't do his problems according to the book.

Rocket scientist Wernher von Braun was reported to have failed math and physics in his teens.

Sound familiar? Even if you weren't the greatest student, don't despair. First Corinthians 1:26–27 reassures us: "Not many of you were wise by human standards; not many were influential; not many were of noble birth. But God chose the foolish things of the world to shame the wise; God chose the weak things of the world to shame the strong." Christ loves you just as you are, and he has a wonderful plan for your life. Jesus Christ has become wisdom for us, and there's no better kind of wisdom to have. No matter what the world may think of you, remember that God loves you. You matter to him!

TODAY'S POWER POINT

Success is how high you bounce when you hit bottom.—George Patton

August 17

TODAY IN HISTORY

1807—Robert Fulton's steamboat sailed from New York City
1935—First patent issued for a wrench
1948—Alger Hiss denied being a Communist agent
1977—Soviet nuclear-powered icebreaker became first surface ship to reach the North Pole
1978—First transatlantic helium balloon crossing (from Maine to Paris in 137 hours)
1987—Death of Rudolf Hess, age ninety-three, last of Hitler's colleagues, in West German prison
1998—President Bill Clinton told nation of affair with White House intern Monica Lewinsky
1999—Seventeen thousand people killed in earthquake in Izmit, Turkey
2001—Ford Motor Company laid off five thousand workers

BORN TODAY

Frontiersman Davy Crockett 1786
Actress Mae West 1892
Actress Maureen O'Hara 1920
Actor Robert DeNiro 1943
Actor Robert Joy 1951
Tennis player Guillermo Vilas ... 1952

Singer Belinda Carlisle 1958
Actor Sean Penn 1960
Basketball player Christian Laettner
   1969
Tennis player Jim Courier 1970

EARLY WORSHIP

When we think of the early church, many think of the 8:00 service instead of the 10:30. But the early church of the first few centuries was made up of a group of on-fire, committed believers who changed the world. We can learn much from their example.

We see, for instance, that early believers were dedicated. Bible teacher, pastor, and author H. A. Ironside wrote that the persecuted early church met in the dead of night or in the early morning. (How many pastors today could get their congregations to meet at these times?) Their worship consisted of the singing of hymns, reading from the Scriptures, and eating a simple meal of bread and diluted wine.

Early believers were loyal as well. Ironside reported the early church encouraged one another to be subject to the government and to pray for all people.

The church today could do well to become more dedicated and loyal—learning from the example of the early Christians. Pray that as members of the church today we would be as faithful in our Christian love and witness as was the early church.

TODAY'S POWER POINT

It is only when men begin to worship that they begin to grow.—Calvin Coolidge

August 18

TODAY IN HISTORY

1840—First class photograph taken (at reunion of Yale class of 1910)
1872—Montgomery Ward published first mail-order catalog
1896—Adolph Ochs named to head the *New York Times*
1926—First televised weather map (Arlington, Virginia)
1931—First patent issued for a plant (the continually blooming New Dawn rose)
1985—Sixty-five thousand cheering fans welcomed singer Bruce Springsteen back
      to his home state of New Jersey
2004—Google, Inc., went public at $85 a share

BORN TODAY

Virginia Dare (first child of English
  parents to be born in North America)
. . . . 1587
Explorer Meriwether Lewis. 1774
Actress Shelley Winters. 1922
Baseball player Roberto Clemente
. . . . 1934

Actor Robert Redford. 1937
Actor Martin Mull 1943
Actor Patrick Swayze 1954
Actor Christian Slater;
  actor Edward Norton 1969
Actor Malcolm-Jamal Warner. . . . 1970

TELLING THE TRUTH

How important it is to always speak the truth. When writer Dr. John Todd was a young boy, his critically ill father sent him to the druggist for medicine. Todd didn't want to go, so he made up a story that the druggist did not have the needed medicine. Later, as his father's condition worsened, Todd was again sent to get the medicine. But it was too late.

Upon his return Todd found his father nearly dead. Weakly, his father told him: "Love me and always speak the truth, for the eye of God is always upon you." Imagine Todd's regret at being untruthful with his father and for not having gone for help the first time!

Do you tell the truth even when it isn't convenient? Make the psalmist's prayer your prayer today: "Keep me from deceitful ways; be gracious to me through your law. I have chosen the way of truth" (Psalm 119:29–30).

TODAY'S POWER POINT

Always tell the truth—it's the easiest thing to remember.—David Mamet

August 19

TODAY IN HISTORY

1782—Last major battle of the American Revolution

1812—USS *Constitution* earned the name "Old Ironsides" by defeating the HMS *Guerrièr* in War of 1812 battle

1942—First German plane shot down by U.S. pilot in World War II (Dieppe, France)

1960—First space capsule captured in midair (off Honolulu, Hawaii)

1976—Gerald Ford and Robert Dole ousted Ronald Reagan to become the leading Republican contenders for president

1977—Death of comedian Julius Henry "Groucho" Marx, age seventy-seven

2002—CNN aired al Qaeda videos showing how to fire missiles and build bombs; 117 killed when Russian helicopter crashed in Chechen minefield

2003—Deadliest attack in UN history, twenty-three killed in bombing of UN compound in Iraq

BORN TODAY

Clockmaker Seth Thomas. 1785

Aviation pioneer Orville Wright . . 1871

Poet Ogden Nash 1902

Publisher Malcolm Stevenson Forbes Sr.
. . . . 1919

Star Trek creator Gene Roddenberry
. . . . 1921

President Bill Clinton. 1946

Actor Gerald McRaney. 1948

Actor Peter Gallagher 1955

Actor Adam Arkin 1956

Singer LeAnn Womack. 1966

Actor Matthew Perry 1969

HOLDING OUT HOPE

A deacon in a small country church once told a visiting evangelist, "I'm afraid the preachers around here are not called to preach. They have no tears when they preach. Nobody is ever converted. There seems to be no burden for souls and no power to win them."

The evangelist responded, "They're probably called, but perhaps they have not been anointed to preach. One needs not only divine instruction . . . but also a holy empowering to melt his heart, give him compassion, and endue him with power to win souls."

Maybe one reason some churches today aren't as effective as they once were is because they've lost their first love. Are you concerned about the eternal destiny of folks around you—your neighbors, acquaintances, fellow workers, and friends? Simply reach out in love to those you meet each day and lovingly share the story of what God has done for you. Ask God to infuse your pastor with God's strength and anointing. And don't forget to ask him to give you opportunities today—and every day—to share your faith with others.

TODAY'S POWER POINT

Where there is no vision, there is no hope.—George Washington Carver

TODAY IN HISTORY

1741—Danish explorer Vitus Bering discovered Alaska for Russia

1910—First gun fired by an airplane pilot (at Sheepshead Bay, New York)

1920—First licensed commercial radio station in United States owned by a newspaper (*The Detroit News*), 8MK (WWJ) Detroit, began daily programming

1940—Exiled Russian leader Leon Trotsky attacked and killed in Mexico City

1968—Soviet troops invaded Czechoslovakia

1971—Texas Instruments introduced first battery-operated "pocket" calculator (weighing 2.5 pounds) in Dallas, Texas

1974—Former New York governor Nelson Rockefeller nominated by President Gerald Ford to be forty-first vice president

1988—Cease-fire called in Iran-Iraq war

1992—George H. W. Bush and Dan Quayle nominated to head GOP presidential ticket for second time

1998—U.S. missiles hit terrorist targets in Afghanistan and Sudan

2003—With more than three million signatures collected, opposition leaders in Venezuela demand recall of President Hugo Chavez

BORN TODAY

President Benjamin Harrison 1833
Poet Edgar Guest 1881
Baseball player Al Lopez 1908
Novelist Jacqueline Susann 1921
Singer Jim Reeves 1924
Boxing promoter Don King 1931

Musician and actor Isaac Hayes . . 1942
Broadcast journalist Connie Chung . . 1946
Singer Robert Plant 1948
TV personality Al Roker 1954
Actress Joan Allen 1956
Baseball player Todd Helton 1973

GOING INTO DEBT

It took sixty years and eleven presidents before the United States had spent its first billion dollars. Now the government spends that much every four hours (a total of more than $400 billion per year). And people are making money on others' debt—a Dallas firm was reportedly charging 58 percent interest annually to its indigent customers. One victim borrowed twenty dollars for a medical bill and was still paying off the debt nine years later. By then the interest had mushroomed to $1,053.

While we should be cautious in assuming financial debt, God has promised to provide for our legitimate needs through his bountiful riches in heaven. "My God will meet all your needs according to his glorious riches in Christ Jesus" (Philippians 4:19).

TODAY'S POWER POINT

Credit is a system whereby a person who cannot pay gets another person who cannot pay to guarantee that he can pay.—Charles Dickens

August 21

TODAY IN HISTORY

1833—Slave rebellion in Virginia resulted in 160 deaths
1847—Mormon Tabernacle Choir's first public performance
1862—First U.S. paper currency to be issued in denominations of five, ten, twenty-five, and fifty cents
1912—Arthur Elred (of Oceanside, New York) became first Eagle Scout
1923—First illuminated airport runways
1944—Conference involving United States, United Kingdom, and USSR laid groundwork for establishing United Nations
1951—United States ordered construction of first nuclear-powered submarine
1959—Fiftieth state, Hawaii, admitted to Union
2000—Russian official said budget cuts prevented rescue of sunken *Kursk* crew

BORN TODAY

Illustrator Aubrey Beardsley 1872
Musician Count Basie 1904
Britain's Princess Margaret 1930
Basketball player Wilt Chamberlain. . 1936
Singer Kenny Rogers 1938

Singer Jackie DeShannon 1944
Actress Kim Cattrall 1956
AOL founder Steve Case 1958
Football player Jim McMahon . . . 1959
Actress Alicia Witt 1975

INVISIBLE GOVERNMENT

While the government keeps society functioning, what is the "invisible government" that keeps individuals under control? For Christians, the Holy Spirit governs us. J. A. Clarke wrote of a time when young Charles Spurgeon was warned that he was in for a tongue-lashing from a quarrelsome woman. Sure enough, it wasn't long before he encountered this busybody who unleashed a flood of verbal abuse.

When she was done, Spurgeon smiled and said, "Yes, thank you. I'm quite well. I hope you are the same."

Then came another verbal blast, after which the preacher said, "Yes, it does look as if it might rain. I think I had better be getting on." And with that, he turned and walked away.

"Bless the man," the woman later said, "he's as deaf as a post."

Spurgeon's "invisible government" had kept his temper under control. The woman never again tried criticizing Spurgeon to his face.

Gaining control over the self is a lifelong struggle in which every believer must prevail daily in order to be effective for God. Ask God today to help you win the victory over your inner self so that you can serve him more effectively.

TODAY'S POWER POINT

The best government is that which teaches us to govern ourselves.—Johann Goethe

■ 233 ■

TODAY IN HISTORY

1787—Side-wheel steamboat demonstrated

1865—Liquid soap patented (made from hard soap diluted to consistency of molasses)

1902—Theodore Roosevelt became first U.S. president to ride in an automobile (a Columbia Electric Victoria, on tour of Hartford, Connecticut)

1911—*Mona Lisa* stolen from the Louvre

1939—Julian Kahn patented first spray can (to dispense whipped cream, paint, or insecticide)

1984—Ronald Reagan and George H. W. Bush won nomination to head the Republican presidential ticket

2002—United States blocked sales of high-tech equipment to North Korea in reaction to their selling Scud missile parts to Yemen

BORN TODAY

Cartoonist George Herriman 1880

Writer Dorothy Parker 1893

Author Ray Bradbury 1920

Baseball player Carl Yastrzemski . . 1939

Football coach Bill Parcells 1941

Actress Cindy Williams 1948

Baseball player Paul Molitor 1956

Singer Howie Dorough 1973

THE MASTER'S WINNING MOVE

Early in the 1800s an artist, who was also an avid chess player, depicted in a painting a young man in a chess game with Satan. It seemed obvious that Satan was soundly defeating the hopeless, hapless youth. For years no one challenged that analysis until an undefeated chess champion studied the painting. He stared at the work with great concentration, in his mind playing and replaying every possible move and outcome.

Suddenly the chess master gave a shout of joy: "Young man, make that move. That's the move!" The veteran chess champion had discovered a way for the young man to achieve victory that even the creating artist had overlooked. With the help of the great master, the outmatched young man would be able to defeat his opponent handily.

Does it ever seem that Satan is just one move away from defeating you? It doesn't have to end that way. The Great Master is able to help you snatch victory from the jaws of defeat. When you feel powerless, backed into a hopeless situation, and unsure what your next move should be, remember the words of the apostle John: "You, dear children, are from God and have overcome them, because the one who is in you is greater than the one who is in the world" (1 John 4:4). You can beat the devil!

TODAY'S POWER POINT

To know where you can find a thing is the chief part of learning.—Source Unknown

August 23

TODAY IN HISTORY

1784—Franklin (three counties in what is now eastern Tennessee) became first "state" denied admission to the Union (its "governor," John Sevier, later became Tennessee's first governor in 1796)

1860—First hotel elevator began operation (in six-story Fifth Avenue Hotel, New York City)

1948—World Council of Churches organized

1977—First human-powered flight (of one mile) made by Bryan Allen at Shafter, CA

1981—Survey showed African Americans increasingly pessimistic over government inaction regarding NAACP-backed causes

1982—Exxon announced plans to close 850 service stations in Northeast and Midwest due to lack of demand; Israel forced one thousand Palestinian guerillas to leave Lebanon

2001—Chinese officials said current AIDS epidemic triggered by ineffective government steps to control the disease

2004—President George W. Bush called for ban on third-party political ads

BORN TODAY

Commodore Oliver Perry 1785
Author Edgar Lee Masters 1869
Actor Gene Kelly 1912
Comedian Mark Russell 1932
Football player Sonny Jurgensen . . 1934

Actor Richard Sanders 1940
Singer Rick Springfield;
    actress Shelley Long 1949
Actor Jay Mohr 1970
Basketball player Kobe Bryant . . . 1978

FROM CRADLE TO GRAVE

Change is one of the few constants in life. But God's love and care for us never change. Hebrews 13:8 reminds us, "Jesus Christ is the same yesterday and today and forever." That means that the same God who was big enough for you as a child, will be big enough to carry you until the last of your days. The God who loved you and guided you through your difficult youth and hectic middle years will walk with you every step of your journey into old age. Our relationship with God runs from cradle to grave, and it can grow closer and richer with each passing day.

God said: "You whom I have upheld since you were conceived, and have carried since your birth. Even to your old age and gray hairs I am he, I am he who will sustain you. I have made you and I will carry you; I will sustain you and I will rescue you" (Isaiah 46:3–4). What a wonderful promise! We need not fear old age, for God will be with us just as he has been all along.

TODAY'S POWER POINT

In this life the old believe everything, the middle-aged suspect everything, and the young know everything.—Source Unknown

August 24

TODAY IN HISTORY

79—Mount Vesuvius erupted, burying the Roman cities Pompeii, Herculaneum, and Stabiae in volcanic ash

1814—Burning of Washington DC by British in War of 1812 (August 24–25)

1853—First potato chips made (in Saratoga Springs, New York)

1869—Waffle iron patented (by Cornelius Swarthout of Troy, New York)

1891—Motion-picture camera patented by Thomas A. Edison

1954—Communist Party outlawed in United States

1991—Mikhail Gorbachev resigned as leader of USSR; Ukraine declared independence from USSR

2004—Vice President Dick Cheney voiced support for same-sex marriage

2006—Astronomers announced that Pluto would no longer be considered a planet but rather an "icy dwarf"

BORN TODAY

British statesman William Wilberforce 1759
Pianist Louis Teicher 1924
Composer Mason Williams 1938
Actor Michael Richards 1950
Boxer Gerry Cooney 1956

Baseball player Cal Ripken Jr. . . . 1960
TV host Craig Kilborn 1962
Basketball player Reggie Miller; actress Marlee Matlin 1965
Comedian Dave Chapelle. 1973
Actor Chad Michael Murray 1981

GOING HOME

A refugee from Hitler's Europe said a sad farewell to his family as he left for a new life in America—a place he had heard much about but had never seen. So convinced was his mother that he was going to a better place that she told her son, "You are going home while I am staying in a foreign land."

Herb Vander Lugt once told of an elderly believer who was soon to be facing eternity. Suffering from the effects of a devastating stroke, stomach surgery, and the amputation of one leg, the senior saint still displayed a cheerful attitude, telling one visitor, "Brother, each of those blows has been a boost. Each one has drawn me closer to Christ and made me more eager for heaven."

Vander Lugt recalled a similar tale from a new believer struggling with terminal cancer. While still hoping for a medical cure, the patient was also said to be looking forward with expectation to heaven and seeing Christ's face. As Vander Lugt noted, "the world can't match that kind of anticipation."

When our loved ones in Christ pass from this life, it should comfort our hearts to know that although they're no longer here, they've been promoted to glory. Where is your eternal home?

TODAY'S POWER POINT

All this and heaven too.—Matthew Henry

August 25

TODAY IN HISTORY

1814—James Madison became first sitting president to experience enemy gunfire (in battle near Bladensburg, Maryland, during War of 1812)

1916—U.S. National Park Service established

1991—Former Soviet republics Latvia, Estonia, and Lithuania declared independence

1997—Texas established coded software system for astronauts to cast secret ballots from space

2004—Ninety killed as two Russian planes crashed within minutes of each other

BORN TODAY

Conductor Leonard Bernstein . . . 1918
Game-show host Monty Hall. . . . 1923
Tennis player Althea Gibson. 1927
Actor Sean Connery. 1930

TV host Regis Philbin 1933
Director Tim Burton 1958
Singer Billy Ray Cyrus 1961
Food personality Rachel Ray 1968

THE WAR WITHIN

President Abraham Lincoln led this country during one of its fiercest, most difficult wars. But the Civil War was just one of the critical struggles he fought. As with most people who aspire to live good lives and be good people, Lincoln grappled with his inner self; yet it was a battle he was resolved to win. He once said, "My desire is to so conduct the affairs of this administration that if at the end, when I come to lay down the reins of power, I have lost every other friend on earth, I shall have at least one friend left—the friend deep down inside of me. . . . I do the very best I know how; the very best I can; and I mean to keep on doing it to the end."

Lincoln recognized the importance of fighting the good fight within oneself. The first step toward winning that fight is resolving to win it and to live a life of integrity and obedience to God. But the resolution is insufficient to ensure success, for the enemy is strong. Even the apostle Paul couldn't win the battle on his own. He wrote, "I know that nothing good lives in me, that is, in my sinful nature. For I have the desire to do what is good, but I cannot carry it out" (Romans 7:18).

So if even an apostle can't get it right, what chance do we have? The same chance as Paul. "What a wretched man I am!" he lamented. "Who will rescue me from this body of death?" (Romans 7:24). Then Paul answered his own question: "Thanks be to God—through Jesus Christ our Lord! . . . Because through Christ Jesus the law of the Spirit of life set me free from the law of sin and death" (Romans 7:25; 8:2).

Through Jesus you can be set free from the sinful nature that wars against your desire to do good. With his help, you can win the battle within.

TODAY'S POWER POINT

We may pretend that we're basically moral people who make mistakes, but the whole of history proves otherwise.—Terry Hands

August 26

TODAY IN HISTORY

1873—St. Louis School board established first kindergarten

1883—Volcano in East Indies triggered tsunami, leaving 35,000 dead

1920—Nineteenth Amendment ratified, giving women the right to vote

1938—First broadcast of a prerecorded program (on WQXR radio, New York)

1939—First televised baseball game (Reds-Dodgers at Ebbets Field in Brooklyn, New York)

1976—Mysterious flulike disease (dubbed Legionnaire's Disease) killed twenty-eight, mostly conventioneers at American Legion conference in Philadelphia

1978—Pope John Paul I became new pontiff after August 6 death of Pope Paul VI

2003—Congressional report forecast U.S. budget deficit of $5.8 trillion by 2013

2004—Judge ruled ban on D&C abortions illegal, as it did not provide exemption to protect life of the mother

BORN TODAY

Inventor Lee DeForest 1873

Author Christopher Isherwood. . . 1904

Microbiologist Albert Sabin 1906

Publisher Benjamin Bradlee 1921

News correspondent Irving R. Levine 1922

Politician Geraldine Ferraro 1935

Actor Macaulay Culkin 1980

Musician Branford Marsalis 1960

Actor Christopher Burke 1965

WOMEN'S RIGHTS

Voting rights for women were a long time coming, with more than a few struggles. Years ago a debate was held in Kansas on the question of whether women were capable of handling the right to vote. Some opposed to women voting claimed that women could not be relied upon to exercise good judgment in voting, as they change their minds too often. But a young woman silenced these critics by simply questioning: "I would like to ask my honorable opponents if they've ever tried to change a woman's mind once it was made up."

End of debate.

Women didn't win the right to vote in America until this day in 1920, but in God's eyes, the issue of women's rights was settled long ago. Inspired by the Holy Spirit, Paul wrote: "You are all sons of God through faith in Christ Jesus. . . . There is neither Jew nor Greek, slave nor free, male nor female, for you are all one in Christ Jesus" (Galatians 3:26, 28). God is no respecter of persons but rather loves all of us equally—regardless of racial, social, financial, or gender concerns. No one is a second-class citizen in God's kingdom. So hold your head high and treat all your fellow citizens with respect and dignity.

TODAY'S POWER POINT

The battle for women's rights has been largely won.—Margaret Thatcher

August 27

TODAY IN HISTORY

1665—First play presented in the Colonies (satire *The Bare and the Cubb*, in Accomack, Virginia)

1859—First commercial oil well in the United States began operation (in Titusville, Pennsylvania)

1939—First flight of jet airplane

1981—Divers located safe from sunken passenger ship the *Andrea Dorea*

1985—Continued racial unrest in South Africa resulted in the rand (basic monetary unit) dropping in value to just thirty-five cents—lowest exchange rate ever

2002—Congressional report predicted 6.6 percent lower tax revenues for year

BORN TODAY

Author Theodore Dreiser 1871
President Lyndon Johnson 1908
Mother Teresa 1910
Comedienne Martha Raye 1916
Singer Tommy Sands 1937
Musician Daryl Dragon 1942

Actress Tuesday Weld 1943
Actor Paul Rubens 1952
Baseball player Jim Thome 1970
Actress Sarah Chalke;
    tennis player Carlos Moya. . . . 1976
Actress Alexa Vega 1988

A MIGHTY FORTRESS

Sometimes just when we feel safest, we're most vulnerable to attack. The story is told of burglars who broke into the offices of a company that produced "burglar proof" glass. An embarrassed company spokesman admitted, "It never occurred to us to use burglar-proof glass in our door."

Too often we make ourselves vulnerable and put ourselves at risk because we trust in the wrong things. Thieves break in and steal. The stock market may crash. Mighty armies are laid low by an unexpected attack. Even family and friends disappoint us, hurt us, or may not be there when we need them. But followers of God have a safe tower we can run to for protection—a mighty fortress. Read Psalm 46 for a stirring, strong promise of God's protection. Then consider the words of the hymn it inspired, Martin Luther's "A Mighty Fortress." It'll make you feel safe, but this is no false feeling of security; it's a promise as solid as God, our Rock.

As Edward Elson noted, "Throughout the ages men have been stirred by the realization that the Eternal God is available to them and that nothing, literally nothing, can overwhelm or destroy a man when he lives this faith." Who's guarding your fort?

TODAY'S POWER POINT

All that I have seen teaches me to trust the Creator for all I have not seen.—Ralph Waldo Emerson

August 28

TODAY IN HISTORY

1609—Delaware Bay first encountered by white man (English explorer Henry Hudson)

1922—First broadcast commercial aired (over WEAF radio, New York, for Queensboro Realty Co. in Jackson Heights, New York—ad was ten minutes long)

1957—Strom Thurmond set record for longest Senate filibuster (twenty-four hours, eighteen minutes)

1963—Two hundred thousand demonstrators marched in peaceful civil-rights gathering in Washington DC

1976—After nine years of trying, an MIT biologist succeeded in synthesizing the functioning of a gene through revolutionary recombinant DNA technology

1986—Convicted spy Jerry Whitworth sentenced to 365 years in prison for involvement in spy ring

2000—Blaze in 1,772-foot Moscow broadcast tower extinguished

2003—North Korea announced plans to become a nuclear power and test a nuclear bomb; report linked thousands of deaths in Peru since 1980 to Maoist guerillas

BORN TODAY

Philosopher Johann von Goethe. . 1749
Actor Charles Boyer 1889
Actor Ben Gazzara 1930
Baseball manager Lou Piniella . . . 1943
Baseball player Ron Guidry 1950
Actor Daniel Stern 1957

Olympic ice skater Scott Hamilton
. . . . 1958
Actress Emma Samms 1960
Singer Shania Twain 1965
Actor Jason Priestley 1969
Singer LeAnn Rimes 1982

PAID IN FULL

Bill Gold, writing in the *Washington Post*, told of a little girl who had saved up enough money to buy her father a present for Father's Day, but she still had one concern. "I can't get downtown every month to make payments," she said to her mother, "Is there a store where they'll let you pay the whole thing at once?"

God has done just that for us through the sinless sacrifice of Christ on the cross. He has prepaid our sin-debt in full—something our own feeble attempts at good works have no power to accomplish. To believe that we can earn our way to heaven through our own efforts is to go through life attempting to buy forgiveness on credit when God has already paid for it in full.

Have you accepted God's payment for your sins, or are your still struggling to earn what has already been paid? Take God at his Word. Confess your sins to him, repent, and ask him to stamp your account "paid in full."

TODAY'S POWER POINT

God's gifts put man's best dreams to shame.—Elizabeth Barrett Browning

August 29

TODAY IN HISTORY

1839—Slave ship *Amistad* seized by U.S. forces and towed to New London, Connecticut
1896—Chop suey introduced in New York City
1916—U.S. Marine Corps Reserve organized
1949—Soviets test-fired their first atom bomb (in Kazakhstan)
1958—U.S. Air Force Academy (in Colorado Springs, Colorado) opened
1974—Professional basketball player Moses Malone became highest-paid teenage athlete in United States (total earnings could exceed $3 million)
1989—*Voyager 2* transmitted startling new information about planet Neptune
2002—Supreme Court called for new look at death penalties for juveniles

BORN TODAY

Author Oliver Wendell Holmes . . 1809
Actress Ingrid Bergman 1915
Actor Elliott Gould 1938
Actor Richard Gere 1949
Actress Rebecca De Mornay 1959
Hockey player Pierre Turgeon 1969
Baseball player Roy Oswalt 1977

SELF-SACRIFICE

Charles Dickens masterfully portrayed sacrificial love in his epic work *A Tale of Two Cities*. In this story Sydney Carton, a man who has lived an empty, selfish life, falls in love with a woman he cannot have. She is in love with—and eventually marries—another man, Carton's colleague Charles Darnay. When Darnay is arrested and condemned to death on the guillotine, Carton makes a heroic decision. Bearing a striking resemblance to Darnay, Carton visits him in prison, where he tricks him into changing clothes with him, then drugs him and takes his place. His great love motivates him to trade his life to save his rival's.

Do you know anyone who would do that for you? Someone already has! Jesus said, "Greater love has no one than this, that he lay down his life for his friends" (John 15:13). Romans 5:7–8 takes it one step further: "Very rarely will anyone die for a righteous man, though for a good man someone might possibly dare to die. But God demonstrates his own love for us in this: While we were still sinners, Christ died for us."

Such sacrificial love is bestowed on us freely, but it comes with a responsibility. Jesus said, "My command is this: Love each other as I have loved you" (John 15:12). That means loving those who sin against us, loving those who are still enemies—and sacrificing ourselves for them. Are you up to the challenge? Who is God calling you to love today?

TODAY'S POWER POINT

He who would accomplish little must sacrifice little; he would achieve much must sacrifice much; he would attain highly must sacrifice greatly.—James Allen

August 30

TODAY IN HISTORY

1663—John Ratliffe hired to bind two hundred Bibles for Indians, making him the first bookbinder in the New World

1890—Congress passed first meat-inspection law

1963—Communications "hot line" linking White House and Kremlin connected

1967—Thurgood Marshall confirmed as first African American Supreme Court justice

2000—President Bill Clinton told Columbians $1.3 billion in U.S. aid was earmarked to combat drugs, not to target rebels

2002—World Trade Organization ruled against U.S. plans to provide tax breaks to exporters

2004—U.S. president George W. Bush expressed doubts war on terrorism could ever be won

BORN TODAY

Physicist Ernest Rutherford 1871
Politician Huey Long 1893
Civil-rights leader Roy Wilkins. . . 1901
Actor Fred MacMurray. 1908
Baseball player Ted Williams 1918

Singer Kitty Wells. 1919
Olympic skier Jean Claude Killy. . 1943
Basketball player Robert Parish. . . 1953
Actress Cameron Diaz 1972
Tennis player Andy Roddick. 1982

THE UNSINKABLE SHIP

A story is told about church services in Belfast, Ireland, the Sunday after the "unsinkable ship," the *Titanic* (built in Belfast), sank in the depths of the icy Atlantic, claiming more than fifteen hundred lives. In the congregation were scores of new widows and orphans and countless shipyard executives and workers whose loved ones, friends, or both had gone down with the ship on its maiden voyage to America.

In light of the tragedy, the preacher chose as his sermon title "The Unsinkable Ship." He wasn't talking about the *Titanic* but rather the delicate little boat that carried Jesus and his disciples across raging, stormy waters. While the winds swirled seemingly uncontrollably around the tiny vessel, the Master was sound asleep in the back of the boat. He was not concerned about the howling winds and frothy waves. He knew that with God in the boat, it truly is unsinkable. When the disciples woke Jesus, he rebuked the storm, and the winds ceased immediately.

In a later passage (Mark 6:45–52) the Bible tells of the time Jesus walked on the surface of the water out to the boat where his disciples were. What awesome power! Nowhere are we more secure in the vastness of God's great universe than in the "unsinkable boat" of his loving hand.

TODAY'S POWER POINT

Don't try to hold God's hand; let him hold yours. Let him do the holding and you do the trusting.—Source Unknown

August 31

TODAY IN HISTORY

1803—Start of Lewis and Clark expedition

1886—First major earthquake to strike eastern United States killed one hundred near Charleston, South Carolina

1887—Thomas Edison patented the kinetoscope (early motion-picture viewer)

1955—General Motors unveiled first solar-powered automobile prototype (in Chicago)

1994—Cease-fire called by IRA in Northern Ireland

1997—Britain's Princess Diana and two others killed in Paris car crash

1998—North Korea launched missile over Japan

2000—President Bill Clinton refused to repeal the estate tax

2004—Russia blamed terrorists for crash of two passenger planes six days earlier

BORN TODAY

Educator Maria Montessori 1870

Entertainer Arthur Godfrey 1903

Comedian Buddy Hackett 1924

Actor James Coburn. 1928

Baseball player Frank Robinson . . 1935

Singer Van Morrison 1945

Baseball player Hideo Nomo 1968

Actor Chris Tucker. 1972

ONLY ASK

Have you noticed that our heavenly Father often lets us run the course with our own efforts before he steps in? Theology professor and author Eugene Peterson related a struggle he once had with his lawn mower. Turning the unit on its side, he toiled to remove the blade for sharpening. But try as he might, the blade just wouldn't budge. When his biggest wrench wouldn't turn the nut, he slipped a length of pipe over its handle to give him more leverage, but still he had no success. Frustrated, he began beating on the pipe with a large rock.

Hearing the commotion, a neighbor came over and quietly suggested that perhaps the lawn mower bolt was threaded the other way. Sure enough, when Peterson reversed the wrench, the nut came off easily. Peterson noted that his neighbor's correction had saved him from both frustration and failure.

In the same way, God is standing ready to provide guidance and strength when we just call on him. Jeremiah 29:12–13 says, "Call upon me and come and pray to me, and I will listen to you. You will seek me and find me when you seek me with all your heart."

So next time things are difficult and you just can't seem to make it work on your own, don't get frustrated—get the Father's help. He's standing back, watching, and waiting for you to seek him in prayer.

TODAY'S POWER POINT

Ask and it will be given to you; seek and you will find; knock and the door will be opened to you. For everyone who asks receives; he who seeks finds; and to him who knocks, the door will be opened.—Matthew 7:7–8

TODAY IN HISTORY

1807—Aaron Burr cleared of treason

1939—Nazi Germany invaded Poland, launching World War I

1974—U.S. pilot James Sullivan flew from New York to London in less than two hours

1983—Korean jetliner shot down, killing 269 (Soviets suspected)

1985—Wreckage of ocean liner *Titanic* found off coast of Newfoundland

2004—Start of Beslan school hostage crisis: Islamic-militant Chechen separatists stormed the school, taking more than 1,300 hostages

2006—Missile defense test succeeds when interceptor rocket in California downs a target missile launched from Alaska

BORN TODAY

Author Edgar Rice Burroughs . . . 1875

Boxer Rocky Marciano 1923

Singer Conway Twitty 1933

Actress Lily Tomlin 1939

TV host Dr. Phil McGraw 1950

Basketball player Tim Hardaway . 1966

MORE POWER

When Ezra Roth's family first crossed the Rocky Mountains, it was in a vintage car that huffed and puffed. It overheated, and the radiator often boiled over. All the beauties of the mountain scenery went unnoticed due to the continued problems with the car, for it was struggling under its own limitations.

Some years later the family made the trip again, this time in a somewhat newer vehicle that performed a bit better. But the engine still lacked the necessary strength to cross the mountain peaks well.

The third trip was a different story. This time the group traveled in a modern car with all the power needed to conquer even the steepest mountain road. Only with sufficient power was the family able to stop and enjoy the scenery without worrying that their car might not make it over the next rise.

It's the same in our spiritual lives. Too many people putt along with their puny engines, straining to climb mountains that are out of their league. But no Christian has to struggle on without sufficient power to crest the mountains in their paths. God is our power source, and he has power to conquer any mountain. As believers, we can accomplish the seemingly impossible because God will supply all we need to complete the task according to his will.

Have you availed yourself of God's power, or are you still struggling in your own strength? God wants you to use his power to complete the job he has called you to do. Like Paul, you too will be able to say, "I can do everything through him who gives me strength" (Philippians 4:13).

TODAY'S POWER POINT

What lies behind you and what lies in front of you pales in comparison to what lies inside of you.—Ralph Waldo Emerson

September 2

TODAY IN HISTORY

1666—Fire swept through London, destroying thirteen thousand houses

1752—September 3–13 skipped with adoption of Gregorian calendar

1789—U.S. Treasury Department established

1945—World War II officially ended with Japan's signing of surrender terms; North Vietnam recognized by Communists

1947—Treaty of Rio de Janeiro, pledging mutual defense, signed by nineteen Western nations

1963—*CBS Evening News* extended to a half hour

1983—Yitzhak Shamir elected to succeed Menachem Begin as Herut Party leader (and likely new prime minister) of Israel

2004—UN-backed proposal encouraging Lebanese to resist Syrian pressure to extend current Lebanese leader's term

BORN TODAY

Poet Eugene Field. 1850

Baseball commissioner Peter Ueberroth 1937

Quarterback and sportscaster Terry Bradshaw 1948

Actor Mark Harmon 1951

Tennis player Jimmy Connors . . . 1952

Football player Eric Dickerson . . . 1960

Actor Keanu Reeves 1964

Boxer Lennox Lewis 1965

PATIENCE

The missionary candidate arrived for his scheduled interview shortly after 8:00 a.m., but he had a long wait. His interviewer didn't arrive until four o'clock in the afternoon and then asked the candidate simply to spell *flavor*. The candidate complied and spelled the word, then was asked, "What is three plus five?" The candidate answered correctly again. Then the interviewer announced, "Very good, you've passed the test. I'll recommend that you be appointed for missionary service."

Later the interviewer explained the real tests the candidate had passed: punctuality—he arrived for the interview on time; patience—he waited eight hours to be interviewed and never complained about the delay; temper—no sign of anger despite the frustrating setting; humility—he gladly answered questions an eight-year-old could get right without being offended. In short, he was not antagonized by his "trial" and therefore was considered emotionally qualified for missionary service.

Would you have passed this test? Take some time and think about it—if you have the patience.

TODAY'S POWER POINT

He that can have patience can have what he will.—Benjamin Franklin

TODAY IN HISTORY

1783—Treaty of Paris ended Revolutionary War
1935—World auto-speed record set (304 mph)
1939—World War II spread as Britain and France declared war on Germany
1943—Italy surrendered to Allies
1976—U.S. *Viking II* spacecraft sent back first close-up, color pictures of Mars
1978—Pope John Paul I installed
1981—Newsman David Brinkley left NBC after thirty-eight-year stint (moved to ABC)
2004—Medicare premiums set to increase 17 percent; U.S. jobless rate dropped to
    5.4 percent with creation of 144,000 new jobs

BORN TODAY

Actress Kitty Carlisle 1915
Cartoonist Mort Walker 1923
Actress Ann Jackson 1926
Actress Eileen Brennan 1935
Actress Pauline Collins 1940
Actress Valerie Perrine 1943
Football player Eric Dickerson . . . 1960
Actor Charlie Sheen 1965

ABOVE THE LAW

Pranksters thought it funny when they removed the stop sign from a busy rural intersection, but it wasn't long before they learned the devastating consequences of their crime. A car neared the intersection at full speed, unaware of an approaching vehicle. Following a grinding crash, the grim toll became clear: the driver of the first vehicle was killed instantly and his wife hospitalized with broken legs—the children and driver of the approaching car were also injured, all because of someone who acted as if he were above the law.

Did part of you just say to yourself, "I would never do something like that," with just a whiff of self-satisfaction? You don't have to be a criminal or even break a traffic law to be guilty of the same offense—thinking you're above the law. The most pious, strictly religious people of Jesus's day, the Pharisees, were especially guilty of this one. They were craftier than most lawbreakers. Instead of blatantly breaking the law, they rationalized it away and established their own traditions that benefited them. Eventually they allowed their traditions to supersede the law given by God.

Are you guilty of the same mental gymnastics that help you rationalize why some of God's laws don't apply to you? Don't fool yourself. You're certainly not fooling God. "Do not be deceived: God cannot be mocked. A man reaps what he sows. The one who sows to please his sinful nature, from that nature will reap destruction" (Galatians 6:7–8). No one is above God's laws or above reaping the consequences of breaking those laws.

TODAY'S POWER POINT

In times of trouble leniency becomes crime.—Ancient Proverb

September 4

TODAY IN HISTORY

1781—Los Angeles incorporated
1882—New York City got first electric power
1888—Kodak roll-film camera patented
1951—President Harry Truman's speech in San Francisco inaugurated coast-to-coast TV
1983—U.S. claimed Russian spy plane was flying in area of downed Korean jetliner
2003—*New England Journal of Medicine* reported PPY hormone reduces human appetite in all body types (fat and thin)
2004—Hurricane Frances caused $40 billion damage across Florida
2006—TV's Crocodile Hunter Steve Irwin, 44, dies from sting ray dart to the chest

BORN TODAY

Composer Anton Bruckner 1824
Architect Daniel Burnham 1846
Broadcaster Paul Harvey. 1918
Actress Mitzi Gaynor 1931
Golfer Tom Watson 1949

Comedian and actor Damon Wayans
. . . . 1960
Baseball player Mike Piazza 1968
Singer Dan Miller : 1980
Singer Beyoncé Knowles. 1981

A GODLY EXAMPLE

It's refreshing to read of a recent survey in which 70 percent of U.S. teenagers said the people they most admired were their parents—even more than athletes and TV stars. With such admiration comes responsibility to be worthy of respect and emulation. This responsibility should drive us to depend on the Lord to help us be godly examples for our children.

As a parent, role model, or leader, what can you do to faithfully discharge your role as a godly example to your son or daughter? Writer David Brannon emphasizes the importance of pursuing the following five principles to help guide youths and set a good example of loving and honoring God:

1. Acknowledge that "life's main purpose is to trust Christ and live for him."
2. Let them know that you "care enough for them to protect them."
3. Impress on them that "it is better to please God than to please people."
4. Determine that what is expected of them, they'll see first in you.
5. Show them that "they can't go anywhere and get more love than they can at home (not even from a boyfriend or girlfriend)."

By teaching young people around you such principles, "they'll have the best reasons to admire you."

TODAY'S POWER POINT

The first great gift we can bestow on others is a good example.—Morell

TODAY IN HISTORY

1870—Three Catholic universities founded in one day: St. John's in Long Island, Loyola in Chicago, and Canisius in Buffalo

1881—Massive forest fire in Michigan killed 125 and left thousands homeless

1882—First Labor Day parade drew ten thousand marchers

1972—Palestinian terrorists killed eleven Israeli Olympic athletes in Munich

1975—Charles Manson follower Lynette "Squeaky" Fromme failed in attempt to assassinate president Gerald Ford

1984—U.S. space shuttle *Discovery* returned after successful six-day maiden voyage

1987—Invading forces from Chad destroyed major Libyan base

1995—France exploded nuclear device, generating widespread protests

1997—Death of Mother Theresa, age eighty-seven

2001—Mexican president Vicente Fox urged U.S. president George W. Bush to quickly define status of millions of illegal Mexican immigrants in United States

2002—Afghan president Hamid Karzai escaped attempted assassination; Senate overwhelmingly approved arming of U.S. airline pilots; Institute of Medicine doubled recommended daily exercise for adults to one hour

2003—United Nations reported former Liberian leader Charles Taylor escaped with over $100 million

BORN TODAY

Researcher Arthur Nielsen 1897
Actress Raquel Welch 1942
Producer Darryl Zanuck. 1902
Actor Dennis Dugan 1946
Composer John Cage 1912
Cartoonist Cathy Guisewite 1950
Comedian Bob Newhart 1929
Singer Dweezil Zappa. 1969
Actor William Devane 1939
Actress Rose McGowan 1973

THE POWER OF A GODLY WOMAN

Motivated women have contributed much to the heritage of our nation. One such individual in history was Sarah Hale. As a magazine editor, Hale began campaigning for a national Thanksgiving Day. She tirelessly wrote letters and contacted national leaders from the president on down in an effort to persuade them to approve Thanksgiving as a national holiday. But success did not come quickly. A full thirty-five years after she began her crusade, in the midst of the Civil War, president Abraham Lincoln declared the fourth Thursday of November as the official "National Thanksgiving Day." All because of one dedicated woman who would not be discouraged or defeated in her cause.

TODAY'S POWER POINT

Women who seek to be equal with men lack ambition.—Timothy Leary

September 6

TODAY IN HISTORY

1901—President William McKinley gunned down in Buffalo, New York

1920—First championship boxing match broadcast (on WWJ radio Detroit)

1952—Television launched in Canada

1986—Two Palestinian gunmen opened fire in Istanbul synagogue, killing twenty-two

2001—United States withdrew plan to break up Microsoft in favor of a less-drastic reorganization

2002—For only second time in history, Congress convened outside Washington DC (to honor 9/11 victims and rescuers in New York City)

BORN TODAY

Statesman Marquis de Lafayette . . 1757	Comedienne JoAnne Worley 1937
Social worker Jane Addams. 1860	Actress Swoosie Kurtz. 1944
Diplomat Joseph Kennedy 1888	Actress Jane Curtin. 1947
Producer Billy Rose 1899	Comedian Jeff Foxworthy. 1958

GOOD SAMARITANS

A young girl reaching into a cage at the zoo cried out in terror as a lion grabbed her arm in its teeth. Seeing the emergency unfold, a watchman nearby quickly drew his gun and shot the lion dead. The force of the lion's fall knocked both the girl and the guard to the ground, which triggered another random shot that struck the girl in the leg.

The girl's parents filed suit against the zoo, the guard, and the government agency that owned the zoo. The jury hearing testimony in the case denied all damages except those against the zoo for not having the cage sufficiently inaccessible. The guard was not held liable based on the fact that he was being a "good Samaritan" and should not be punished for accidentally wounding the girl in the course of trying to save her.

A lawsuit-happy society has made many people afraid to help others. It's enough to make an ordinary citizen duck his or her head and look the other way.

But God doesn't call us to be ordinary. Read again the story of the good Samaritan in Luke 10:30–37. This person helped a stranger because it was the right thing to do, even though it was inconvenient, it cost him something, and it was dangerous—and even when he knew there was little chance he'd ever be thanked. That's what good Samaritans do. And what did Jesus say about the Samaritan's heroics? "Go and do likewise" (Luke 10:37).

TODAY'S POWER POINT

The first question which the priest and the Levite asked was: "If I stop to help this man, what will happen to me?" But . . . the good Samaritan reversed the question: "If I do not stop to help this man, what will happen to him?"—Martin Luther King Jr.

September 7

TODAY IN HISTORY

1936—Boulder Dam began operation

1977—President Jimmy Carter signed treaty transferring control of Panama Canal to Panama in 1999

2001—U.S. jobless rate rose to 4.5 percent in August, highest one-month increase in six years

2003—U.S. president George W. Bush asked Congress for $87 billion in aid for defense and reconstruction of Iraq

2004—Death toll of U.S. forces in Iraq reached one thousand; military records of president George W. Bush released

BORN TODAY

Painter Grandma Moses 1860
Director Elia Kazan 1909
Pianist Arthur Ferrante 1921
Singer Buddy Holly 1936
Singer Gloria Gaynor 1949
Actor Corbin Bernsen 1954
Pianist Michael Feinstein 1956
Soccer player Briana Scurry 1971

WHERE SCIENCE IS SILENT

In recent years a divide between the proponents of science and believers in the Bible seems to be growing as evolutionists battle for control of school curriculums with those who want "intelligent design" to be at least considered in schools. But outside the question of how life began, belief in both the Bible and science is easily reconciled. Although the Bible was not intended to be a science textbook, it addresses many questions for which science has no answers.

This fact was highlighted by Dr. Joseph Parker, who asked a group of students, "What does science have to say to a woman who has lost her only son?" Silence ensued. "Does existence end with death? We're awaiting an answer."

Still no response.

"Then we must turn to Scripture," he said. Opening the Bible, he read: "I will go to him, but he will not return to me" (2 Samuel 12:23). "The dead will be raised imperishable, and we will be changed. For the perishable must clothe itself with the imperishable, and the mortal with immortality" (1 Corinthians 15:52–53). "I saw the dead, great and small, standing before the throne" (Revelation 20:12).

The Bible speaks where science is silent—on the life hereafter, on love, on justice, pain, loneliness, joy, and a relationship with God. The Bible speaks to the issues that really affect your life—those that keep you awake at night. What's keeping you awake at night? Go to the best answer book available and find God's solutions.

TODAY'S POWER POINT

Everywhere you look in science, the harder it becomes to understand the universe without God.—Robert Hermann

September 8

TODAY IN HISTORY

1935—U.S. senator Huey P. "Kingfish" Long of Louisiana shot and mortally
wounded in state capitol, motivation for shooting still cloaked in mystery

1939—Nazi troops besieged Warsaw

1941—Leningrad surrounded by Nazis

1966—Television premiere of *Star Trek*

1971—Opening of Kennedy Center in Washington

1974—Stuntman Evel Knievel's attempt to rocket 1,600 feet across a canyon
fell short (but he survived); new president Gerald Ford pardoned his
predecessor, Richard Nixon

1982—Three Lutheran denominations voted to merge to become third-largest
protestant group in the United States

1986—Television premiere of *The Oprah Winfrey Show*

1998—Mark McGwire's sixty-second home run of the season broke Roger Maris's
longstanding record

2003—Recording Industry Association of America (RIAA) sued hundreds of people
for illegal sharing of songs via the Internet

BORN TODAY

Composer Antonin Dvorak	1841	Actress Heather Thomas	1956
Comedian Sid Caesar	1922	Basketball player Latrell Sprewell	1970
Comedian Peter Sellers	1925	Actor David Arquette	1971
Singer Patsy Cline	1932	Actor Jonathan Taylor Thomas	1981

GOOD CITIZENS

Is it possible to be a Christian as well as a good citizen—or even to fight as a
soldier? Let's look to the Bible for some examples. Weren't David, Joshua, and
Gideon all soldiers while at the same time being good citizens and children of
God? In more modern times we have the examples of Stonewall Jackson, an active
Presbyterian deacon who established a Sunday school for impoverished blacks,
and Robert E. Lee, who regularly spoke to others about being "right with God."
Both were Confederate generals with reputations as men of strong faith and moral
conviction as well as valiant warriors. And General George Washington's heartfelt
prayer in the snows of Valley Forge, calling upon the Almighty for strength in
battle, is still an inspiration and model for us today.

All of these were Christian citizens whose lives demonstrated what they
believed. What does your life demonstrate about what you believe?

TODAY'S POWER POINT

It is not the function of our government to keep the citizen from falling into
error; it is the function of the citizen to keep the government from falling into
error.—Supreme Court Justice Robert Jackson

TODAY IN HISTORY

1850—Thirty-first state, California, joined the Union

1972—Television premiere of cartoon *Fat Albert*

1982—Princess Grace of Monaco (formerly Grace Kelly) died of injuries suffered in an earlier car accident

2002—One hundred people killed in train derailment in northeast India

2003—Resolution called on Iran to allow UN inspections and to disclose information on its nuclear program; U.S. Army said troops might remain in Iraq and Kuwait for up to one year; Boston archdiocese settled 550 sexual-abuse lawsuits for $85 million

2004—House blocked new rules that would have kept some employees from getting overtime pay

BORN TODAY

William the Conqueror 1087
Author Leo Tolstoy. 1828
Entrepreneur Colonel Harlan Sanders
. . . . 1890
Actor Cliff Robertson. 1925
Singer Billy Preston 1946
Quarterback Joe Theisman 1949
Actress Angela Cartwright 1952
Actor Hugh Grant 1960
Comedian and actor Adam Sandler
. . . . 1966
Actress Michelle Williams. 1980

AN APPLICATION LETTER

Remember the last time you applied for employment? You no doubt stressed your qualifications for the job on your application. Imagine the mood of the church that received the following: "I understand your pulpit is currently vacant. Allow me to state my credentials: I have been a good leader in most of the places where I have been and am generally considered to be a good preacher. Although I have done some writing, I am over fifty years of age and not in the best of health. I have never preached in one place for more than three years, and that usually in small churches. I had to leave some places when riots and disturbances broke out. I have been threatened several times and have gone to jail for witnessing. Does your church want to hire me? (signed) Paul of Tarsus."

What seemed on the surface like less-than-desirable qualities were actually the result of Paul's being effective for God. Sometimes working for God can bring difficulties. Have you suffered in some way in the course of faithful ministry? Don't be discouraged. Sometimes progress comes at a price—but God sees all, and just as he used Paul to help establish the early church, he can use you to build his kingdom—no matter what your resume looks like.

TODAY'S POWER POINT

A man who qualifies himself well for his calling never fails of employment.
—Thomas Jefferson

September 10

TODAY IN HISTORY

1919—New York City gave gigantic salute to General John Pershing and victorious
    army troops returning from World War I
1955—Television premiere of *Gunsmoke*
1969—Oil leases brought $900 million to Alaska
1993—Television premiere of *The X-Files*
2000—Indiana University fired controversial coach Bobby Knight
2002—Nation went on high alert as first anniversary of 9/11 terrorist attacks neared
2003—President George W. Bush called for broadened powers in revised Patriot Act

BORN TODAY

Golfer Arnold Palmer 1929   Actress Amy Irving 1953
Baseball player Roger Maris 1934   Baseball player Randy Johnson . . . 1963
Singer Jose Feliciano 1945   Actor Ryan Phillippe 1974

KNOWING YOUR ENEMY

Just after the outbreak of World War I, the British War Ministry sent messages to all its outposts: "War declared. Arrest all enemy aliens in your area." Back to headquarters came this reply: "We have arrested ten Germans, six Belgians, four Frenchmen, two Italians, three Austrians, and an American. Please advise immediately who we are at war with."

It's difficult—if not impossible—to fight a successful war until you clearly identify your enemy. This is extremely difficult when the enemy is within. Terrorists within a country are harder to identify and therefore potentially even more dangerous than an enemy nation. Strong walls of defense guard most nations from outside attack, but who can defend against the surprise offensive from those who have been accepted into the community as friends and comrades? "If an enemy were insulting me, I could endure it; if a foe were raising himself against me, I could hide from him. But it is you, a man like myself, my companion, my close friend, with whom I once enjoyed sweet fellowship as we walked with the throng at the house of God" (Psalm 55:12–14).

The point is not to be suspicious of all those around us. But neither should we be surprised—nor allow ourselves to be undone—when someone close to us betrays us or turns out to be a hidden enemy. God is the just and faithful arbiter. Eventually righteousness will be rewarded and wickedness punished. In the meantime, we can call out to God. He will be faithful to sustain and save us when we cry out to him.

TODAY'S POWER POINT

If we could read the secret history of our enemies, we should find in each man's life sorrow and suffering enough to disarm all hostilities.—Henry Wadsworth Longfellow

TODAY IN HISTORY

1609—Manhattan Island "discovered" by Henry Hudson
1959—Food stamps introduced in United States
1967—Television premiere of *The Carol Burnett Show*
1985—Baseball's Pete Rose got 4,192nd career hit, breaking Ty Cobb's record
1998—Independent counsel announced charges in impeachment case against President Bill Clinton
2001—Terrorists flew hijacked jetliners into Pentagon and World Trade Center towers, and one hijacked jet crashed in field in Pennsylvania: thousands killed in worst terrorist attack on U.S. soil

BORN TODAY

Singer Jenny Lind. 1850
Producer Brian De Palma. 1940
Actress Lola Falana. 1943
Softball player Donna Lopiano. . . 1946
Actress Amy Madigan. 1951
Actress Kristy McNichol. 1962
Actress Virginia Madsen. 1963
Singer Moby. 1965
Singer Harry Connick Jr. 1967
Actress Ariana Richards 1979

WALKING IN THE LIGHT

One of the more visually interesting of all God's creatures is the colorful chameleon. These small lizards are intriguing to watch as they change colors, fading from light brown to pale green within just a few moments. Many people believe the chameleon's colorful camouflage is determined by its surroundings (e.g., turning green to match the leaf it's on), but scientists tell us that's not so. Rather, the chameleon's hue is triggered by the light and temperature of its surroundings.

For chameleons, this feature is a matter of survival. But the Bible talks about another kind of chameleon—"chameleon Christians." These are believers whose actions and behaviors adapt to their worldly surroundings to the point where it's nearly impossible to tell them apart from the non-Christians with whom they live and work. In 1 John we are reminded that God's Word, and not our daily surroundings, should decide our spiritual "color." John was writing to believers who, like you and I today, are often surrounded by activities and attitudes that are disappointing and contrary to God. But rather than taking on the color of our atmosphere, we need to resolve to stay true and pure. What is your spiritual color today?

TODAY'S POWER POINT

The number one cause of atheism is Christians. Those who proclaim God with their mouths and deny him with their lifestyles are what an unbelieving world finds simply unbelievable.—Karl Rahner

September 12

TODAY IN HISTORY

1814—Baltimore survived battle of Fort McHenry

1959—Television premiere of *Bonanza*

1976—National Academy of Sciences urged limitations on usage of fluorocarbon gases

1979—Record-setting hurricane blasted coastal Alabama with 100-mph winds

1994—Small plane crashed into White House (no one injured)

2000—Selma, Alabama, heart of 1960s-era racial strife, elected first African American mayor

2002—President George W. Bush laid out case against Iraq in UN address

2004—Justice Department reported U.S. property- and violent-crime rates the lowest in thirty years; for second time, U.S. Airways filed for bankruptcy protection

BORN TODAY

Newspaperman Charles Warner . . 1829

Journalist H. L. Mencken. 1880

Olympic runner Jesse Owens 1913

Actor Ian Holm 1931

Singer Maria Muldaur 1943

Actor Peter Scolari 1954

Actress Rachel Ward. 1957

Actor Paul Walker 1973

Singer Ruben Studdard 1978

Basketball player Yao Ming. 1980

DOING SOMETHING ABOUT HUNGER

What are you doing to feed the world's hungry? Some churches have sponsored "starvation banquets" to underscore the problem of worldwide hunger. Typically, each banquet guest is served half a cup of soup, half a slice of plain bread, and a cup of black tea. Following the banquet an offering is collected for world missions. One such project at a major university netted over $12,000 for famine relief during a single semester of once-a-week rice lunches.

As God's representatives here on earth, we Christians need to be especially conscious of the needy and the hungry and do what we can to assist. We have to be more than concerned. Wringing our hands in grief and just talking about the problem won't make it go away. James 2:15–16 says, "Suppose a brother or sister is without clothes and daily food. If one of you says to him, 'Go, I wish you well; keep warm and well fed,' but does nothing about his physical needs, what good is it?"

What action can you take today—not tomorrow, not next week or sometime in the future—to help feed the hungry? Do it. As James 2:14 says, "What's the use of saying you have faith if you don't prove it by your actions?" (NLT) Have you put your faith in God? Prove it!

TODAY'S POWER POINT

Anyone who gives you a cup of water in my name because you belong to Christ will certainly not lose his reward.—Mark 9:41

TODAY IN HISTORY

1503—Michelangelo began work on his sculpture David
1971—Thirty-seven killed in four-day standoff at Attica (New York) prison; Liberty University opened
1976—California adopted first right-to-die law to avoid life-prolonging treatment
1990—Television premiere of *Law and Order*
2001—Osama bin Laden named prime suspect in 9/11 terrorist attacks

BORN TODAY

Surgeon Walter Reed	1851	Actress Jacqueline Bisset	1944
General John Pershing	1860	Baseball player Bernie Williams	1968
Singer Mel Torme	1925	Designer Stella McCartney	1971
Producer Fred Silverman	1937	Actor Ben Savage	1980

BEING TRUTHFUL

Some years ago a study was conducted to determine what qualities American and Canadian church people looked for in their pastors. As reported by *Christianity Today*, the study of more than five thousand people revealed that congregations wanted their spiritual leaders to be humble and good Christian examples, but more than anything else, they wanted leaders to be honest. It's not surprising that churches expect their pastors to be truthful above all else.

It has become increasingly difficult to recognize and guard the truth in this day of increasingly complex and technological communication. Bloggers spout biased opinions immediately after an event occurs. Even news photos have been occasionally doctored or staged to manipulate our sympathies. Sophisticated computer software makes it easy to find and manipulate facts and images to support almost any viewpoint. But although the techniques are new, the concept is not. People have been shading the truth to manipulate and con others since the beginning of time (consider Satan's manipulative half-truth to Eve in the Garden of Eden).

But Christians are to avoid even the slightest hint of such manipulation or distortion of reality and cling tenaciously to the truth, the whole truth, and nothing but the truth. Like Paul, we must be able to say, "We reject all shameful and underhanded methods. We do not try to trick anyone, and we do not distort the word of God. We tell the truth before God, and all who are honest know that" (2 Corinthians 4:2 NLT).

Are you as honest as you could be? Tell the truth!

TODAY'S POWER POINT

If any man seeks for greatness, let him forget greatness and ask for truth, and he will find both.—Horace Mann

September 14

TODAY IN HISTORY

1814—Francis Scott Key drafted words to "The Star Spangled Banner" while observing battle at Fort McHenry, Maryland

1901—Vice President Theodore Roosevelt assumed the office of president upon the death of president William McKinley

1927—Bob Jones University opened

1948—Groundbreaking for UN headquarters building in New York City

1963—Mary Ann Fischer gave birth to first surviving U.S. quintuplets

1972—Television premiere of *The Waltons*

1975—Knife-wielding vandal attacked Rembrandt painting in Amsterdam

1994—MLB strike resulted in cancellation of World Series and remaining games of the season

2001—Day of Mourning held in memory of 9/11 victims and families; in unanimous vote, Senate authorized president to use "all necessary and appropriate force" in response to terrorist attacks

BORN TODAY

Physiologist Ivan Pavlov 1849
Feminist Margaret Sanger. 1879
Actress Zoe Caldwell 1933
Writer Kate Millett. 1934
Producer Walter Koenig 1936
Actress Joey Heatherton 1944
Actor Sam Neill 1947
Actress Faith Ford. 1964

PREPARED FOR ANYTHING

Few people today know that evangelist Billy Graham preached his first sermon in jail. Graham—fresh from high school—and his friend Grady Wilson were spending the summer working as Fuller Brush salesmen when an evangelist invited them to attend his jail service. During the service Billy was asked to give his testimony, a talk that launched his worldwide ministry of preaching to millions of people. It all began on a warm afternoon when a young salesman was prepared to share his salvation story in prison.

What opportunities is God giving you today? Don't be afraid to reach out and grab them. "Preach the Word," Paul encouraged in 2 Timothy 4:2. "Be prepared in season and out of season; correct, rebuke and encourage—with great patience and careful instruction." You may not be a preacher, but you can tell your story. You may not be a theologian, but you can tell what you believe and know to be true. You may be only a brush salesman or a _____ (you fill in the blank), but you can encourage someone else who's struggling or discouraged. You don't even have to go out of your way. God will bring the opportunities to you. All that's required of you is to be prepared. Are you ready?

TODAY'S POWER POINT

To be prepared is half the victory.—Miguel de Cervantes

TODAY IN HISTORY

1933—Nazis passed Nuremberg Laws, sharply curtailing rights of Jews in Germany

1940—Seventy-eight German planes shot down during Battle of Britain

1949—Television premiere of *The Lone Ranger*

1982—Start of publication of *USA Today*

1983—U.S. Senate unanimously condemned Soviet attack on Korean Airlines jet, which killed 269

1984—Princess Diana gave birth to second son, Henry ("Harry"), third in line of succession to the British throne behind his father, Charles (the Prince of Wales) and older brother, Prince William

2000—Summer Olympics opened in Sydney, Australia

2003—Court ordered delay of California's gubernatorial recall election (to update voting equipment)

2004—President George W. Bush asked for $3.4 billion earmarked for war in Iraq to be spent on strengthening U.S. homeland defenses

BORN TODAY

Novelist James Fenimore Cooper . 1789

Writer Robert Benchley 1889

Author Agatha Christie 1890

Singer Roy Acuff 1903

Actor Jackie Cooper 1922

Baseball player Gaylord Perry 1938

Director Oliver Stone;

    actor Tommy Lee Jones 1946

Football player Dan Marino 1961

Britain's Prince Harry 1984

KNEE MAIL

Who today hasn't used e-mail? Whether it's Instant Messenger or simply checking the inbox on your laptop (or cell phone), it seems we're in constant contact with others. But have you ever wondered, *Is my e-mail getting to its destination? Is anybody reading it? When will I receive a response? Will I ever?*

We never have to worry about such things when using "knee mail"—prayer, or talking to our heavenly Father. The Bible promises (in Psalm 66:18) that if the channels aren't blocked by sin, our prayers will always be heard by God himself. And even when we do fall short, God is always willing to forgive (and forget) our wrongs (see 1 John 1:9). While an e-mail message could go unread for days, that'll never happen with your messages to God. He's available 24/7, and you may be certain he's never too busy to hear from you. Not only that, but you can be sure of his care and his loving response. The psalmist wrote, "You are forgiving and good, O Lord, abounding in love to all who call to you" (Psalm 86:5). So we can call out to God with confidence: "Hear my prayer, O Lord; listen to my cry for mercy. In the day of my trouble I will call to you, for you will answer me" (Psalm 86:6–7).

TODAY'S POWER POINT

Prayer is not overcoming God's reluctance; it is rather laying hold of his highest willingness.—Archbishop Trench

TODAY IN HISTORY

1620—Pilgrims departed for the New World aboard *Mayflower*

1630—Boston, Massachusetts, adopted present name

1776—General George Washington scored first major victory in Revolutionary War in battle of Harlem Heights, New York

1974—President Gerald Ford announced immunity from prosecution for Vietnam-era draft evaders

1985—For first time in seventy-one years, the United States became a debtor nation

1993—Television premiere of *Frasier*

2000—Albert Lasker medical awards given to six scientists for drastically reducing risk of transmitting hepatitis virus through blood transfusions

2004—Government report said Saddam Hussein clearly intended to produce weapons of mass destruction

BORN TODAY

Historian Francis Parkman 1823

Producer Allen Funt 1914

Actress Lauren Bacall 1924

Actor Peter Falk 1927

Basketball player Elgin Baylor . . . 1934

Editor Mark McEwen 1954

Illusionist David Copperfield 1956

Baseball player Orel Hershiser . . . 1958

Actress Molly Shannon 1964

Golfer Tina Barrett 1976

WORTH THE TROUBLE

Diamonds are lackluster and unattractive in their natural state. Only after they are subjected to repeated abrasion and cutting do they become the sparkling gems so prized for their radiant beauty. But only diamonds have the hardness to wear down other diamonds, so the abrasives used to polish diamonds are themselves quite expensive. Diamonds are so valuable that some companies go to the trouble of searching through 180 million parts of diggings to retrieve just one part diamond.

In the diamond we can get an idea of how God sees mankind. Looking at the world, it's hard to imagine how God could stoop down and love lost humanity, hardened by sin. Yet in the Master's hand the surrendered soul becomes a new being. Through the rough-and-tumble events of life, our lives become polished to the point of radiantly reflecting God's brilliant glory.

If you're going through a difficult time that's wearing you down, take heart. God may be polishing you into a shining gem of rare beauty in his artful and loving hands. Don't fight the polishing; embrace it.

TODAY'S POWER POINT

Guard well your spare moments. They are like uncut diamonds. Discard them and their value will never be known. Improve them and they will become the brightest gems in a useful life.—Ralph Waldo Emerson

TODAY IN HISTORY

1920—NFL founded (in Canton, Ohio)

1972—Television premiere of *M*A*S*H*

1978—Fighter Muhammad Ali won heavyweight boxing title for unprecedented third time (defeating Leon Spinks)

1983—Vanessa Williams crowned first African American Miss America

1987—Bicentennial of U.S. Constitution celebrated in Philadelphia

1997—Swiss pledged to release funds to Holocaust survivors from estimated $100 million left in dormant World War II–era bank accounts

2003—Retired army general Wesley Clark entered Democratic race for president;

BORN TODAY

General Frederic von Steuben	1730	Basketball coach Phil Jackson	1945
Singer Hank Williams	1923	Actor John Ritter	1948
Actor Ruddy McDowall	1928	Football player Mark Brunell	1970
Actress Anne Bancroft	1931	Basketball player Rasheed Wallace	1974

VIRTUE

We live in an age in which society is struggling to find moral guidance. Never before has ethics been such a focus in the business world. Executives pay hundreds of dollars to attend seminars to help them determine what's right and wrong. While the Bible clearly spells out the absolutes, there are other areas of conviction and preference which—in themselves—may be neither clearly right nor clearly wrong unless they cause others to stumble.

We don't have to live our lives by a list of rules, watching closely to be sure we get everything to which we're entitled, not wanting to step over the line and be guilty but neither wishing to abstain from anything that is just the slightest on the right side of legal or moral. How much freer we can be when we stop nitpicking the letter of the law and start striving to be the best we can be. How can we make this switch? The apostle Peter said, "His divine power has given us everything we need for life and godliness through our knowledge of him" (2 Peter 1:3).

With God's help we can escape the corruption in the world and participate in his divine nature. Imagine not having to worry about what's right or wrong—or not even having a desire for things that are bad. Better yet, imagine having the desire to do what's noble and right. Growing in faith, goodness, knowledge, self-control, perseverance, godliness, brotherly kindness, and brotherly love keeps us from being ineffective and unproductive and keeps us from falling. That's the way to true success in God's book.

TODAY'S POWER POINT

With virtue you can't be entirely poor; without virtue you can't really be rich.
—Chinese Proverb

TODAY IN HISTORY

1793—Capitol cornerstone laid in Washington DC
1851—*New York Times* first published
1927—CBS network launched with sixteen radio stations
1947—U.S. Air Force separated from the Army
1957—Television premiere of *Wagon Train*
1975—Patty Hearst found safe in San Francisco nineteen months after her kidnapping
1978—U.S. president Jimmy Carter, Egyptian president Anwar Sadat, and Israeli prime minister Menachem Begin ended Camp David summit with historic peace agreement
1998—Senate failed to overturn veto of late-term abortion procedure
2001—U.S. pledged billions of dollars in aid to U.S. airlines struggling after 9/11 terrorist attacks; in antiterrorism move, U.S. broadened powers to arrest immigrants

BORN TODAY

Lexicographer Samuel Johnson. . . 1709
Actress Greta Garbo 1905
Actor Rossano Brazzi 1916
Hockey coach Scotty Bowman . . . 1933
Singer Frankie Avalon. 1939
Baseball player Ryne Sandberg . . . 1959
Actor James Gandolfini 1961
Cyclist Lance Armstrong 1971

SHINING A LIGHT

A passenger on a ship en route to India became too ill to venture from his cabin. During the middle of one particularly turbulent, difficult night, he heard the cry, "Man overboard!" The sick man was filled with compassion for the unknown soul who had plunged into the troubled sea, but he felt helpless, perplexed about what he could do to help. Then he hit upon an idea. He grabbed a light from his cabin and held it up to the porthole so that it might be seen at sea. He was thrilled a few moments later to hear the cry, "There he is. Throw him the line and pull him to safety." In a matter of minutes the endangered man had been pulled back aboard the ship and saved.

The next day the sick passenger was told that it was only by some timely light which shone upon the overboard man that the crew had been able to spot him and throw out the rope to pull him to safety. The man's little lamp was the light by which a man's life was saved.

You can have an equally vital role in holding out light to those around you who are floundering in darkness. God has called you to "shine like stars in the universe as you hold out the word of life" (Philippians 2:15–16). What are you doing to spread the hope and light of God's love to those around you?

TODAY'S POWER POINT

God likes help when helping people.—Irish Proverb

TODAY IN HISTORY

1676—Jamestown Colony, Virginia, burned to the ground by Nathaniel Bacon Jr. during Bacon's Rebellion

1796—President George Washington's farewell address published

1881—Vice President Chester Arthur assumed presidency upon death of President James Garfield

1928—Mickey Mouse debuted in Walt Disney's animated cartoon, *Steamboat Willie*

1970—Premiere of television's *The Mary Tyler Moore Show*

1985—Series of earthquakes in Mexico City, killing ten thousand people

1994—Premiere of television's *ER*

2002—President George W. Bush requested congressional approval to use "all appropriate means" to remove Saddam Hussein from power in Iraq

2003—Three-foot tall rodent fossil unearthed in South America

BORN TODAY

Actor Adam West 1928
Columnist Mike Royko 1932
Actor David McCallum 1933
Composer Paul Williams 1940
Sportscaster Joe Morgan 1943
TV cohost Joan Lunden 1951
Singer Trisha Yearwood. 1964
Baseball player Jim Abbott 1967

TRUST

Years ago the *Covenant Companion* carried the story of a man who wished to teach his young daughter the meaning of total trust in the face of hardship. One day he asked the youngster if she loved her daddy enough to give up her prized glass beads. She replied, "Yes," and sorrowfully surrendered them to her father. Nothing more was said until several weeks later, on her birthday. Her father called the little girl over to him and handed her a small box. Gently the girl slid off the ribbon and lifted the lid to see an exquisite string of genuine pearls! Proudly she put them around her neck and told her smiling father, "Oh Daddy, I didn't understand, but now I do."

The little girl learned the value of implicit trust in a loving father whom she wished to honor and obey. She learned that he only took her small, worthless trinkets for a short time and replaced them with something of far greater beauty and lasting value.

The apostle Paul knew how to trust God like that. In Philippians 3:8, he said: "I consider everything a loss compared to the surpassing greatness of knowing Christ Jesus my Lord, for whose sake I have lost all things. I consider them rubbish, that I may gain Christ." Like Paul and like the little girl in this story, do you trust your heavenly Father?

TODAY'S POWER POINT

Though he slay me, yet will I trust in him.—Job 13:15 KJV

September 20

TODAY IN HISTORY

1519—Ferdinand Magellan began around-the-world exploration
1952—Premiere of television's *The Jackie Gleason Show*
1973—Billie Jean King beat Bobby Riggs in tennis "Battle of the Sexes"
1984—Premiere of television's *The Cosby Show*
2000—Prosecutor for six-year Whitewater investigation cleared President Bill
    Clinton and wife, Hillary, of committing any crimes

BORN TODAY

Novelist Upton Sinclair	1878	Actress Anne Meara	1929
Jazz pianist Jelly Roll Morton	1885	Actress Sophia Loren	1934
Basketball coach Red Auerbach	1917	Actor Gary Cole	1957
Psychologist Dr. Joyce Brothers	1928	Actress Kristen Johnson	1967

OUR GODLY HERITAGE

While the world today tells us that America is a secular nation, it's inspiring to recall what some of America's greatest leaders had to say about the Bible.

Abraham Lincoln noted, "I believe the Bible is the best gift God has ever given man. All the good from the Savior of the world is communicated to us through this book." But he was by no means alone.

The famous Civil War general Ulysses S. Grant advised, "Hold fast to the Bible as the anchor of your liberties; write its precepts in your hearts, and practice them in your lives. To the influence of this Book we are indebted for all the progress made in true civilization, and to this we must look as our guide in the future." Another Civil War general, Robert E. Lee, acknowledged, "In all my perplexities and distresses, the Bible has never failed to give me light and strength."

America's third president, Thomas Jefferson, saw the benefits of the Bible for his nation: "The Bible is the cornerstone of liberty. . . . I have always said, I always will say, that the studious perusal of the Sacred volume will make better, citizens, better fathers, and better husbands."

But perhaps one of the most eloquent comments on the Scriptures came from the great orator Patrick Henry, who said, "If I could leave each of my children a million dollars, but could not leave them a heritage of faith in God, I would leave them nothing of value and unfit to face life. . . . The Bible is worth more than all other books which have ever been printed."

What heritage are you leaving your children? What will their most cherished memory of you be? May it be that of a godly parent humbly committed to God and his Word.

TODAY'S POWER POINT

If we will not be governed by God, then we will be ruled by tyrants.—William Penn

September 21 First Day of Autumn Colossians 3:23–24

TODAY IN HISTORY

1792—France became a republic
1948—Premiere of television's *The Milton Berle Show*
1970—Premiere of television's *Monday Night Football*
1985—Upward of one hundred thousand homes heavily damaged in earthquakes near Mexico City
1989—Hurricane Hugo hit U.S. east coast, causing $8 billion in damage
2000—Government statistics showed no significant difference in murder rates in states with death penalty to those without one
2001—Stock prices took second largest drop ever in response to 9/11 terrorist acts
2004—President George W. Bush defended war on Iraq in annual UN address

BORN TODAY

Historian H. G. Wells 1866
Actor Larry Hagman 1931
Songwriter Leonard Cohen 1934
Broadcast journalist Bill Kurtis . . . 1940
Actress Fannie Flagg 1944
Writer Stephen King 1947
Comedian and actor Bill Murray . 1950
Actor David James Elliott 1960
Singer Faith Hill 1967
TV personality Nicole Richie 1981

HARD WORK

A sculptor was hired to carve a large statue, but before he could finish, he became ill. Needing the job completed on time, his employers brought in a young sculptor to fill in. Although the young man could refer to the first artist's drawings, he had no idea what the carving was for or how long he might be working on it before the first man was well enough to work again. He knew it was unlikely that he would receive any credit for his job, but he was determined to do his best work anyway. Week after week he sculpted the stone, patiently chiseling a leaf here and a flower there. At last the job was finished and the carving shipped to its destination.

Years passed, and one day the young sculptor walked through a beautiful building, appreciating the elegant architecture and classic decor. As he glanced admiringly around the expansive halls, a splendid marble pillar caught his eye. Following its majestic lines upward, he was stunned to see at the top the beautiful piece he had carved. Overcome by emotion, he removed his cap and said reverently, "Thank God I did that job well."

Have you ever considered what you're doing today to be a ministry? Every believer's occupation is just that—a holy calling, something that God has ordained for him or her to do. No matter what your occupation or calling may be, do your best, as unto God.

TODAY'S POWER POINT

We should work to become, not to acquire.—Elbert Hubbard

September 22

TODAY IN HISTORY

1776—Nathan Hale executed by British for spying, considered the first U.S. martyr

1789—Samuel Osgood appointed first postmaster general by President George Washington

1862—First part of Emancipation Proclamation released

1927—Jack Dempsey failed to reclaim heavyweight boxing championship, losing again to Gene Tunney in the famed "Fight of the Long Count" in Chicago

1964—Broadway premiere of *Fiddler on the Roof*

1994—Premiere of television's *Friends*

2000—Major international banks shored up the euro to strengthen world economy

2004—Congressman Porter Goss named to head CIA

BORN TODAY

Scientist Michael Faraday 1791
Actor John Houseman 1902
Baseball manager Tom Lasorda . . . 1927
Singer Debby Boone 1956
Singer Joan Jett 1960
Actor Scott Baio 1961
Actress Bonnie Hunt 1964
Soccer player Ronaldo 1976

A PENNY'S WORTH OF CONTENTMENT

Perhaps the American president most often associated with poverty and humble roots is Abraham Lincoln, who was born in a lowly log cabin. It was Lincoln who said, "The Lord must love the common people, he has made so many of them." But did you know why Lincoln was selected to appear on the penny?

There was much controversy over whether a person should appear on the nation's coinage. But President Theodore Roosevelt, who was responsible for the decision, was impressed by a sculpture of Lincoln by immigrant Victor David Brenner. Because more pennies would be minted than any other coin and more of them would be found in the pockets of the common people, the humble face of Lincoln seemed a natural for the penny—the first U.S. coin to bear the motto "In God We Trust," which had first been approved by Congress during Lincoln's presidency.

Are you a penny person—comfortable with what you own even if it's less than someone else has? The Bible tells us, "Godliness with contentment is great gain. For we brought nothing into the world, and we can take nothing out of it. But if we have food and clothing, we will be content with that" (1 Timothy 6:6–8).

Are you content with what you have? If not, watch out. "People who want to get rich fall into temptation and a trap and into many foolish and harmful desires that plunge men into ruin and destruction" (1 Timothy 6:9). Money is not evil, but loving money is a root cause of all kinds of evil. Surely you can find something more worthy to love.

TODAY'S POWER POINT

The greatest man in history was the poorest.—Ralph Waldo Emerson

September 23

Matthew 7:20-27

TODAY IN HISTORY

1642—Harvard conducted first college commencement in the New World

1780—Benedict Arnold's treason exposed when his instructions to the British on how to take the fort at West Point were intercepted

1806—Conclusion of Lewis and Clark expedition

1938—Time capsule buried at New York World's Fair

1952—Richard Nixon's "Checkers" speech kept him on the Eisenhower ticket

1962—Lincoln Center's Philharmonic Hall opened; premiere of cartoon *The Jetsons*

1979—Lou Brock stole record 938th base after scoring his three-thousandth hit of the season

1999—$125 million U.S. spacecraft reported missing from Mars orbit

2003—In UN address, President George W. Bush called for international cooperation to help rebuild Iraq

2006—Published reports quote U.S. intelligence czar John Negroponte as saying that "the Iraq war has made the overall terrorism problem worse"

BORN TODAY

Educator William McGuffey 1800
Actor Mickey Rooney. 1920
Singer Ray Charles 1930
Singer Julio Iglesias. 1943
Actor Paul Petersen. 1945
Singer Bruce Springsteen 1949
Actor Jason Alexander 1959
Singer Ami DiFranco 1970

TIME TO PLAN

French surgeon Nelaton once said that if he had just four minutes to perform surgery to save a life, he would take the first minute to plan how to do it. How many times do we get into trouble because we either fail to plan or we run ahead of God's plan for our lives? To truly succeed, we must be in step with God every day through reading his Word and praying.

PLANNING AHEAD

A godly woman was confined to an assisted-living home in her later years. However, she always seemed to be happy and to have a radiant testimony for the Lord. Time went by, and she lay dying. She told the chaplain she had but one last request, that someone sing her favorite hymn at her funeral. The chaplain later recalled, "I never will forget that day; a rich contralto voice sang out, 'I'm a Child of the King' over the humble pine box. By planning ahead and accepting Christ as her Savior, she had moved from the lowly poor house to God's great mansion in the sky."

How far ahead have you planned for your future?

TODAY'S POWER POINT

Plan your work for today and every day, then work your plan.—Norman Vincent Peale

266

September 24

TODAY IN HISTORY

1742—Boston's historic Faneuil Hall opened
1934—Babe Ruth played his last baseball game as New York Yankee
1951—Premiere of television's *Love of Life*
1955—President Dwight Eisenhower suffered heart attack (not fatal)
1957—U.S. troops ordered to Little Rock, Arkansas, to implement school integration
1968—Premiere of television's *60 Minutes*
1984—President Ronald Reagan, in UN address, called for new arms controls
1987—Premiere of television's *A Different World*
2001—Antiterrorist drive in Afghanistan buoyed by promise of Russian support
2002—U. S. Census Bureau reported number of U.S. poor stood at nearly 33 million, up 1.3 million over earlier figures
2003—Federal court blocked FTC plan to implement telemarketing "Do Not Call" list, saying Congressional approval required (later obtained)

BORN TODAY

Novelist F. Scott Fitzgerald 1896
Sportscaster Jim McKay 1921
Actress Sheila MacRae 1923
Actor Anthony Newley 1931
Muppets creator Jim Henson 1936
Musician Linda McCartney 1941
Actor Gordon Clapp;
    comedian Phil Hartman 1948
Actress Nia Vardalos 1962
Gymnast Paul Hamm 1982

BIRDS OF A FEATHER

A man had a sparrow he wanted to teach to sing, so he found a canary with a sweet song and placed their two cages together. As the birds lived side by side day after day, an interesting thing happened. Instead of the sparrow's learning to sing like the canary, the canary began to chirp like the lowly sparrow. True, one bird had taught the other, but the wrong bird had learned the wrong thing!

Be careful about with whom you choose to spend your time. It's only natural for people who spend time together to grow more like each other. That's why it's important for us to choose friends and associates who have traits we admire and want to emulate. Friends can help us grow better, or they can lead us down a path to trouble and heartache. As the apostle Peter warned, "Be on your guard so that you may not be carried away by the error of lawless men and fall from your secure position. But grow in grace and knowledge of our Lord and Savior Jesus Christ" (2 Peter 3:17–18).

Birds of a feather flock together. If you don't want to be a real dodo, stay away from birdbrained friends.

TODAY'S POWER POINT

A man is known by the company he keeps out of.—Alexander Craig

TODAY IN HISTORY

1513—Spanish explorer Balboa first saw the Pacific
1789—U.S. Bill of Rights ratified
1882—Baseball's first doubleheader
1964—Premiere of television's *Gomer Pyle, USMC*
1974—Scientists first reported that they believe aerosol gases are destroying the earth's ozone layer
1978—At least 150 known dead after 727 jetliner collided with a small private plane over San Diego
1981—Sandra Day O'Connor became first woman justice on U.S. Supreme Court
2003—United States gave Iraqis deadline of six months to draft new constitution

BORN TODAY

Novelist William Faulkner 1897
Composer Dimitri Shostakovich . 1906
Journalist Barbara Walters 1931
Actor Mark Hamill. 1951
Actor Christopher Reeve 1952
Actress Heather Locklear 1962
Basketball player Scottie Pippen . . 1965
Actor Will Smith 1968
Actress Catherine Zeta-Jones 1969

FORGIVEN

A kindly country doctor had died, and a judge was going through his accounts. Across many of them the doctor had written, "Forgiven—too poor to pay." After his death, someone asked whether the old accounts could be collected, as some of the patients now could pay. "No indeed," said the judge. There's no court in the land that could order a collection of funds where the account has been marked, "forgiven."

All of us have debts that we could never repay—to our parents, a mentor, some helpful friend. But our greatest debt is to the Creator of the universe. Everyone has fallen short of the stringent demands of his righteousness and holiness. We willfully go our own way, are selfish or lazy, or fail to do what is right because it's not convenient. But God is also merciful and gracious: "The LORD is compassionate and gracious, slow to anger, abounding in love. . . . He does not treat us as our sins deserve or repay us according to our iniquities. For as high as the heavens are above the earth, so great is his love for those who fear him; as far as the east is from the west, so far has he removed our transgressions from us" (Psalm 103:8, 10–12).

Have you experienced the peace of knowing that God has marked your debt, "Forgiven—paid in full"?

TODAY'S POWER POINT

To err is human, to forgive divine.—Alexander Pope

TODAY IN HISTORY

1892—Composer John Philip Sousa led Marine Corps Band in first performance as bandmaster

1907—New Zealand gained independence from Britain

1960—First televised presidential debate (between John F. Kennedy and Richard Nixon)

1962—Premiere of television's *The Beverly Hillbillies*

1968—Premiere of television's *Hawaii Five-O*

2000—Euro rejected by Danish voters, slowing political integration of Europe; scientists in Texas isolated diabetes II gene

2001—Canada joined United States in antiterrorist drive

2003—U.S. poor rose to 12.2 percent of population, up 1.7 million over previous year

2004—Pakistani officials reported the killing of noted al Qaeda terrorist Amjad Farooqi (alias Amjad Hussain), linked to two failed assassination attempts against Pakistan president Pervez Musharraf and allegedly involved in murder of journalist Daniel Pearl; for fourth time in one season

BORN TODAY

Naturalist Johnny Appleseed 1774
Poet T. S. Eliot 1888
Composer George Gershwin 1898
Fitness expert Jack LaLanne 1914
Singer Julie London 1926

Singer Lynn Anderson 1947
Singer Olivia Newton-John 1948
Author Jane Smiley 1949
Actor James Caviezel 1968
Tennis player Serena Williams . . . 1981

MAKING GOOD USE OF TIME

Wishing to be surrounded by fresh blooms throughout the day, noted botanist Linnaeus once planted a "clock of flowers." It was so named because the various blooms would open at different times during the day—like clockwork. Awareness of the plants' blooming habits and careful, ordered planting enabled Linnaeus to establish a continually blooming array.

Do we make productive use of our time, or do we live as if this is just another day we have to get through? Shouldn't we structure our lives so that they reflect God's work and blessing all throughout the day? One thing is sure. We must one day all give account to God for how we've used our time. What will you report?

TODAY'S POWER POINT

The less one has to do, the less time one finds to do it in.—Lord Chesterfield

September 27

TODAY IN HISTORY

1941—USS *Patrick Henry* launched, first of more than 2,751 emergency World War II–era U.S. Liberty ships

1954—Premiere of NBC's *The Tonight Show*

1964—Warren Commission report said Lee Harvey Oswald acted alone in murdering President John F. Kennedy

1975—After seven months of Karen Ann Quinlan's being in a coma, her parents filed a petition with the court seeking to cease her life support (first such publicized case), leading to the establishment of "living wills"

1982—President Ronald Reagan said U.S. troops would remain in Lebanon until Syria and Israel withdrew their forces

2001—National Guard called to assist with airport security in light of 9/11 attacks

2002—George W. Bush administration called on United Nations to approve resolution granting "immediate, unlimited" access to suspected terrorism sites in Iraq

2003—Russia denied U.S. request to stop assisting Iran in developing its nuclear energy program

BORN TODAY

Patriot Samuel Adams 1722
Political cartoonist Thomas Nast . 1840
Actor William Conrad 1920
Filmmaker Arthur Penn 1922

Actress Jayne Meadows. 1924
Baseball player Mike Schmidt. . . . 1949
Actor and singer Shaun Cassidy . . 1959
Basketball player Steve Kerr 1965

HERE ALL THE TIME

Remember watching the old Superman cartoons? Every time the caped crusader appeared on screen, the soundtrack would shout, "He's everywhere, he's everywhere!" While this is merely entertaining fiction in the fantasy world of children's cartoons, it's true of God in the real world.

A young boy was riding the bus home from church when a fellow traveler noticed the boy's Sunday-school paper. Thinking he'd have some fun with the child, the rider inquired, "Son, tell me where God is, and I'll give you an apple." The sincere boy answered, "Sir, I'll give you a whole barrel of apples if you can tell me where God is not." There's a lot of truth in those words, for we cannot get away from God. The psalmist understood this when he wrote, "If I go up to the heavens, you are there; if I make my bed in the depths, you are there" (Psalm 139:8).

We never need to feel alone. God is here (and everywhere) all the time.

TODAY'S POWER POINT

Life's greatest tragedy is to lose the sense of God's presence and not miss it. —David Egner

September 28

TODAY IN HISTORY

1066—Norman Conquest began when William the Conqueror invaded England

1820—Widely believed myth that tomatoes were unsafe to eat put to rest when Robert Johnson ate an entire bushel of them in Salem, Massachusetts

1920—Eight Chicago White Sox players arrested for deliberately losing 1919 World Series (to Cincinnati)

1970—Death of Egyptian president Gamal Abdel Nasser

2000—FDA approved sale of RU-486, "morning after" abortion pill

2001—UN Security Council passed U.S. resolution calling on all UN members to take an active stand against terrorist groups

2002—Iraq said it would not comply with UN demand for full disclosure of weapons and unrestricted access to weapons sites

BORN TODAY

Educator Frances Willard 1839
Entertainer Ed Sullivan 1901
Cartoonist Al Capp 1909
Actor Marcello Mastroianni 1924
Actor Arnold Stang. 1925

Comedian Jerry Clower 1926
Actress Brigitte Bardot 1934
Actress Janeane Garofalo 1964
Actress Gwyneth Paltrow 1973
Actress Hilary Duff. 1987

NOT DOUBTING

While it may seem we live in an age of doubt, when no one believes anything without proof, doubt is nothing new. Even John the Baptist—prophet, God's messenger, the one of whom Jesus said there was no one greater—had his doubts at one time. His doubts came not when he was on the front lines working, preaching, and baptizing, but rather when he was on the sidelines in prison. In Luke 7:19 we learn that John sent some of his followers to ask Jesus what he already knew and had been preaching: "Are you the one who was to come, or should we expect someone else?"

Jesus sent the men back with an eyewitness report of the miracles they had seen and this word of encouragement: "Blessed is the man who does not fall away on account of me" (Luke 7:23).

If you've noticed doubts creeping into your mind about God and the Bible lately, perhaps it's time to get off the sidelines and back to the frontline of your relationship with God. A rolling stone gathers no moss, and working Christians lose those doubts and fears as we bump against the work God is doing around us. So don't just sit there; get on with the work he has for you to do.

TODAY'S POWER POINT

Doubt your doubts before you doubt your beliefs.—Walt Allmand

September 29

TODAY IN HISTORY

1829—British launched Scotland Yard police force
1892—First nighttime football game played (at Mansfield, Pennsylvania)
1899—Veterans of Foreign Wars (VFW) established
1953—Premiere of television's *Make Room for Daddy*
1981—President Ronald Reagan said $1.3 trillion debt is nation's foremost problem
2004—Two terrorists sentenced to death for bombing the USS *Cole* in 2000

BORN TODAY

Naval hero Horatio Nelson. 1758
Nuclear physicist Enrico Fermi. . . 1901
Actor Gene Autry. 1907
Actress Greer Garson 1908
Actress Anita Ekberg 1931
Singer Jerry Lee Lewis 1935
Sportscaster Bryant Gumbel. 1948
Actress Emily Lloyd 1970

TIME TO READ

Someone has determined that is takes seventy hours and forty minutes to read the Bible aloud at the pace a preacher would read from the pulpit. Broken down, this means the Old Testament can be read aloud in fifty-two hours and twenty minutes, while the New Testament can be read through completely in less than a day—in eighteen hours and twenty minutes. A church in Scotland seems have to set the world's record for reading the Bible nonstop, completing their reading in just under sixty-three hours.

Yet it's not how quickly we read through the Scriptures that counts but how fully the truths of the Bible penetrate our hearts and minds. In the words of renowned nineteenth-century evangelist Charles Spurgeon, "A man who has his Bible at his fingers' ends, and in his heart's core, is a champion in any conflict; you cannot compete with him; you may have an armory of weapons, but his Scriptural knowledge will overcome you."

With so many Bible translations and study helps available online, not to mention audio versions of the Bible on CD and even DVD, there's no reason not to take advantage of them and spend a few minutes each day letting God's Word sink into your heart and mind. Do you have a long commute? Listen to the Bible being read as you drive. Have a few minutes between appointments? Why not download the Scriptures to your iPod and listen in your spare time. You'll be glad you did!

TODAY'S POWER POINT

Some people like to read so many [Bible] chapters every day. I would not dissuade them from the practice, but I would rather let my soul soak in half a dozen verses all day than rinse my hand in several chapters. Oh, to be bathed in a text of Scripture, and to let it be sucked up in your very soul, till it saturates your heart!—Charles Haddon Spurgeon

September 30

TODAY IN HISTORY

1641—First annual fair in America

1846—First use of ether (as a dental anesthetic)

1927—Babe Ruth hit sixtieth home run of the season for New York Yankees

1935—George Gershwin's *Porgy and Bess* premiered in Boston

1951—Premiere of television's *The Red Skelton Show*

1955—Actor James Dean killed in car crash

1960—Premiere of cartoon *The Flintstones*

2001—President George W. Bush approved aid to groups in Afghanistan opposing the Taliban

2004—President George W. Bush and Senator John Kerry engaged in first of three televised presidential debates; twin car-bomb explosions killed forty-one people in Iraq, thirty-four of them children; thirty died in firefight in Gaza refugee camp, worst total in two years;

BORN TODAY

Actress Deborah Kerr 1921

Author Truman Capote 1924

Author Elie Wiesel 1928

Actress Angie Dickinson. 1931

Singer Johnny Mathis. 1935

Singer Marilyn McCoo. 1943

Singer Deborah Allen;

    actress Victoria Tennant 1953

Actress Fran Drescher. 1957

Actress Jenna Elfman 1971

JUSTICE AND MERCY

The Bible records a number of instances of "poetic justice" in which the treatment given to others later comes back to haunt the giver. Remember how Jacob cheated Esau out of his birthright? Later he was cheated by Laban, who substituted Leah for Rachel at Jacob's wedding. Then there was King David, who stole Uriah's wife and then had some of his wives taken by his own son Absalom. And Haman was hanged on gallows he built for Mordecai. Clearly, justice eventually was served in these cases.

We cheer when other people get the justice they deserve, yet how would our lives change if we all got exactly what we deserve? For most of us, that's a scary thought. Even small errors or oversights could have deadly consequences—such as looking briefly away while driving can lead to a fatal accident. "Because of the LORD's great love we are not consumed, for his compassions never fail. They are new every morning" (Lamentations 3:22–23). How thankful we should be that God not only is a God of justice but of mercy and grace as well.

TODAY'S POWER POINT

Every offense is avenged on earth.—Johann Wolfgang von Goethe

October 1

TODAY IN HISTORY

1908—First Model T rolled off Ford assembly line

1940—First major U.S. toll road, Pennsylvania Turnpike, opened; U.S. Army parachute division opened at Fort Benning, Georgia

1943—U.S. troops captured Naples, Italy, in World War II

1949—Communist People's Republic of China established

1961—Roger Maris hit sixty-first home run of the season, breaking longtime record set by Babe Ruth

1971—Disney World opened in Florida

1974—Premiere of television's *The Lucy Show*

1987—Six died, one hundred hospitalized when earthquake rocked Los Angeles

2000—Vatican canonized 120, including eighty-seven Chinese martyrs

2004—Mount St. Helens eruption spread volcanic steam and ash but caused no deaths, damage, or injuries

BORN TODAY

Naval officer James Lawrence 1781

Writer Faith Baldwin 1893

Actor Walter Matthau 1920

President Jimmy Carter 1924

Actress Julie Andrews 1935

Actor Randy Quaid 1950

Actor Esai Morales 1952

Baseball player Mark McGwire. . . 1963

A MYSTERY

Like a good mystery? The Bible speaks of the great mystery of how we will all be changed into new beings at the end times. "Listen, I tell you a mystery: We will not all sleep [die], but we will all be changed—in a flash, in the twinkling of an eye, at the last trumpet. For the trumpet will sound, the dead will be raised imperishable, and we will be changed" (1 Corinthians 15:51–52). Although we can't comprehend all the details this side of eternity, the Bible gives us at least an idea of what our new bodies will be like. They will be imperishable—not breaking down, getting sick, or dying—and immortal. Our new bodies will never age, wear out, weaken, or die. Our old bodies die in weakness and dishonor, but they'll be raised as spiritual bodies, in power and glory. As we've borne the image of our earthly families here on earth, in heaven we'll bear the image of Christ.

What these spiritual bodies will look like—whether we'll look like ourselves or something totally new—no one can say for sure. It's a mystery. But God knows the answer to this and all mysteries. All we need to know is that the ultimate enemy, death, will be swallowed up in victory. What a great ending to this mystery!

TODAY'S POWER POINT

Death is no more than passing from one room into another. But there's a difference for me, you know. Because in that other room I shall be able to see.—Helen Keller

October 2

TODAY IN HISTORY

1870—Rome voted to merge with Italy, ending the pope's rule of that city

1918—Surrounded U.S. soldiers in World War I "Lost Battalion" began one-hundred-hour holdout against dominant German forces in Argonne Forest of France

1950—*Peanuts* comic strip first published

1955—Premiere of television's *Alfred Hitchcock Presents*

2001—Fed cut prime interest rate for ninth time in 2001 (to a new thirty-nine-year low)

2006—Gunman enters Amish schoolhouse in Pennsylvania, shooting ten girls and himself, the third fatal U.S. school shooting within one week

BORN TODAY

Indian nationalist and spiritual leader
  Mahatma Gandhi 1869
Comedian Groucho Marx 1895
Actor Spanky McFarland 1928
Baseball player Maury Wills 1938
Film critic Rex Reed 1939
Designer Donna Karan 1948
Musician Sting 1950

JUST PASSING THROUGH

A number of years ago a family was traveling to Florida for a vacation. The van was packed to the roof, and the drive proved long and tiresome, so they pulled into a motel for the night. Wanting to get an early start the next day and being exhausted from the long drive, the family went directly to their room, plopped on the beds, and went to sleep in their clothes. Why? Because the motel was just a stop en route to their destination. They never intended to make the motel visit a featured part of the trip.

The same can be said for believers' days on this earth. Life here is not the main attraction of our existence, or even an attraction at all compared with what's in store for us in heaven. In fact, outside of what we do for God, whatever we might manage to obtain or accomplish in this life has little eternal consequence.

Despite this fact, it's easy and tempting to get attached to the things of this life. Eighteenth-century English writer William Law noted hundreds of years ago, "the world is now a greater enemy to the Christian than it was in apostolic times. It is a greater enemy," he said, "because it has greater power over Christians by its favors, riches, honors, rewards, and protection than it had by the more obvious dangers of fire and fury of its persecutors." Christians live in the world, but they are not to be "of the world." We're just passing through. Are you keeping your eyes on eternity?

TODAY'S POWER POINT

Worldliness today is no longer viewed as an enemy. Thus people are easily influenced by it. Don't let Satan trick you into going along with the world. Accept no substitutes for God's amazing grace.—William Law

October 3

TODAY IN HISTORY

1789—President George Washington proclaimed first national Thanksgiving Day

1863—President Abraham Lincoln declared the last Thursday in November annual Thanksgiving Day

1922—Rebecca Felton appointed first woman U.S. senator (from Georgia)

1960—Premiere of television's *The Andy Griffith Show*

1974—Frank Robinson became first African American baseball manager

1990—East and West Germany reunited (after forty-five years)

2000—Congress asked states to adopt uniform .08-percent blood-alcohol standard for drunk driving

2005—White House counsel Harriet Miers nominated to replace U.S. Supreme Court justice Sandra Day O'Connor

BORN TODAY

Historian George Bancroft 1800	Author Gore Vidal 1925
Hymn writer Carolina Berg 1832	Singer Chubby Checker 1941
Novelist Thomas Wolfe 1900	Baseball player Dave Winfield . . . 1951
Cartoonist Herb Block 1909	Musician Tommy Lee 1972

A PARABLE OF PEACE

Winston Churchill is credited with telling a parable of peace that went something like this: Long ago all the zoo animals decided to disarm, so they arranged "peace talks" to work out the details. The rhinoceros asked for a strict ban against the use of teeth in war. The stag and porcupine agreed, but the lion and the tiger defended teeth and even claws as being honorable weapons. The bear, however, wanted both teeth and horns to be banned and suggested that all animals be allowed to give each other a good hug when they quarreled. This only served to offend all the other animals and so they never could agree.

Have you ever noticed how much easier it is to make rules for other people to follow than it is to hold ourselves to rules that impact us? Sometimes, like these animals, we're so protective of our own interests that we can't see the legitimate concerns of others. The Bible raises our sights and gives us a worthy challenge on this issue: "Do nothing out of selfish ambition or vain conceit, but in humility consider others better than yourselves. Each of you should look not only to your own interests, but also to the interests of others" (Philippians 2:3–4).

Next time you feel the need to look out for your own best interest, stop. Try looking at the situation from the other person's point of view. You just might learn something new.

TODAY'S POWER POINT

All men desire peace, but very few desire those things that make for peace. —Thomas à Kempis

October 4

TODAY IN HISTORY

1931—Comic strip *Dick Tracy* first published
1957—Soviets launched space age by orbiting *Sputnik* satellite
1958—First passenger jetliner service across Atlantic
1965—Arrival in America of Pope Paul VI, first pontiff to visit United States
1995—Pope John Paul II began four-day visit to United States
2000—Telecommunications mogul John Kluge gave record $60 million gift to
　　　Library of Congress
2001—Airliner crashed in Black Sea, killing seventy-six, apparently struck down by
　　　stray Ukrainian missile

BORN TODAY

Artist Jean Millet . . . . 1814　Actor Charlton Heston. 1922
President Rutherford B. Hayes . . . 1822　Baseball manager Tony LaRussa . . 1944
Poet Frances Gurney. . . . . 1858　Actress Susan Sarandon 1946
Artist Frederick Remington . . . . . 1861　Actress Alicia Silverstone 1976

TURNING AROUND

It is said that former Princeton University president Dr. James McCosh always made it a point to pray with graduating seniors before they left the campus to make their mark on the world. However, when he asked one new graduate to pray with him, the young man refused, instead extending his hand to bid the president farewell.

Years went by, and one day a man appeared in the president's study. "You probably don't remember me," the man said. "I was the young man who refused to pray with you. But all along, my godly mother was praying on my behalf. Her prayers have won out, and I am back to enter the seminary. Before I go, could I ask you to kneel down with me and offer that long-postponed prayer?"

Have you ever invested yourself in the life of another with seemingly few results? Perhaps it was a child or some other relative. Maybe it was a young person you mentored or taught. It might even have been a friend or colleague. Making a positive difference in someone's life can be a long, ungratifying process. Sometimes we can't see the growth, reflection, and grappling with the truth that is occurring under the surface. But it's important not to give up. Faithfully do your part, and trust God to do his part of changing a heart or a life.

Today, like the psalmist, make this your pledge on behalf of someone whose life you hope to impact: "I will instruct you and teach you in the way you should go; I will counsel you and watch over you" (Psalm 32:8).

TODAY'S POWER POINT

You cannot escape the responsibility of tomorrow by evading it today.—Abraham Lincoln

October 5

TODAY IN HISTORY

1947—President Harry Truman delivered first televised White House address
1950—Premiere of television's *You Bet Your Life*
1982—Tylenol removed tainted capsules from store shelves in massive recall
1984—Spacecraft *Challenger* lifted off with largest crew to go to space (seven astronauts)
1993—China conducted nuclear-weapons test despite moratorium
1998—Largest U.S. budget surplus in thirty years reported
2001—Barry Bonds hit seventy-first home run, breaking Mark McGwire's home-run record
2003—Condoleezza Rice named to head reconstruction efforts in Iraq and Afghanistan
2006—Recovering from earlier dot-com meltdown, recession, and 9/11 terrorist attacks, U.S. stock market reaches 11,866.69—third record high in one week

BORN TODAY

Theologian Jonathan Edwards . . . 1703
Writer Denis Diderot 1713
President Chester Arthur 1830
Cartoonist Bil Keane 1922
Architect Maya Lin 1959
Race-car driver Michael Andretti . 1962
Hockey player Mario Lemieux . . . 1965
Actress Kate Winslet. 1975

EXTRAORDINARY STRENGTH

It's always encouraging to read of God's conversation with Moses, who tried to talk God out of calling him. Moses even gave what he felt was a valid excuse—perhaps a speech impediment. But God wasn't buying any excuses. He knew what Moses was capable of accomplishing—with God's help. He told Moses, "Who gave man his mouth? Who makes him deaf or mute? Who gives him sight or makes him blind? Is it not I, the LORD? Now go; I will help you speak and will teach you what to say" (Exodus 4:11–12).

Maybe you've also felt the urge to tell God, "O Lord, please send someone else to do it" (Exodus 4:13). But God's not buying your excuses either. As author David Roper reminds us, God often uses "our impairments, our disabilities, our handicaps" to glorify him. For "if our weaknesses cause us to seek God and rely on him, they actually help us instead of hinder us. In fact, they become the best thing that could happen to us, because our growth in courage, power and happiness depends upon our relationship with the Lord," and the extent of our reliance on him.

What's your excuse for not being all God has called you to be? Don't look at the strikes against you, but strike out in God's strength. As the apostle Paul wrote, "That is why, for Christ's sake, I delight in weaknesses, in insults, in hardships, in persecutions, in difficulties. For when I am weak, then I am strong" (2 Corinthians 12:10). With God's help, you can do it.

TODAY'S POWER POINT

I can't believe that God put us on this earth to be ordinary.—Lou Holtz

October 6

TODAY IN HISTORY

1889—First motion pictures demonstrated (by Thomas A. Edison)
1927—*The Jazz Singer* introduced as first U.S. talking feature movie
1969—New York Mets won National League championship
1979—Pope John Paul II became first pontiff to visit the White House
1998—Gay college student Matthew Shepard fatally beaten in Wyoming
2000—Premiere of television's *CSI: Crime Scene Investigation*
2004—U.S. official reported Saddam Hussein's intention to resume weapons program
    after "essentially destroying" all illegal weapons following 1990 Iraqi war

BORN TODAY

Singer Jenny Lind. 1820
Inventor George Westinghouse. . . 1846
Architect Le Corbusier 1887
Explorer Thor Heyerdahl 1914
Journalist Shana Alexander 1925
Actor Fred Travelena. 1942
Producer David Zucker 1947
Musician David Hidalgo 1954
Actress Stephanie Zimbalist 1956
Basketball player Rebecca Lobo . . 1973

CARRYING US THROUGH

A man was struggling under a heavy workload that seemed to require more than the usual exercise of his faith. About this time his little girl, a paralytic, begged to carry his package in to her mother. "How could you possibly carry it," he asked. "Oh, Daddy!" she exclaimed, "if you give me the package, I can hold it while you carry me." It was then that he saw God's lesson for him—that despite his emotional hurts and handicaps, his heavenly Father was there to carry him through the difficult challenges of life.

ENOUGH

The Gospel Herald told the story of a pastor who phoned in his Sunday sermon topic to the local newspaper. "The Lord is my Shepherd," he said. The editor asked, "Is that all?" The preacher replied, "That's enough."

When the church page was published, it listed the sermon topic as "The Lord is my Shepherd—that's enough." Liking the change, the pastor enlarged his sermon to incorporate the new title.

Are you trusting God to carry you through life's crises? His tender, loving care is enough for any situation or difficulty. "The LORD is my shepherd, I shall not be in want" (Psalm 23:1).

TODAY'S POWER POINT

As your faith is strengthened, you will find that there is no longer the need to have a sense of control, that things will flow as they will, and that you will flow with them, to your great delight and benefit.—Emmanuel Teney

TODAY IN HISTORY

1826—First U.S. railroad began operation

1896—Daily Dow Jones Industrial Average listing began

1950—Premiere of television's *Your Hit Parade*

1982—Broadway premiere of *Cats*, second-longest-running production in Broadway history (eighteen years), behind *Phantom of the Opera*

1994—U.S. troops ordered to Persian Gulf

2001—U.S. and British forces hit targets within Afghanistan

2003—Actor Arnold Schwarzenegger victorious in California gubernatorial race

2005—International Atomic Energy Agency shared Nobel Peace Prize with its leader, Mohamed ElBaradei

BORN TODAY

Poet James Whitcomb Riley 1849

Physicist Niels Bohr 1885

Singer Al Martino 1927

Archbishop Desmond Tutu 1931

Singer John Mellencamp 1951

Russian president Vladimir Putin . 1952

Cellist Yo-Yo Ma 1955

Singer Toni Braxton 1967

ALONG FOR THE RIDE

Have you ever tried to find your way to an unfamiliar location? You stop to ask directions and proceed cautiously on a course you hope will lead to your destination. But as you travel farther, you grow increasingly desperate with each wrong turn and wonder if you'll ever reach your intended destination. Think of how much better it would be (and how many fewer mistakes you would make) if someone were willing to personally lead you. A person's instructions are harder to ignore or get wrong when he or she is present with us than when we just try on our own to follow what they said.

As a general rule we're more strongly influenced by what people do than by what they say. For example, have you ever noticed that when the driver of a car buckles up, everyone else in the car usually follows suit? But if the driver doesn't buckle up, others rarely do either. People tend to do what they see, more so than following the advice they hear. That's why the message we proclaim with our lives is even more important than the message we proclaim with our mouths. Paul's instructions to Timothy apply to us as well: "Set an example for the believers in speech, in life, in love, in faith and in purity" (1 Timothy 4:12).

Don't just give people instructions—on how to get to heaven, how to follow God, or how to be happy. Instead, fasten your seatbelt and ask them to go along with you for the ride.

TODAY'S POWER POINT

When people are free to do as they please, they usually imitate each other.—Eric Hoffer

October 8

TODAY IN HISTORY

1871—Chicago fire killed 250 and left nearly one hundred thousand homeless; Peshtigo, Wisconsin, fire charred 1.5 million acres and killed between 1,200 and 2,500 people

1918—Legendary sergeant Alvin York killed twenty-five German soldiers and captured 132 in one day

1956—Yankees pitcher Don Larsen threw perfect (no-hit, no-run) World Series game against Brooklyn Dodgers

2002—Terrorists blamed for shooting death of U.S. Marine in Kuwait; President George W. Bush ordered locked-out longshoremen back to work at West Coast ports

2005—More than fifty thousand killed and 2.5 million left homeless when a massive earthquake rocked Kashmir, another eight hundred dead in India

2006—Funeral for fifth Amish schoolgirl killed in October 2 shooting in Lancaster County, Pennsylvania

BORN TODAY

Aviator Eddie Rickenbacker 1890
Comedian Chevy Chase 1943
Actor Paul Hogan 1939
Actress Sigourney Weaver 1949
Actor David Carradine 1940
Actor Matt Damon 1970
Civil-rights leader Jesse Jackson . . 1941
Football player Rashaan Salaam . . 1974

FAR FROM THE EDGE

A tourist was riding up a winding mountain pass aboard a rickety old bus. To the left rose the sheer face of the mountainside. To the right—with no guardrail—lay an awesome precipice dropping hundreds of feet to the canyon floor below. The guide, wanting to show off to his rider, boasted, "I can drive right at the edge of the cliff. Want to see how close I can get?" The shocked visitor replied, "No, please don't. I want to arrive in one piece, so let's see how far away from the edge we can stay."

Some people insist on doing their own thing despite the risks. Like the foolish bus driver, too many try to see just how close they can get to the edge instead of staying as far from possible spiritual and physical danger as they can get. The Bible warns us: "Pride goes before destruction, a haughty spirit before a fall" (Proverbs 16:18).

Only a fool plays with fire or needlessly risks a devastating fall. The wise person takes care to avoid spiritual danger, steering as far from evil as possible: "The highway of the upright avoids evil; he who guards his way guards his life" (Proverbs 16:17).

TODAY'S POWER POINT

The path is smooth that leadeth to danger.—William Shakespeare

October 9

TODAY IN HISTORY

1701—Yale University chartered

1962—Ugandan independence

1984—Egyptian president Hosni Mubarak traveled to Jordan—first visit to Arab nation since the Israeli peace accord

2002—European Union approved ten new member nations: Hungary, Latvia, Poland, Czech Republic, Slovenia, Slovakia, Estonia, Cyprus, Malta, and Lithuania

2004—Voters turned out in record numbers to elect new Afghani leader, interim president Hamid Karzai favored to win

BORN TODAY

Composer Camille Saint-Saens. . . 1835

Editor Edward Bok 1863

Historian Bruce Catton 1899

Cartoonist Russell Myers 1938

Beatle John Lennon 1940

Football player Mike Singletary . . 1958

Golfer Annika Sorenstam 1970

Actor Zachery Ty Bryan 1981

SPIRITUAL FOOD

Have you ever watched how newborn babies eat? They certainly don't start out on steak. At first their nutrition consists mainly of milk, which they hungrily drink every few hours. But over time they develop a greater appetite and the capacity to digest solid foods. The same is true of our spiritual appetites. We begin with the simplest biblical concepts, but with time and spiritual growth, we develop a hunger for meatier truths from God's Word. The apostle Peter advised, "Like newborn babies, crave pure spiritual milk, so that by it you may grow up in your salvation" (1 Peter 2:2). We should hunger for biblical truths that help us to grow spiritually.

Reformer Martin Luther described his system of spiritual growth: "I study my Bible as I gather apples. I first search the Bible as a whole, like shaking the whole tree. Then I shake every limb—study book after book. Then I shake every branch, giving attention to the chapters. . . . Then I shake every twig for a careful study of the paragraphs and sentences and words and their meanings."

Biblical scholar W. A. Criswell advises Bible students to "work hard to understand exactly what it [the Bible text] means. . . . Immerse yourself in the history and culture of those ancient times. But when you've cracked open the secrets and . . . [extracted] the truth of God's holy inspired Word, then sit back quietly and read the words again. Only this time, let their exquisite beauty wash over you like a cooling rain on a hot summer day."

It takes food to grow physically as well as spiritually. Are you feasting on God's Word every day?

TODAY'S POWER POINT

Never a night goes by, be I ever so tired, but I read the Word of God before I go to bed.—Douglas MacArthur

October 10

TODAY IN HISTORY

1802—First settlers began arriving in Oklahoma

1845—U.S. Naval Academy opened in Annapolis, Maryland

1886—"Tuxedo" dinner jacket worn for first time

1973—U.S. vice president Spiro Agnew resigned under fire for tax evasion, (first vice president to resign since John C. Calhoun in 1832)

2000—In first such meeting with a U.S. chief executive, North Korean leader Kim Jong Il met with President Bill Clinton to explore peace initiatives between North and South Korea

2001—Nancy Pelosi elected minority whip, second-ranking House Democrat

2002—Indians overwhelmingly defeated ruling party in Kashmir election following three weeks of violence; House and Senate voted support to defend against "the continuing threat posed by Iraq"

2005—Germany elected Angela Merkel as its first female chancellor

BORN TODAY

Composer Giuseppe Verdi 1813

Actor Ben Vereen 1946

Author Nora Roberts 1950

Singer David Lee Roth 1955

Tennis player Martina Navratilova . .1956

Singer Tanya Tucker 1958

Journalist Daniel Pearl 1963

Football player Brett Favre 1969

Actor Mario Lopez 1973

Race-car driver Dale Earnhardt Jr. 1974

COMFORT IN THE DARK

A father and his little girl returned to an empty home after burying their wife and mother. Nothing seemed the same. The youngster was tucked into bed as usual, but sleep would not come. For a while all was quiet, then the little girl called out through the darkness, "Daddy, you can love through the dark can't you?" Choking back tears, her father replied, "Yes, dear, you can." The little girl, reassured of her mother's love even when she couldn't see her, soon drifted off to sleep. The man then silently thanked God for the lesson of how love conquers fear.

What do you fear? Don't fear those things that may cause physical harm but can't touch your soul. You can trust God to be especially near in your darkest night: "He will cover you with his feathers, and under his wings you will find refuge; his faithfulness will be your shield and rampart. You will not fear the terror of night" (Psalm 91:4–5). God's love penetrates the darkness of fear and reassures his children of his constant presence and love.

TODAY'S POWER POINT

Remember, fear doesn't exist anywhere except in the mind.—Dale Carnegie

October 11

Psalm 127:1–5

TODAY IN HISTORY

1779—General Casimir Pulaski killed in Revolutionary War
1887—Adding machine patented
1890—Daughters of American Revolution organized
1928—Roscoe Robinson named first African American army general
1975—Premiere of television's *Saturday Night Live*
1999—United Nations reported that world population had reached six billion
2000—One-hundredth U.S. space-shuttle flight launched
2005—Sunni leaders pledged support for new Iraqi constitution following
    agreement allowing postreferendum changes

BORN TODAY

Parson Mason Weems. 1759
Food pioneer John Heinz 1844
First lady Eleanor Roosevelt 1884
Journalist Joseph Alsop. 1910
Choreographer Jerome Robbins . . 1918
Singer Dottie West 1932
Musician Daryl Hall. 1948
Actor David Morse. 1953
Baseball player Orlando Hernandez
    1969

NO PLACE LIKE HOME

Home sweet home: what truth is proclaimed in those wonderful words. But in order to make the best home life possible, we must make it fit around Christ and not reshape or resize him to fit the space we have made available to him. How well does Christ fit into your home?

A good place to start is to make Christ the center of your family life. Of the nineteen children raised by Samuel and Susannah Wesley, several went on to become great Christian leaders in large part because Mrs. Wesley "brought her little ones into close contact with the Bible stories." The Wesleys' fifteenth child, John, went on to found the Methodist Church, while his younger brother Charles is known for the dozens of hymns he wrote, many of them still sung today.

Another remarkable Christian family was that of noted author Andrew Murray. Five of his eleven children became ministers, and four of Murray's daughters married ministers. This pattern of Christian service extended into the next generation of Murrays, as ten of his grandsons became ministers, and thirteen were missionaries.

For both the Wesleys and the Murrays, it all began with a solid foundation—a Christian home with dedicated, spiritually involved parents. The same is true for your home. And you too will find that the effort is well worthwhile.

TODAY'S POWER POINT

We adults spend far too much time preparing the path for our youth and far too little time preparing our youth for the path.—Source Unknown

■ 284 ■

TODAY IN HISTORY

1492—Christopher Columbus arrived in Hispaniola, "discovering" America

1792—White House cornerstone laid by George Washington

1950—Television premiere of *The George Burns and Gracie Allen Show*

1964—Soviets launched first two-person space capsule

1979—Cuban leader Fidel Castro called on industrialized nations to aid Third World countries

1985—Death of producer Orson Welles, age seventy

2000—Bomb blast killed seventeen sailors aboard USS *Cole* in Yemen

2001—Instant-picture producer Polaroid declared bankruptcy

2002—Al Qaeda found to be linked to Bali nightclub bombing

2003—Six killed as bomb blasted Baghdad hotel housing Americans and Iraqi governing-council members; Texas lawmakers approved new congressional boundaries likely to give Republicans a majority

2005—Syrian politician Ghazi Kanaan found dead of an apparent suicide following questioning about murder of former Lebanese prime minister Rafik Hariri

BORN TODAY

Comedian Dick Gregory 1932	Singer Susan Anton 1950
Architect Alan Meier 1934	Journalist Chris Wallace 1947
Opera singer Luciano Pavarotti . . 1935	Actor Adam Rich 1968
Sportscaster Tony Kubek 1936	Actor Kirk Cameron. 1970

ADOPTED

A lowly, flea-bitten kitten came to the door of a country farmhouse. The children pleaded with their mother to let them adopt the unhappy creature. They fed it warm milk, and soon it became part of the family—they wouldn't have been able to get it to leave if they had wanted to.

In the same way God adopts poor, shopworn sinners into his eternal family though we have nothing to offer him. Paul says, "In him we were also chosen" (Ephesians 1:11). It was God's pleasure and will to adopt us as his sons and daughters through Jesus Christ. We, who have and are nothing on our own, become heirs of God with a guarantee of an inheritance as sons and daughters. With Paul we can exult: "Praise be to the God and Father of our Lord Jesus Christ, who has blessed us in the heavenly realms with every spiritual blessing in Christ" (Ephesians 1:3).

TODAY'S POWER POINT

God does not love us because we are valuable. We are valuable because God loves us.—Fulton J. Sheen

TODAY IN HISTORY

1843—B'nai B'rith (Sons of the Covenant) founded
1969—President Richard Nixon promised not to be affected by Vietnam War protests
1977—Oil industry chided by President Jimmy Carter for not accepting energy plan
1983—William Clark named to succeed controversial James Watt as secretary of the
    interior
1985—Atom smasher started—physicists hoped it would help United States regain
    leadership in high-energy physics
1994—Protestants called for cease-fire in Northern Ireland dispute
1999—U.S. tobacco companies acknowledged harmful effects of smoking
2001—Uzbekistan approved U.S. base as staging area in fight against Taliban in
    nearby Afghanistan
2003—Texas governor signed state-redistricting bill into law after minority
    Democrats staged walkout

BORN TODAY

Comedian Nipsey Russell 1924
British prime minister Margaret
    Thatcher 1925
Singer Paul Simon 1941
Singer Marie Osmond 1959
Basketball coach Doc Rivers 1961
Actress Kelly Preston 1962
Skater Nancy Kerrigan 1969
Basketball player Jermaine O'Neal
    1978

REVEALING GOD'S IMAGE

The great sculptor Michelangelo was once asked how he could make such a lifelike statue as the *Pieta* or *David* from a formless block of stone. He replied, "It's easy— I just chisel away what's not needed, and there is the statue."

Without some serious shaping and cutting away, our lives are like formless blocks of marble. We must ruthlessly, painstakingly, and sometimes painfully remove all that hides the image of God. The apostle James described the process this way: "Get rid of all moral filth and the evil that is so prevalent and humbly accept the word planted in you, which can save you" (James 1:21).

The work of revealing God's image in us is a continuing process in which both God and we play important parts. John Newton, writer of the well-known hymn "Amazing Grace," described the process this way: "I am not what I ought to be, nor what I wish to be, nor yet what I hope to be, [but] I can truly say I am not what I once was—a slave to sin."

Are you in the process of being sculpted into the image of the Master? Let the Master Sculptor help you chip away the refuse of evil so you can live a life of spiritual beauty.

TODAY'S POWER POINT

The time is always right to do what is right.—Martin Luther King Jr.

TODAY IN HISTORY

1066—England claimed for the Normans
1905—First all-shutout World Series
1960—Peace Corps founded
1961—Broadway premiere of musical *How to Succeed in Business Without Really Trying*
1964—Martin Luther King Jr., age thirty-five, won Nobel Peace Prize (youngest recipient ever)
1968—U.S. *Apollo 7* crew sent first live television broadcast from outer space
1983—National Council of Churches published *An Inclusive Language Lectionary*, new gender-neutral Bible translation, sparking conservative protests
2001—United States acted to stem bioterrorism as anthrax threat widened

BORN TODAY

President Dwight Eisenhower. . . . 1890
Actress Lillian Gish. 1893
Travel writer Eugene Fodor 1905
Physician C. Everett Koop 1916
Actor Roger Moore. 1928

Designer Ralph Lauren. 1939
Singer Cliff Richard 1940
Actor Harry Anderson 1952
Golfer Beth Daniel. 1956

LOVE AS A LUBRICANT

In his book, *Love as a Lubricant*, Dr. C. H. Parkhurst recalled the story of one train commuter who noticed that the train's door squeaked every time it opened. He reached inside his pocket, retrieved a small oilcan, and squirted a few drops on the squeaky part. Returning to his seat, the man explained to his surprised fellow passengers, "I always carry an oilcan in my pocket, for there are so many squeaky things a drop of oil will correct."

So, too, love acts as a "lubricant" in life, making relationships in the home and community harmonious. Consider this description of godly love: "Love is patient, love is kind. It does not envy, it does not boast, it is not proud. It is not rude, it is not self-seeking, it is not easily angered, it keeps no record of wrongs. Love does not delight in evil but rejoices with the truth. It always protects, always trusts, always hopes, always perseveres" (1 Corinthians 13:4–7). Imagine how smoothly your home would run if you demonstrated love like that. Are you prepared to lubricate your world with a dose of love to help smooth over the rough spots you encounter with others today?

TODAY'S POWER POINT

A new command I give you: Love one another. As I have loved you, so you must love one another. By this all men will know that you are my disciples, if you love one another.—John 13:34–35

October 15

TODAY IN HISTORY

1939—La Guardia Airport opened in New York City

1951—Premiere of television's *I Love Lucy*

1974—Federal troops requested by Massachusetts to quell racial violence in Boston suburbs

1991—Following turbulent hearings, U.S. Senate confirmed Clarence Thomas to the Supreme Court

2001—Anthrax-tainted letters received in office of Senator Tom Daschle, also at NBC News and at a Microsoft office in Reno, Nevada

2003—China became third country to successfully launch a human into space

2004—New vaccine credited for halting majority of life-threatening malaria cases in Mozambique

2005—Iraqi voters turned out in force to ratify new constitution

BORN TODAY

Poet Virgil . . . . 70 BC

Philosopher Friedrich Nietzsche . . 1844

Author P. G. Wodehouse 1881

Historian Arthur Schlesinger 1917

Industrialist Lee Iacocca 1924

Director Penny Marshall 1942

Sportscaster Jim Palmer 1945

Artist Joni Eareckson Tada 1949

Britain's Duchess of York,

   Sarah Ferguson 1959

NO GUARANTEE OF TOMORROW

Once there was a successful farmer whose crops and herds grew and increased. But he resisted all attempts to discuss spiritual things. In fact, the man often replied, "I must make my fortune first, then I shall attend to those matters." One day he became seriously ill and had to be rushed home. As he lay dying, he was visited by a neighbor who had often tried to speak to him about spiritual things. The farmer cried out bitterly, "I'm a loser. At last I have gained the world, but have lost my soul."

The farmer found out too late what all of us should know: no one is guaranteed tomorrow. All we have is today, right now. James reminds us: "You do not even know what will happen tomorrow. What is your life? You are a mist that appears for a little while and then vanishes" (James 4:14).

Before that mist vanishes, it's up to us to take care of those things that are most important. Don't put off until tomorrow what would be left tragically undone if your life ended today. That includes making things right with God and those who matter most to you. Take care of things right now—today!

TODAY'S POWER POINT

What good is it for a man to gain the whole world, yet forfeit his soul?—Mark 8:36

October 16

TODAY IN HISTORY

1859—Harper's Ferry, Virginia, invaded by John Brown and twenty-one fellow abolitionists

1916—First U.S. birth-control dispensary opened (in Brooklyn)

1940—President Franklin D. Roosevelt signed bill enacting first peacetime draft in United States

1969—New York Mets won World Series for the first time (over Baltimore Orioles)

1987—Baby Jessica McClure rescued from a narrow oil-well shaft where she'd been trapped for more than two days

1995—Hundreds of thousands of African Americans participated in Million Man March in Washington DC

2001—New anthrax cases reported in New York and Florida

2002—North Korean official said his nation had been working on nuclear arms for several years

2003—UN approved U.S.–led multinational force to oversee Iraq's redevelopment

BORN TODAY

Lexicographer Noah Webster 1758
Writer Oscar Wilde 1854
Playwright Eugene O'Neill. 1888
Actress Angela Lansbury. 1925

Author Charles Colson. 1931
Baseball player Juan Gonzalez. . . . 1969
Football player Kordell Stewart. . . 1972
Actress Kellie Martin 1975

THE GOLDEN RULE

A chaplain was assisting injured troops on the battlefield when he came across a young man who had just been wounded. The chaplain asked if the man would like him to read from the Bible. The soldier replied, "I'm so thirsty, could I have a drink of cold water instead?" The chaplain obliged and drew a cold drink for the injured youth. Later the kind minister arranged a pillow for the man and even covered him with his own coat when he was cold. The wounded man thanked the chaplain sincerely, then added feebly: "If there's anything in that Book in your hand that makes a man do for another what you have done for me, please read it to me."

What's known as the Golden Rule comes from the Bible: "In everything, do to others what you would have them do to you" (Matthew 7:12). This summarizes one of the overriding messages of the Law and the Prophets—it's that important. The chaplain knew the importance of the Golden Rule. That's why he risked his life to show kindness to the wounded soldier. How about you? Are you willing to risk anything to minister to others in the manner you'd want someone to minister to you?

TODAY'S POWER POINT

The greatest thing a man can do for his heavenly Father is to be kind to some of his other children.—Henry Drummond

October 17

TODAY IN HISTORY

1777—British surrendered to Colonial forces at Saratoga, New York
1933—Albert Einstein arrived in United States after fleeing Nazis
1994—Israel and Jordan signed peace treaty
2003—Congress approved hundreds of billions of dollars for funding war in Iraq; Pope John Paul II marked twenty-fifth year as pontiff, only fourth pope in history to serve that long

BORN TODAY

Food manufacturer Charles Kraft . 1880
Playwright Arthur Miller 1915
Actress Rita Hayworth 1918
Stuntman Evel Knievel 1938
Actress Margot Kidder 1948
Singer Alan Jackson 1958

ENCOURAGEMENT

What do you do to lift up someone who is discouraged? One college professor reported that whenever he encounters someone in his class who is discouraged, he gives the student a higher score than he or she had earned. "Almost invariably," said the professor, "the student perks up and earns that mark the next time around. Maybe not exactly according to Hoyle—but it works!"

AN ENCOURAGER

One great encourager was a welder described by H. A. Ironside. After working on his knees all week, welding steel rails, the man spent his Saturdays encouraging those confined in hospitals and jails. For the families who were desperately poor, he would leave a cash gift. Then, when Sunday came around, he would say, "My, I was worn out Friday, but I had a wonderful time yesterday, and now I am all rested up!" For relaxation, he used his free time to encourage others and in doing the work of the Lord.

SUGGESTIONS FOR ENCOURAGING OTHERS

One source lists these suggestions for encouraging others: "Work for improvement, not perfection. Commend the effort, not the results. Let the person work at his own speed. Stimulate and support, don't push. Stress cooperation and contribution rather than winning. Help the person develop the courage to be imperfect and to take mistakes in stride."

TODAY'S POWER POINT

Those who are lifting the world upward and onward are those who encourage.
—Elizabeth Harrison

October 18

TODAY IN HISTORY

1767—Mason-Dixon Line established between Maryland and Pennsylvania

1867—Alaskan Territory transferred from Russian to U.S. control

1892—First long-distance telephone line completed (between New York and Chicago)

1896—First newspaper comic strip published

1977—West German commandos freed eighty-six hostages aboard Lufthansa plane minutes before terrorists said it would explode

1983—UN group reported that twenty-two African nations faced food shortages and possible starvation

2000—Senate voted to end forty-year ban on food sales to Cuba but set new limits

2002—Vatican ordered U.S. bishops to enact zero-tolerance policy for priest sexual abuse

BORN TODAY

Journalist A. J. Liebling 1904
Politician Jesse Helms. 1921
Singer Chuck Berry 1926
Actor George C. Scott 1927
Poet Shel Silverstein 1932

Football coach Mike Ditka. 1939
Actress Pam Dawber. 1951
Actor Jean-Claude Van Damme . . 1960
Musician Wynton Marsalis. 1961

WHOM GOD BLESSES

Who among us has not been moved by first lady of song Kate Smith's stirring rendition of "God Bless America"? These famous soaring lyrics may cause one to wonder, just why has God blessed America in such an unusual way over the years?

In his book *Democracy in America,* nineteenth-century French political thinker Alexis de Tocqueville wrote: "I sought for the greatness and genius of America in her commodious harbors and her ample rivers—and it was not there . . . in her fertile fields and boundless forests—and it was not there . . . in her rich mines and her vast world commerce—and it was not there . . . in her democratic Congress and her matchless Constitution—and it was not there. Not until I went into the churches of America and heard her pulpits flame with righteousness did I understand the secret of her genius and power. America is great because she is good, and if America ever ceases to be good, America will cease to be great."

There's no secret to gaining God's blessing, whether on a home, an organization, or a nation. As the psalmist reminds us, "Blessed is the nation whose God is the LORD" (Psalm 33:12). Putting God first will bring God's blessing upon any people. Are you doing your part to keep firsts things first today, honoring God so that he, in turn, can honor you, your family, and your nation?

TODAY'S POWER POINT

We are called to love God, serve people, and use money. But oftentimes we use people, serve money, and neglect God.—Source Unknown

October 19

TODAY IN HISTORY

1781—American Revolutionary War ended with British surrender at Yorktown, Virginia

1960—U.S. blocked most exports to Cuba

1978—Twenty-seven-year-old Anatoly Karpov defeated Soviet defector Viktor Korchnoi in world chess championship

1987—Worst trading day to date on Wall Street, with market losing over 22 percent of its value in one day; U.S. Navy disabled three Iranian oil rigs in retaliation for repeated ship attacks by Iran in the Persian Gulf

2001—War in Afghanistan intensified with night helicopter raids following thirteen days of bombing (United States struck Taliban headquarters and airfield); President George W. Bush conferred with Chinese leaders, reported international support for war against terror in Afghanistan

2003—United Nations joined with World Bank to apportion funds for rebuilding Iraq; Mother Theresa beatified, called "icon of the Good Samaritan" by pope

2005—Beginning of Saddam Hussein's first trial, former dictator pleaded not guilty to charges of killing 140 Iraqis

BORN TODAY

Author and Campus Crusade for Christ founder Bill Bright 1921
Journalist Jack Anderson 1922
Author John Le Carre. 1931
Actor Robert Reed 1932
Artist Peter Max 1937
Feminist Patricia Ireland. 1945
Boxer Evander Holyfield 1962

POOR BUT NOT NEEDY

Evangelist John R. Rice told of the times when, as a poor farm boy in a small town in Texas, he rode to the general store. Often when the family had no money, he would tell the grocer what he needed and then say, "Charge it to Will Rice," and the grocer would always give him what he asked for. Rice's father, who had sent him to town to get the things, had given the youngster authority to charge them to his account, and the grocer knew the father was good for the money. The son simply had to ask in his father's name to get what he needed.

So it is when God's children come before him in prayer—we have nothing to offer him, nor do we even truly know what we need. But as Rice said, "When I find out what Jesus wants and ask it of my heavenly Father, I can honestly ask for it in Jesus's name and expectantly wait to receive it."

What needs do you have? Ask for them "In Jesus's name," and in accordance with God's will, things will start to happen!

TODAY'S POWER POINT

I have found out in later years that my family was very poor [when I was a child], but . . . we didn't know it.—Dwight Eisenhower

October 20

TODAY IN HISTORY

1803—Louisiana Purchase approved by U.S. Congress

1820—Spanish president signed treaty granting ownership of Florida to United States

1906—Radio vacuum tube patented

1944—General Douglas MacArthur arrived in Philippines with seven hundred ships and 160,000 U.S. Marines to liberate that country from Japan

1968—Wedding of Jacqueline Kennedy and Aristotle Onassis

1975—Supreme Court ruling permitted spanking in public schools

1976—Ship collision in Mississippi River north of New Orleans killed seventy-eight people

1999—Elizabeth Dole withdrew from U.S. presidential race

2003—President George W. Bush offered security guarantee to North Korea in exchange for dismantling nuclear-weapons program

BORN TODAY

Architect Christopher Wren 1632
Educator John Dewey 1859
Actor Bela Lugosi 1882
Columnist Art Buchwald 1925
Baseball player Mickey Mantle . . . 1931
Actor Jerry Orbach 1935
Baseball player Keith Hernandez . 1953
Actor Viggo Mortensen 1958
Musician Jim Sonnefeld 1964
Rapper Snoop Dogg 1971

LOVING THE UNLOVELY

The great author C. S. Lewis once said, "I remember that when Christian teachers told me long ago that I must hate a bad man's actions but not the man, I used to think this a silly straw-splitting distinction: how could you hate what a man did and not hate the man? But years later it occurred to me that there was one man to whom I had been doing this all my life—namely myself."

Just as we overlook our faults and love rather than hate ourselves, so we are to extend that grace to others. Jesus said, "You have heard that it was said, 'Love your neighbor and hate your enemy,' But I tell you: Love your enemies and pray for those who persecute you" (Matthew 5:43–44).

The Golden Rule once described a wealthy New Yorker who spent his life living in a house just five feet wide. As the story goes, the man had tried unsuccessfully to sell the five-foot strip of land to his neighbor, so he built a five-foot wide "spite house" on the property and spent the rest of his life living there in misery.

How sad. We're told that "they shall know we are Christians by our love." How do your actions make you known to others?

TODAY'S POWER POINT

We should conduct ourselves toward our enemy as if he were one day to be our friend.—John Henry Newman

TODAY IN HISTORY

1797—Navy launched USS *Constitution*
1879—Thomas A. Edison demonstrated first incandescent lamp
1916—First college ROTC units established
1923—World's first planetarium opened in Munich
1959—New York's Guggenheim Museum opened to the public, housed in
    dramatically modern structure designed by architect Frank Lloyd Wright
1967—Thousands of demonstrators marched near the Pentagon to protest U.S.
    involvement in Vietnam
2003—Senate passed ban on late-term abortions
2005—Women elected to more than twenty-five percent of seats in Afghanistan's
    new parliament

BORN TODAY

Poet Samuel Coleridge 1772
Inventor Alfred Nobel 1833
Conductor George Solti 1912
Musician Dizzy Gillespie 1917
Baseball player Whitey Ford 1928
Singer Manfred Mann 1940
Singer Elvin Bishop 1942
Singer Steven Curtis Chapman;
    actress Carrie Fisher; 1956
Actor Jeremy Miller 1976

PAYING THE PRICE

Have you ever taken a shortcut you thought would save time or money, only to discover that just the opposite was true? In the days of the Wild West, a young man planned to take a journey on a stagecoach. When buying a ticket, he noticed that he could save substantially by purchasing a third-class ticket rather than paying for first- or second-class fare. Reasoning that all the seats were alike, the man bought the cheapest ticket.

On the long journey, all went well for a while, and the young man prided himself on making a thrifty decision. But then the coach neared the foot of a steep hill. The driver stopped the coach and shouted, "First-class passengers, keep your seats. Second-class passengers, get out and walk; third-class passengers, get out and push."

How many people have prided themselves on being smart, only to later discover how foolish they were. Proverbs 14:12 warns: "There is a way that seems right to a man, but in the end it leads to death." There are no shortcuts to wisdom. God's way is always best, no matter what the short-term costs and considerations may be.

TODAY'S POWER POINT

Wickedness is always easier than virtue; it takes the shortcut to everything.
—Samuel Johnson

October 22

TODAY IN HISTORY

995—First saints canonized

1746—Princeton University established

1907—Tented extravaganzas consolidated as Ringling Brothers bought Barnum and Bailey circus

1962—President John F. Kennedy established naval barricade to block Soviet weapons from entering Cuba

1975—Death of historian Arthur Toynbee, the man who called history "God revealing himself" to man, age eighty-six

1979—Shah of Iran arrived in New York for medical tests

1983—Day-long concert marked one-hundredth birthday of New York's Metropolitan Opera

2001—Two Washington DC postal workers died from anthrax poisoning

2003—Senate unanimously approved restrictions on senders of unsolicited e-mails (spam)

BORN TODAY

Artist Robert Rauschenberg 1925

Actor Christopher Lloyd 1938

Actor Tony Roberts 1939

Actress Annette Funicello 1942

Actress Catherine Deneuve 1943

Actor Jeff Goldblum 1952

Olympic skater Brian Boitano . . . 1963

Baseball player Ichiro Suzuki 1973

GOD'S ECONOMY

French banker Baron de Rothschild's personal valet was said to be eagerly studying socialism. But after a time the baron noticed his assistant was no longer taking part in socialist gatherings. Puzzled, he inquired why the young man had lost interest in the philosophy he had pursued so diligently before.

"Sir," the young man replied, "it has been determined that if the national wealth was equally divided among all its citizens, each would have 2,000 francs."

"So?" the baron inquired.

"But I now have 5,000 francs!"

Bible scholars have noted that the Bible has more to say about money and the ownership of the things money can buy than about heaven. Although we may acquire money and possessions, we really don't own anything—it all belongs to God. He just gives us temporary stewardship over it. As he reminds us, "Every animal of the forest is mine, and the cattle on a thousand hills . . . and the creatures of the field are mine" (Psalm 50:10–11). The apostle Paul said, "God will meet all your needs according to his glorious riches in Christ Jesus" (Philippians 4:19).

Be assured that, as a child of God, whatever you need, God will provide, for he owns it all.

TODAY'S POWER POINT

God's will done God's way will never lack God's supply.—Source Unknown

TODAY IN HISTORY

1915—Twenty-five thousand women paraded in New York City, demanding right to vote

1945—Jackie Robinson became first African American major-league baseball player

1947—Physicians Carl and Gerty Cory became first husband-and-wife team to win Nobel prizes (for research on blood sugar)

1973—President Richard Nixon agreed to turn over taped White House conversations

1976—Widow of Chinese leader Mao Zedong jailed for plotting a coup

1983—Terrorist explosion at U.S. Marine barracks in Beirut, Lebanon, killed 241 American military personnel

1998—Abortion doctor killed at his home in suburban Buffalo, New York; Israeli prime minister Benjamin Netanyahu and Palestinian president Yasser Arafat signed historic land-for-peace agreement

2003—United States eased travel restrictions to Cuba

BORN TODAY

Inventor Nicolas Appert 1752
Director Ang Lee 1954
TV host Johnny Carson 1925
Singer Dwight Yoakam 1956
Golfer Juan "Chi-Chi" Rodriguez . 1934
Football player Doug Flutie; football
Soccer player Pelé 1940
  player Mike Tomczak 1962
Author Michael Crichton 1942
Basketball player Keith Van Horn . 1975

GOD'S PROTECTION

God's protection covers us 24/7, wherever we may go. Legendary missionary David Livingstone described God's "invisible hedge" about him. In one instance angry men from the heart of Africa had completely surrounded Livingstone's position and were threatening his life. Later he wrote in his diary: "I read that Jesus said, 'I am with you always, even unto the end of the world.' Should such a man as I flee? Nay, verily I feel quite calm now, thank God!" The Lord gave him peace and shielded him against the threat of violence.

When troubles surround you and threaten your life or your peace, like David Livingstone and like the psalmist, call out to God: "Do not withhold your mercy from me, O LORD; may your love and your truth always protect me. For troubles without number surround me" (Psalm 40:11–12). Remember, your strength and protection comes from God. "Blessed is the man who makes the LORD his trust" (Psalm 40:4). Rest secure in God's love, knowing that your trust is in the all-powerful, all-knowing God.

TODAY'S POWER POINT

Fear of God can deliver us from the fear of man.—John Witherspoon

October 24

TODAY IN HISTORY

1931—George Washington Bridge opened between New York City and New Jersey
1939—Nylon stockings first went on sale
1945—United Nations chartered
1978—Japan and China signed friendship pact in Tokyo
1984—Baboon heart transplanted into a fifteen-day-old infant
2000—Sixty reported dead in Ebola-virus outbreak in Uganda; Clinton administration posted $237 billion U.S. budget surplus, third straight year of gains

BORN TODAY

Scientist Anton van Leeuwenhoek 1632
Football player Y. A. Tuttle 1926
Actor David Nelson 1936
Actor Murray Abraham 1939
Actor Kevin Kline 1947
Civil-rights leader Kweisi Mfume . 1948
Actor B. D. Wong 1962
Singer Monica 1980

THE MIRACLE WITHIN

Have you considered the phenomenal automatic performances taking place within every human body? Scientists say that within twenty-four hours, the human heart beats 103,680 times, pushing the bloodstream some 43 million miles. You'll inhale 438 cubic feet of air in twenty-three thousand breaths. Three and one-fourth pounds of food will be digested, along with a half gallon of liquid. Two pounds of water will evaporate through perspiration while the body generates 450 tons of energy. That's not all. Your nails will grow (by 1/200 of an inch), and each hair will add 1/100 of an inch to its length overnight.

Who keeps watch over this system to be sure it operates properly? Could it be the omnipotent God who created mankind? Who else but God could accomplish it? Psalm 139:13–14 sums up this truth, and it should stir our hearts: "You created my inmost being; you knit me together in my mother's womb. I praise you because I am fearfully and wonderfully made; your works are wonderful, I know that full well."

And that's just the start. God's knowledge of us goes beyond the basic mechanics of our physical bodies to what makes us who we are—unique individuals. "O LORD, you have searched me and you know me. . . . You perceive my thoughts from afar. . . . You are familiar with all my ways. Before a word is on my tongue you know it completely." (Psalm 139:1–4).

How does this knowledge affect how you feel about God? About yourself? The God who sets the universe in order is intimately involved with your life. Now that's a miracle of God's love.

TODAY'S POWER POINT

Our body is the most gracious gift God has given us.—Oswald Chambers

TODAY IN HISTORY

1930—Beginning of air-passenger service linking U.S. coasts
1944—U.S. forces successful in battle of the Philippine Sea
1971—China admitted to United Nations
1972—First female FBI agents sworn in
1983—Two thousand U.S. Marines and Army Rangers invaded Caribbean island of Grenada following an earlier coup that had made it a Soviet-Cuban colony
1999—Mysterious small-plane crash killed pro golfer Payne Stewart and five others
2001—Scores missing in intense blaze sparked by truck crash deep within Swiss tunnel
2002—Small-plane crash in Minnesota killed Senator Paul Wellstone and seven others
2005—Iraqis passed new constitution with nearly 80 percent of the vote

BORN TODAY

Artist Pablo Picasso 1881
Explorer Richard E. Byrd 1888
Naval aviator Floyd Bennett 1890
Comedienne Minnie Pearl 1912
Actress Marion Ross 1936
Basketball coach Bobby Knight . . 1940
Singer Helen Reddy 1942
Olympic wrestler Dan Gable 1948
Singer Chely Wright 1970
Baseball player Pedro Martinez . . . 1971

FEEDING FAITH

A war widow and mother of young children found herself in a desperate situation. It was the week before Christmas, and she had no more food—and no money to buy any. The poor woman entered a store and asked the grocer to show her some small kindness by giving her food to feed her children. She told him that her husband had been killed in the war and that she had nothing to give for the food but a prayer.

"Write it on paper," the unimpressed grocer said harshly before turning to wait on other customers. He let her wait for a while, then grabbed the paper with the woman's prayer and placed it on one side of his scale. "We'll see just how much food your prayer is worth," he muttered skeptically.

But much to the grocer's amazement, the scale seemed weighted on the side of the paper, even as he piled more and more food on the other. Exasperated and a bit unnerved, he finally tossed the woman a bag and told her to go ahead and pack up the food. When she had gone, the grocer opened the crumpled note to read: "Please, Lord, give us today our daily bread" (Matthew 6:11).

If you have the faith of this woman, God can supply your needs as well. Thank him for meeting your needs today.

TODAY'S POWER POINT

He who abandons himself to God will never be abandoned by God.—Source Unknown

October 26

TODAY IN HISTORY

1825—Erie Canal opened

1954—Chevrolet unveiled first V-8 engine

1955—South Vietnamese independence

1970—*Doonesbury* cartoon strip debut

1972—Henry Kissinger declared, "Peace is at hand" in Vietnam

1982—Polish parliament outlawed Solidarity (free-trade union); premiere of television's *St. Elsewhere*

1989—NFL named Paul Tagliabue new commissioner

1990—Death of CBS founder William Paley, age eighty-nine; Wayne Gretzky first player to score two thousand points in hockey

1995—House passed balanced-budget bill

2000—Yankees beat the Mets to win "subway" World Series

2001—Misdirected U.S. air strikes nearly demolished Kabul Red Cross headquarters in Afghan capital

2002—Russian troops stormed besieged Moscow theater, rescuing 650 hostages from Chechen rebels (who killed 117 captives)

BORN TODAY

Inventor Joseph Hanson. 1803

Philanthropist Amy Rockefeller . . 1874

Publisher John Knight 1894

Singer Mahalia Jackson. 1911

Writer Pat Conroy 1945

TV personality Pat Sajak 1946

First Lady and senator Hillary Clinton; actress Jaclyn Smith. 1947

TV host Jeff Probst. 1962

Basketball player Nick Collison . . 1980

TIME TO TALK

Pastor Martin Niemöller was confined in a Nazi prison camp for eight years for opposing state control of churches. When he was released, reporters rushed to get his story. But rather than talking about himself, Niemöller talked about God's grace and help, even preaching a stirring gospel message. One disappointed reporter remarked, "Imagine all those years in prison, and all he can talk about is Jesus Christ." Yet what a testimony to God's power in his life Niemöller gave!

How bold are you in speaking out about God? Sometimes opportunities come when we least expect them. Like the apostle Paul, we should pray for boldness and the right words to say: "Pray also for me, that whenever I open my mouth, words may be given me so that I will fearlessly make known the mystery of the gospel" (Ephesians 6:19).

Be alert for every opportunity you may have today. When it's your turn to speak, will you talk about yourself, or will you talk about God?

TODAY'S POWER POINT

Deeds, not stones, are the true monuments of the great.—John Motley

TODAY IN HISTORY

1492—Columbus first landed on Cuba

1858—Macy's opened first store in New York City

1873—Barbed wire patented

1890—Postal street-letter-box patented

1904—New York subway began operation

1925—Waterskis invented

1927—Release of first news sound film, *Movietone*

1928—Israel's Menachem Begin and Egypt's Anwar Sadat named joint winners of Nobel Peace Prize

1954—Premiere of Walt Disney's television show *Disneyland* (later *The Wonderful World of Disney*)

1999—United States reported second annual back-to-back budget surplus (of $123 billion)

BORN TODAY

Violinist Nicolo Paganini 1782

President Theodore Roosevelt. . . . 1858

Poet Dylan Thomas 1914

Pianist Floyd Cramer 1933

Actor John Cleese. 1939

Satirist Fran Lebowitz. 1950

Actress Marla Maples 1963

Singer Scott Weiland 1967

NOT IDLE

History gives us numerous examples of hard workers with prolific works. Sir Walter Scott awoke at four o'clock each morning and thus was able to write a book every two months. Violinist Fritz Kreisler, despite his great talent and natural ability, spent eight to ten hours a day practicing. And John Wesley was said to have preached three sermons a day for fifty-four years, written more than eighty works, and traveled 290,000 miles.

Industry is important. While we must avoid improper attitudes like greed and selfish ambition, we should never fear hard and honest work. The Bible says, "Sow your seed in the morning, and at evening let not your hands be idle, for you do not know which will succeed, whether this or that, or whether both will do equally well" (Ecclesiastes 11:6).

Don't be among those who are too easily dissuaded from work. Conditions will never be perfect for that new business venture or for your ministry to expand, but that shouldn't stop you from starting with determination, working hard, and finishing strong. "Whoever watches the wind will not plant; whoever looks at the clouds will not reap" (Ecclesiastes 11:4). Don't be a wind watcher; work!

TODAY'S POWER POINT

What is right is often forgotten by what is convenient.—Bodie Thoene

October 28

TODAY IN HISTORY

1636—Harvard University founded

1886—Statue of Liberty dedicated

1904—Fingerprints first used in police investigation

1919—Law enforcing prohibition passed despite presidential veto

1927—Pan Am made first scheduled international passenger flight

1950—Television premiere of *The Jack Benny Program*

1961—Brian Epstein first heard performance by the Beatles (became their manager)

1965—Pope Paul VI cleared Jews of guilt in crucifixion of Jesus Christ; Gateway Arch completed in St. Louis

1980—Ford Motor Company reported record $595 million loss in third quarter, highest loss ever for any U.S. company

1984—Huge celebration marked thirty-five years of Communism in China

BORN TODAY

Explorer James Cook	1728	Computer executive Bill Gates	1955
Actress Jane Alexander	1939	Actress Jami Gertz	1965
Actor Dennis Franz	1944	Actress Julia Roberts	1967
Actress Telma Hopkins	1948	Singer Brad Paisley	1972

GOD'S INTEREST

Some time ago a pastor decided to put the parable of the talents to a modern-day test. He told his congregation that each member could take $10 from church funds providing they each returned it in two months along with any proceeds they had earned from it. Some members were skeptical that the church would even get back the $3,500 members had taken. But when the offering was collected at the end of the period, it totaled $10,207.24—nearly three times the original amount. The pastor said the experiment proved the power of putting faith in people to be good stewards.

In the parable of the talents (or minas—both forms of money), the Bible reminds us of the importance God places on being good stewards of the possessions he has given us. You have been commissioned to manage your financial affairs for the Lord and must account to God someday for how well you've done—what you spent your money on, how much you gave to God and others, the attitude you had toward money and possessions. How good a steward are you? What do you think Jesus would say about the way you handle your finances? At the end of your life, will he say to you, "Well done, my good servant!" (Luke 19:17)?

TODAY'S POWER POINT

I don't believe in principle, but I do in interest.—James Russell Lowell

TODAY IN HISTORY

1929—Historic U.S. stock-market collapse set off the Great Depression
1940—Start of armed-services draft lottery
1969—Beginning of Internet age: computers at UCLA and Stanford first exchanged data
1974—Billions of dollars pledged at Arab League Summit to assist Arab nations who have fought Israel
1975—President Gerald Ford blamed city officials for New York City's financial crisis
1979—More than one thousand protestors arrested in Wall Street antinuclear demonstration
1997—Iraq expelled U.S. members of UN weapons-inspection team
1998—John Glenn became oldest man in space
2003—Death toll in four 9/11 attacks scaled back from 3,035 to 2,995 (including 2,752 at the World Trade Center)
2004—Yasser Arafat flew to Paris hospital for treatment of stomach ailment (from which he never recovered)

BORN TODAY

Biographer James Boswell. 1740
Cartoonist Bill Mauldin 1921
Singer Melba Moore. 1945
Actor Richard Dreyfus 1947
Actress Kate Jackson. 1948
Actress Joely Fisher. 1965
Singer Toby Smith 1970
Actress Winona Ryder 1971

THE KEYS

Who ultimately has ownership of all that you have? The answer is God—he owns it all. We are merely stewards (managers) of what God has entrusted to us. When we have this relationship clearly in mind, it removes a great burden from us. If everything is God's to begin with, why worry when things go wrong?

At one time Dr. F. B. Meyer felt that his ministry was no longer fruitful and that he was lacking in spiritual power. Dr. Meyer says it was as if Christ were suddenly standing beside him saying, "Let me have the keys to your life." Meyer actually got out his key ring. The Lord then asked, "Are all the keys here?" Meyer responded, "Yes, Lord, all except the key to one small room in my life." Christ replied, "Well, if you cannot trust me to have access to every room in your life, then I cannot accept any of the keys." Meyer became overwhelmed by the feeling that God was leaving his life, and so he cried out, "Come back, Lord. Here are the keys to all the rooms of my life."

Who holds the keys to your life, you or God?

TODAY'S POWER POINT

The best things in life aren't things.—Art Buchwald

October 30

TODAY IN HISTORY

1894—Time clock patented

1925—First TV picture beamed to London

1938—Orson Welles's radio dramatization of H. G. Wells's *War of the Worlds* broadcast set off nationwide panic

1961—Body of Joseph Stalin ordered removed from Red Square; Soviets conducted fifty-eight-megaton hydrogen-bomb test

1975—Dr. Mary Leakey announced discovery of human remains she said date back 3.75 million years

1984—Pro-Solidarity union priest found slain near Warsaw, Poland

1995—By a slim margin, Quebec voters decided not to part from Canada

2000—Kosovo revolutionary Ibrahim Rugova elected to lead Albania

2002—Governing alliance dissolved in Israel over budget dispute; former vice president Walter Mondale agreed to run as Democratic candidate for U.S. Senate from Minnesota (replacing the late Paul Wellstone on the ballot)

BORN TODAY

Author Emily Post 1872

Admiral Bull Halsey 1882

Poet Ezra Pound 1885

Bodybuilder Charles Atlas 1893

Football coach Dick Vermeil 1936

Actor Henry Winkler 1945

Journalist Andrea Mitchell 1946

Actor Harry Hamlin 1952

Actor Kevin Pollak 1958

Singer Kassidy Osborn 1976

OPEN DOORS

Evangelist Paul Rader often shared his faith with a New York banker, but the man never seemed interested. One day Rader felt an urgent need to visit this man again, so he boarded a train and hurried to the bank. When he arrived, he found the banker standing in the doorway waiting for him.

"Rader," he cried, "I was just going to send you a telegram begging you to come." "That's OK," said the preacher, "I got the message on heaven's 'telegraph.'" He talked to the man at length, stressing the urgency of making a decision for Christ right away. Impressed by Rader's well-timed visit and under deep conviction, the banker surrendered fully to God. Moments later the banker groaned and fell into the evangelist's arms, dead.

Like the Old Testament prophet Samuel, who answered God's call by saying, "Here am I, Lord," we need to be ready to respond to God's call instantly. The Bible says Christians are to be ready at all times to give a reason for the hope within them. Are you?

TODAY'S POWER POINT

Electric communication will never be a substitute for the face of someone who . . . encourages another person to be brave and true.—Charles Dickens

October 31

TODAY IN HISTORY

1517—Martin Luther posted his famous "Ninety-Five Theses"

1864—Thirty-sixth state, Nevada, added to Union

1918—Government reported massive flu outbreak had claimed the lives of 195,000 U.S. victims during October, making it the deadliest month in American history (epidemic spread, eventually killing twenty million people worldwide)

1956—First plane landed at the South Pole

1968—President Lyndon Johnson announced end to all U.S. bombing of North Vietnam

1983—Nineteen hundred U.S. Marines began "mopping-up" action in Grenada, where sixteen Americans had been killed and seventy-seven injured

2000—Napster began charging fees for music downloads; three astronauts blasted off to become first residents of International Space Station

2001—President George W. Bush sought to make it an international crime to acquire or build biological weapons for terrorist attacks

2003—U.S. economy recorded fastest expansion in nine years

BORN TODAY

Poet John Keats 1795

Girl Scout founder Juliet Low . . . 1860

Chinese leader Chiang Kai-shek . . 1887

TV newsman Dan Rather 1931

Actor Michael Landon 1936

Actress Deidre Hall 1948

TV host Jane Pauley 1950

Actor Rob Schneider 1963

GROWTH THROUGH GOD'S WORD

As the phenomenal success of *The Purpose Driven Life* and the *Left Behind* books, as well as the movie *The Passion of the Christ* clearly demonstrates, the search for biblical truth is a powerful force today. In fact, author Elmer Towns noted that the ten fastest growing churches in America are not only conservative, but are boldly biblically based in their doctrine.

Undoubtedly the best example of a fast-growing, successful church is the early church as recorded in the book of Acts. That first church saw incredible growth—it increased by three thousand in just one day! Miraculous signs and wonders filled everyone with awe. Regular, sincere fellowship led believers to share everything they had with others. But all of these amazing things sprang from one essential component we dare not leave out of our churches today: "They devoted themselves to the apostles' teaching" (Acts 2:42).

Do you want your church to grow? Study and proclaim God's Word. Do you want to grow in your own spiritual life? Study and put into practice the Word. It's as basic as that.

TODAY'S POWER POINT

To read the Bible is to take a trip to a fair land where the spirit is strengthened and faith renewed.—Dwight Eisenhower

TODAY IN HISTORY

1800—President John Adams moved into the Presidential Mansion, later called the White House (first president to reside there)
1848—First medical school for women opened (Boston Female Medical School)
1864—First money orders sold in United States
1870—U.S. Weather Bureau opened
1894—*Billboard* magazine began publication
1952—United States tested first H-bomb
1957—Mackinac Bridge opened, its five-mile span linking upper and lower Michigan
1959—Hockey mask invented
1968—First movie ratings began in United States
1985—Microsoft released Windows 1.01
1994—Chicago Bulls retired Michael Jordan's uniform
2000—Yugoslavia joined the United Nations

BORN TODAY

Artist Benvenuto Cellini 1500
Author Stephen Crane 1871
Columnist James Kilpatrick 1920
Golfer Gary Player 1935
Actress Marcia Wallace 1942
Singer Lyle Lovett. 1957
Actress Jenny McCarthy 1972

UNDERSTANDING THE WATERMELON

American statesman and presidential nominee William Jennings Bryan is probably best known for his stand against Darwinism in the famed Scopes' Trial of 1925. But he is also known for his watermelon story, illustrating the creative power of God.

As Bryan told it, one tiny seed was placed into the ground, watered, and heated by the sun. From somewhere, Bryan explained, that tiny seed drew in matter two hundred times its own weight and forced it through a narrow stem to create a forty-pound watermelon. But where, he wondered, did the watermelon receive its shiny green coat, the white rind, or the juicy red pulp, interlaced with thousands of seeds capable of doing the same thing all over again? Where does the watermelon get its flavor or coloring? How did that little seed build a watermelon? As Bryan observed, "The most learned man in the world cannot explain a watermelon. And until you can explain a watermelon, he noted, you cannot set limits on the power of the Almighty."

Are you facing impossible hurdles today? Does it seem like things are hopeless and there's no way out? Remember that God specializes in things thought impossible, and go to him for help.

TODAY'S POWER POINT

All things are possible with God.—Mark 10:27

November 2 ___

TODAY IN HISTORY

1889—North and South Dakota became thirty-ninth and fortieth states
1917—Britain designated Palestine as home for the Jewish people
1920—KDKA (Pittsburgh) broadcast first regularly scheduled radio programs
1931—Synthetic rubber introduced
1947—World's largest airplane (the "Spruce Goose") made first and only flight
    (Howard Hughes lost interest in the plane after proving it could fly)
2001—Unemployment at five-year low (5.6 percent) in October
2004—By a more than two-thirds approval, Californians voted to fund embryonic
    stem-cell research

BORN TODAY

Pioneer Daniel Boone 1734
France's queen Marie Antoinette. . 1755
President Warren G. Harding. . . . 1865
Actor Burt Lancaster 1913
Political pundit Pat Buchanan . . . 1938
Golfer Dave Stockton. 1941

Actress Stefanie Powers;
   author Shere Hite 1942
Actress Alfre Woodard 1953
Singer k. d. lang 1961
Actor Danny Cooksey 1975

AN UNEXPLAINED MIRACLE

They had headed out of town late at night, their car loaded down with three kids and supplies for the seven-hundred-mile journey to Grandma's house. After a while they noticed the gas gauge indicating they were near empty. At first the couple was not concerned—they were on a major highway, and they had seen lots of gas stations at exits along the way. But as they traveled on, they watched the gauge creep ever lower, with no gas stations in sight. What had begun as only a minor concern was growing into a major crisis.

It seemed the car was now running on fumes, as the fuel indicator had long ago dropped below E. Still the couple kept driving, sure they would spot a station around the next bend. But none came into view.

Finally, desperate and about to run out of fuel on the deserted highway, the wife prayed for God to keep them going until they could refuel. Sure enough, within a few more miles they saw a gas-station sign off in the distance. They reached the exit and filled up the tank. Somehow, miraculously, God had kept their car running for many miles after the gauge had dropped well below the empty mark.

Are you looking for a miracle in your life today? Turn your needs over to God in prayer.

TODAY'S POWER POINT

I believe in miracles, for I believe in God.—Source Unknown

November 3

TODAY IN HISTORY

1783—Continental Army disbanded

1900—New York City hosted first national auto show

1948—Famous incorrect headline, "Dewey Defeats Truman," published

1952—First frozen loaves of bread sold (by a bakery in Port Chester, New York)

1953—First coast-to-coast live color telecast (an unnamed program broadcast from New York to Burbank, California)

1959—Russians launched first animal (a dog) into space

1964—Washington DC residents got first opportunity to vote for president; President Lyndon Johnson won reelection by record margin

1976—Jimmy Carter elected first Deep-South president in 132 years

1992—Bill Clinton defeated incumbent president George H. W. Bush

2004—Hamid Karzai formally named winner of Afganistan presidential election

BORN TODAY

Texas pioneer Stephen Austin. . . . 1793

Poet William Cullen Bryant 1794

Baseball player Bob Feller 1918

Actor Charles Bronson 1921

Actor Ken Berry 1933

Actor Steve Landesberg 1945

Comedian and actor Dennis Miller; comedienne Roseanne Barr . . . 1953

Singer Adam Ant; actress Kathy Kinney 1954

Football player and sportscaster Phil Simms 1956

SOMEONE TO HOLD ON TO

A story is told of two men who were standing watch on a ship. The sea was dark and turbulent, and when a sudden storm blew in overnight, one of the sailors was swept overboard. The next day the crew discovered that the man lost at sea had been in a sheltered part of the ship, while the sailor who survived had stood in an area bearing the brunt of the storm. So how was he able to survive while the other man drowned? The sailor who was lost had nothing to hold on to.

When life is peaceful, it's easy to feel self-sufficient; but when things get tough, look out for a fall. Why? Because when we reject God's assistance, we have nothing left to hold on to and are easily overcome.

When you trust in the Lord and do his will, you have both an advocate and a guide to see you through the tempests of life. The pressures that would quickly overwhelm you otherwise, you can now take in stride because you are God-powered, relying on his strength to see you through.

Psalm 91:2 says, "He is my refuge and my fortress; my God, in whom I trust." To whom do you cling in times of trouble? Thank God today for always being there for you.

TODAY'S POWER POINT

When we lose hold of God, it is not God who is lost.—Source Unknown

TODAY IN HISTORY

1842—Abraham Lincoln married Mary Todd

1879—Cash register patented

1922—King Tut's tomb discovered in Egypt

1979—Four people killed and eighteen injured in Greensboro, North Carolina, when a group of whites fired on demonstrators opposed to the Ku Klux Klan; hundreds of Iranian students seized the U.S. embassy in Tehran, taking fifty-two Americans hostage (and holding them for 444 days)

1980—Ronald Reagan, age sixty-nine, elected fortieth president of the United States (oldest presidential candidate to be elected)

1985—Following an apparent effort to distract the CIA from identifying Soviet "moles," senior KGB official Vitaly Yurchenko returned to Russian custody after briefly defecting to the United States

1991—Five U.S. presidents (Nixon, Ford, Carter, Reagan, and George H. W. Bush) dedicated Reagan Presidential Library

1992—START disarmament treaty approved by Russia

1995—Israeli prime minister Yitzhak Rabin killed in Tel Aviv

2004—Ailing Palestinian leader Yasser Arafat lapsed into coma; wife of Democratic presidential candidate John Edwards revealed she would undergo treatment for breast cancer

BORN TODAY

Humorist Will Rogers 1879

News anchor Walter Cronkite . . . 1916

Actor Art Carney;
   actor Cameron Mitchell 1918

Actor Martin Balsam 1919

Actress Loretta Swit 1937

First Lady Laura Bush 1946

Actor Matthew McConaughey . . . 1969

Rapper Sean "Puffy" Combs 1970

Football player Orlando Pace 1975

BECOMING SALTY

In this age of frozen foods and canned goods, it's good to recall the original purpose of salt. Before refrigeration, salt was often used as a preservative—especially to keep meat edible over extended periods of time. The Bible refers to salt, too, when Jesus said, "You are the salt of the earth. But if the salt loses its saltiness, how can it be made salty again? It is no longer good for anything, except to be thrown out and trampled by men" (Matthew 5:13). In other words, once we become Christians, God has us stay here on earth for a while to act as a preservative in society—to stand up for godliness and hold back the floodgates of evil. When others see you, do they know you as a "salty Christian"?

TODAY'S POWER POINT

He who shall introduce into public affairs the principles of Christianity, will change the face of the world.—Benjamin Franklin

November 5

TODAY IN HISTORY

1895—First U.S. automobile patent granted
1930—Sinclair Lewis won Nobel Prize in literature, first American to do so
1940—Franklin D. Roosevelt won unprecedented third term as U.S. president
1956—Premiere of television's *The Nat King Cole Show*
1977—Death of bandleader Guy Lombardo, age seventy-five
1996—President Bill Clinton reelected
2002—GOP regained majority in Senate
2003—President George W. Bush signed bill outlawing late-term abortions
2004—Labor Department reported more than 335,000 new jobs created

BORN TODAY

Socialist Eugene V. Debs 1855
Singer and actor Roy Rogers. 1912
Singer Art Garfunkel 1941
Basketball player Bill Walton 1952
Singer/songwriter Bryan Adams . . 1959
Actress Tatum O'Neal 1963
Baseball player Javy López 1970
Basketball player Jerry Stackhouse 1974

RESTITUTION

Too many people seem to want something that doesn't belong to them. But stealing is against the law—including God's Law. The eighth commandment says quite simply: "You shall not steal" (Exodus 20:15). Ephesians 4:28 addresses those already caught up in the lure of getting something for nothing: "He who has been stealing must steal no longer, but must work, doing something useful with his own hands, that he may have something to share with those in need." This is a positive first step, but it's not enough. The Bible calls believers to restitution—repaying what was stolen.

Years ago the War Department received a letter from a veteran of World War I. In the letter the man said he had stolen equipment and clothing worth about fifty dollars. He enclosed a check for that amount, adding, "God has wonderfully saved me, and I'm now seeking to make everything right that I can."

Zacchaeus was perhaps the champion of restitution. When Christ changed his life, he offered to repay four times the amount he had stolen. In the Old Testament God had instructed that a thief should add one fifth of the value to what he had stolen and give it to the rightful owner (see Leviticus 6:1–5). So Zacchaeus's restitution went above and beyond the letter of the law. What a change of heart this showed! When Christ changes someone's heart, he really changes it!

Has God changed your heart? Is there anything you need to do to show it and make things right?

TODAY'S POWER POINT

Thieves respect property. They merely wish the property to become their property that they may more perfectly respect it.—G. K. Chesterton

November 6

TODAY IN HISTORY

1860—Abraham Lincoln elected president
1869—First college football game played
1928—First lighted news sign displayed election returns in Times Square
1947—Television premiere of *Meet the Press*
1955—*The Constant Husband* became first coast-to-coast movie premiere (on network TV)
1959—Box-office premiere of *The Sound of Music*
1967—Television premiere of *The Phil Donahue Show*
1975—Premiere of television's *Good Morning America*
1984—New York Stock Exchange stayed open on Election Day (first time in almost two hundred years)—market gained fifteen points
1994—Former president Ronald Reagan announced he had Alzheimer's disease
2001—U.S. doctors banned from prescribing fatal doses of drugs for terminal patients; Fed cut interest rate for tenth time in 2001
2002—Fed cut prime interest rate to forty-one-year low
2003—U.S. unemployment fell to 6 percent with net gain of 126,000 jobs

BORN TODAY

Composer John Philip Sousa 1854
Basketball game inventor James Naismith. 1861
Writer James Jones 1921
Director Mike Nichols 1931
Journalist Maria Shriver 1944
Actress Sally Field. 1946
Musician Glenn Frey 1948
Actor Nigel Havers. 1949
Actor Ethan Hawke 1970
Actress Rebecca Romijn 1972

SERVING GOD

A man once hired two laborers but soon noticed they weren't out working on the task he had assigned them. After searching for some time, he found one of them, Joe, fast asleep. Soon he found the other loafing nearby. Confronting him, the boss asked, "Ted, what have you been doing?" The man quickly replied, "Why I've been helping out Joe."

Too many Christians are content just to "help out Joe" by warming a pew and not becoming actively involved in the work of the Lord. Taking care of God's business is every believer's job. God doesn't call every Christian to be involved in full-time ministry, but he does call us into various avenues of service—each one important. God has work for you to do. Ask your pastor where you might use your gifts and interests to serve God in your church or community. Determine how God has gifted you, and then gladly use your gifts.

TODAY'S POWER POINT

A good servant is a real godsend.—Martin Luther

November 7

TODAY IN HISTORY

1874—GOP elephant symbol first used
1876—Cigarette-making machine patented (by Albert Hook)
1885—Canadian Pacific Railway linked Canada coast-to-coast
1914—*The New Republic* magazine first published
1917—Communist takeover of Russia
1930—Pennsylvania voters modified blue law to allow sports on Sunday
1944—Franklin D. Roosevelt won unprecedented fourth presidential term
1946—New York City displayed coin-operated TV (showing *Felix the Cat*)
1954—Television premiere of *Face the Nation*
1963—Elston Howard became first African American named American League's
      Most Valuable Player
1973—Girls first allowed to play on New Jersey Little League teams
1989—First African American governor elected, Virginia's Douglas Wilder
2001—Shirley Franklin elected first African American woman mayor of Atlanta
2002—Terrorist car bomb blast killed nearly two hundred people in Bali nightclub

BORN TODAY

Physicist Marie Curie 1867
Actor Dean Jagger 1903
Writer Albert Camus 1913
Evangelist Billy Graham 1918
Musician Al Hirt 1922
Singer Joan Sutherland 1926
Singer Mary Travers 1937
Singer Johnny Rivers;
   singer Joni Mitchell 1942
Actor Barry Newman 1948
Conductor Keith Lockhart 1959
Actors Jason and Jeremy London . 1972

ALWAYS FAITHFUL

In the tragic destruction of Pompeii, many people were buried alive under lava and volcanic ash from the eruption of Mount Vesuvius. Some victims were discovered in isolated cellars while others were found out in the open; all were "frozen in time." Excavators found the remains of one Roman sentry still standing guard outside the gate, grasping his weapon—obedient to his captain's orders. Despite the choking ash and terrifying roar of the volcano, the sentry stood firm at his post, faithful to the end.

When God inspects your life in the hereafter, will he find that you were faithful to the end—doing whatever it is he has called you to do? The apostle Paul wrote, "Stand firm. Let nothing move you. Always give yourselves fully to the work of the Lord, because you know that your labor in the Lord is not in vain" (1 Corinthians 15:58). Determine to be found faithful in doing the work of God as he has called you to do it.

TODAY'S POWER POINT

It is better to be faithful than famous.—Theodore Roosevelt

TODAY IN HISTORY

1793—Opening of the Louvre Museum in Paris

1889—Forty-first state, Montana, added to Union

1895—X-rays discovered

1942—U.S. and British forces landed in French North Africa to join battle against Axis forces in World War II

1954—NFL approved Philadelphia Athletics move to Kansas City

1960—John F. Kennedy became first Catholic and youngest U.S. president

1965—Premiere of television's *Days of Our Lives*

1966—Edward Brooke became first popularly elected African American U.S. senator

1988—George H. W. Bush elected U.S. president, defeating Michael Dukakis

2002—UN Security Council voted unanimously to call on Iraq to disarm

2005—France declared state of emergency in wake of escalating youth labor riots

BORN TODAY

Astronomer Edmond Halley 1656

Psychiatrist Hermann Rorschach . 1884

Singer Patti Page. 1927

Journalist Morley Safer. 1931

Actress Virna Lisi 1937

Singer and musician Bonnie Raitt 1949

TV personality Mary Hart 1951

Musician Rickie Lee Jones 1954

Actor Leif Garrett. 1961

Actress Courtney Thorne-Smith . . 1967

BLOCKED PRAYERS

Have you ever had the feeling that your prayers weren't going any higher than the ceiling? It may be because there's something in your life that's blocking communication with your heavenly Father.

A mother was tucking her young son into bed for the night when abruptly, in the middle of saying his bedtime prayer, the boy suddenly jumped up and ran downstairs. A few moments later he returned to his knees in the bedroom and resumed his prayer. Once the covers were pulled up, his mom asked what he'd had to do that was so important. The youth replied, "When I was praying, 'If I should die before I wake,' I realized that I had left all the toys downstairs in a pile, hoping it would bug my brother. Then I thought, if I should die, I wouldn't want him to remember me that way, so I had to make things right."

The mother brushed a tear from her cheek as she turned out the light, thinking that adults should be that sensitive in their relationship with God. How are things going in your life today? Can you say that all is well with your soul? If not, turn everything over to God in prayer.

TODAY'S POWER POINT

If God is not where he once was in your life, guess who moved?—Source Unknown

November 9

TODAY IN HISTORY

1799—Napoleon declared himself head of France
1857—*Atlantic Monthly* began publication
1911—Neon sign patented
1918—Germany declared itself a republic
1933—Civil Works Administration established to create Depression-era jobs
1938—Tens of thousands of Jews arrested, synagogues and businesses ravished in overnight raids on Jews in Germany
1964—*The Wizard of Id* first appeared on comic pages
1967—*Rolling Stone* magazine first published
1976—United Nations condemned apartheid in South Africa
1984—Vietnam Veterans Memorial unveiled
1985—Russian Gary Kasparov, age twenty-two, became world chess champion
1989—Berlin Wall permanently opened between East and West Germany,
2005—Reporter Judith Miller resigned from the *New York Times* after serving nearly ninety days in jail for not revealing her sources in "Plamegate"

BORN TODAY

Publisher Elijah P. Lovejoy 1802
Novelist Margaret Mitchell. 1900
Pastor and author Stuart Briscoe. . 1930
Baseball player Bob Gibson 1935
Musician Tom Fogerty 1941
Golfer Tom Weiskopf. 1942
Actor Lou Ferrigno. 1951
Golfer David Duval 1971
Singer Nick Lachey; singer Sisqo . 1973
Baseball player Adam Dunn 1979

BEING BOLD FOR CHRIST

Having a holy boldness can greatly enhance your effectiveness for God. One of the first concerns of a certain new pastor was to confront city administrators about their obvious corruption. After seeking God in meditation and prayer, he made an appointment to meet with the mayor. As J. E. Conant tells the story, the pastor congratulated the mayor on being selected to the office, then said: "A far greater honor awaits you—something much bigger than the office of mayor of a city like this. You ought to be a servant of Jesus Christ." The mayor was astonished. "No one ever spoke to me like this before," he said.

It wasn't long before the pastor received a phone call from the mayor. "I must see you," he said. Within two weeks the pastor welcomed into his church not only the mayor but the fire and police chiefs and five aldermen as well.

People can't say yes to God until they've been asked to do so. Who have you asked recently? With God's power, be faithful in communicating the gospel to friend and foe alike.

TODAY'S POWER POINT

Fortune befriends the bold.—John Dryden

TODAY IN HISTORY

1775—Continental Marines (precursor to the U.S. Marine Corps) established
1951—Direct-dial long-distance calling introduced, with eighty-four area codes
(more than 285 today)
1969—Premiere of television's *Sesame Street*
1975—Wreck of the *Edmund Fitzgerald*: ore carrier sank in Lake Superior, killing
crew of twenty-nine in the worst shipwreck on the Great Lakes
1983—Microsoft advanced from DOS to Windows with graphical user interface
1994—Bill Gates bought Da Vinci's *Codex Leicester* manuscript for $30.8 million
1996—Quarterback Dan Marino threw for NFL-record 50,000th career yard
2001—In his initial UN address, President George W. Bush told General Assembly
that "every country is vulnerable to terrorist attacks" and thus has a
responsibility to fight terror
2004—Alberto Gonzales named to replace outgoing John Ashcroft as U.S. attorney
general

BORN TODAY

Reformer Martin Luther. 1483
Announcer George Fenneman . . . 1919
Actor Richard Burton. 1925
Actor Roy Scheider. 1935
Activist Russell Means 1940
Lyricist Tim Rice 1944
Singer Donna Fargo 1949
Comedian and actor Sinbad 1956
Actress Mackenzie Phillips 1959
Football player Isaac Bruce 1972

EVERLASTING LIFE

It's nearly impossible for the human mind to comprehend the scope of life eternal, yet even scientists have found reasons to believe in life after death. Dr. Wernher von Braun, known for his contributions to the space program, said, "Science has found nothing that can disappear without a trace. Nature does not know extinction. All it knows is transformation. If God applies the fundamental principle to the most minute and insignificant parts of the universe, doesn't it make sense to assume that he applies it to the masterpiece of his creation—the human soul? I think it does."

This isn't a new concept. Jesus said something similar two thousand years ago: "I tell you the truth, whoever hears my word and believes him who sent me has eternal life and will not be condemned; he has crossed over from death to life. I tell you the truth, a time is coming and has now come when the dead will hear the voice of the Son of God and those who hear will live" (John 5:24–25).

Your present life is only the beginning. Your future life will last forever. This life is just a brief stop on the road to eternity.

TODAY'S POWER POINT

Forever is a long bargain.—German Proverb

TODAY IN HISTORY

1647—First Colonial compulsory-education law enacted (in Massachusetts)

1889—Forty-second state, Washington, added to Union

1918—World War I ended with defeat of Germany

1919—First Armistice Day (Veterans Day) observed; first concrete ship manufactured

1921—First unknown soldier buried at Arlington cemetery

1933—"Black blizzard" (giant dust storm) blanketed Great Plains

1935—First photograph taken showing curvature of the earth's horizon

1938—Kate Smith introduced the song "God Bless America"

2005—Ellen Johnson-Sirleaf elected president of Liberia, first woman head of state in Africa

BORN TODAY

Author Fyodor Dostoevsky 1821

General George Patton 1885

Novelist Kurt Vonnegut Jr. 1922

Comedian Jonathan Winters 1925

Golfer Fuzzy Zoeller 1951

Actress Demi Moore 1962

Actress Calista Flockhart 1964

Actor Leonardo DiCaprio 1974

PRESERVING THE NATION

As quoted in *Christianity Today*, Henry Leiper illustrated the wealth of our nation in the following example: "Imagine that we could compress the world's population into one town of 1,000 people. In this town there would only be sixty Americans who would receive half the income for the entire town! They would have an average life expectancy of seventy years in contrast to less than forty years for all the others. The sixty Americans would own fifteen times as much as their neighbors and would eat 72 percent more than the maximum food requirements (while many of the others go hungry). The lowest income group among the Americans would be far better off than the average of the other townsmen."

America is truly a blessed land. But with the blessings come responsibilities to bless others—and danger if we don't remember the God who has blessed us. Moses's warning to the Israelites in Deuteronomy 8:10–14 is relevant for Americans today: "When you have eaten and are satisfied, praise the LORD your God for the good land he has given you. Be careful that you do not forget the LORD your God, failing to observe his commands, his laws and his decrees that I am giving you this day. Otherwise, when you eat and are satisfied, when you build fine houses and settle down, and when your herds and flocks grow large and your silver and gold increase and all you have is multiplied, then your heart will become proud and you will forget the LORD your God."

When was the last time you thanked God for creating and blessing our nation? In your bounty, don't forget God. Thank him for blessing you.

TODAY'S POWER POINT

The more I saw of foreign countries, the more I loved my own.—De Delloy

November 12

TODAY IN HISTORY

1920—First commissioner of baseball elected

1927—Joseph Stalin became lone Soviet ruler

1932—President Herbert Hoover invited President-elect Franklin D. Roosevelt to White House—first time this courtesy was ever extended

1946—First auto (drive-through) bank opened in Chicago

1948—Japan's World War II premier General Hideki Tojo sentenced to death

1974—United Nations voted to suspend South Africa over apartheid

1975—Supreme Court justice William Douglas resigned after longest term ever (more than thirty-six years); first dog hotel opened in New York City

1981—President Ronald Reagan refused budget director David Stockman's resignation for Stockman's admitted "poor judgment and loose talk"

1982—Former KGB chief Yuri Andropov named new leader of USSR

1984—Space-shuttle astronauts successfully retrieved passing satellite for first time

1987—Blizzard shut down U.S. northeast

1989—Brazil held free elections (first in nearly thirty years)

1990—British computer expert Tim Berners-Lee proposed hypertext system, which he labeled the World Wide Web

2002—Recorded voice of Osama bin Laden praised recent terror attacks

BORN TODAY

Suffragist Elizabeth Cady Stanton. 1815
Sculptor Auguste Rodin 1840
Princess Grace of Monaco 1929
Sportscaster Al Michaels. 1944
Singer Neil Young 1945
Gymnast Nadia Comaneci 1961
Actor David Schwimmer 1966
Baseball player Sammy Sosa 1968

WARMED BY THE SUN

There once was an old violinist whose music always impressed the audience with its soothing, mellow sound. His performances received a warm and enthusiastic response from all who heard them. When asked to explain the secret of his lilting music, the old man pointed to his instrument and said, "a great deal of sunshine must have gone into this wood. What has gone in comes out."

How much of God's sunshine has entered your life? How much do you radiate his glory? The Bible says, "Arise, shine, for your light has come, and the glory of the LORD rises upon you. . . . Then you will look and be radiant, your heart will throb and swell with joy" (Isaiah 60:1, 5). God's presence in our lives changes us. He brings peace and joy. Our lives should reflect the character and glory of God. When people look at you, do they see God?

TODAY'S POWER POINT

The sun, the hearth of affection and life, pours burning love on the delighted earth.—Arthur Rimbaud

November 13

TODAY IN HISTORY

1927—Holland Tunnel, linking New York and New Jersey, opened
1933—First sit-down strike (at Hormel meat packing plant in Austin, Minnesota)
1940—Box-office premiere of Disney's feature-length cartoon *Fantasia*
1942—Minimum draft age lowered from twenty-one to eighteen
1956—Supreme Court banned segregation on public buses
1985—Dwight Gooden, youngest pitcher to win twenty games, won Cy Young
　　　award; Xavier Suarez sworn in as Miami's first Cuban-born mayor
2003—Alabama chief justice Roy Moore relieved of duty after ignoring federal court
　　　order to remove Ten Commandments monument from state courthouse

BORN TODAY

Physicist James Clerk Maxwell . . . 1831 　Actress Sheila Frazier 1948
Writer Robert Louis Stevenson. . . 1850 　Actress Whoopi Goldberg 1949
Author Nathaniel Benchley . . . . . 1915 　Football player Vinny Testaverde . 1963
Producer Garry Marshall . . . . 1934 　Actress Rachel Bilson 1981

LIBERTY OR DEATH

Two baby eagles, abandoned in infancy, were taken in by a gentleman who raised
them with great care. One day, when they had fully grown, the door to their cage
was accidentally left open, and they escaped. Unaware of the dangers outside its
cage, the first eagle roosted in the low branches of a tree, where it was shot and
killed by a passing hunter. The other eagle, never able to strengthen its wings in
the cage or learn to fly well, fell into a river and drowned.

Eagles were created to soar on high mountain peaks, not languish in the
confines of a cage—no matter how loving the care. For the eagles, the cage was
not a place of safety but the ultimate cause of their deaths, for they never learned
what they needed to know to fly free.

Patrick Henry knew the importance of freedom. His famous speech that spurred
reluctant legislators to take military action to fight for America's independence
concluded with these words: "Is life so dear, or peace so sweet, as to be purchased
at the price of chains and slavery? Forbid it, Almighty God! I know not what
course others may take; but as for me, give me liberty or give me death!"

The apostle Paul would have agreed. He said, "It is for freedom that Christ
has set us free. Stand firm, then, and do not let yourselves be burdened again by a
yoke of slavery" (Galatians 5:1).

Do you value your freedoms? Stay alert to those things that threaten to
enslave—whether spiritually, physically, or politically—and resist them.

TODAY'S POWER POINT

They who give up essential liberty to obtain a little temporary safety deserve
neither liberty nor safety.—Benjamin Franklin

TODAY IN HISTORY

1666—First recorded blood transfusion

1832—First streetcar ran (in New York City)

1906—President Theodore Roosevelt first president to leave United States while in office (to visit Panama Canal zone)

1910—First flight launched from deck of a ship

1935—Franklin D. Roosevelt granted freedom to Philippines

1942—Captain Eddie Rickenbacker and seven others rescued following Pacific air crash

1969—Richard Nixon first U.S. president to attend manned space launch

1972—Dow Jones average topped one thousand for first time

1982—Solidarity leader Lech Walesa freed after nearly a year in Polish jail

2002—Nancy Pelosi became first woman House minority leader; White House approved independent board to investigate 9/11 attacks

BORN TODAY

Inventor Robert Fulton 1765
Artist Claude Monet 1840
Composer Aaron Copland 1900
Actor Dick Powell 1904
Actress Barbara Hutton 1912
Actor Brian Keith. 1921
Actor McLean Stevenson 1929
Britain's Prince Charles. 1948
Stateswoman Condoleezza Rice . . 1954
Baseball player Kurt Schilling. . . . 1966

THE BLESSING OF BELONGING

All of us need someone to belong to, but not all of us can claim that privilege naturally. This dramatic story underscores that point: A businessman commuted to his workplace each day by ferry. To help pass the time, he often patronized a smiling shoeshiner who enthusiastically polished the man's shoes. Eventually, whenever the man boarded the ferry, the boy would come up to him and begin brushing off his clothing and would help carry his belongings, never expecting a reward. Puzzled by such personal attention, the man finally asked the youth why he was so attentive. The boy explained, "Sir, when I first met you, you called me, 'my boy.' Until then I felt I belonged to no one, because both my parents are dead. But since you've been so kind and loving, there's nothing I wouldn't do for you."

Touched by the young man's story, the wealthy businessman took steps to see that the boy was well cared for. This brings to mind 2 Corinthians 6:18, where we read, "I will be a Father to you, and you will be my sons and daughters, says the Lord Almighty." Do you feel lonely or that no one cares about you? God does. He's waiting with open arms for you today.

TODAY'S POWER POINT

I'm safe in the arms of Jesus.—Fanny Crosby

November 15

TODAY IN HISTORY

1791—Opening of Georgetown, first Catholic college in the United States

1896—Hydroelectric power from Niagara Falls first used to light a city (Buffalo, New York)

1926—First network, NBC, went on the air (over twenty-four radio stations)

1937—Senate and House convened in newly air-conditioned chambers

1940—First peacetime draft called up seventy-five thousand men

1974—First self-adhesive postage stamp issued

1990—Pop music group Milli Vanilli admitted it did not do the singing on its album

1996—Texaco agreed to $176 million settlement of race-discrimination suit

1999—China and United States reached historic trade agreement

2001—U.S. Congress agreed on measure requiring hiring of twenty-eight thousand employees to screen airport passengers and baggage

2005—Major League Baseball adopted "three strike" rule, banning for life players who failed third steroid drug test

BORN TODAY

Artist Georgia O'Keefe 1887
Judge Joseph Wapner 1919
Singer C. W. McCall 1928
Actor Ed Asner 1929
Singer Petula Clark 1932
Actor Sam Waterston 1940
Singer Janet Lennon 1946
Actress Beverly D'Angelo 1954
Bandleader Kevin Eubanks 1957
Actor Johnny Lee Miller 1972

HOPING IN GOD

Many years ago a submarine was rammed by another ship and quickly sank off the coast of Massachusetts. Although rescue was impossible at that depth, a diver was dispatched to determine if there was still life aboard the disabled vessel. The diver placed his helmeted ear against the sub's hull and heard a faint tapping sound. Carefully he made note of the dots and dashes and decoded the following question: "Is . . . there . . . any . . . hope?" With great remorse he slowly signaled back: "Hope . . . in . . . God . . . alone."

People need hope. But hope is vain unless we place it in something worthy of that hope. Is your situation bleak? Have you exhausted all options, all possible sources of help but still find yourself facing something too big, too terrible for any relief? Hope remains. God is powerful, and he is kind. Take comfort—and draw hope—from the psalmist's repeated refrain: "Why are you downcast, O my soul? Why so disturbed within me? Put your hope in God, for I will yet praise him, my Savior and my God" (Psalm 42:5, 11; 43:5–6).

TODAY'S POWER POINT

The word which God has written on the brow of every man is *hope.*—Victor Hugo

November 16

TODAY IN HISTORY

1801—First publication of *New York Evening Post*
1841—First cork life preserver patented
1901—Automobile first exceeded 60 mph
1907—Forty-sixth state, Oklahoma, added to Union
1955—Motorboat first exceeded 216 mph
1959—Broadway premiere of *The Sound of Music*
1961—Metropolitan Museum of Art bought Rembrandt painting for then-record
    price of $2.3 million
1993—Senate approved measure to protect people who seek or provide abortions

BORN TODAY

Composer W. C. Handy 1873
Composer Paul Hindemuth 1895
Actor Burgess Meredith 1907
Voice actor Daws Butler 1916
Actress Marg Helgenberger 1958
Baseball player Dwight Gooden . . 1964
Actress Lisa Bonet 1967
Olympic skater Oksana Baiul 1977

TO RESCUE THE PERISHING

A group of college students in Chicago banded together to form an amateur rescue team to help save drowning victims from Lake Michigan. Early one November day the group was called to rescue the crew of a shipwrecked vessel not far from shore. In the face of numbing cold and crashing waves, one student, Ed Spencer, showed unusual bravery. Swimming to the wrecked ship time and again, Spencer rescued ten people before stopping to warm his nearly frozen body by the fire.

But as he stood there, he saw more men, women, and children desperately waiting to be rescued. Ignoring the pleas of those on shore who warned him that he wouldn't survive going in again, Spencer plunged into the frigid water again and managed to rescue six more victims. Returning safely to shore with the last remaining passenger, Spencer finally stopped to rest. Yet his thoughts were not of himself but of those he hadn't been able to rescue on that frigid November day. This amateur rescuer was a full-fledged hero to those he saved that night.

The Bible instructs us to conduct ourselves pretty much as Ed Spencer did: preparing ourselves for the task, then rescuing others when the opportunity arises. "Keep yourselves in God's love as you wait for the mercy of our Lord Jesus Christ to bring you to eternal life. Be merciful to those who doubt; snatch others from the fire and save them" (Jude 1:21–23). Ask God to give you opportunities to share the eternal hope of the gospel with others today.

TODAY'S POWER POINT

God is not saving the world; it is done. Our business is to get men and women to realize it.—Oswald Chambers

November 17

TODAY IN HISTORY

1797—First clock patented
1800—First Washington DC session of Congress
1869—Suez Canal opened
1919—First bank reached $1 billion in deposits, New York's National City Bank
1949—First large-scale U.S. Air Force (C-74) transport carried one hundred
passengers across Atlantic (in twenty-three hours of flying time)
1969—United States and Soviet Union discussed strategic weapon restrictions
1993—House passed North American Free Trade Agreement (NAFTA)
1997—Egyptian militants killed sixty-two people at Luxor
2003—Arnold Schwarzenegger sworn in as California's governor

BORN TODAY

Mathematician August Mobius .. 1790
Olympic runner Bob Mathias. . . . 1930
Singer Gordon Lightfoot 1938
Director Martin Scorsese 1942
Actress Lauren Hutton; TV host Daisy
Fuentes; actor Danny Devito . 1944
Basketball player Elvin Hayes. . . . 1945
Actor Justin Cooper 1988

MENDING THE FENCE

It was bedtime, and a father was telling his young son the story of the lost sheep. The boy was spellbound as the father explained how the little lamb had slipped through a hole in the fence and drifted far from home. The kindly shepherd went searching for his wandering sheep and rescued it just as a hungry wolf was preparing to attack. As the story ended, the boy was transfixed at the dramatic rescue from the jaws of death. After a moment he asked, "Dad, did they fix the hole in the fence?"

In his childhood innocence, the boy had made a valid point: in a home where children are loved, there needs to be a spiritual "fence" to keep the little "lambs" from wandering from the fold and to keep out any intruders who would capture their hearts and try to steal their souls. If you have young children, ask yourself, "How strong is our fence?" Are you, as a family, reinforcing the spiritual barriers around your youngsters through daily Bible reading and prayer as a family? Have you provided wholesome activity for your youngsters, or is there a gap in your fence? Want to keep your family spiritually safe? Be sure to mend the fence.

TODAY'S POWER POINT

Character may be manifested in the great moments, but it is made in the small ones.—Phillip Brooks

November 18

TODAY IN HISTORY

1820—Antarctica discovered
1874—Woman's Christian Temperance Union (WCTU) founded
1894—First Sunday comic section published
1928—Mickey Mouse first appeared (in cartoon *Steamboat Willie*)
1949—Jackie Robinson became first African American named baseball's MVP
1963—First push-button telephone introduced
1972—First navy ship with female sailors assigned, USS *Sanctuary*
2003—Massachusetts Supreme Court cleared the way for same-sex marriages

BORN TODAY

Inventor Louis Daguerre 1789
Songwriter William Gilbert 1836
Analyst George Gallup 1901
Comedienne Imogene Coca 1908
Astronaut Alan Shepard 1923
Actress Linda Evans 1942
Actress Susan Sullivan. 1944
Baseball player Gary Sheffield. . . . 1968

ON BEING FARSIGHTED

Remember your last eye exam, looking at the eye chart on the wall and attempting to identify the smallest letters? Many of us, without corrective lenses, cannot drive, play team sports, or even read a computer screen.

In today's Scripture passage we read of ordinary people who were farsighted in a different way. They acted in faith, believing God to carry out his promises in his own good time—even if that meant they never got to see it.

Noah demonstrated his farsighted faith by bulding a huge ark on dry ground in front of a mocking crowd that had never even seen rain. Yet, in his time, God fulfilled his promise to bring a flood and save only those inside the ark.

Abraham, the man God had called "the father of nations," was ninety-nine years old before his wife conceived and later bore a son, Isaac, from whom the ancient nation of Israel would spring.

Remember Joshua, who believed God's pledge to take his people to the Promised Land? Yet forty years passed before they took possession of the land God had promised them.

Like them, we also need to persevere so that despite all appearances, when we have done God's will the best we know how, we will receive what he has promised (see Hebrews 10:36). All of these heroes believed God would keep his promise, and he did. They were spiritually farsighted. How well would you pass God's vision test?

TODAY'S POWER POINT

Faith is to believe what we do not see; and the reward of this faith is to see what we believe.—Source Unknown

November 19

TODAY IN HISTORY

1620—The *Mayflower* landed off coast of Massachusetts
1850—System for projecting "magic lantern" slides patented
1863—Lincoln delivered Gettysburg Address
1872—Printing adding machine patented
1954—First automatic road-toll collector installed on New Jersey's Garden State Parkway
2001—United States offered $25 million for capture of Osama bin Laden
2003—Human and technical errors at an Ohio electric utility blamed for nation's largest blackout

BORN TODAY

President James Garfield. 1831
Evangelist Billy Sunday 1862
Talk-show host Larry King. 1933
TV executive Ted Turner 1938
Designer Calvin Klein 1942
Actress Glynnis O'Connor 1956
Actress Meg Ryan. 1961
Actress Jodie Foster. 1962
Olympic gymnast Kerri Strug. . . . 1977
McCaughey septuplets 1997

SEEING CHRIST

The German sculptor Dannaker toiled for several years to carve a likeness of Christ in stone. He wanted to ensure that it closely resembled the Savior, so he summoned a young child to his studio for a neutral observer's opinion of who was depicted in the sculpture. "A great man," was her reply. Dannaker was crushed.

Sensing his failure, he returned to his studio and worked six more years. Again he invited a little girl to his studio and, pointing to the statue, questioned, "Who is that?" Suddenly the youngster began to sniffle and said, "Suffer the little children to come unto me." His goal was achieved—he had fashioned a likeness of Christ so real that even a small child could visualize the Savior carved in the stone. Then he disclosed that in his hours of deepest discouragement, he had personally turned to Christ as Savior. In so doing the sculptor was then able to carve into marble the vision of Christ he had already "seen."

It was necessary for the apostle Thomas to see Christ as well. After the Resurrection, the other disciples told him, "We have seen the Lord!" But Thomas vowed he wouldn't believe unless he saw Jesus for himself: "Unless I see the nail marks in his hands and put my finger where the nails were, and put my hand into his side, I will not believe it" (John 20:25). Jesus told Thomas, "Because you have seen me, you have believed; blessed are those who have not seen and yet have believed" (John 20:29). Through faith we, too, can know Christ without ever having "seen" him.

TODAY'S POWER POINT

The more you know about Christ, the less you will be satisfied with superficial views of him.—Charles Spurgeon

TODAY IN HISTORY

1866—First university for African Americans, Howard University, opened
1888—Time clock patented
1914—Passport photographs first required
1925—First nighttime photo taken from a plane
1978—*Wall Street Journal* became first newspaper to be relayed via satellite
1984—McDonald's sold fifty-billionth burger
1990—Saddam Hussein ordered 250,000 Iraqi troops into Kuwait
1993—Brady Bill signed, limiting firearms purchases
1998—Tobacco company settlement of $208 billion accepted by forty-six states

BORN TODAY

Poet Thomas Chatterton 1752
Astronomer Edwin Hubble 1889
Journalist Alistair Cooke. 1908
TV host Richard Dawson. 1932

Comedian Dick Smothers 1939
Guitarist Duane Allman. 1946
Actress Bo Derek 1956
Actress Ming-Na Wen 1967

PLANTING SEEDS

A Swiss physician spent the better part of his flight to Paris in deep conversation with a fellow traveler. The stranger had many doubts and questions concerning Christianity, and the doctor carefully answered each with wisdom from the Bible and his own experience with God. But the skeptic remained unconvinced.

When the physician disembarked in Paris, he may have felt that he had failed. But he had done his part. In God's game plan, evangelism is a team sport, not an individual event. As the apostle Paul explained it: "The Lord has assigned to each his task. I planted the seed, Apollos watered it, but God made it grow" (1 Corinthians 3:5–6).

Years later the physician received a letter from the former doubter, saying that he had become a Christian. Referring to the spirited discussion en route to Paris, the man said that by quoting Scripture, "You made me feel as if I was not fighting you, but God."

The physician had been faithful in planting the seed of God's Word. Others undoubtedly watered that seed, and God made it grow. Years later it produced the fruit of a changed life.

Just like the physician, we have an assigned task in God's harvest. "The man who plants and the man who waters have one purpose, and each will be rewarded according to his own labor. For we are God's fellow workers" (1 Corinthians 3:8–9). Do your best to faithfully plant or water—then leave the rest to God!

TODAY'S POWER POINT

I am not ashamed of the gospel, because it is the power of God for the salvation of everyone who believes.—Romans 1:16

November 21

TODAY IN HISTORY

1783—First manned, untethered balloon flight

1789—Twelfth state, North Carolina, ratified the U.S. Constitution

1918—Wartime Prohibition Act passed, banning sale of alcoholic beverages in United States

1921—First licensed educational radio station (WOI) began broadcasting

1922—*Laconia* first cruise ship to set sail around the world

1952—First U.S. postage stamp printed in two colors

1964—Verazanno-Narrows Bridge linked Brooklyn to Staten Island

1977—Egyptian president Anwar Sadat pledged "no more war" with Israel

1980—"Who Shot J. R.?" *Dallas* episode drew then-record 86.6 million viewers

1985—President Ronald Reagan and Soviet leader Mikhail Gorbachev held longest summit conference to date between Russian and American leaders

1999—China launched its first spacecraft

2002—NATO expanded to include Latvia, Lithuania, Estonia, Bulgaria, Romania, and Slovenia

2005—Ariel Sharon launched Kadima, more moderate political party in Israel

BORN TODAY

Author Voltaire. 1694
Surgeon William Beaumont 1785
Financier Hetty Green 1835
Baseball player Stan Musial. 1920
Actress Marlo Thomas 1938
Actress Goldie Hawn 1945
Actress Lorna Luft 1952
Quarterback Troy Aikman 1966
Baseball player Ken Griffey Jr. . . . 1969
Gymnast Tasha Schwikert 1984

FARAWAY AND FORGOTTEN

Perhaps one of the most reassuring passages of Scripture is Psalm 103:12, which reminds us that "as far as the east is from the west, so far has he removed our transgressions from us." How far is the east from the west? It's an inconceivable distance. Micah 7:19 describes it this way: "You will again have compassion on us; you will tread our sins underfoot and hurl all our iniquities into the depths of the sea."

When missionaries first visited the Eskimos, there was no word in their language for forgiveness. After considering a number of possibilities, a new word was coined—one with an unmistakable meaning. The new word means, "Not being able to think about it anymore." What an apt description of what God has done in our lives! Thank God for his gracious mercy: he forgives our sin and remembers it no more.

TODAY'S POWER POINT

God pardons like a mother, who kisses the offense into everlasting forgiveness.
—Henry Ward Beecher

TODAY IN HISTORY

1904—First direct-current electric motor patented

1906—SOS radio distress signal adopted

1924—First college football game played that drew one hundred thousand fans (California versus Stanford)

1927—Snowmobile patented

1963—President John F. Kennedy assassinated in Dallas

1965—Broadway premiere of *Man of La Mancha*

1977—Cigar and pipe smoking banned on all U.S. planes

1984—Mr. Rogers's sweater presented to Smithsonian museum

1996—O. J. Simpson testified he did not kill his ex-wife, Nicole Brown, and her friend Ron Goldman

1998—Dr. Jack Kevorkian administered lethal drugs in televised assisted suicide (later sentenced to ten years in prison for second-degree murder)

BORN TODAY

Author George Eliot. 1819

Aviator Wiley Post 1898

Songwriter Hoagie Carmichael. . . 1899

Comedian Rodney Dangerfield . . 1921

Actor Robert Vaughan 1932

Actress Jamie Lee Curtis. 1958

Tennis player Boris Becker 1967

Actress Scarlett Johansson. 1984

CREATION SPEAKS

God's concern for detail can be realized in the smallest things of life. The smallest of all known plants is the Coccolithophoridae—startlingly beautiful plankton with an elaborate outer armor made of a chalklike material. Invisible to the naked eye, under a microscope these plants are as beautiful as the mammoth California redwood on the opposite of end of the size scale.

What does the complexity of these tiny creatures and the care with which they were created tell us about God? "Ask the animals, and they will teach you, or the birds of the air, and they will tell you; or speak to the earth, and it will teach you, or let the fish of the sea inform you. Which of all these does not know that the hand of the Lord has done this? In his hand is the life of every creature and the breath of all mankind" (Job 12:7–10). The same God who created all the species of plants and animals on the earth, big and small, also created you in your unique complexity. It is he who sustains and gives you life. Praise God for the uniqueness and beauty of his creation and for his care in creating you.

TODAY'S POWER POINT

In the vast and the minute we see the unambiguous footsteps of the God who gives its luster to an insect's wing and wheels his throne upon the whirling worlds.
—William Cowper

November 23

TODAY IN HISTORY

1835—Mechanized horseshoe machine patented
1903—Enrico Caruso's New York debut at the Metropolitan Opera (in *Rigoletto*)
1936—First issue of *Life* magazine published
1948—Zoom lens patented
1969—First news conference televised from outer space (orbiting *Apollo 12* astronauts answered questions from reporter in Houston)
1971—Mainland ("Red") China seated on UN Security Council (replacing Nationalist China)
1973—Baby born to first U.S. representative to give birth while in office (Y. B. Burke)
1980—Earthquakes killed 4,800 people in southern Italy
1992—Death of singer Roy Acuff, age eighty-nine
1996—Hijacked Ethiopian jet crashed in Atlantic, killing 125 people
2001—Militant Hamas leader Mahmoud Abu Hunud killed in Jerusalem

BORN TODAY

President Franklin Pierce 1804
Actor Boris Karloff 1887
Comedian Harpo Marx 1888
Composer Jerry Bock 1928
Basketball player Oscar Robertson . 1938
Actress Susan Anspach 1945
Pianist Bruce Hornsby 1954
Comedian Steve Harvey 1956
Basketball player Vin Baker 1971
Actor Austin Majors 1995

ALWAYS GIVING THANKS

This is the time of year when the thoughts of many traditionally turn to giving thanks. Although 1621 is often considered the first Thanksgiving feast, the traditional November celebration began in 1863 when president Abraham Lincoln declared the last Thursday of each November as "a day of Thanksgiving and Praise to our beneficent Father."

But beyond the good food and fellowship of the Thanksgiving holiday, let us remember to give thanks daily to our heavenly Father, the God who single-handedly set our world in motion and who sustains it by his power. One needn't look far to see God's creation, for all the world reflects his handiwork. That alone should be reason enough for us to give thanks to the One who gives us the very air we breathe and who grants eternal life through faith in Christ. For what are you thankful today?

TODAY'S POWER POINT

Let us remember that, as much has been given us, much will be expected from us, and that true homage comes from the heart as well as from the lips, and shows itself in deeds.—Theodore Roosevelt

TODAY IN HISTORY

1871—National Rifle Association incorporated

1903—Automobile electric starter patented

1954—Lockheed VC-121 christened *Air Force One*, first such U.S. presidential plane

1963—In first (inadvertently) televised murder, Lee Harvey Oswald (accused assassin of President Kennedy) shot and killed on live TV

1971—Hijacker and extortionist D. B. Cooper parachuted from jetliner with $200,000 in marked bills and disappeared

1974—President Gerald Ford and Soviet leader Leonid Brezhnev reached tentative agreement to limit strategic nuclear arms

1981—Premiere of television's *Simon & Simon*

1992—U.S. troops left Philippines (after nearly one-hundred-year presence)

1995—Voters in Ireland overturned ban on divorce

2003—Convicted DC sniper John Allen Muhammad sentenced to death

BORN TODAY

President Zachary Taylor 1784

Painter Henri de Toulouse-Lautrec . 1864

Composer Scott Joplin 1868

Author Dale Carnegie 1888

Author William F. Buckley Jr. . . . 1925

Baseball player Steve Yeager 1948

GLORY TO GOD

Whether it's a football receiver praying in the end zone after catching the scoring pass or entertainers or government leaders openly espousing their faith in God, it's refreshing to see people who recognize that they owe their success to God.

The psalmist warned about the dangers of pride and failing to recognize that position and success come from God and not our own cleverness or worthiness: "I warned the proud, 'Stop your boasting!' . . . For no one on earth . . . can raise another person up. It is God alone who judges; he decides who will rise and who will fall" (Psalm 75:4–7 NLT).

General George Washington recognized how much he needed to rely upon God's help if he—and the American cause—were to succeed. Some time ago the *Sunday School Times* told of a farmer who observed Washington on his knees in prayer at Valley Forge and told his wife, "The Americans will gain their independence."

"Oh, what makes you so sure?" she asked.

"I heard him praying out in the woods today, and the Lord will surely hear his prayer—you may rest assured he will." And, of course, God did.

When success comes your way, recognize God's role and humbly give credit and glory to him.

TODAY'S POWER POINT

To God be the glory, great things he hath done!—Fanny Crosby

November 25

TODAY IN HISTORY

1715—First British patent assigned to an American (for machine to process corn)

1780—British warship carrying a fortune in gold sank in New York Harbor

1867—Dynamite invented (by Alfred Nobel)

1920—First play-by-play college football radio broadcast (College Station, Texas)

1960—First atomic reactor for research began operation

1969—United States banned use of bacteriological weapons by its forces in warfare

1973—President Richard Nixon imposed a 55-mph driving-speed limit to cut energy consumption

1986—President Ronald Reagan revealed secret arms deal involving Iran and Nicaraguan anti-Communist guerillas, the Contras

1992—Czechoslovakia's parliament approved division into two nations

2001—Hundreds of U.S. Marines established base in Afghanistan followed by air attacks on Taliban forces

2003—Senate approved $400 billion Medicare bill including prescription-drug coverage, sending it to the president for signing

BORN TODAY

Industrialist Andrew Carnegie . . . 1835
Baseball player Joe DiMaggio 1914
Actor Ricardo Montalban. 1920
Actress Kathryn Crosby 1933
Football coach Joe Gibbs 1940

Actor John Larroquette. 1947
Baseball player Bucky Dent 1951
Singer Amy Grant 1960
Football player Bernie Kosar. 1963
Actress Christina Applegate 1971

EXPLORING THE POSSIBILITIES

In Acts 12:1–16 a lot of people had a hard time believing something that seemed too good to be true—even when it was something they had been praying for. Peter was in prison, bound with chains to two soldiers, with two more soldiers guarding the entrance to his cell. But an angel appeared and released Peter from prison.

At the home where the believers were praying for Peter, the servant girl, Rhoda, believed it was Peter but was so overjoyed she ran to tell the others—leaving Peter standing outside. No one inside believed that Peter could be outside, but Peter kept knocking until they came to see for themselves.

How long does it take to go to the door and see who's knocking? How many good things do we miss out on because we never take the trouble to open the door to a new opportunity? God doesn't call us to be gullible, but it's always a good idea to be alert to possibilities and the unusual ways they often come to us.

TODAY'S POWER POINT

All I have seen teaches me to trust the Creator for all I have not seen.—Ralph Waldo Emerson

November 26

TODAY IN HISTORY

1716—First lion exhibited in America (in Boston, Massachusetts)

1825—First fraternity, Kappa Alpha, established (at Union College, Schenectady, New York)

1867—Refrigerated railroad car patented

1950—China entered Korean War

1966—First major tidal power plant opened in France

1973—President Richard Nixon's secretary claimed to have caused eighteen-minute erasure on key White House tape

1977—Philippine politician Benigno Aquino sentenced to death on murder and other charges, claimed charges stemmed from his opposition to president Ferdinand Marcos

1990—Russia told Iraq to leave Kuwait; MCA sold to Matsushita for $6.6 billion

2002—New law required companies to insure buildings against losses from foreign attackers up to $10 billion; UN reported female AIDS cases equaled male cases worldwide for the first time

BORN TODAY

Scholar John Harvard 1607
Poet William Cowper 1731
Physician Mary Walker 1832
TV commentator Eric Sevareid . . 1912
Cartoonist Charles Schulz 1922
Singer Robert Goulet 1933
Singer Tina Turner;
    impressionist Rich Little 1938
Actress Olivia Cole 1942
Snowboarder Shannon Dunn 1972

FURTHERING THE PEACE

Peace has been the longtime goal of mankind. Perhaps the best-known international award is the annual Nobel Peace Prize, yet few know the story behind its creation. At age thirty-four Alfred Nobel patented dynamite, and over the next three decades he became extremely wealthy from the manufacture of explosives. Noting how his invention was increasingly being used for making weapons of war, Nobel determined to be remembered for more than his invention. So, in his will, he established a trust to establish annual awards for noteworthy accomplishments in the pursuit of peace. Today, after more than one hundred years, the annual awards continue as a memorial to his name. In fact, Nobel is rarely known outside scientific circles for creating dynamite. He is predominately known as the founder of these renowned awards for furthering peace.

As a child of God, do your best to be remembered for living in peace with those around you.

TODAY'S POWER POINT

It is far easier to make war than to make peace.—Georges Clemenceau

November 27

TODAY IN HISTORY

1912—Post Office issued first stamps in a series (one-cent stamps)

1951—Nike missile first rocket to strike an airplane (over New Mexico)

1960—Gordie Howe became first hockey player to exceed one thousand points

1966—First NFL game with sixteen touchdowns scored (Redskins versus Giants)

1980—Study showed that monkeys use basic language skills

1983—Tens of thousands of Filipinos celebrated birthday of Benigno Aquino

2001—United Nations backed broad-based new government for Afghanistan

2002—UN inspectors launched initial weapons search in Iraq; Germany promised weapons support for Israel's defense

2003—President George W. Bush made surprise Thanksgiving visit to U.S. troops in Iraq, first visit to Iraq by any U.S. president

BORN TODAY

Scientist Anders Celsius 1701
Historian Charles Beard 1874
Producer David Merrick. 1912
Entertainer "Buffalo" Bob Smith . 1917
Author Gail Sheehy 1937

Actor Bruce Lee 1940
Guitarist Jimi Hendrix 1942
Basketball player Nick Van Exel . . 1971
Actor Jaleel White 1976
Basketball player Jimmy Rollins . . 1978

RICHES

The Upper Room told of a pioneering preacher who had temporarily deserted the pulpit to join prospectors in panning for gold. Before long he realized how much time his prospecting was taking and decided to reexamine what was really important. He saw that he had let his desire for short-term monetary gain get in the way of his everlasting spiritual rewards. So after some thoughtful reflection, he slowly opened the handkerchief that held the precious gold particles he had so painstakingly recovered and shook the contents out into the wind.

Be sure that the love of money has not overtaken you. The Bible warns us: "People who want to get rich fall into temptation and a trap and into many foolish and harmful desires that plunge men into ruin and destruction. For the love of money is a root of all kinds of evil. Some people, eager for money, have wandered from the faith and pierced themselves with many griefs. But you, man of God, flee from all this, and pursue righteousness, godliness, faith, love, endurance and gentleness" (1 Timothy 6:9–11).

What will you pursue, wealth or godliness?

TODAY'S POWER POINT

Money has never yet made anyone rich.—Lucius Annaeus Seneca

TODAY IN HISTORY

1520—Magellan launched exploration of the Pacific
1821—Panama gained independence from Spain
1922—First skywriting demonstrated
1942—Boston nightclub fire killed nearly five hundred people
1963—Beatles' "I Want to Hold Your Hand" became first song to sell more than
      one million copies before its release
1967—John Shalikashvili first draftee promoted to army general
1977—Rhodesia announced willingness to give black majority full voting rights
1981—Alabama's Bear Bryant won 315th game to become college football's
      winningest coach
2005—Saddam Hussein's trial resumed after nearly six-week recess

BORN TODAY

Author John Bunyan 1628
Poet William Blake. 1757
Critic Brooks Atkinson. 1894
Motown founder Barry Gordy Jr. . 1929
Actress Hope Lange 1933

Singer Randy Newman. 1943
Bandleader Paul Shaffer 1949
Actor Judd Nelson 1959
Comedian Jon Stewart 1962
Baseball player Matt Williams . . . 1965

GROWING DANGER

How easy it is for a "small" sin to grow rapidly into a great evil that soon consumes your life. E. Gorham Clark told of a circus trainer who had worked long and hard with a twenty-five-foot boa constrictor. He had bought it when it was only a few days old and had handled it daily for more than twenty years. It seemed perfectly harmless and under his control.

The trainer worked with many animals in his act, but he always reserved the boa constrictor for the grand finale. This time the trainer, dressed as a hunter, was making his way through a wooded setting when he was confronted by the mammoth reptile. He gave the cue, and the snake began to coil around his master. Higher and higher it coiled around the man, as it had done countless times before. But suddenly the serpent reverted to its deadly nature. It clutched its master in an ever-tightening grip, crushing bones until the trainer's life was squeezed from him.

What a picture of the deadly power of sin. At first we think we can control it and use it for our own benefit. But eventually, unexpectedly, the trap is sprung and we are caught in its deadly grip, powerless to free ourselves. Never underestimate the destructive power of sin. Never overestimate your own power to control it and avoid its deadly consequences. "Sin, when it is full-grown, gives birth to death" (James 1:15). The only safe plan is to avoid all sin, no matter how small it may seem.

TODAY'S POWER POINT

Evil enters like a needle and spreads like an oak tree.—Ethiopian Proverb

November 29

TODAY IN HISTORY

1775—Foreign Service Committee (first diplomatic service in what would become the United States) authorized by Continental Congress

1877—Thomas A. Edison demonstrated first wind-up phonograph

1890—First Army-Navy football game

1929—Richard Byrd made pioneering flight over South Pole

1944—First open-heart surgery performed

1951—First underground atomic-explosion test (at Frenchman Flat, Nevada)

1961—Chimpanzee "Enos" first animal launched into earth orbit

1963—Warren Commission established to investigate assassination of President John F. Kennedy

1978—More than nine hundred bodies recovered from mass suicide in Jonestown, Guyana (followers of cult leader Jim Jones)

1985—Earliest known appearance of "crack" cocaine on New York City streets

1987—Riots in Haiti postponed first democratic transfer of power in thirty years

1991—Dust storm triggered one-hundred-vehicle pileup in San Joaquin Valley, near San Francisco, leaving seventeen dead, 151 injured

2001—Death of Beatles lead guitarist George Harrison, age fifty-eight

BORN TODAY

1st U.S. secretary Charles Thomson . . 1729
Author Louisa May Alcott 1832
Author C. S. Lewis. 1898
Sportscaster Vin Scully 1927
Actress Diane Ladd. 1932

Musician Chuck Mangione 1940
Comedian Gary Shandling. 1949
Actor Howie Mandel 1955
Actress Kim Delaney 1961
Baseball player Mariano Rivera. . . 1969

KEEPING YOUR FOCUS ON GOD

Ever notice how easy it is to get sidetracked when reading the Bible or praying? It suddenly seems as if every distraction imaginable pops into your mind once you open God's Word. If you've had this experience, you are not alone. Your enemy, who does not want you to concentrate on God (or on anything wholesome), will constantly attempt to distract you with highly appealing diversions from your spiritual purpose or with spiritual "shortcuts."

The Bible says, "There is a way that seems right to a man, but in the end it leads to death" (Proverbs 14:12). With so many voices in the world today, all claiming to be "right," which one(s) are you following? Don't allow yourself to be distracted or lose your focus. Daily consult God's map for your life through regular Bible reading and prayer.

TODAY'S POWER POINT

Satan trembles when he sees the weakest saint upon his knees.—William Cowper

November 30

TODAY IN HISTORY

1782—Treaty with Britain granted U.S. independence

1887—First indoor softball game

1939—Dwight Eisenhower issued airplane-pilot's license (later first licensed pilot to become U.S. president)

1954—Elizabeth Hodges first human known to have been struck by a meteor (crashed through roof of her home at Sylacauga, Alabama—she survived with no permanent injuries)

1988—Soviets stopped jamming U.S. station Radio Liberty's beaming programs into Russia (first time in thirty-eight years)

2001—Deadly anthrax discovered on mail delivered less than a mile away from earlier victim in Oxford, Connecticut (source still unknown)

BORN TODAY

Writer Jonathan Swift	1667	Entertainer Dick Clark	1929
Writer Mark Twain	1835	Radio host G. Gordon Liddy	1930
British PM Winston Churchill	1874	Singer Billy Idol	1955
Actor Efrem Zimbalist Jr.	1923	Actor Ben Stiller	1965
Actor Robert Guillaume	1927	Actress Elisha Cuthbert	1982

FORWARD

To succeed in life we must persistently strive to reach our goals. C. E. McCartney explained the importance of continuing to move forward when it comes to airplanes. He said that all others vehicles—trains, buses, cars, boats, bicycles—can stop or reverse their direction with no serious consequence. But because airplane engines have no "reverse," they cannot back up. The plane must keep moving forward in flight at all times. If the plane should lose momentum and forward thrust, it would quickly crash.

In the same way, our lives as Christians should be like the airplane's flight—constantly moving forward toward the goal. What is our goal? The apostle Paul articulated it: "I want to know Christ and the power of his resurrection" (Philippians 3:10). Distractions, dead-ends, and detours, no matter how compelling, must be ignored if we are to reach our goals. To stall is to crash and be destroyed. Keep your attention fixed on God, and make Paul's resolution in Philippians 3:13–14 your own: "Forgetting what is behind and straining toward what is ahead, I press on toward the goal to win the prize for which God has called me heavenward in Christ Jesus."

TODAY'S POWER POINT

The difference between the impossible and the possible lies in a person's determination.—Tommy Lasorda

TODAY IN HISTORY

1891—Game of basketball invented
1921—First blimp filled with helium gas
1929—Game of bingo created
1955—Civil-rights activist Rosa Parks arrested for not giving up seat on bus in Montgomery, Alabama
1959—First color photo of earth taken from space
1988—Pakistan chose Benazir Bhutto to be first Islamic woman prime minister
2004—Tom Brokaw's last broadcast: retired as NBC *Nightly News* anchor

BORN TODAY

Writer Rex Stout 1886
Baseball manager Walter Alston . . 1911
Actress Mary Martin. 1914
Singer Lou Rawls 1936
Golfer Lee Trevino 1939
Singer and actress Bette Midler. . . 1945
Actor Treat Williams. 1952
Actress Julie Condra. 1970

STANDING YOUR GROUND

The crucial battle of Dunkirk marked a turning point in history. Forty-seven British ships had been sunk in the sea off Norway, and the Royal Air Force was diminished by 40 percent. This was Britain's darkest hour: it seemed inevitable that she would be conquered by invading Nazi forces. Yet despite the gloomy outlook, Winston Churchill challenged his countrymen not to give up but to resist the enemy: "We shall not flag or fail. We shall go on to the end. . . . We shall defend our Island, whatever the cost may be; we shall fight on the beaches, we shall fight on the landing grounds, we shall fight in the fields and in the streets, we shall fight in the hills; we shall never surrender."

This should also be true in your Christian walk. The apostle Paul rallied Timothy to defend spiritual treasure: "Guard the good deposit that was entrusted to you—guard it with the help of the Holy Spirit who lives in us" (2 Timothy 1:14). In our own strength, this is difficult: our battles are not physical but spiritual. But like Paul, we can be confident of God's power to help and sustain us. We can boldly assert: "I know whom I have believed, and am convinced that he is able to guard what I have entrusted to him for that day" (2 Timothy 1:12). Don't fear the enemy, "for God did not give us a spirit of timidity, but a spirit of power, of love and of self-discipline" (2 Timothy 1:7). Stand up and fight for what God has given you.

TODAY'S POWER POINT

Life yields only to the conqueror. Never accept what can be gained by giving in. You will be living off stolen goods, and your muscles will atrophy.—Dag Hammarskjöld

December 2 Deuteronomy 4:1–14

TODAY IN HISTORY

1816—First savings bank opened (in Philadelphia)
1942—First self-sustaining nuclear reaction
1952—First telecast of human birth in United States
1954—Senate voted overwhelmingly to censure Senator Joseph McCarthy for reckless (and largely unsubstantiated) charges of various government officials having Communist ties
1982—Patient fitted with first permanent artificial heart
1999—Beginning of self-rule in Northern Ireland
2001—Record-setting bankruptcy declared by Enron, one of world's largest energy firms
2005—TSA lifted ban on scissors aboard aircraft; Pentagon acknowledged it paid for news coverage in Iraqi press

BORN TODAY

Painter Georges Seurat 1859
Composer Adolph Green 1914
Singer Maria Callas 1923
Actress Julie Harris 1925
Actress Cathy Lee Crosby 1948
Broadcast journalist Stone Phillips 1954
Actor Dennis Christopher 1955
Figure skater Randy Gardner 1958
Actress Lucy Liu 1967
Tennis player Monica Seles 1973
Singer Britney Spears 1981

BOTTLING A PICKLE

A little boy was at his grandmother's house, captivated by a huge pickle in a soda bottle. While it was preserved in vinegar, all who saw it prominently displayed on the mantle wondered how such a huge pickle could have ever been put into such a small-necked container. On every visit the boy would ponder this. Finally the grandmother could keep the secret no longer. She explained that while the pickle was still a thin cucumber on the vine, it was slipped easily through the narrow bottleneck and allowed to grow unhindered. Then, at harvest, when the pickle had reached full size, the vinegar was added, and it was preserved for all to see—a huge pickle inside a narrow necked bottle.

That pickle serves as a poignant example of how to raise a godly child. While they are still youngsters, surround them with regular prayer and biblical instruction. Get them safely "in the bottle" of God's loving arms when they're small, and they'll be less likely to step outside those encircling arms when they're older.

TODAY'S POWER POINT

Big trees from little acorns grow.—Source Unknown

December 3

TODAY IN HISTORY

1818—Twenty-first state, Illinois, added to the Union
1833—Oberlin College first to enroll male and female students on equal basis
1922—First movie shown in Technicolor
1933—Earliest radio broadcast of U.S. Congress
1947—Broadway premiere of *A Streetcar Named Desire*
1950—Paul Harvey began his long-running national radio broadcast
1952—First television broadcast in Hawaii
1967—Final run of 20th Century Limited, famous luxury train service between
    New York and Chicago
2003—Three Rwandan media leaders convicted of genocide in provoking attacks
    among warring tribes

BORN TODAY

Painter Gilbert Stuart	1755	Race-car driver Rick Mears	1951
Author Joseph Conrad	1857	Actress Daryl Hannah	1961
Singer Ferlin Husky	1927	Actress Holly Marie Combs	1973
Singer Andy Williams	1930	Actor Brian Bonsall	1981

LEARNING OBEDIENCE

Many times people are led into sin because they have neither anticipated the temptations they would encounter nor armed themselves accordingly. The story is told of a wealthy banker whose rebellious son left home to join the military. There the boy had the same problems obeying the officers' orders as he had obeying his father while at home. Exasperated, his commanding officer finally took him aside to remind him that while the service was not able to force him to do anything, they would certainly make him wish he had obeyed.

Obedience is a lesson best learned early. This is true of earthly authority as well as of God's ultimate authority. We can either follow God and obey his laws now, or later wish that we had. In Isaiah 45:22–23 God warned: "Turn to me and be saved, all you ends of the earth; for I am God, and there is no other. By myself I have sworn, my mouth has uttered in all integrity a word that will not be revoked: Before me every knee will bow." Obedience to God is mandatory. The only question is how and when you will bow to him: willingly as a loving child, or forced as a vanquished enemy at the end of time to acknowledge his lordship? Have you chosen to obey God today?

TODAY'S POWER POINT

No principal is so noble, and there is none more holy than that of true obedience.
—Henry Giles

December 4

TODAY IN HISTORY

1779—First law school opened at a U.S. college (College of William and Mary)
1867—National Grange founded
1877—Thomas A. Edison's phonograph demonstrated
1917—First transatlantic voyage by self-powered submarine began (from Newport, Rhode Island, to the Azores and back)
1977—Central African Empire (one of world's poorest nations) held $20 million coronation for new leader
1987—Cuban inmates ended eleven-day siege in Atlanta Federal Prison
1996—First electric car mass-produced in United States, GM's EVI
2002—Israel agreed to Palestinian state in areas of Gaza and West Bank once Yasser Arafat was no longer in power; United Airlines, said to be losing $8 million a day, turned down for government-loan guarantees

BORN TODAY

Writer Thomas Carlyle 1795
Actress Lillian Russell 1861
Nurse Edith Cavell 1865
Actress Deanna Durbin 1921
Actor Max Baer Jr. 1937
Singer Dennis Wilson. 1944
Actor Jeff Bridges 1949
Actress Patricia Wettig 1951
Singer Cassandra Wilson 1955
Supermodel Tyra Banks 1973

FAIR-WEATHER FANS

In 1908 Richard "Rube" Marquard, a highly touted southpaw, was signed to pitch for the New York Giants for the fantastic sum of $11,000. Fans were elated—at first. He tried hard in his first two seasons, but his performance just couldn't match the high expectations of fans and experts alike. He was soon called the "$11,000 lemon."

But Marquard was just getting warmed up. From 1911 through 1913 he led the Giants to three straight pennants. In 1912 he won his first nineteen consecutive games and later won two more pennants with other teams. It seems safe to say that after that year's performance, the team—and the fans—had no regrets for keeping him in the lineup through the lean years.

Are you going through some lean years? Wondering if you'll ever live up to the high expectations of others—or yourself? Don't despair. God is no fair-weather fan. He believes in you, is rooting for you, and will stick with you through the good times as well as the bad. His love for you is constant and unchanging. He sees your past. He knows your potential. And he sees the future that can be yours if you don't give up in discouragement. So keep on pitching. Tomorrow starts a new season.

TODAY'S POWER POINT

I have no regrets because I know I did my best—all I could do.—Midori Ito

December 5

TODAY IN HISTORY

1776—First college fraternity (Phi Beta Kappa) founded
1908—Numerals first used on U.S. football uniforms
1922—First commercial electric power line installed
1933—End of Prohibition
1951—Opening of first automated parking garage
1952—Premiere of television's *The Abbott and Costello Show*; beginning of a choking, four-day smog that smothered London, leaving more than four thousand dead
1955—American Federation of Labor and Congress of Industrial Organizations (AFL-CIO) created; start of bus-riding boycott in Montgomery, Alabama
1996—Madeleine Albright appointed first female secretary of state
2005—First witnesses in trial of Saddam Hussein told of unspeakable torture purportedly approved by the fallen Iraqi leader

BORN TODAY

President Martin Van Buren 1782
Producer Walt Disney 1901
Director Otto Preminger 1905
Singer Little Richard 1935
Singer José Carreras 1946
Football player Art Monk 1957
Comedienne Margaret Cho 1968
Actor Frankie Muniz 1985

GIVING LARGELY

A well-to-do farmer vowed to assist a poor family who had lost everything in a fire. He promised not only money but also a large ham from his smokehouse. On the way to get the ham, though, a little voice inside his head encouraged him to give the smallest ham he had. The man listened a moment, but then called upon God's strength to overcome the temptation. "If you don't keep still," he threatened the voice, "I'll give that poor man every ham in my smokehouse." No doubt the farmer recognized the spiritual benefit he'd receive simply by sharing his blessings.

Have you noticed that the more you give to God, the more he gives back to you? This might be called the believer's advantage. You can be certain that when we're generous, God will return multiplied material blessings as well. Jesus said, "You won't regret it. No one who has sacrificed home, spouse, brothers and sisters, parents, children—whatever—will lose out. It will all come back multiplied many times over in your lifetime. And then the bonus of eternal life!" (Luke 18:29–30 MSG).

Don't listen to that little voice inside telling you to give less. Give largely; give your best, knowing that this pleases God and benefits everyone.

TODAY'S POWER POINT

Giving to the Lord is but transporting our goods to a higher floor.—Source Unknown

TODAY IN HISTORY

1768—Encyclopædia Britannica first published

1849—Harriet Tubman escaped from slavery (and later became a famed abolitionist)

1902—First postage stamp issued portraying an American woman (Martha Washington)

1907—Underground blasts killed 350 West Virginia coal miners

1917—Finland's independence; munitions ship collision in Nova Scotia triggered blast that killed 1,600 and injured four thousand

1979—"Democracy Wall" torn down in Peking after being papered with anti-Communist slogans

2002—President George W. Bush removed treasury secretary Paul O'Neill over criticism of the recent income-tax cut

2004—Al Qaeda blamed for five deaths in attack on U.S. diplomatic post in Saudi Arabia

BORN TODAY

Poet Joyce Kilmer. 1886
Lyricist Ira Gershwin 1896
Photographer Alfred Eisenstaedt. . 1898
Pianist Dave Brubeck. 1920
Football player Otto Graham 1921

Actor James Naughton 1945
Actor Thomas Hulce 1953
Comedian Steven Wright 1955
Actress Janine Turner 1962
Singer Macy Gray. 1969

LOOKING UP

The young girl knew she was in big trouble. She had snatched her older sister's class ring away from her only to have it clatter to the floor and disappear—apparently for good—into the heating vent. Her sister stepped toward her, a look of anger and shock on her face. The younger girl instinctively sank to the floor, fearing the blows and seeking to make herself a smaller target. But from her new perspective near the floor, she caught a glint of gold in a fold of the bedsheet draped on the floor. It was the ring: it had bounced off the hardwood floor and lodged in the soft material near the vent. Things were starting to look up.

Sometimes we have to get to our very lowest point before we can start going up. When it seems life has dealt you a harsh blow, recognize your need to depend on God. Fall to your knees, look up to him, and ask him for strength to carry you through the temporary crisis. Don't curse the crisis or the low points in life. They're often prerequisites for the high points still to come.

TODAY'S POWER POINT

Press on. Obstacles are seldom the same size tomorrow as they are today.—Robert H. Schuller

December 7

TODAY IN HISTORY

1787—First state, Delaware, ratified U.S. Constitution
1842—First New York Philharmonic concert
1903—First radio distress signal sent from U.S. ship
1926—Gas refrigerator introduced
1941—Japanese attack on Pearl Harbor Naval Base, Hawaii
1944—First million-dollar day of sales recorded (Macy's)
1975—President Gerald Ford completed tour of China and South China Sea
1976—Kurt Waldheim nominated for second five-year term as head of UN
1978—Appeals court ordered U.S. military to accept homosexuals into military
1983—First execution by lethal injection
1988—Soviet leader Gorbachev told UN that Soviets would unilaterally reduce
     their armed forces by five hundred thousand troops
2004—IBM sold its Thinkpad personal computer division to Chinese firm
2005—Air marshals killed mentally ill airline passenger claiming to have a bomb

BORN TODAY

Museum creator Marie Tussaud . . 1761
Author Willa Cather. 1873
Actor Eli Wallach 1915
Actress Ellen Burstyn 1932
Singer Harry Chapin 1942

Baseball player Johnny Bench. . . . 1947
Basketball player Larry Bird 1956
TV announcer Edd Hall. 1958
Baseball player Tino Martinez . . . 1967
Singer Aaron Carter 1987

PRAISE THE LORD!

Despite life's hardships, we always need to praise the Lord. A poor elderly woman whose hard life had seen its share of troubles and sorrow still managed to praise the Lord loudly during sermons at her church. Eventually her pastor, who lost his train of thought each time she shouted out, "Praise the Lord!" In exasperation the pastor offered the woman several warm blankets (which she desperately needed) if she would simply refrain from shouting out during the service.

She got the blankets and did her best to earn them. She did well for several weeks until a guest speaker visited the church and began preaching on the forgiveness of sin. As the sermon went on, the woman found praise for God's goodness bubbling up within her in spite of her best efforts. At last she could hold back no longer and cried, "Blankets or no blankets, praise the Lord!"

Is God's blessing evident in your praise? Think of all the ways in which God has blessed you. Doesn't it make you want to rejoice and praise him?

TODAY'S POWER POINT

Let everything that has breath praise the LORD.—Psalm 150:6

December 8

TODAY IN HISTORY

1792—First cremation in United States
1941—U.S. declared war on Japan
1948—First "split screen" telecast
1949—Chiang Kai-shek moved China's Nationalist government to Formosa
1959—China travelogue first movie to use scent
1978—Death of Israel's first woman prime minister, Golda Meir, age eighty
1980—Singer John Lennon gunned down outside his New York City apartment
2001—Uzbekistan opened bridge to allow humanitarian aid to reach needy Afghans
2003—Medicare prescription drug coverage benefit approved by President George W. Bush
2004—UN figures showed worldwide continual hunger stood at 852 million, up eighteen million in four years

BORN TODAY

Inventor Eli Whitney 1765
Composer Jean Sibelius 1865
Author James Thurber 1894
Entertainer Sammy Davis Jr. 1925
Comedian Flip Wilson 1933
Musician James Galway 1939
Singer Greg Allman 1947
Actress Kim Basinger 1953
Actress Teri Hatcher 1964
Singer Sinead O'Connor 1966

GENEROSITY

A young boy was given two cookies and asked to share with his sister. "Remember to be generous," his mother cautioned him. Eyeing the larger cookie hungrily, he asked his mom if she wouldn't please give his sister the cookies so *she* could be generous. Many of us like generosity when it's someone else who's doing the giving. But as we mature, we should start to enjoy the flip side of generosity—being on the giving end.

A wealthy businessman, George Peabody, was once asked which he enjoyed more, making money or giving it away. He thought a moment and then responded, "I sincerely like making money, and when it was first suggested that I give it away, I resisted the idea. But after I saw the happiness and joy of those who lived in the new housing I built for the poor, I gave more, and the feeling increased. Today I can truly say that as much as I have enjoyed making money, I now enjoy giving it away a great deal better."

Have you learned the joy of giving? What do you have that you could give to someone whose need is greater than your own? When you give with a generous heart and open hand, you too will find the joy and blessing of giving. Try it today.

TODAY'S POWER POINT

Generosity is giving more than you can.—Kahlil Gibran

December 9

TODAY IN HISTORY

1621—First printed sermon

1907—Christmas Seals first sold as fund-raiser (by Delaware chapter of American Red Cross, with proceeds designated to fight tuberculosis)

1917—British assumed control of Jerusalem

1940—First contract signed to air commercials on FM radio

1958—John Birch Society established

1990—Polish presidential runoff won by labor leader Lech Walesa

1992—Britain's Prince Charles and Princess Diana filed formal separation papers

2002—Fifteen Scud missiles found aboard North Korean–manned ship in Gulf of Aden; United Airlines filed for bankruptcy

2003—U.S. limited contracts for rebuilding Iraq to Coalition members only

2004—Report from Congress indicated only about three-fourths of all factory-reinforced Humvees needed by troops had been delivered

BORN TODAY

Poet John Milton 1608

Writer Joel Chandler Harris 1848

Actor Kirk Douglas 1916

Comedian Redd Foxx 1922

Actor Dick Van Patten 1928

Actor Beau Bridges 1941

Actor John Malkovich 1953

Entertainer Donny Osmond 1957

KEEPING CHRIST IN CHRISTMAS

You've probably noticed that we're entering the busiest time of year. Everyone's busy getting the house ready for company, gifts bought and wrapped, children dressed for school pageants, cookies baked, decorations hung, cards written, . . . the list goes on and on. With all this busyness, it's especially important to not lose sight of the reason for the season: Christ's birth.

Many parents make it a point to read the Christmas story with their families during this time, as it makes clear to young and old alike the true message of Christmas. Some families may divide up the passages and memorize the story. Others might help children decorate the Christmas tree with symbols of the season. Whatever traditions are established in your home, be sure to plan in advance to make the spiritual meaning of Christ's birth the center of your holiday activities.

All too soon these weeks will pass by, and with them a golden opportunity to share your faith while God is on everyone's mind. Remember to rejoice and honor the Lord in all you do this holiday season.

TODAY'S POWER POINT

Christmas began in the heart of God. It is complete only when it reaches the heart of man.—Source Unknown

December 10

TODAY IN HISTORY

1672—First postal delivery between cities announced (between New York and
   Boston, a trip on horseback that took three weeks each way)
1817—Twentieth state, Mississippi, admitted to Union
1869—Wyoming women given right to vote
1898—End of Spanish-American War
1903—Nobel Prize first won by a woman (Marie Curie, for physics)
1904—New York City established motorcycle police
1927—First broadcast of the *Grand Ole Opry* (over WSM radio, Nashville)
1936—England's King Edward VIII abdicated throne to marry American divorcee
1963—Zanzibar regained independence from Great Britain (merged with
   Tanganyika into Tanzania April 26, 1964)
1975—Wife of Nobel Prize winner Andrei Sakharov (who was under house arrest in
   the USSR for his liberal views on human rights) accepted prize for him
1978—Egyptian president Anwar Sadat and Israel's Menachem Begin won joint
   Nobel Prize
1979—Mother Theresa named Nobel Prize winner
1983—Solidarity's Lech Walesa won Nobel Peace Prize
1986—Survivor of Nazi death camp, Elie Wiesel, won Nobel Prize
1989—First human-powered helicopter demonstrated
2003—Supreme Court ruled the Bipartisan Campaign Reform Act constitutional

BORN TODAY

Educator Thomas Gallaudet 1787
Poet Emily Dickinson 1830
Actress Dorothy Lamour 1914
Actor Harold Gould 1923
Evangelist John Ankerberg 1945
Actress Gloria Loring 1946
Actress Susan Dey 1952
Actress Raven Symone 1985

HOLDING YOUR TONGUE

A young man once went to Socrates in hopes that the wise man could teach him
how to speak. Noting the fellow's inclination to talk constantly, Socrates asked for
double his usual fees. Not surprisingly, the youth objected: "Why charge me two
fees?" Socrates replied, "Because I have to teach you two skills—how to hold your
tongue and how to speak. The first is more difficult, but if you are not skilled at
it, you will suffer greatly and create trouble without end."

Ever notice how easily your tongue can get you into trouble, sometimes even
before you realize what you've done? Holding the tongue is a difficult discipline
to master, but it's well worth the effort. Proverbs 10:19 warns, "When words are
many, sin is not absent, but he who holds his tongue is wise." How wise are you?

TODAY'S POWER POINT

Halfwits talk much but say little.—Benjamin Franklin

TODAY IN HISTORY

1816—Nineteenth state, Indiana, joined the Union
1844—Anesthetic first used by a dentist
1866—The *Henrietta*, the *Vesta*, and the *Fleetwing* began first yacht race across the Atlantic (205-ton *Henrietta* won)
1882—First U.S. theater with electric lights opened (in Boston)
1946—United Nations International Children's Emergency Fund (UNICEF) established
1980—Premiere of television's *Magnum, PI*
2001—AOL CEO Gerald Levin announced plans to retire from media giant
2003—Dow Jones stock average closed above ten thousand for first time in eighteen months

BORN TODAY

Composer Hector Berlioz. 1803
Politician Fiorello LaGuardia 1882
Producer Carlo Ponti 1913
Writer Aleksandr Solzhenitsyn . . . 1918
Actress Rita Moreno. 1931
Actress Donna Mills. 1942
Singer Brenda Lee 1944
Actress Teri Garr. 1949
Singer Jermaine Jackson 1954
Actor Rider Strong. 1979

SELF-SACRIFICING LOVE

Godly marriage, in which a man shows love for his wife, is a parallel of Christ's love for the church. One young college student was poor and had to forego much just to get by. Yet when his fiancée wanted candy that cost $1.50 per pound (in the days of the nickel candy bar), he made sure she got it. When they were apart, he wrote to her every day. The young man recalled, "No work was hard if she was pleased with it, and no road was too long if she were at the end of it. . . . I never thanked God for a blessing without pouring out to her my joys."

This is how God loves each of us—with an all-encompassing love—even those who don't love him in return. Believe it or not, this is the same kind of expansive love God requires us to show toward others. The Bible tells us, "Be imitators of God, therefore, as dearly loved children and live a life of love, just as Christ loved us and gave himself up for us as a fragrant offering and sacrifice to God" (Ephesians 5:1–2).

How do you show this kind of love to those around you? It's perhaps the most basic lesson children learn in Sunday school, but it's one of the most important: "Love each other as I [Jesus] have loved you" (John 15:12). Find a way to love sacrificially today.

TODAY'S POWER POINT

Young love is a flame; very pretty, often very hot and fierce, but still only light and flickering. The love of the older and disciplined heart is as coals, deep-burning, unquenchable.—Henry Ward Beecher

TODAY IN HISTORY

1787—Pennsylvania second state to ratify U.S. Constitution
1789—First English Catholic Bible introduced
1862—First warship to be sunk by a mine
1925—First U.S. motel opened (in San Luis Obispo, California)
1937—First mobile TV truck
1955—Ford Foundation gave half a billion dollars to U.S. colleges and hospitals
1977—Edward Koch sworn in as New York City's 105th mayor
1985—President Ronald Reagan signed Gramm-Rudman bill designed to force a balanced budget
2000—Supreme Court ruled in favor of George W. Bush in landmark decision, thus ending disputed presidential election
2003—Former director of finance Paul Martin became prime minister of Canada

BORN TODAY

Statesman John Jay 1745
Singer Frank Sinatra 1915
TV host Bob Barker 1923
Politician Edward Koch 1924
Singer Connie Francis 1938
Singer Dionne Warwick 1941
Olympic gymnast Cathy Rigby . . 1952
Tennis player Traci Austin 1962
Actress Jennifer Connelly 1970
Actress Mayim Bialik 1975

TRIUMPH OVER DEATH

The thread of life is so fragile within us that, when overcome by death, the forces of destruction quickly take over. Doctors tell us that for human body parts to be used for transplants, they must be removed within minutes after death. A surgeon described the process this way: "The human body is filled with 'invaders' who are held in check by life. When death comes, these invaders sweep out to destroy the body. Within two hours their damage has become so extensive that nothing may be salvaged for a living human being."

That pretty accurately reflects our spiritual condition as well. With Adam's sin, Satan's invaders moved and so permeated the human race that they left nothing good to restore spiritual life or growth. Only through Christ's death, burial, and resurrection, which conquered sin, do we have any hope at all of eternal life. As Romans 5:17 tells us, "The sin of this one man, Adam, caused death to rule over us, but all who receive God's wonderful, gracious gift of righteousness will live in triumph over sin and death through this one man, Jesus Christ" (NLT).

Are you living in triumph over sin and death through Jesus? You can do so today. Then we need not fear death—no matter how fragile life may be.

TODAY'S POWER POINT

If we really think that home is elsewhere . . . why should we not look forward to the arrival?—C. S. Lewis

December 13

TODAY IN HISTORY

1769—Dartmouth College chartered

1809—First abdominal surgery performed

1928—Broadway premiere of George Gershwin's *An American in Paris*

1978—First U.S. coin featuring a woman introduced (Susan B. Anthony silver dollar)

1996—Kofi Annan named UN secretary-general

2001—United States released video showing Osama bin Laden boasting that the 9/11 attacks were more damaging than expected

2002—Mass smallpox inoculations approved for five hundred thousand military troops in response to possibility of biological terrorism

2003—Former Iraqi dictator Saddam Hussein captured by U.S. troops in an underground hideaway near his hometown, Tikrit

2004—Bill and Melinda Gates Foundation pledged more than $42 million to develop inexpensive treatment for malaria

BORN TODAY

Poet Heinrich Heine 1797

Clergyman Phillips Brooks 1835

Boxer Archie Moore 1913

Actor Dick Van Dyke 1925

Actor Christopher Plummer 1929

Actor Tim Conway 1933

Singer John Davidson 1941

Musician Ted Nugent 1948

Actor Jamie Foxx 1967

Actress Christie Clark 1973

THE REST OF THE STORY

Have you ever listened to Paul Harvey's radio segment, "The Rest of the Story," which gives the little-known story behind historic events or well-known people? Knowing the rest of the story can sometimes change our opinion of a person or situation. It's good to know the background story before we pass judgment.

In the Christian life there's also more to the story than what first meets the eye. More and more these days, it seems we hear preachers promote what some call a prosperity gospel—that if we have enough faith, think positively, and give generously, we can expect God to reward us with abundance. While the Bible contains numerous references to thinking positively and giving to the work of the Lord, sometimes the prosperity message emphasizes these so much that they overshadow the Bible's other teachings concerning Christ's sacrifice for sin and his desire that we live godly lives. As Dennis De Haan notes, "Our God is not only loving, good, and generous; he is also righteous, holy, and demanding. He hates sin and will not compromise with evil."

While God is the author of all success, he expects us to live a life pleasing to him. And that's the "rest of the story."

TODAY'S POWER POINT

It is good to dream, but it is better to dream and work.—Thomas Gaines

December 14

TODAY IN HISTORY

1793—Kentucky became first state to subsidize road construction
1799—Death of American founding father George Washington
1807—First recorded meteorite landing
1819—Twenty-second state, Alabama, admitted to Union
1902—Completion of first transpacific telegraph cable
1911—Norwegian Roald Admunsen first explorer to reach South Pole
1934—Streamlined steam locomotive introduced
1939—Box-office premiere of *Gone with the Wind* (in Atlanta)
1974—Death of Pulitzer Prize–winning columnist Walter Lippmann, age eighty-five
2004—World's highest bridge (one thousand feet) opened in southern France
2005—House extended Patriot Act to allow continued government surveillance of suspected terrorists

BORN TODAY

Astronomer Tycho Brahe 1546
Aviator Jimmy Doolittle 1896
Bandleader Spike Jones. 1911
Singer Charlie Rich 1932
Actress Lee Remick. 1935
Actress Patty Duke 1946
Baseball player Craig Biggio 1965
Soccer player Michael Owen 1979

UPLIFTING YOUR SPOUSE

The TV quiz-show host asked the woman contestant the secret of happiness in her marriage. "Why, my husband is boss," she said.

"And who made the decision that he was to be the boss?" the host persisted.

"Why naturally, I did," she exclaimed.

While the audience chuckled at this humorous exchange, the Bible does address the relationship between a husband and wife in Ephesians 5:21–33.

How should husband and wife respond to the trials of life? An excellent starting place is for couples to share a time of Bible reading and prayer together each day. In this time together before God, the customary bumps and abrasions of married life can be healed. Each spouse might ask the other what displeasing thing he or she is doing that could be improved or better understood. Additionally, partners should pray for and with each other. Truly happy couples will discover that the closer they draw to God, the closer they are to each other and the stronger their marriage. "Come near to God and he will come near to you" (James 4:8). Do this and you'll discover that James 4:8 applies as much to couples, families, and friends as it does to individuals. Uplift the one you love and encourage him or her spiritually. You'll both become more Christlike when you do.

TODAY'S POWER POINT

Marriage is that relation between a man and woman in which the independence is equal, the dependence mutual, and the obligation reciprocal.—Louis Anspacher

December 15

TODAY IN HISTORY

1791—Bill of Rights ratified
1854—First street-cleaning machine introduced
1944—Bandleader Glenn Miller vanished on flight over English Channel
1965—First rendezvous in outer space conducted by U.S. astronauts
1973—After more than one hundred years, American Psychiatric Association redefined homosexuality as not being a mental illness
1989—Romanians deposed Communist leaders and government
2002—Former vice president Al Gore announced he would not run against President George W. Bush again in 2004 race
2004—Missile-defense system suffered setback due to early shutdown during test launch (cause unknown)
2005—Estimated eleven million Iraqis turned out to vote in first parliamentary elections since fall of Saddam Hussein

BORN TODAY

General "Mad Anthony" Wayne. . 1745
Engineer Alexandre Eiffel 1832
Musician Stan Kenton 1911
Actor Jeff Chandler 1918
Author Edna O'Brien. 1931
Comedian Tim Conway. 1933
Musician Dave Clark 1942
Actor Don Johnson 1949
Actress Helen Slater 1963
Actor Adam Brody 1979

FREE TO WORSHIP

When asked why he attended church, the board chairman of Sun Oil Company, J. Howard Pew, was quoted as saying, "I go to church to hear heralded the mind of Christ, not the mind of man. I want to hear expounded the timeless truth contained in the Scriptures, the kind of preaching that gets its power from, 'Thus saith the Lord.' Such preaching is hard to find these days."

Every week each citizen, consciously or not, "votes" on the issue of religious freedom. By attending church, they are voting for the opportunity to worship as they please. Likewise, by staying away, they are casting a negative vote (in effect, against the opportunity for free worship). Which way will you vote this week? If you've found a good, gospel-preaching church, be sure to cast your positive vote by being faithful to your church. And if you haven't yet found such a church, ask God to direct you to one. Thank God for the freedom to worship in peace. Then take advantage of that freedom by worshiping in God's house each week.

TODAY'S POWER POINT

It is only when men begin to worship that they begin to grow.—Calvin Coolidge

TODAY IN HISTORY

1773—Boston Tea Party
1835—Six hundred New York City buildings destroyed in first great urban U.S. fire
1884—First coin-operated liquid vending machine patented
1893—Dvorak's *New World Symphony* premiered
1899—First children's museum opened in Brooklyn
1908—First credit union opened
1944—Start of Battle of the Bulge
1979—Rocket-powered car broke sound barrier
2001—Yasser Arafat publicly urged militants to halt terror attacks against Israelis
2003—FDA approved sale of controversial RU-485 "morning after" contraceptive pill
2005—Senate voted down extension of Patriot Act, charging the measure did not adequately safeguard civil liberties

BORN TODAY

Composer Ludwig van Beethoven. . 1770
Author Jane Austen 1775
Anthropologist Margaret Mead . . 1901
Actress Liv Ullmann. 1939
Broadcast journalist Lesley Stahl. . 1941
Producer Steven Bocho. 1942
Football player William "Refrigerator" Perry. 1962
Actor Benjamin Bratt. 1963
Actress Halle Hirsh. 1987

BEING A BLESSING

One of the most cherished wedding gifts of a young couple was a modern painting of Christ by Richard Hook, in which the Savior's beckoning smile and eyes seemed to follow the viewer. The couple hung the painting in a prominent place wherever they lived.

As their children grew into teenagers, the couple added action to the smiling face of Christ with a small sign posted at eye level on the front door, reminding the teens to "Be a blessing" every day as they left the house. As a result, those kids were known for doing just that. Every summer for nearly fifteen years, there was always at least one of those teens helping point young kids to Christ as a counselor or helper at summer camp.

Today the "children" have completed college and are out serving the Lord on their own. But it all began with reminding them of Christ every day and of the importance of being a blessing.

You never know what your words of encouragement and kindness can do. Whom will you be a blessing to today?

TODAY'S POWER POINT

When you're feeling despondent, go out and do something kind for somebody. —John Keble

TODAY IN HISTORY

1791—New York City designated first one-way street

1821—Kentucky became first state to outlaw prison sentences for debtors

1903—Orville and Wilbur Wright piloted first powered airplane flight

1939—German crew scuttled battleship *Admiral Graf Spee* to avoid British capture

1944—Nazis gunned down eighty U.S. POWs

1956—New York City's Seagram Building, first bronze-and-glass skyscraper

1959—*On the Beach* first film to have simultaneous international premieres

1975—Two women, Lynette "Squeaky" Fromme and Sarah Jane Moore, found guilty on the same day of separate assassination attempts on President Gerald Ford

1984—Chicago Bears running back Walter Payton set new career rushing record of 12,400 yards (surpassing Jim Brown's old record of 12,317 yards)

BORN TODAY

Poet John Greenleaf Whittier 1807

Conductor Arthur Fiedler 1894

Scientist Willard Libby 1908

Columnist William Safire 1929

Actor Tommy Steele 1936

Actor Bill Pullman 1954

Actor Sean Patrick Thomas 1970

Actress Vanessa Zima 1986

INCREASING KNOWLEDGE

This has been called the "information age"—an era of unprecedented increase in human knowledge. Because of such a knowledge explosion, this is an era of increased specialization in learning. Not many years ago a leading university offered just one psychology class in the philosophy department. Today that same school offers a full-blown psychology program with specializations in clinical, experimental, or educational psychology. In addition, there are numerous subdisciplines such as learning theory, physiological psychology, and social psychology. Similarly, other areas of knowledge are also rapidly expanding.

Although few of us will ever master the great knowledge of the universe, anyone can have knowledge of the Creator of the universe, the One who knows all things. Do you have personal, relational knowledge of God? The Bible says there's no excuse for not knowing him: "Since the creation of the world God's invisible qualities—his eternal power and divine nature—have been clearly seen, being understood from what has been made, so that men are without excuse" (Romans 1:20). You can learn about God through the orderliness of the seasons, the vastness of the universe, the power of a hurricane, and the beauty of a sunset. Get to know him better by reading his Word and studying his creation. You will discover a God of order, who has a deep love for you.

TODAY'S POWER POINT

The purpose of learning is growth, and our minds, unlike our bodies, can continue growing as we continue to live.—Mortimer Adler

December 18

TODAY IN HISTORY

1787—Third state, New Jersey, ratified U.S. Constitution
1796—First Sunday newspaper published in Baltimore, Maryland
1839—One-inch daguerreotype of the moon made, first astronomy photograph
1865—Thirteenth Amendment abolished slavery
1924—Livestock auction first broadcast on radio
1986—Soviets announced plans to resume nuclear testing (which had been stopped since 1985)
1987—Ivan Boesky sentenced to three years in prison and fined $100 million for insider stock trading
1996—FBI agent Earl Pitts arrested for spying for Moscow
2001—United Nations reported 2001 was second-warmest year in more than a century
2002—BET founder Robert Johnson became first African American to own NBA team

BORN TODAY

Hymnist Charles Wesley. 1707
Baseball player Ty Cobb 1886
General Benjamin Davis. 1912
Actor Ossie Davis. 1917
Director Steven Spielberg 1947
Actor Brad Pitt. 1963
Actress Katie Holmes 1978
Singer Christina Aguilera 1980

PRECISION PRAYERS

Sometimes we may wonder why our prayers apparently go unanswered. Could it be we don't see the results we hope for because our prayers are imprecise? As a teenager evangelist John R. Rice learned the importance of precise prayer.

At a rally in West Texas, a country preacher asked Rice to join him in a time of specific prayer for the crusade. After reading Scripture, the two agreed that the Lord was encouraging them to pray for five people to make a decision for Christ that night. At the end of that service, five people did come forward, later testifying that God had cleansed their hearts. The next day the pair prayed that three people would respond to God's gentle calling. That evening, exactly three people acknowledged Christ as Savior. Encouraged by God's answers to specific prayer, they began to pray for people by name, asking God to work in their hearts. Again God responded to the faithful prayers of his children, and the young man who would later be one of Dr. Rice's roommates made a decision to follow Christ that night. As the famed evangelist said, "In those few days it dawned on me that God wants Christians to pray for definite objectives—to be explicit in their requests." If you want specific answers from God, pray specifically for your needs each day.

TODAY'S POWER POINT

Pray as though everything depended on God. Work as though everything depended on you.—Augustine

December 19

TODAY IN HISTORY

1823—Georgia passed first birth-registration law

1871—Corrugated paper (for packing) patented

1939—First televised movie premiere festivities

1950—General Dwight Eisenhower named NATO commander

1958—First message broadcast from orbiting satellite in space (President Dwight Eisenhower's recorded one-minute Christmas greeting)

1972—U.S. Apollo moon program ended with successful splashdown of *Apollo 17*

1998—House voted to impeach President Bill Clinton on charges of perjury and obstruction of justice

1999—Box-office premiere of *Titanic* (at $200 million, most expensive film to date)

2001—AT&T sold cable TV operations to Comcast for $47 billion

2005—Millions of New Yorkers stranded by transit strike, Transport Union fined $1 million a day

BORN TODAY

Explorer William Parry 1790
Historian Carter Woodson 1875
Pastor W. A. Criswell 1909
Actress Cicely Tyson 1939
Anthropologist Richard Leakey . . 1944

Basketball player Kevin McHale . . 1957
Basketball player Tom Gugliotta;
   actress Kristy Swanson 1969
Actress Alyssa Milano 1972

TRYING TIMES

God sometimes uses sharp setbacks to get our attention focused on him and to redirect our lives. A man walked down a windswept street after a storm in a small northeastern town. He walked with his head down and his coat pulled up around his face to protect him from the bitter wind. A man across the street happened to see that the unsuspecting man was heading straight for a high voltage wire downed by the storm's violent winds. He waved his arms and yelled a warning to the man, but he could not be heard over the howling wind. With no time to lose, he decided to take more drastic measures. Grabbing a rock from the graveled edge of the road, he hurled it directly at the man, hitting him squarely in the chest. Stunned, the man stopped and looked at his "attacker," who pointed out the wire and, undoubtedly, saved the man's life.

Do you feel God has dealt you a blow? Perhaps he's using it to warn you to avoid some danger or to draw your attention to some need you should address in your life. The howling winds of life's distractions can drown out God's still, small voice. We can be thankful that in those times he may smack us in the chest to get our attention. Make up your mind to be alert to God's leading at all times.

TODAY'S POWER POINT

These are the times that try men's souls.—Thomas Paine

December 20

TODAY IN HISTORY

1803—United States purchased Louisiana Territory from France
1860—South Carolina became first state to secede from Union
1922—USSR formed
1938—TV cathode ray tube patented
1946—Box-office premiere of *Its a Wonderful Life*
1951—First electrical power generated from nuclear energy
1976—Death of longest-serving Chicago mayor, Richard J. Daley ("Boss Daley"), ending his twenty-one years in office (he had presided over arrests of "Chicago Seven" at 1968 Democratic National Convention, scene of massive protests against Vietnam War)
1979—Senate passed $1.5 billion federal loan guarantees for Chrysler Corporation
2002—Trent Lott resigned as Senate majority leader due to perceived racist statements at Strom Thurmond's birthday party
2005—Teaching of "intelligent design" as alternative to evolution ruled unconstitutional by federal judge in Pennsylvania case

BORN TODAY

Industrialist Harvey Firestone. . . . 1868
Baseball player Branch Rickey . . . 1881
Philosopher Susanne Langer. 1895
Actress Irene Dunne. 1898
Director George Hill 1922
Artist David Levine 1926
Sociologist William J. Wilson. . . . 1935
Actor John Spencer. 1946
Singer Billy Bragg. 1957
Singer JoJo 1990

LIVING WITH POWER

Not long ago a power company in the Philippines became suspicious of one customer's consistently low electric bill. They were even more troubled when they learned that this man earned more than ten thousand pounds per month and could surely afford all the energy he needed. Investigators were sent to check out the situation, and they were amazed to find that this relatively wealthy man had only two light bulbs (and no electric appliances) in his home. Living so meagerly, he was able to limit his power consumption to just one dollar per month.

In spite of the inexhaustible power of our almighty God, too many people live as if there's a power shortage. They use little, if any, almost as if they fear God's power in their lives might run out. But God's power is in no danger of running out. He wants us to live fully in his power. Paul prayed for the Ephesians: "I pray also that the eyes of your heart may be enlightened in order that you may know . . . his incomparably great power for us who believe" (Ephesians 1:18–19). Are you tapping into God's unlimited energy, or are you living like a spiritual pauper?

TODAY'S POWER POINT

I recognize power passing mine, immeasurable, God.—Robert Browning

TODAY IN HISTORY

1898—Radium discovered

1913—First crossword puzzle published (by Simon & Schuster)

1937—Box-office premiere of first film to earn a billion dollars, *Snow White and the Seven Dwarfs* (also first feature-length animated Technicolor film)

1942—U.S. Supreme Court upheld Nevada's six-week divorce law

1968—*Apollo 8* crew became first astronauts to orbit the moon

1970—Elvis met President Richard Nixon in the White House

1988—Pan American jetliner exploded over Lockerbie, Scotland, killing all 259 passengers aboard, terrorist bomb suspected

2005—Iraqi government reported 70 percent voter turnout in recent parliamentary elections

BORN TODAY

Russian leader Joseph Stalin 1879

Football coach Joe Paterno 1926

Talk-show host Phil Donahue . . . 1935

Musician Frank Zappa 1940

Actor Samuel L. Jackson. 1948

Tennis player Chris Evert 1954

Actor Ray Romano. 1957

Actor Kiefer Sutherland 1966

MOTIVATION FOR WORKING

A United Nations worker witnessed an unusual sight recently on the Indonesian island of Java. There he saw countless workers caked with mud, hauling dirt out of a deep pit. They had to carry their loads up a swaying bamboo ladder to the top. The UN worker suggested to another observer that they bring in bulldozers and other heavy equipment to assist, but he was warned not to interfere with the project. "Understand, this is their canal. For the first time they will have something of their own for which they owe no one. Once they learn to believe in themselves, maybe they can believe in the help we can give them."

God has called us to work. We might not always do everything perfectly; we're bound to make some mistakes and even fail from time to time, but that should never stop us from doing our part. Many people work only because it is required. But we pass to a new level of maturity and effectiveness when we come to the point that our work is motivated by love—love for God, for our families and friends, and for others. Who knows, your attitude toward your work may be inspiring or encouraging someone else. Strive to work in such an outstanding manner that Paul's praise for the Thessalonian believers might also apply to you: "We continually remember before our God and Father your work produced by faith, your labor prompted by love, and your endurance inspired by hope in our Lord Jesus Christ" (1 Thessalonians 1:3).

TODAY'S POWER POINT

When love and skill work together, expect a masterpiece.—John Ruskin

December 22

TODAY IN HISTORY

1807—First trade embargo approved by Congress
1845—Earliest demonstration of a synthesized human voice (via the euphonium, which used compressed air to replicate the human voice, in Philadephia)
1894—U.S. Golf Association established
1914—First prohibition vote in Congress
1937—Lincoln Tunnel opened, linking New York and New Jersey
1944—"Nuts," was Major General Anthony McAuliffe's reply to German demand for surrender of encircled U.S. 101st Airborne Division at Bastogne, Belgium
1971—First bank to project movies on a screen for customers to view while waiting in line (Chemical Bank, New York City)
1984—"Subway Vigilante" Bernhard Goetz shot African American youths he said were trying to rob him on New York City subway
1986—Fifty thousand Chinese students demonstrated on behalf of domestic reforms
2004—Growing deficits blamed for U.S. cuts in aid to global food programs

BORN TODAY

Composer Giacomo Puccini	1858	Broadcast journalist Diane Sawyer	1946
Poet Edwin Robinson	1869	Baseball player Steve Garvey	1948
Actress Peggy Ashcroft	1907	Singer Robin Gibb	1949
Actress Barbara Billingsley	1922	Actor Ralph Fiennes	1962
Baseball player Steve Carlton	1944		

ACCEPTING THE NEW

The Belgian Bible Society has converted a vending machine from selling candy to distributing Bibles in various languages. The machine, placed outside the society's offices at a busy bus stop, was reported to be selling about one hundred copies of the Gospels per month. While this could never be the sole means of distributing Bibles, it works well for people on the go in Brussels.

Sometimes it's tempting to protect the status quo. It's comfortable to do things as they've always been done. It's easier, less time consuming, if we don't have to stop and think something through to discover if it's a good idea or a bad one. But times change, and so should our methods. Change for the sake of change is not the answer, but thoughtful, well-considered change can enhance our efforts and multiply our successes—in any area to which we apply this principle. Are you flexible, thoughtful, and forward-thinking, or are you stuck in a rut? Now might be the time to think about how and why you're doing what you do. There just might be a better way.

TODAY'S POWER POINT

Keep changing. When you're through changing, you're through.—Bruce Barton

December 23

TODAY IN HISTORY

1852—Start of first rail-passenger service west of the Mississippi

1913—Federal Reserve System established

1929—Pennsylvania established first statewide police teletype link

1943—*Hansel and Gretel* first opera to be televised in its entirety

1947—Transistor invented, revolutionizing electronics

1954—First successful human organ transplant surgery

1974—MLB approved practice of free agency

1981—First U.S. cases of AIDS reported

1985—President Ronald Reagan signed record $52 billion, three-year farm bill

2002—Republican Bill Frist unanimously elected Senate majority leader (first unanimous election of a GOP leader)

2003—First U.S. case of mad cow disease verified

BORN TODAY

Baseball manager Connie Mack . . 1862

Dancer Jose Greco 1918

Author Robert Bly 1926

Voice actor Harry Shearer. 1943

Actress Susan Lucci 1948

Football player Jim Harbaugh . . . 1963

Actor Corey Haim 1971

Hockey player Scott Gomez 1979

ABOUT FACES

How long do you think you could keep smiling? You'd have to smile for more than ten hours and five minutes to beat the world record established by a beaming twelve-year-old, Lisa Lester of Winnipeg, Canada. Not only did she beat the smiling record in the *Guinness Book of World Records* of seven hours, thirty-two minutes, but also the unofficial record smile of eight hours, twenty minutes recorded in Toronto, Canada.

But have you ever been around someone who never seemed to smile? A little girl once visited a stable, where she was overheard to say, "Oh, horsey, you must be a Christian, for you have such a long face!" Proverbs 27:19 reminds us, "As water reflects a face, so a man's heart reflects the man." What does your face reveal about you and your relationship with Christ?

Ask yourself, "What kind of feeling do others (including my family) have when they see me coming? Are they happier to see me coming or going?" No matter what the circumstances, your face can reflect the peace and joy that comes from trusting God: "Those who look to him are radiant; their faces are never covered with shame" (Psalm 34:5). So look in the mirror, then look into your heart. If your heart is happy, notify your face. Come on, you can do it. Put on your smile!

TODAY'S POWER POINT

Wear a smile and have friends; wear a scowl and have wrinkles.—George Eliot

December 24 Christmas Eve

TODAY IN HISTORY

1707—Poetry first published in a newspaper
1818—"Silent Night" composed by Franz Gruber
1871—World premiere of opera *Aida* in Cairo, Egypt
1889—Bicycle with back-pedal brake patented (in Freeport, Illinois)
1906—First radio program broadcast
1946—First telecast from a church
1968—In worldwide, live telecast, U.S. astronaut Frank Borman read from the
        book of Genesis while aboard *Apollo 8* spacecraft orbiting the moon
1986—Richard Rutan and Jeanna Yeager completed nonstop around-the-world
        flight in nine days, three minutes, and forty-four seconds
1989—Nobel Prize awarded to Dalai Lama

BORN TODAY

Statesman Benjamin Rush 1745
Frontiersman Kit Carson 1809
Physicist James Joule 1818
Industrialist Howard Hughes 1905
Actress Ava Gardner 1922
Novelist Mary Higgins Clark 1929
Singer Ricky Martin 1971
TV host Ryan Seacrest 1974

GREAT NEWS FOR ALL PEOPLE

What was the scene like in Bethlehem the night before Christ's birth? No doubt
the inn was filling up with visitors from distant places coming to their hometown
to register. For the shepherds it was likely a night like many others in that pre-
electric era, seated around flickering campfires. It's no wonder, amid otherwise
all-encompassing darkness, that the shepherds were frightened by the angels'
heavenly appearance.

Why were the shepherds chosen to receive the angelic announcement? At least
two possibilities seem likely: First, the shepherds were outdoors at night, where
they would most likely see (and be impacted by) the herald angels. Also, who
could be a more fitting witness to the birth of the Good Shepherd than men
who were themselves shepherds? Try to imagine their amazement and wonder
to realize that God had sent his Son to earth and had chosen to make the birth
announcement to them!

This announcement is for us today as well. The angel told the shepherds, "I
bring you good news of great joy that will be for all the people" (Luke 2:10).
"Suddenly a great company of the heavenly host appeared with the angel, praising
God and saying, 'Glory to God in the highest, and on earth peace to men on whom
his favor rests'" (Luke 2:13–14). That's reason enough to rejoice this Christmas.

TODAY'S POWER POINT

The simple shepherds heard the voice of an angel and found their Lamb.
—Archbishop Fulton J. Sheen

TODAY IN HISTORY

1066—William the Conqueror crowned

1741—Centigrade temperature scale introduced

1776—General George Washington and 5,400 American troops crossed the
     Delaware River (on their way to battle Britain's hired Hessian troops)

1818—First oratorio (Handel's *Messiah*) performed in Boston

1896—John Phillip Sousa wrote "Stars and Stripes Forever"

1925—First "national Christmas tree" dedicated (in California)

1926—Radio premiere of Metropolitan Opera

1931—Hirohito named new Japanese emperor

1971—AFC playoff between Kansas City Chiefs and Miami Dolphins became first
     U.S. football game to go longer than eighty minutes (with two overtimes)

1991—Resignation of Soviet Union president Mikhail Gorbachev (USSR dissolved
     on the following day)

BORN TODAY

American Red Cross organizer Clara
    Barton 1821

Hotelier Conrad Hilton 1887

Writer Rod Serling 1924

Singer Jimmy Buffett 1946

Baseball player Rickey Henderson;
    Singer Barbara Mandrell 1948

Actress Sissy Spacek 1949

Singer Annie Lennox 1954

Singer Dido 1971

THE COMING OF PEACE

"God so loved the world that he gave his one and only Son, that whoever believes in him should not perish but have eternal life" (John 3:16). Jesus came that first Christmas day not because he had to, but because God loved mankind.

One of the most fascinating characters related to the Christmas story is the godly man Simeon, who had waited years for the arrival of the Messiah. We can scarcely imagine his joy at seeing Jesus in the flesh, the fulfillment of years of anticipation. Simeon took the child in his arms and praised God for allowing him to see God's salvation: "Sovereign Lord, as you have promised, you now dismiss your servant in peace" (Luke 2:29).

Jesus's birth brought peace to Simeon. The angel host who announced and celebrated the baby's birth sang of peace on earth (Luke 2:14). In foretelling Christ's birth, the prophet Isaiah called him the "Prince of Peace" (Isaiah 9:6). Jesus came into the world to bring peace—his gift to us this Christmas is peace with God.

TODAY'S POWER POINT

The soul of peace is love, which . . . comes from the love of God and expresses itself in love for men.—Pope Paul VI

December 26

TODAY IN HISTORY

1776—General George Washington and his army victorious in sneak attack on Hessian camp at Trenton, New Jersey, scoring first major victory by Colonial forces in the American Revolution

1805—Philadelphia established first U.S. art museum

1865—Coffee percolator patented

1878—First store lighted by electric light

1933—FM radio patented

1979—Russians airlifted five thousand troops into Afghanistan

2001—American Diabetes Association issued report saying eating sweets OK as long as blood sugar is controlled

2002—Record (to date) $314.9 million Powerball prize ($113 million after taxes) won by single ticket holder, Jack Whittaker of West Virginia

2003—Bam, Iran, devastated by 6.6-magnitude earthquake, thirty thousand people killed

2004—Massive earthquake triggered far-reaching, devastating tsunami along Pacific rim, Indonesia hardest hit with more than one hundred fifty thousand casualties

BORN TODAY

Mathematician Charles Babbage . 1792	Producer Phil Spector. 1940
Novelist Henry Miller 1891	Baseball player Carlton Fisk 1947
Chinese Chairman Mao Zedong . 1893	Baseball player Ozzie Smith 1954
Entertainer Steve Allen. 1921	Tennis player Marcelo Rios. 1975

RAISING A CHILD

Some people seem to think their children will grow up to be godly, productive adults simply by being left alone. What could be further from the truth? Poet and author Samuel Taylor Coleridge was once talking with a man about raising children. The man said he didn't see any need to direct his children spiritually, preferring to let them grow up and decide for themselves which way is right. Coleridge then beckoned the man to come and look at his garden. "Why it's just a patch of weeds!" exclaimed the visitor. "Quite true," responded the philosopher, "But I decided some time ago to simply let the garden grow its own way. You see I didn't want to influence how it would turn out."

Does this sound familiar? Never let it be said of you that you let your children grow up on their own. Give them spiritual instruction and encouragement, for after all, our families are the only earthly things we can ever take with us to heaven. Make it your prayer that God will help you to be a worthy parent or teacher to the young people God has entrusted to your care.

TODAY'S POWER POINT

Children have never been very good at listening to their elders, but they have never failed to imitate them.—James Baldwin

TODAY IN HISTORY

1845—First anesthetic administered during childbirth
1892—Cornerstone laid for St. John Cathedral in New York City
1932—Radio City Music Hall completed
1934—First U.S. youth hostel opened
1937—First ski lift started operating, in New Hampshire
1945—World Bank organized
1947—Premiere of television's *The Howdy Doody Show*
1951—First mail-delivery vehicle with steering on the right put into service
1983—President Ronald Reagan took responsibility for lack of security in Beirut that allowed terrorists to kill 241 U.S. Marines; Pope John Paul II met with man who attempted to assassinate him

BORN TODAY

Astronomer Johann Kepler. 1571	Psychologist Lee Salk 1926
Inventor George Cayley 1773	Designer Bernard Lanvin 1935
Scientist Louis Pasteur 1822	Actor John Amos 1939
Actress Marlene Dietrich 1901	Journalist Cokie Roberts 1943
Physician William Masters 1915	Actor Gerard Depardieu. 1948

A LESSON FROM STRAWBERRIES

Have you ever planted strawberries? If you have, you know that God has made them to grow in a unique way. Rather than sprouting from a bulb or a seed, the strawberry plant duplicates itself by sending out narrow, thin "runners" that root themselves in the soil and bring forth new plants. Multiply this effect by all the plants in a patch, and you can see why they so quickly come to cover the entire bed.

Perhaps believers could learn from the strawberry plant. Imagine the effect on the spiritual bed of our nation and our world if believers would reproduce themselves as diligently and effectively as strawberry plants. God has planted each believer in a unique spot all his own. With God's help, our influence and witness should spread into the barren spots around us, where no other Christian can reach so well. In the open, fertile soil of neighbors' disappointments, losses, needs, longings, and opportunities, our "runners" of compassion, love, assistance, and testimony should naturally spread until from just one, many more have been rooted and grown. Like the strawberry, believers are to do more than just bear fruit—they are to reproduce themselves. How many new "plants" have been rooted in Christ because of you?

TODAY'S POWER POINT

Christians must produce fruit—if they don't witness, they wilt.—Henry Bosch

December 28

TODAY IN HISTORY

1846—Twenty-ninth state, Iowa, added to the Union
1869—First Labor Day celebrated in United States
1912—First streetcars started operating in San Francisco
1920—Navy commissioned USS *Relief*, the first ship constructed as a hospital
1941—U.S. Navy Seabees established
1942—Robert Sullivan becomes first pilot to fly across Atlantic Ocean one hundred
      times
1948—Pledge of Allegiance officially recognized by Congress
1961—American Airlines first to fly 100 million passengers
1972—First dual channel telecast (on two New York City TV stations)
1981—First U.S. test-tube baby born (from in-vitro fertilization)
2001—Fifty Islamic militants arrested in Pakistan on charges of planning suicide
      attack on India's parliament building
2002—U.S. unemployment benefits interrupted for 750,000 people when Congress
      failed to extend those benefits

BORN TODAY

President Woodrow Wilson 1856
Humorist Sam Levinson. 1911
Actor Lou Jacobi 1913
Singer Johnny Otis. 1921
Actress Maggie Smith. 1934
Golfer Hubie Green 1946
Actor Denzel Washington. 1954
Actor Malcolm Gets. 1964
Tennis player Patrick Rafter 1972
Snowboarder Todd Richards. 1969

KNOWLEDGE

How much does mankind really know? As it turns out, very little—especially in light of an all-knowing God. Thomas A. Edison said of mankind, "We do not know one-millionth part of 1 percent about anything. We do not know what water is. We do not know what light is. We do not know what electricity is. We do not know what gravity is. We don't know anything about magnetism. We have a lot of hypotheses, but that is all."

A man credited with superior knowledge in many areas, Albert Einstein, said, "We know nothing at all. All our knowledge is but the knowledge of schoolchildren. The real nature of things we shall never know."

God has all knowledge and keeps the universe constantly under his control—yet he has time enough to hear the prayers of every one of his children. What a mighty God we serve! Praise God for his knowledge and power, and thank him for all he has done for you this year—and today.

TODAY'S POWER POINT

It is a dangerous thing to think we know everything.—Jack Kuehler

December 29

TODAY IN HISTORY

1845—Twenty-eighth state, Texas, added to Union
1848—First gaslight installed in White House
1851—First Young Men's Christian Association (YMCA) in United States
1867—First stock ticker introduced
1891—First key radio patent issued (to Thomas A. Edison)
1908—Automobile braking system patented
1916—Assassination of monk Gregory Rasputin
1952—First transistor hearing aid introduced
1975—Bomb explosion in locker at LaGuardia Airport killed fourteen people

BORN TODAY

Inventor Charles Goodyear 1800
President Andrew Johnson 1808
Actress Mary Tyler Moore 1936
Actor Jon Voight 1938
Singer Marianne Faithfull. 1946
Actor Ted Danson 1947
Filmmaker Andy Wachowski 1967
Actor Jude Law. 1972

SAYING I LOVE YOU

Historically, couples have acknowledged their love in unusual ways. A Paris artist, Marcel de Leclure, set the world's record for love letters, according to Robert Ripley. In 1875 Leclure sent his true love, Magdalene, a letter containing only three words, "I love you," repeated 1,875,000 times. But that's just part of the story: Leclure individually repeated (and had repeated back to him by his scribe) the phrase—a total of 5,625,000 times, saying "I love you" in speech and writing. Ripley says, "Never was love made manifest by as great an expenditure of time and effort."

A good question might be, did Magdalene read all of those professions of love? Perhaps not, but it would be hard to miss the depth of the feeling behind the words.

God has said, "I love you" to his beloved humanity over and over. He has said it through his creation, his blessings, and his Word. Even when people don't bother to read his declarations of love, it's hard to ignore the action behind those words: "God demonstrates his own love for us in this: While we were still sinners, Christ died for us" (Romans 5:8).

And now God keeps pouring out his love again and again through his scribe, the Holy Spirit (see Romans 5:5). "I love you! I love you! I love you!" he tells us again and again. Now the only question that remains is, are you listening?

TODAY'S POWER POINT

God proved his love on the cross. When Christ hung, and bled, and died, it was God saying to the world, "I love you."—Billy Graham

December 30

TODAY IN HISTORY

1853—United States purchased southern parts of Arizona and New Mexico from Mexico

1854—Pennsylvania Rock Oil Company incorporated (first U.S. oil company)

1877—Rutherford B. Hayes first president to celebrate his silver wedding anniversary in White House

1903—Iroquois Theatre fire killed six hundred people in Chicago

1959—Ballistic missile sub USS *George Washington* commissioned (first sub to have two crews, providing nearly unlimited time at sea)

1978—House panel reported likelihood of conspiracy in the murder of Martin Luther King Jr.

BORN TODAY

Writer Rudyard Kipling 1865
Philanthropist Simon Guggenheim
. . . . 1867
Actor Bert Parks 1914
Baseball player Sandy Koufax 1935
Singer Del Shannon 1939

TV host Meredith Vieira 1953
TV host Matt Lauer 1957
Actress Tracey Ullman 1959
Sprinter Ben Johnson 1961
Golfer Tiger Woods 1975
Basketball player LeBron James . . 1984

A GOOD ROLE MODEL

A senior executive in one of New York's largest banks recalled how he got his start in banking. It began shortly after he was hired as an office boy many years before. One day the bank president called the youth to his office and told him he wanted him to work with him each day. The young man protested that he knew nothing of banking. The president told him, "Never mind, you will learn a lot faster if you just stay by my side and keep your eyes and ears open." The boy did just that and later recalled, "Being with that man made me just like him. I began to do things the way he did, and that accounts for what I am today."

Who has had that sort of influence in your life? Most people owe at least some of their success to a mentor or role model who demonstrated by his or her life the skills, behaviors, and attitudes necessary for success. Why not take a moment to call or write a brief note thanking that person for helping you to become what you are today?

Now look around you. Who could benefit from your example, experience, and knowledge? Make yourself available to someone as a mentor, encourager, teacher, friend, and guide today. What you can accomplish by yourself pales in comparison with what you can accomplish by investing in the life of someone else.

TODAY'S POWER POINT

I think it's an honor to be a role model . . . because you can influence a person's life in a positive light, and that's what I want to do.—Tiger Woods

TODAY IN HISTORY

1781—First modern bank chartered in United States

1879—First public demonstration of Thomas A. Edison's incandescent electric lightbulb

1943—Frank Sinatra opened at New York's Paramount Theatre

1946—President Harry Truman issued proclamation officially ending U.S. involvement in World War II

1948—Louisiana's Russell Long became first U.S. senator to assume office held by both his father (Huey Long) and mother (Rose McConnell Long)

1961—NFL playoff (Packers versus Giants) first football game to gross more than $1 million in overall revenue

1973—U.S. Energy Department announced gas-rationing plan (at height of world oil shortage)

1978—Ohio State coach Woody Hayes fired after striking player in Gator Bowl game

BORN TODAY

Painter Henri Matisse. 1869

Actor Anthony Hopkins. 1937

Actress Sarah Miles. 1941

Actor Ben Kingsley. 1943

Actress Barbara Carrera 1945

Actor Tim Matheson 1948

Actor Val Kilmer 1959

Singer Joe McIntyre 1972

TRAINING CHILDREN

"Train a child in the way he should go, and when he is old, he will not turn from it" (Proverbs 22:6). These words from the Bible form the basis for all Christian education. No parent would expect a child to compete physically against professional athletes every day, and yet this is, in effect, what occurs educationally when children attend non-Christian schools staffed by college-trained professionals. They are not competing in the same arena. Thus it is doubtful if, after twelve years in such an atmosphere, they can emerge with their original beliefs and faith intact.

Listen to these words from the early 1940s: "Day after day young people are subjected to the bombardment of naturalism with all of its animosity toward Christianity. In the formative years of their lives . . . they must listen to and absorb these ideas of man, the world, and religion. With these facts before them, why do . . . [believers] wonder that Christianity has so little influence over their young people?" Who made this observation? Was it a pastor or Christian educator? No, it was none other than longtime New York newspaper columnist Walter Lippman.

Since children are a great gift from God, shouldn't we resolve to love and protect them? It is vital that we ensure they are trained to know and love God.

TODAY'S POWER POINT

Training is everything. The . . . cauliflower is nothing but cabbage with a college education.—Mark Twain